OF THE IMMORTAL

Autumn Frost

publisher
Mike Richardson

series editor
Tim Ervin-Gore

collection editor
Chris Warner

collection designer
Debra Bailey

**English-language version produced by Studio
Proteus for Dark Horse Comics, Inc.**

This volume collects issues seventy-three through
eighty of the Dark Horse comic-book series,
Blade of the Immortal.

Published by
Dark Horse Manga™
A division of Dark Horse Comics, Inc.
10956 SE Main Street
Milwaukie, OR 97222

www.darkhorse.com

To find a comics shop in your area, call the
Comic Shop Locator Service toll-free at 1-888-266-4226.

First edition: December 2003
ISBN: 1-56971-991-8

1 3 5 7 9 10 8 6 4 2

Printed in Canada

BLADE
OF THE IMMORTAL

art and story
HIROAKI SAMURA

translation
Dana Lewis & Toren Smith

lettering and retouch
Tomoko Saito

Autumn Frost

DARK HORSE MANGA™

ABOUT THE TRANSLATION

The Swastika

The main character in *Blade of the Immortal*, Manji, has taken the "crux gammata" as both his name and his personal symbol. This symbol is also known as the *swastika*, a name derived from the Sanskrit *svastika* (meaning "welfare," from *su* — "well" + *asti* "he is"). As a symbol of prosperity and good fortune, the swastika was widely used throughout the ancient world (for example, appearing often on Mesopotamian coinage), including North and South America and has been used in Japan as a symbol of Buddhism since ancient times. To be precise, the symbol generally used by Japanese Buddhists is the *sauvastika*, which moves in a counterclockwise direction and is called the *manji* in Japanese. The arms of the *swastika*, which point in a clockwise direction, are generally considered a solar symbol. It was this version (the *hakenkreuz*) that was perverted by the Nazis. The *sauvastika* generally stands for night, and often for magical practices. It is important that readers understand that the swastika has ancient and honorable origins, and it is those that apply to this story, which takes place in the 18th century [ca. 1782–3]. *There is no anti-Semitic or pro-Nazi meaning behind the* use of the symbol in this story. Those meanings did not exist until after 1910.

The Artwork

The creator of *Blade of the Immortal* requested that we make an effort to avoid mirror-imaging his artwork. Normally, Westernized manga are first copied in a mirror-image in order to facilitate the left-to-right reading of the pages. However, Mr. Samura decided that he would rather see his pages reversed via the technique of cutting up the panels and re-pasting them in reverse order. While we feel that this often leads to problems in panel-to-panel continuity, we place primary importance on the wishes of the creator. Therefore, most of *Blade of the Immortal* has been produced using the "cut and paste" technique. There are, of course, some sequences where it was impossible to do this, and mirror-imaged panels or pages were used.

The Sound Effects & Dialogue

Since some of Mr. Samura's sound effects are integral parts of the illustrations, we decided to leave those in their original Japanese. We hope readers will view the unretouched sound effects as essential portions of Mr. Samura's extraordinary artwork. In addition, Mr. Samura's treatment of dialogue is quite different from that featured in typical samurai manga and is considered to be one of the features that has made *Blade* such a hit in Japan. Mr. Samura has mixed a variety of linguistic styles in this fantasy story, with some characters speaking in the mannered style of old Japan while others speak as if they were street-corner punks from a bad area of modern-day Tokyo. The anachronistic slang used by some of the characters in the English translation reflects the unusual mix of speech patterns from the original Japanese text.

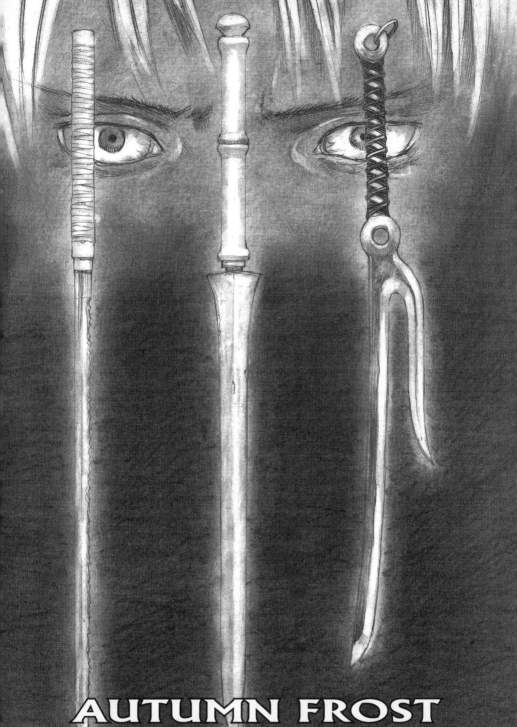

AUTUMN FROST
Part 1

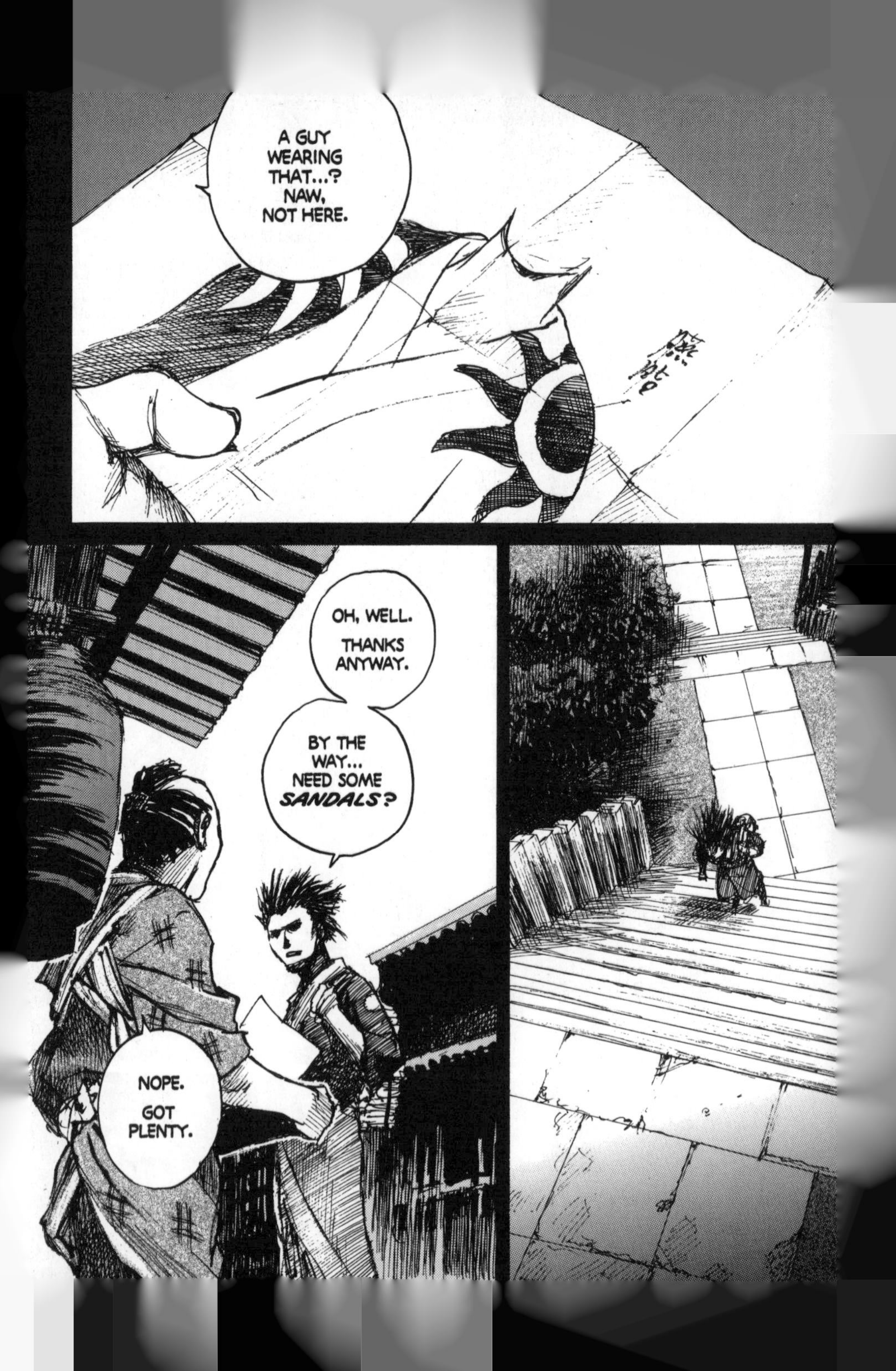
A GUY WEARING THAT...? NAW, NOT HERE.
OH, WELL.
THANKS ANYWAY.
BY THE WAY... NEED SOME *SANDALS*?
NOPE.
GOT PLENTY.

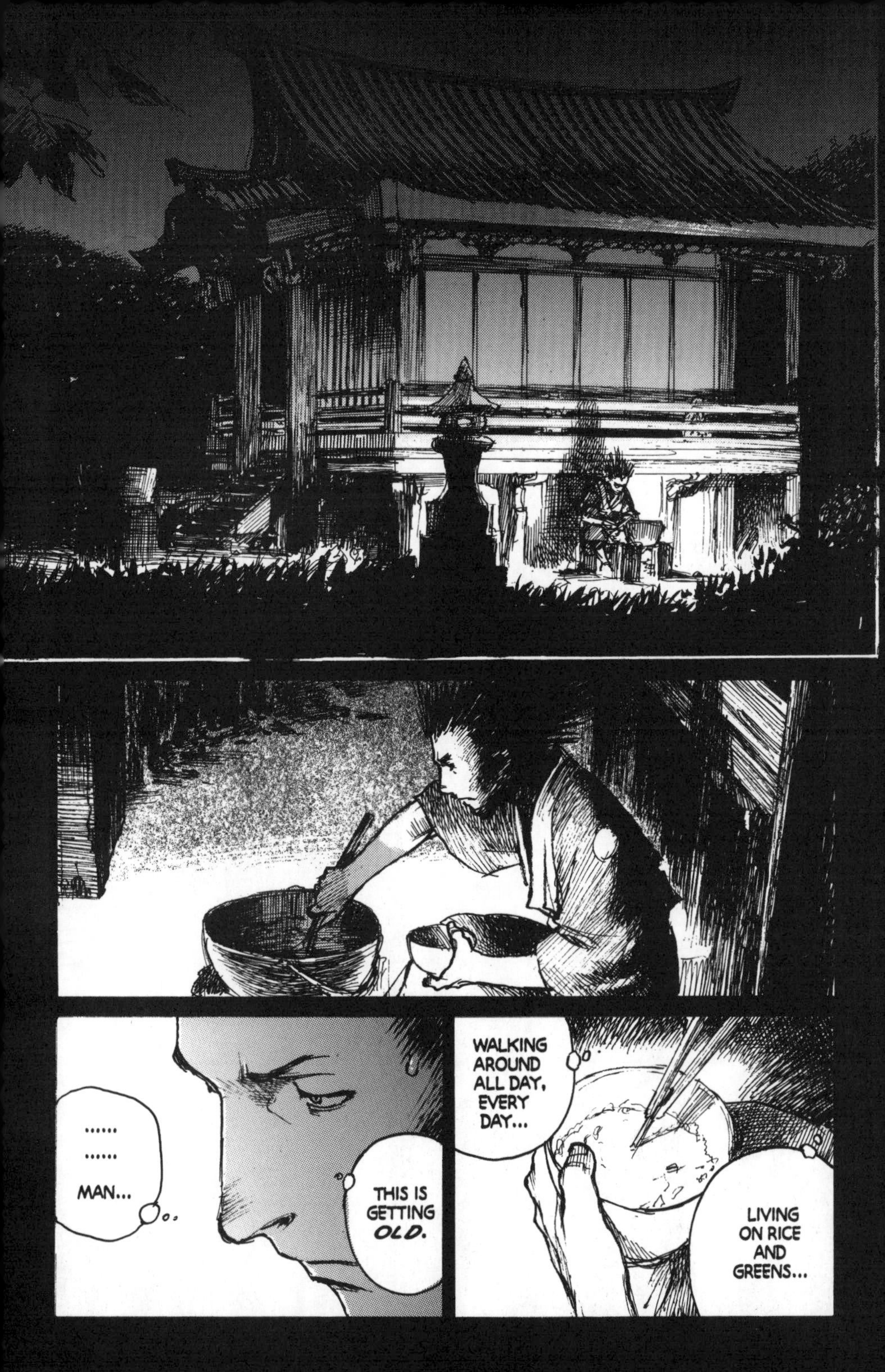
......
......
MAN...
THIS IS GETTING OLD.
WALKING AROUND ALL DAY, EVERY DAY...
LIVING ON RICE AND GREENS...

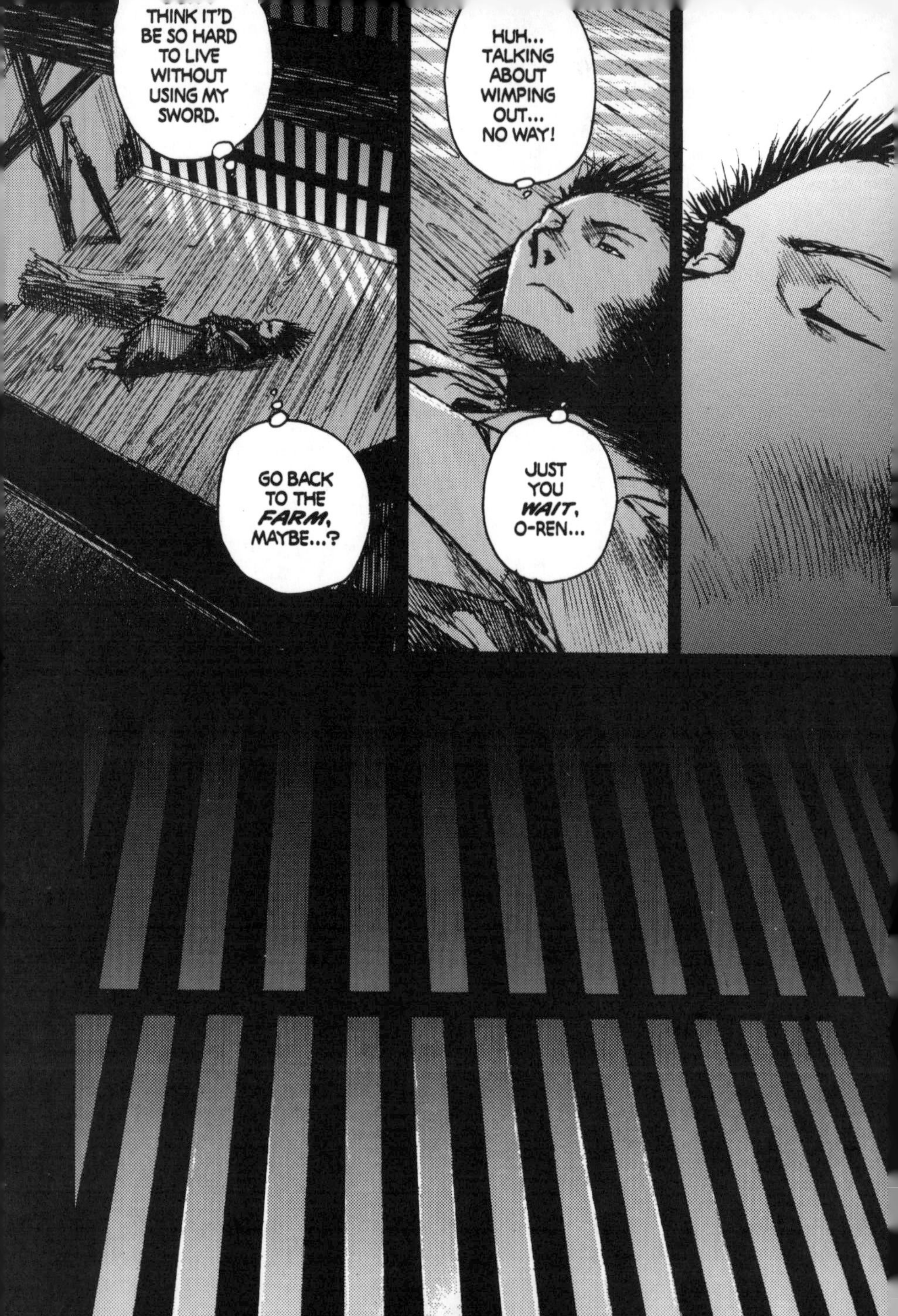
THINK IT'D BE SO HARD TO LIVE WITHOUT USING MY SWORD.
GO BACK TO THE *FARM*, MAYBE...?
HUH... TALKING ABOUT WIMPING OUT... NO WAY!
JUST YOU *WAIT*, O-REN...

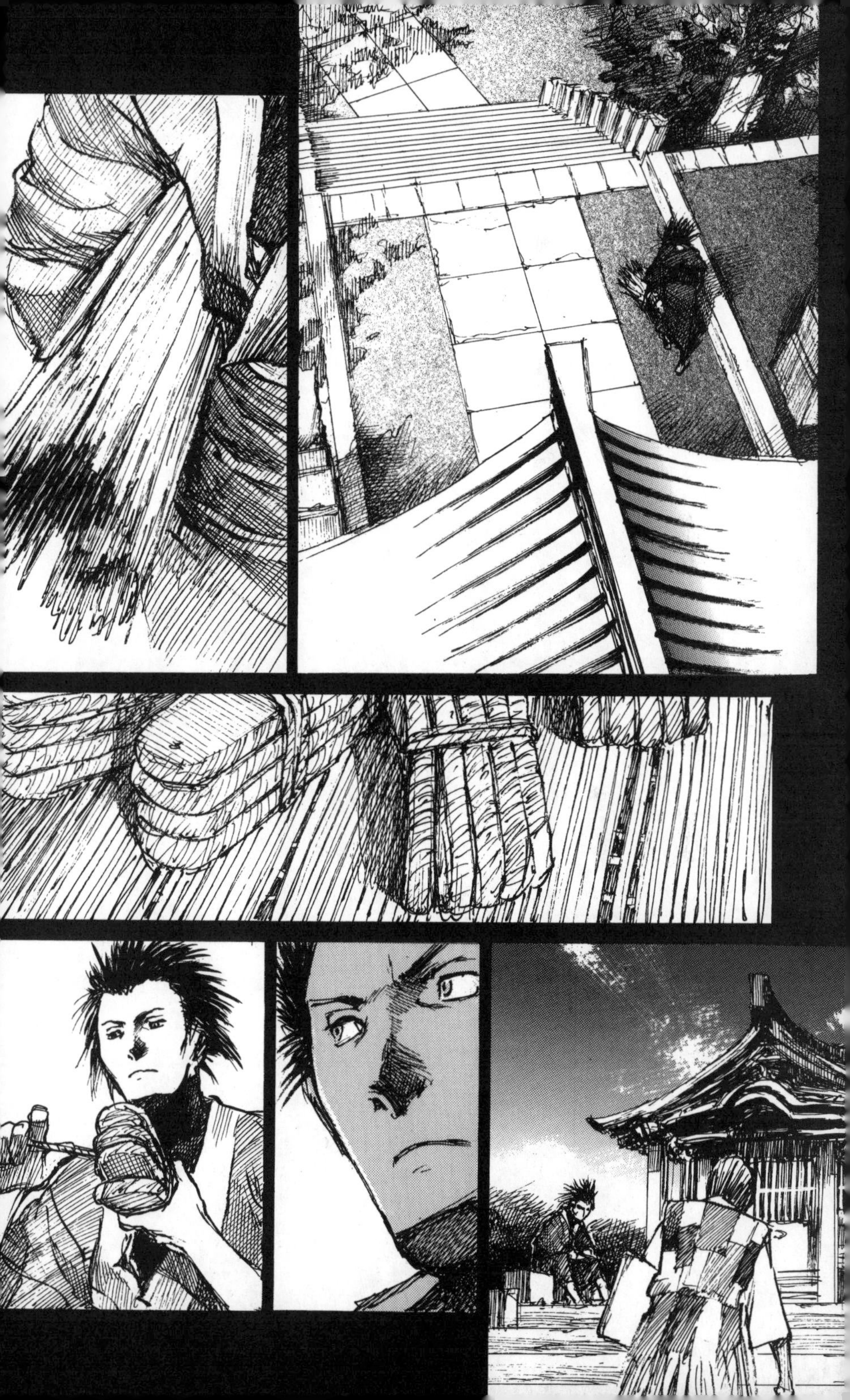

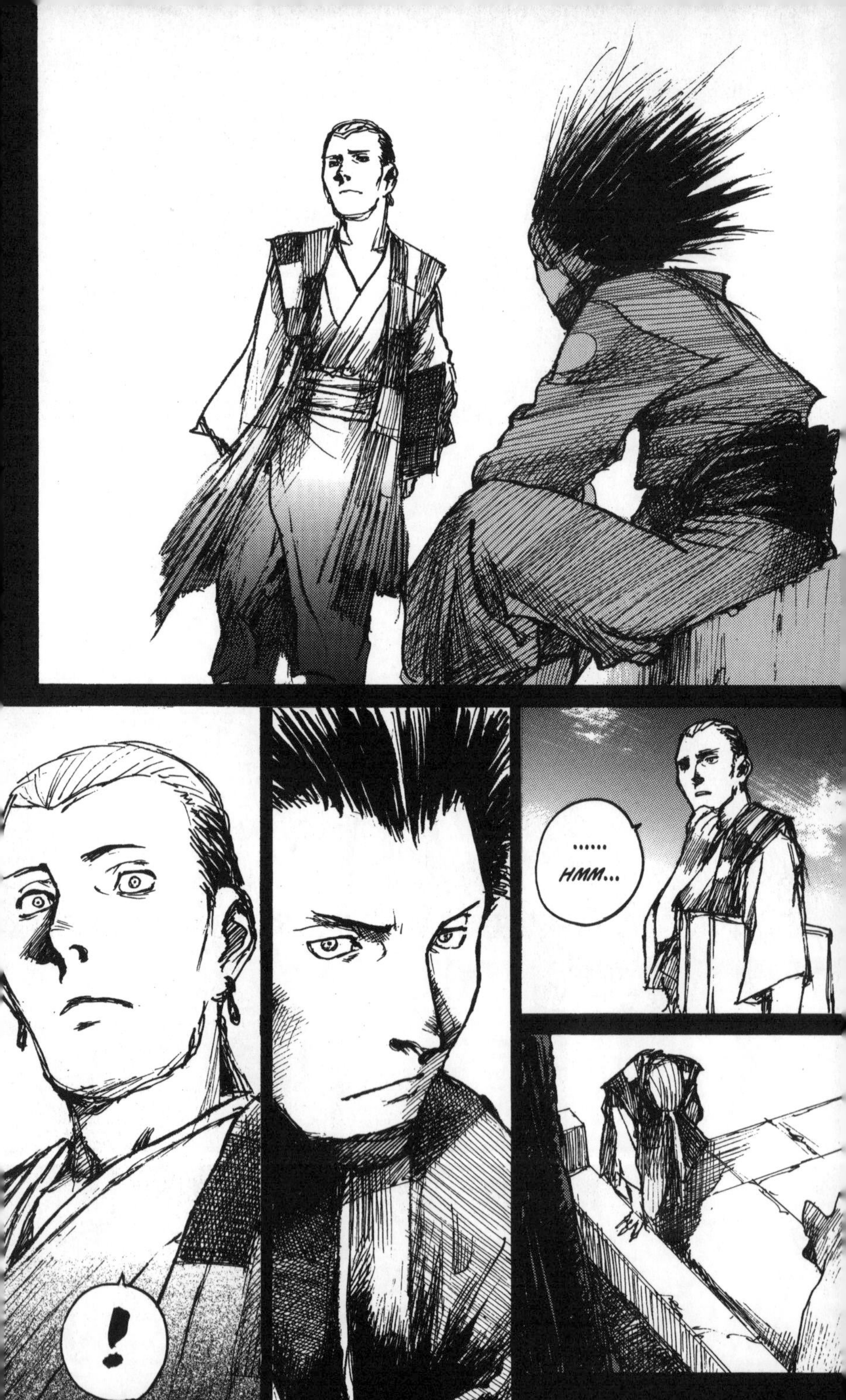

...... HMM...
!

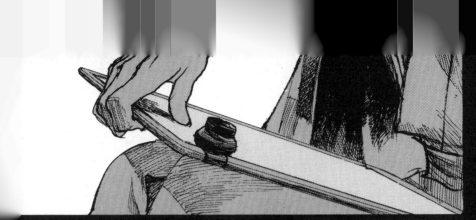

I AM AN *ARTIST*, AS YOU CAN SEE.

DON'T MIND ME. JUST CARRY ON.

......
.....
.....

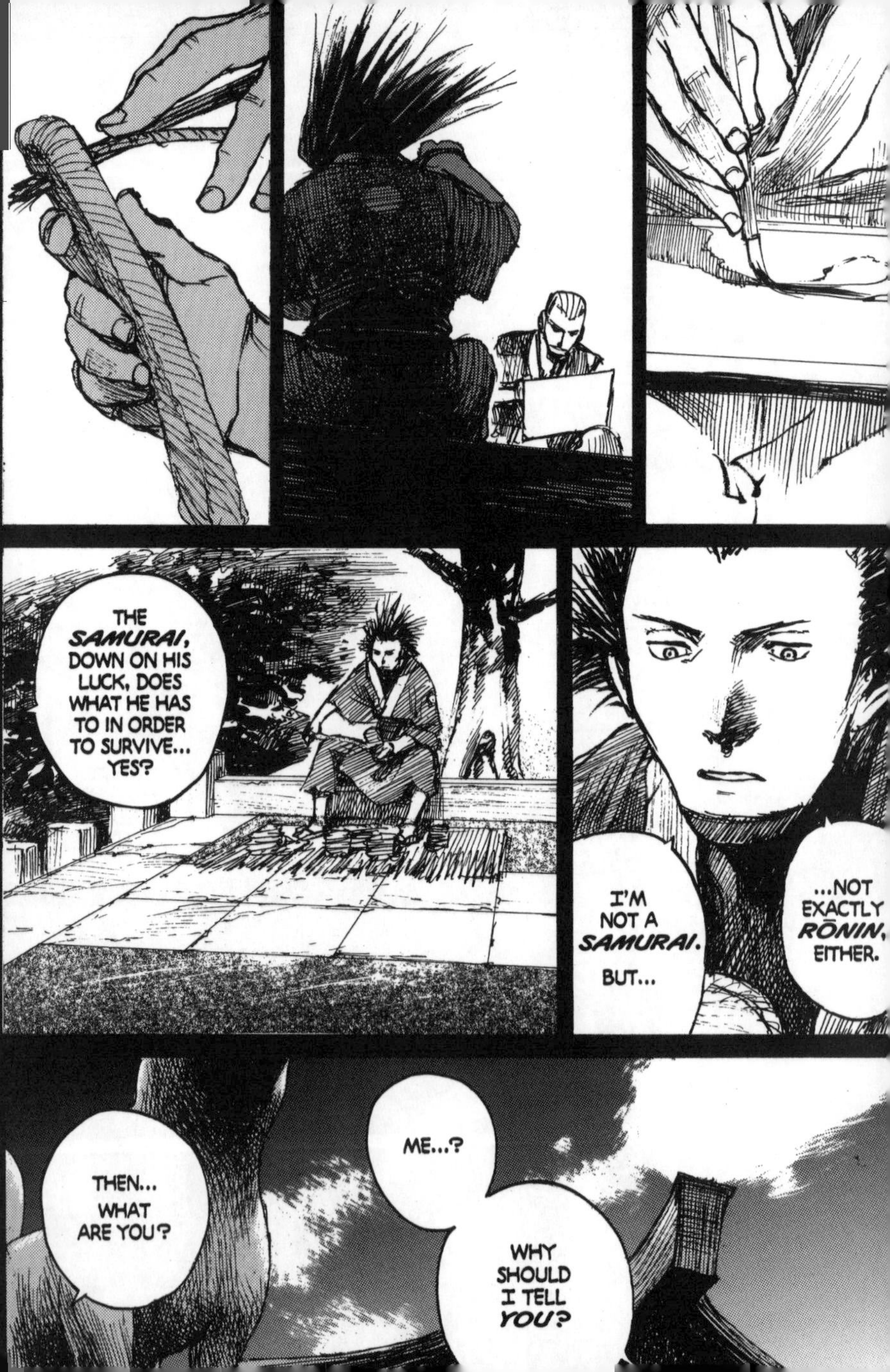
THE *SAMURAI*, DOWN ON HIS LUCK, DOES WHAT HE HAS TO IN ORDER TO SURVIVE... YES?
I'M NOT A *SAMURAI*.
BUT...
...NOT EXACTLY *RŌNIN*, EITHER.
THEN... WHAT ARE YOU?
ME...?
WHY SHOULD I TELL *YOU*?

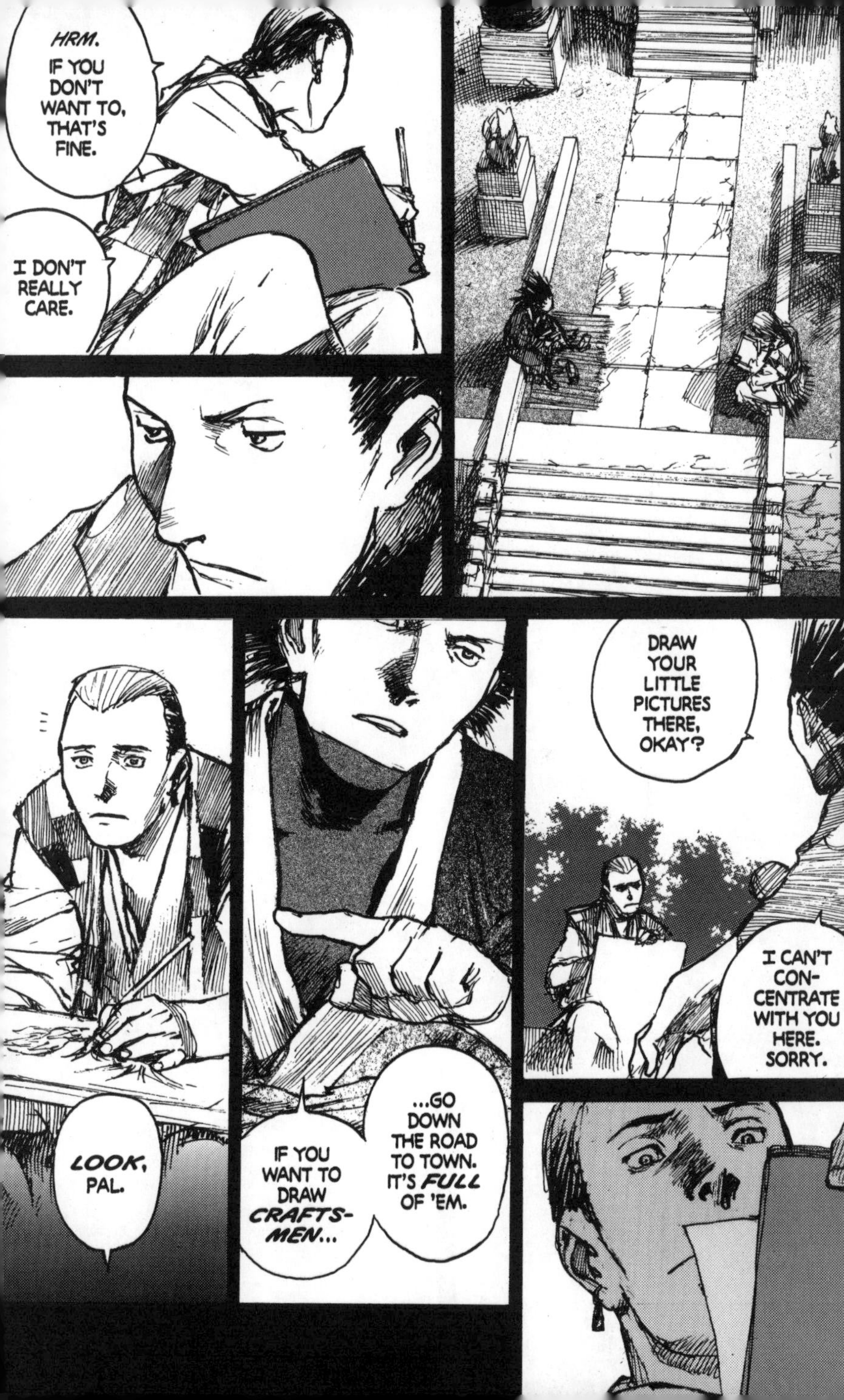
HRM. IF YOU DON'T WANT TO, THAT'S FINE.
I DON'T REALLY CARE.
LOOK, PAL.
IF YOU WANT TO DRAW CRAFTS-MEN...
...GO DOWN THE ROAD TO TOWN. IT'S FULL OF 'EM.
DRAW YOUR LITTLE PICTURES THERE, OKAY?
I CAN'T CON-CENTRATE WITH YOU HERE. SORRY.

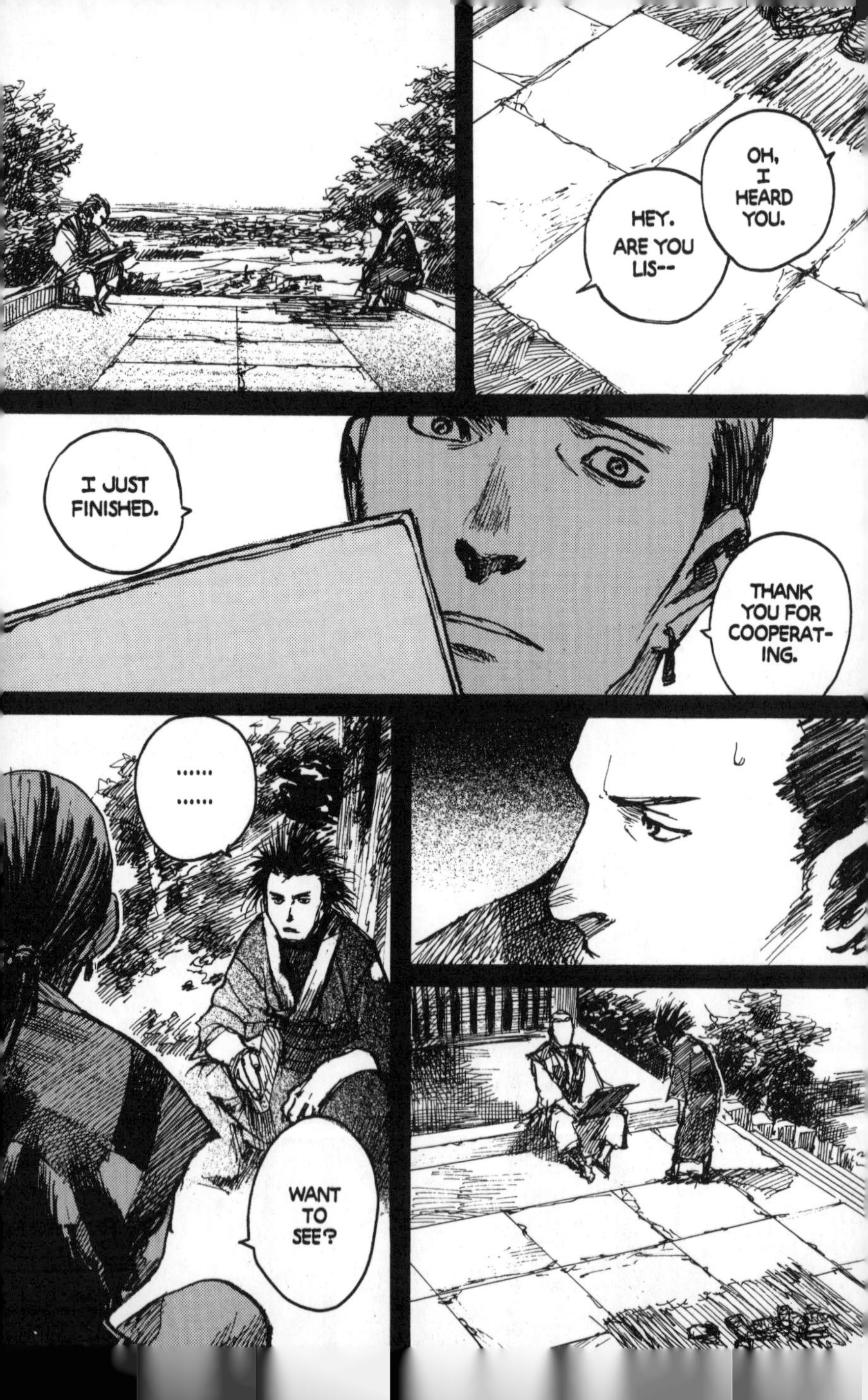
HEY. ARE YOU LIS--
OH, I HEARD YOU.
I JUST FINISHED.
THANK YOU FOR COOPERAT-ING.
......
......
WANT TO SEE?

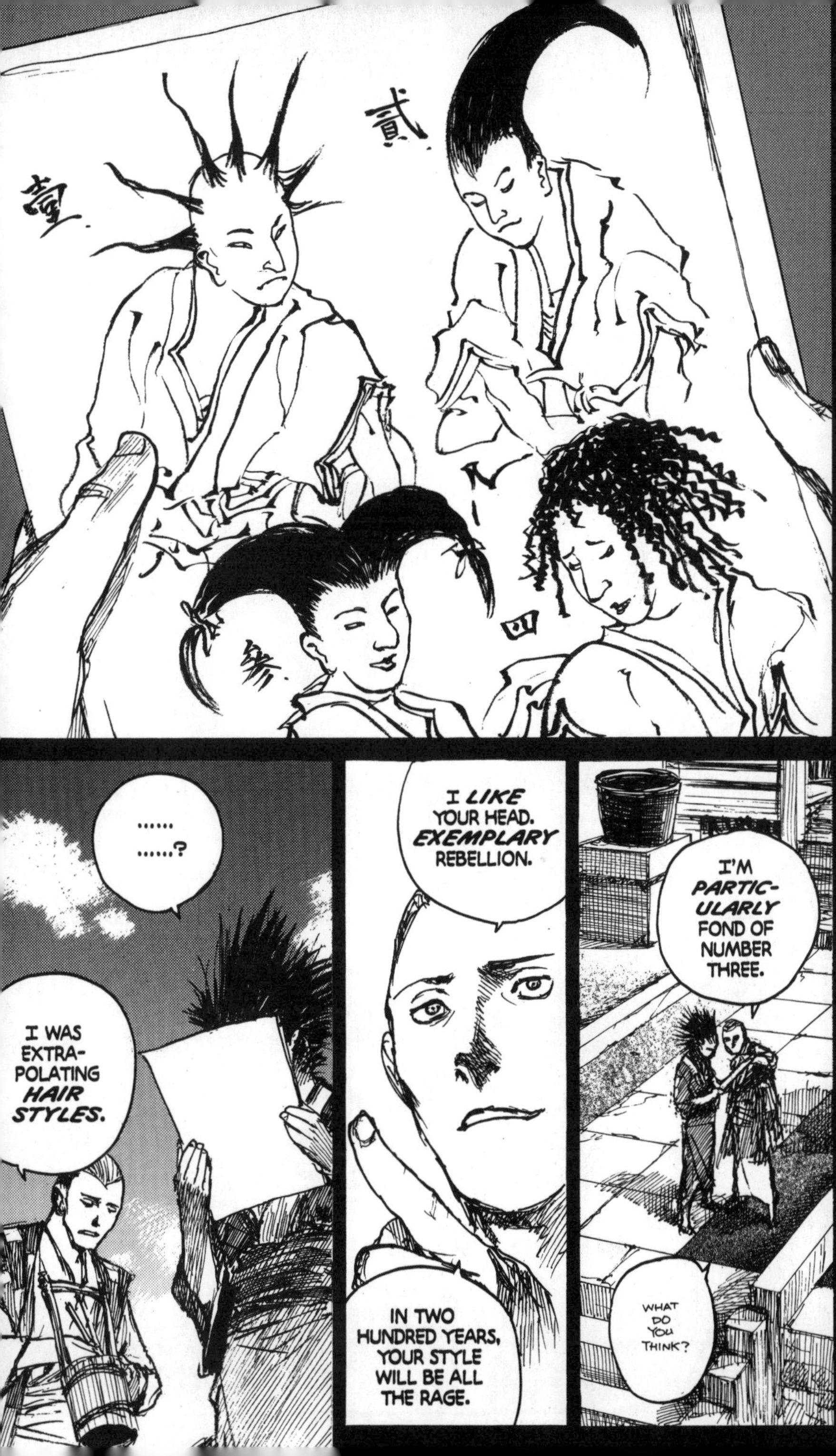
壹
貳
參
四
......
......?
I WAS EXTRAPOLATING *HAIR STYLES*.
I *LIKE* YOUR HEAD. *EXEMPLARY* REBELLION.
IN TWO HUNDRED YEARS, YOUR STYLE WILL BE ALL THE RAGE.
I'M *PARTICULARLY* FOND OF NUMBER THREE.
WHAT DO YOU THINK?

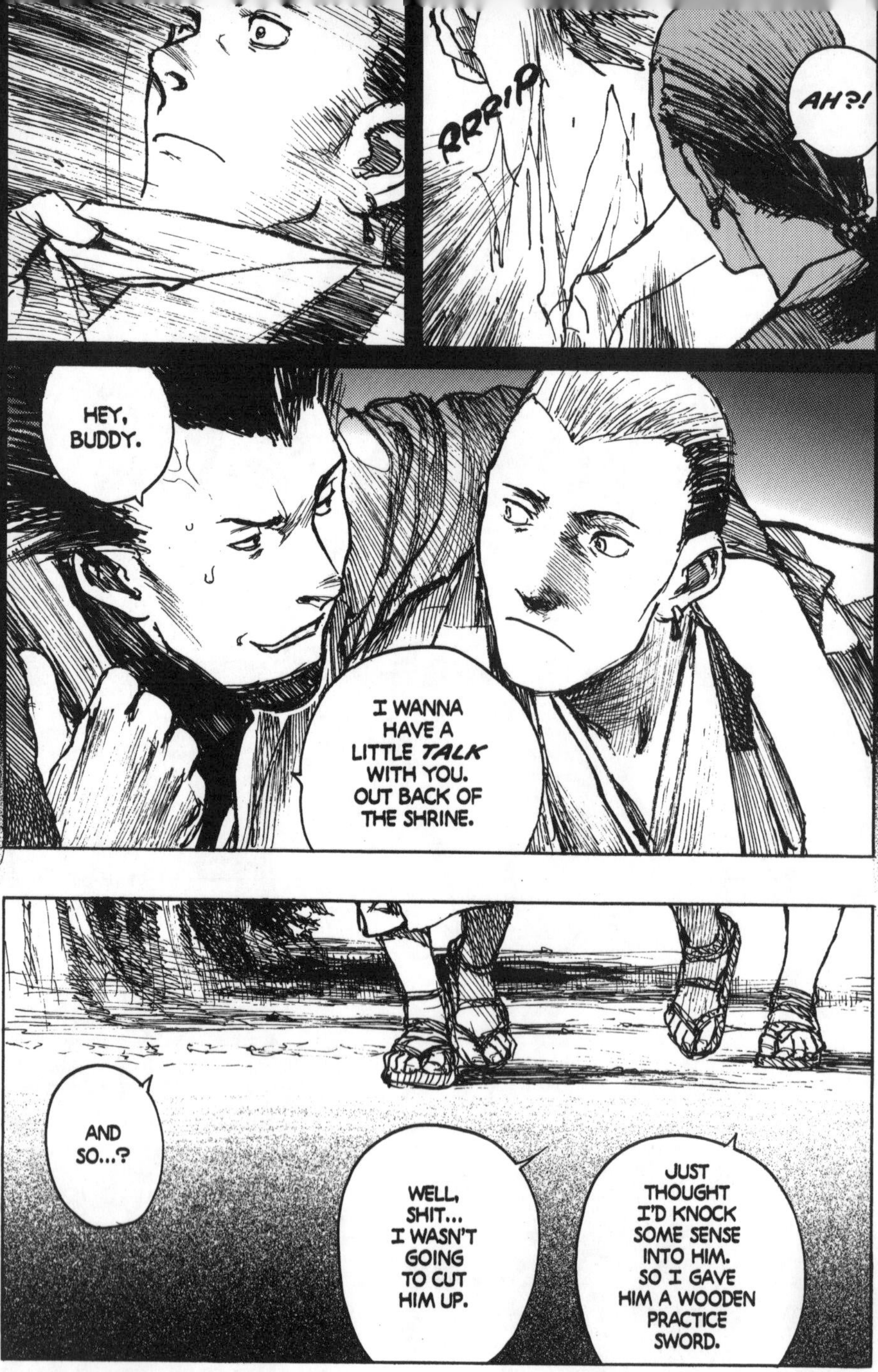
RRRIP
AH?!
HEY, BUDDY.
I WANNA HAVE A LITTLE *TALK* WITH YOU. OUT BACK OF THE SHRINE.
AND SO...?
WELL, SHIT... I WASN'T GOING TO CUT HIM UP.
JUST THOUGHT I'D KNOCK SOME SENSE INTO HIM. SO I GAVE HIM A WOODEN PRACTICE SWORD.

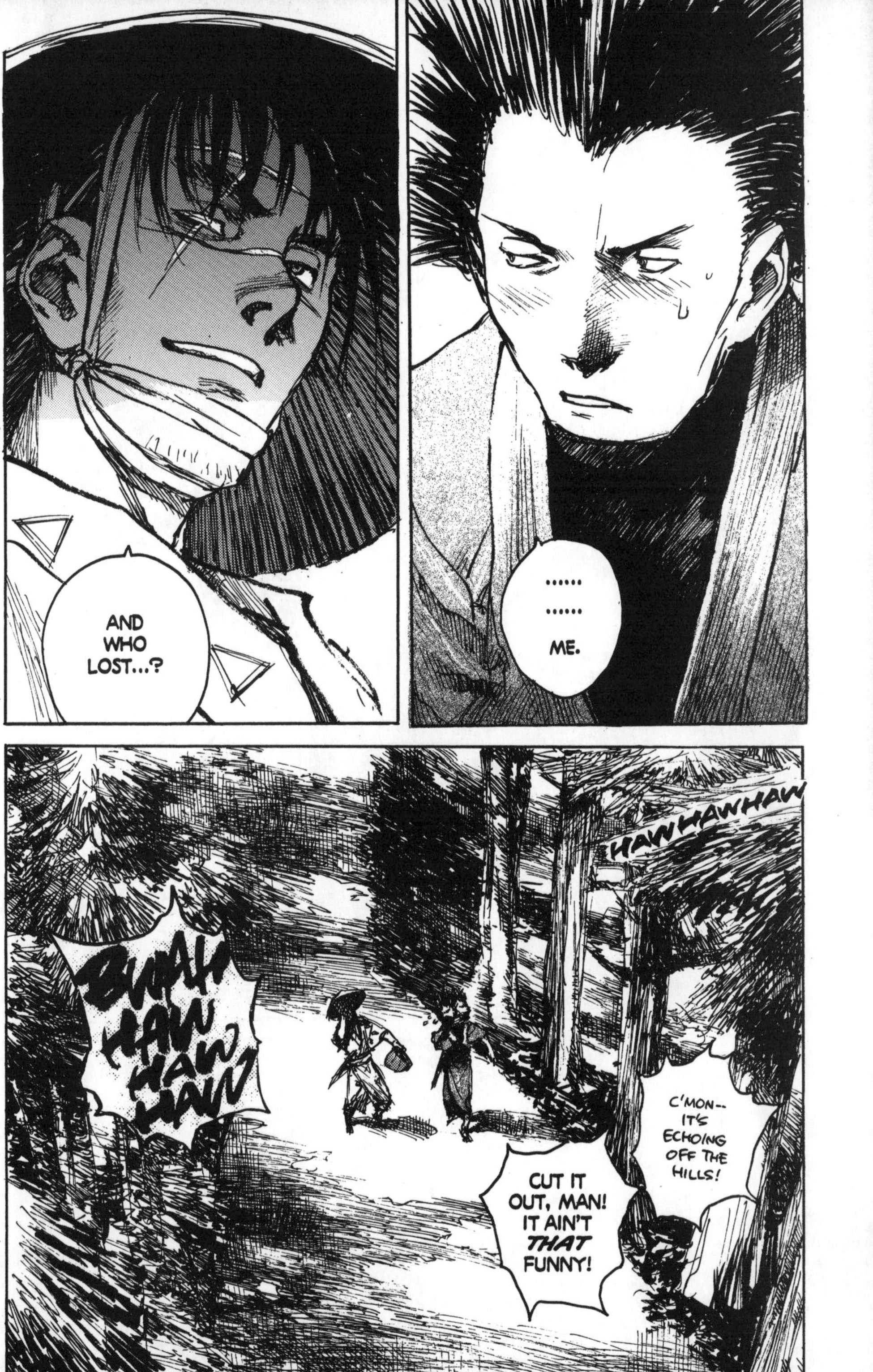
AND WHO LOST...?
......
......
ME.
BUAH HAW HAW HAW
HAWHAWHAW
CUT IT OUT, MAN! IT AIN'T *THAT* FUNNY!
C'MON-- IT'S ECHOING OFF THE HILLS!

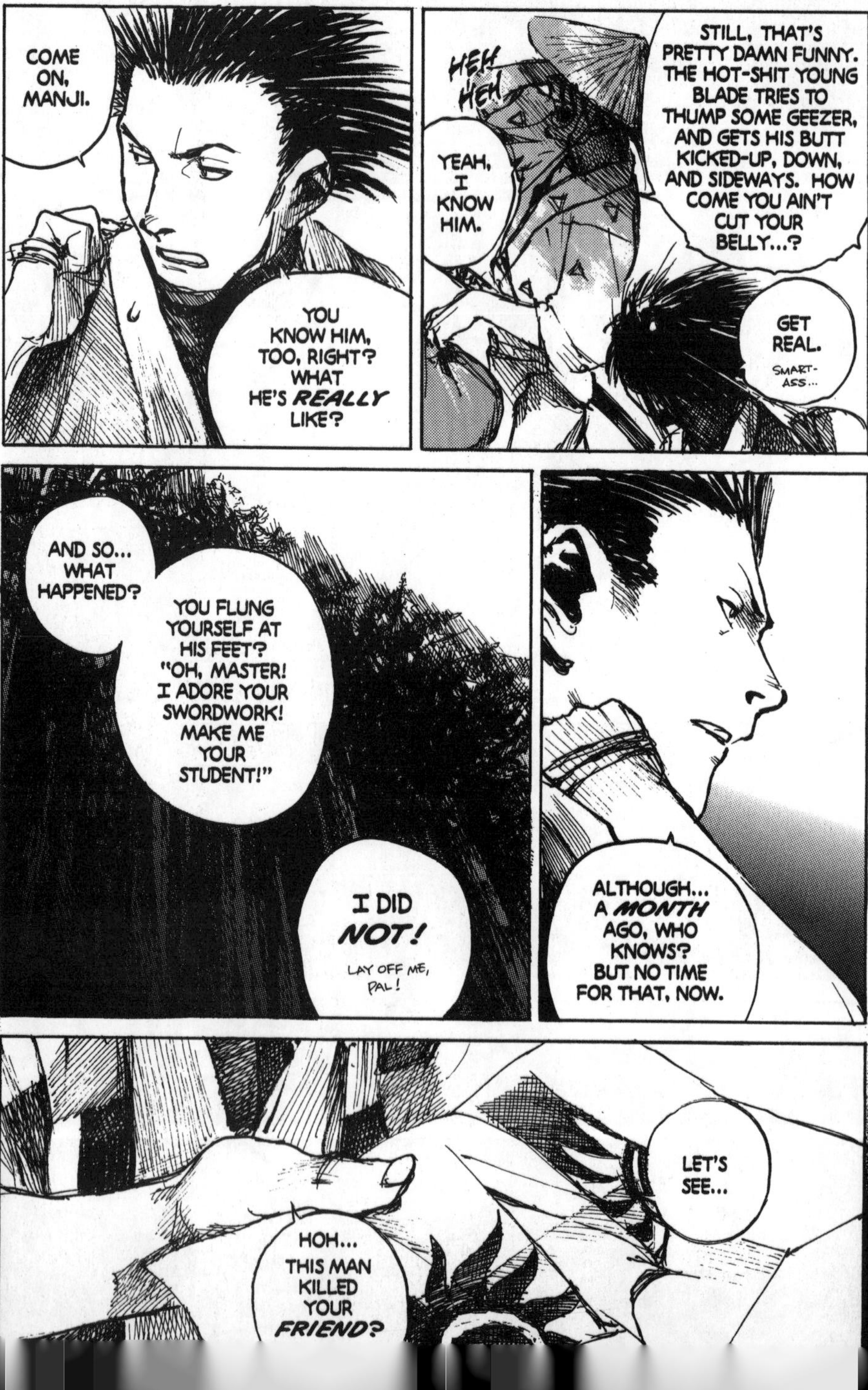
COME ON, MANJI.
YOU KNOW HIM, TOO, RIGHT? WHAT HE'S *REALLY* LIKE?
HEH HEH
YEAH, I KNOW HIM.
STILL, THAT'S PRETTY DAMN FUNNY. THE HOT-SHIT YOUNG BLADE TRIES TO THUMP SOME GEEZER, AND GETS HIS BUTT KICKED-UP, DOWN, AND SIDEWAYS. HOW COME YOU AIN'T CUT YOUR BELLY...?
GET REAL.
SMART-ASS...
AND SO... WHAT HAPPENED?
YOU FLUNG YOURSELF AT HIS FEET? "OH, MASTER! I ADORE YOUR SWORDWORK! MAKE ME YOUR STUDENT!"
I DID *NOT!*
LAY OFF ME, PAL!
ALTHOUGH... A *MONTH* AGO, WHO KNOWS? BUT NO TIME FOR THAT, NOW.
LET'S SEE...
HOH... THIS MAN KILLED YOUR *FRIEND?*

......
......
......

SORRY. DON'T KNOW HIM.

TRY SOMEONE ELSE.

I COULD TELL HE WAS LYING.

BUT WHAT I DON'T GET IS... WHY DID HE *NEED* TO LIE?

MAKE HIM TALK? *THAT* GUY?

NO WAY.

SO I *ACTED* LIKE A STUDENT. FIGURED MAYBE IF I *LIVED* WITH HIM, HE'D SHOW HIS TRUE COLORS...

DAMN, THE KID'S SHARP. BUT IF SŌRI-*SENSEI* WANTS TO PLAY HIM THAT WAY...

...I WON'T GET INVOLVED.

SO, MAGATSU... IS THIS COOL? US HITTING THE ROAD?

HUH?

WHADDA YA MEAN, "HUH?"

YOU'RE HIS *STUDENT*, RIGHT? AND YOU'RE SUPPOSED TO BE GUARDING HIS *HOUSE!*

HEH, HEH... SPEAKING OF SWEET LITTLE TATSU, MANJI MY FRIEND...

...I HEARD SHE WAS YOUR "MOMMY" WHEN YOU WERE SICK.

!?! YOU--!

WHY, THAT LITTLE-- HOW MUCH DID SHE TELL YOU?!

NO SWEAT.

BESIDES, *TATSUBŌ* KEEPS THAT PLACE TOGETHER.

YEAH, YOU CAN SAY THAT AGAIN.

CHEAP LODGINGS

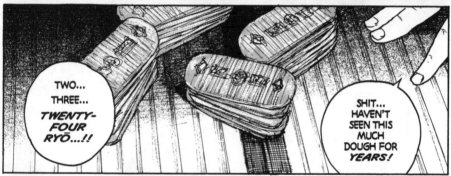

TWO... THREE... *TWENTY-FOUR RYŌ...!!*

SHIT... HAVEN'T SEEN THIS MUCH DOUGH FOR *YEARS!*

EIGHT EACH... . . . .

YOU'RE SOMETHING ELSE, MAN. YOU REALLY *SERIOUS?*

HEH, HEH... WHY NOT?

I LIVE MODESTLY.

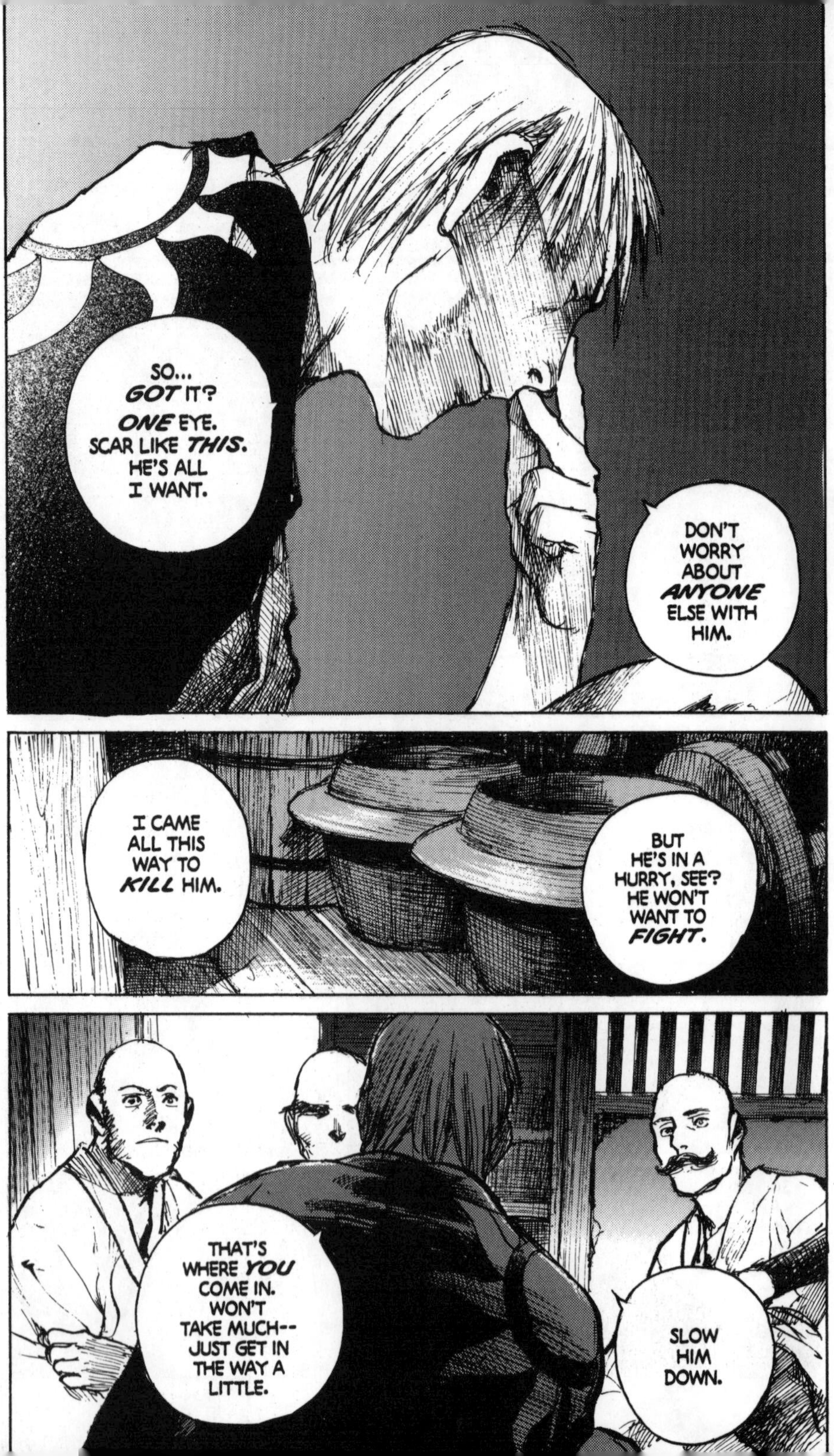

SO... GOT IT? ONE EYE. SCAR LIKE THIS. HE'S ALL I WANT.
DON'T WORRY ABOUT ANYONE ELSE WITH HIM.
I CAME ALL THIS WAY TO KILL HIM.
BUT HE'S IN A HURRY, SEE? HE WON'T WANT TO FIGHT.
THAT'S WHERE YOU COME IN. WON'T TAKE MUCH-- JUST GET IN THE WAY A LITTLE.
SLOW HIM DOWN.

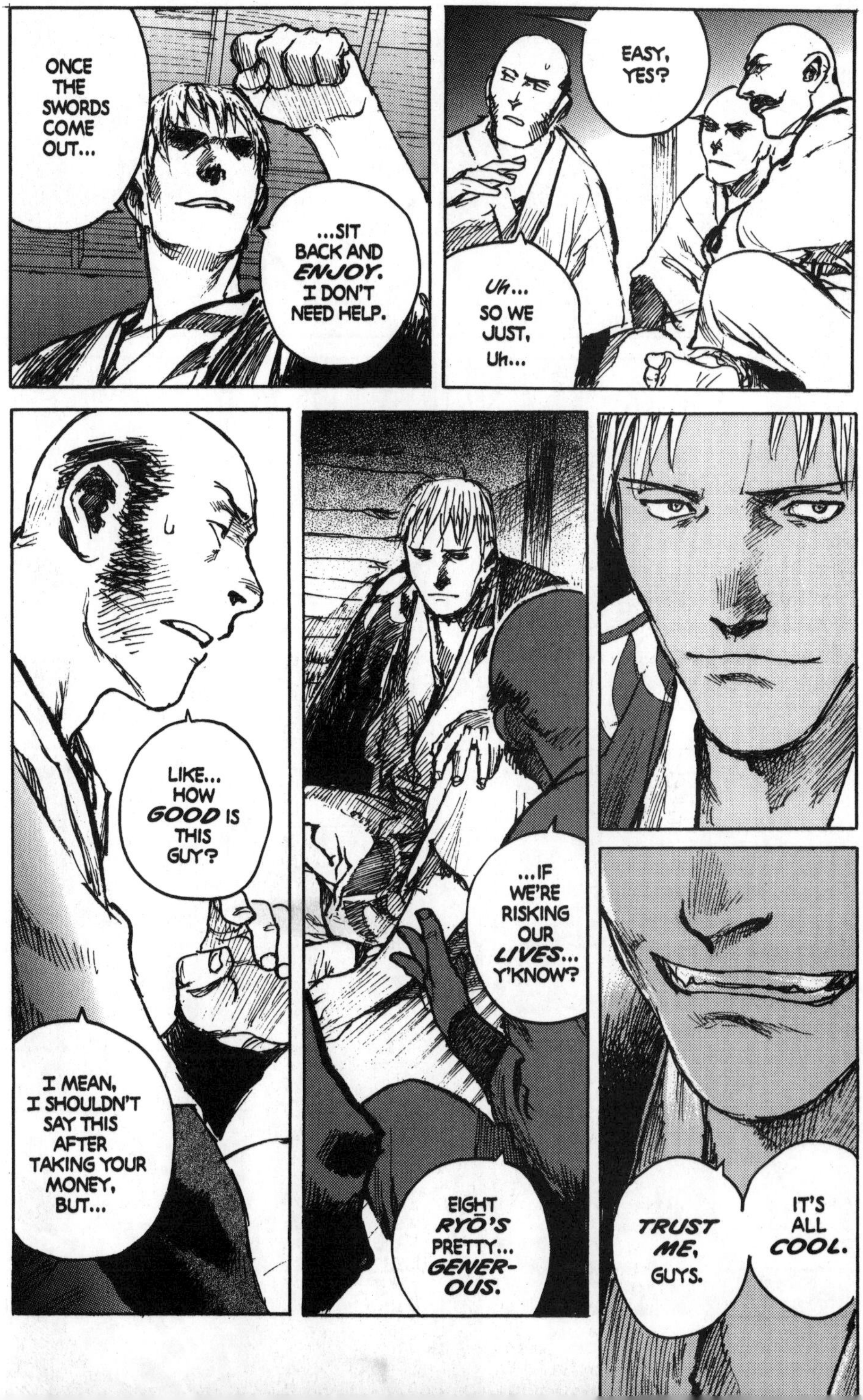
ONCE THE SWORDS COME OUT...
...SIT BACK AND **ENJOY**. I DON'T NEED HELP.
EASY, YES?
Uh... SO WE JUST, *Uh...*
LIKE... HOW **GOOD** IS THIS GUY?
I MEAN, I SHOULDN'T SAY THIS AFTER TAKING YOUR MONEY, BUT...
...IF WE'RE RISKING OUR **LIVES**... Y'KNOW?
EIGHT **RYŌ'S** PRETTY... **GENER-OUS.**
TRUST ME, GUYS.
IT'S ALL **COOL**.

OKAY, I DON'T KNOW ABOUT ONE-ON-ONE...

...BUT *TWO* OF YOU CAN TAKE HIM, EASY.

IN THAT CASE...

YEAH, BUT...

WHY *ALL* OF US? AND ALL THIS *CASH*? I MEAN, IF HE'S JUST--

YOU STUPID ASSHOLES ARE DRIVING ME *NUTS*!!

QUIT JERKING AROUND!! ARE YOU *IN* OR *OUT*?!

NO FREE RIDES IN *LIFE*, MAN!

DECIDE! NOW !!

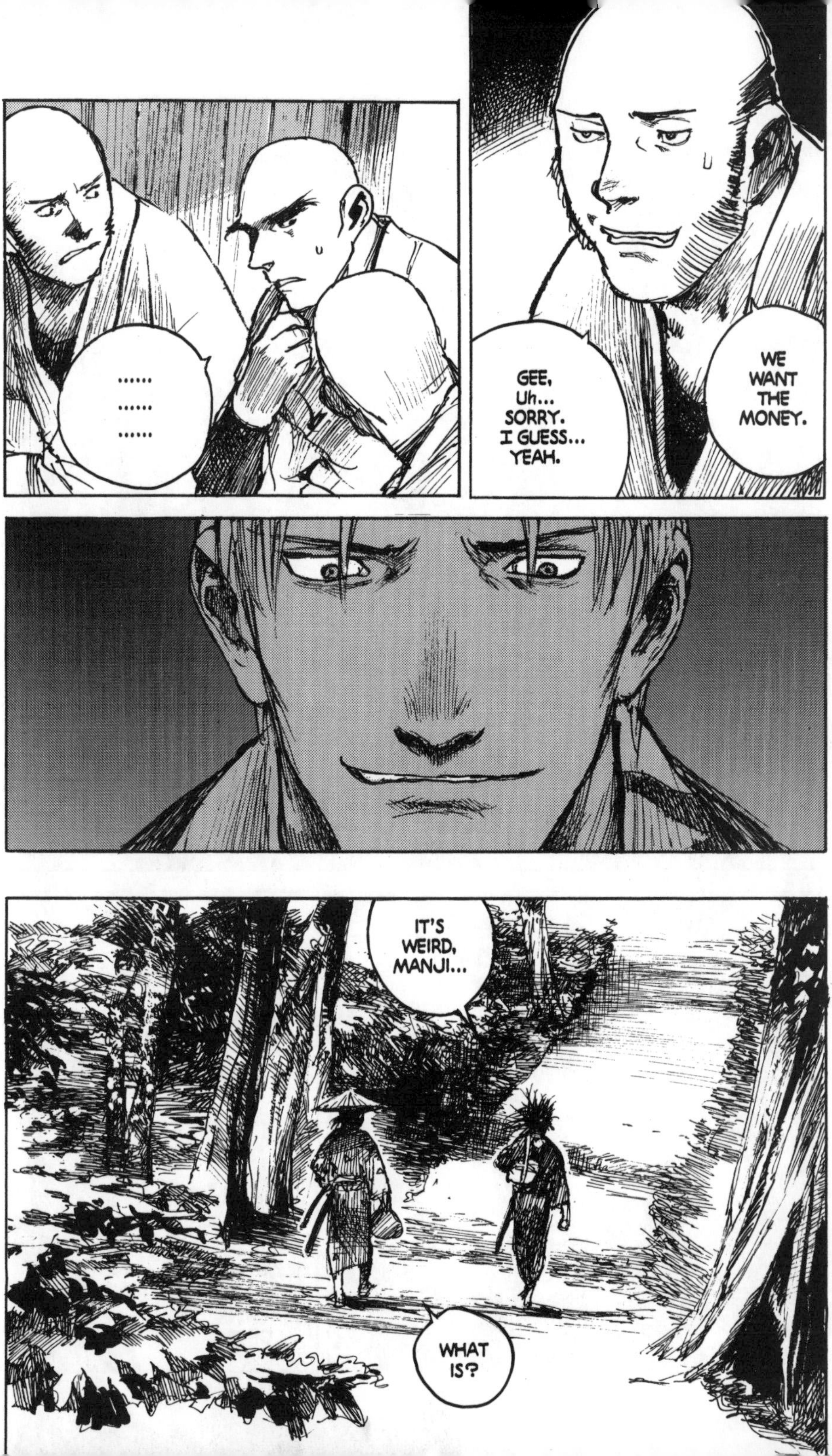
......
......
......
GEE, Uh... SORRY. I GUESS... YEAH.
WE WANT THE MONEY.
IT'S WEIRD, MANJI...
WHAT IS?

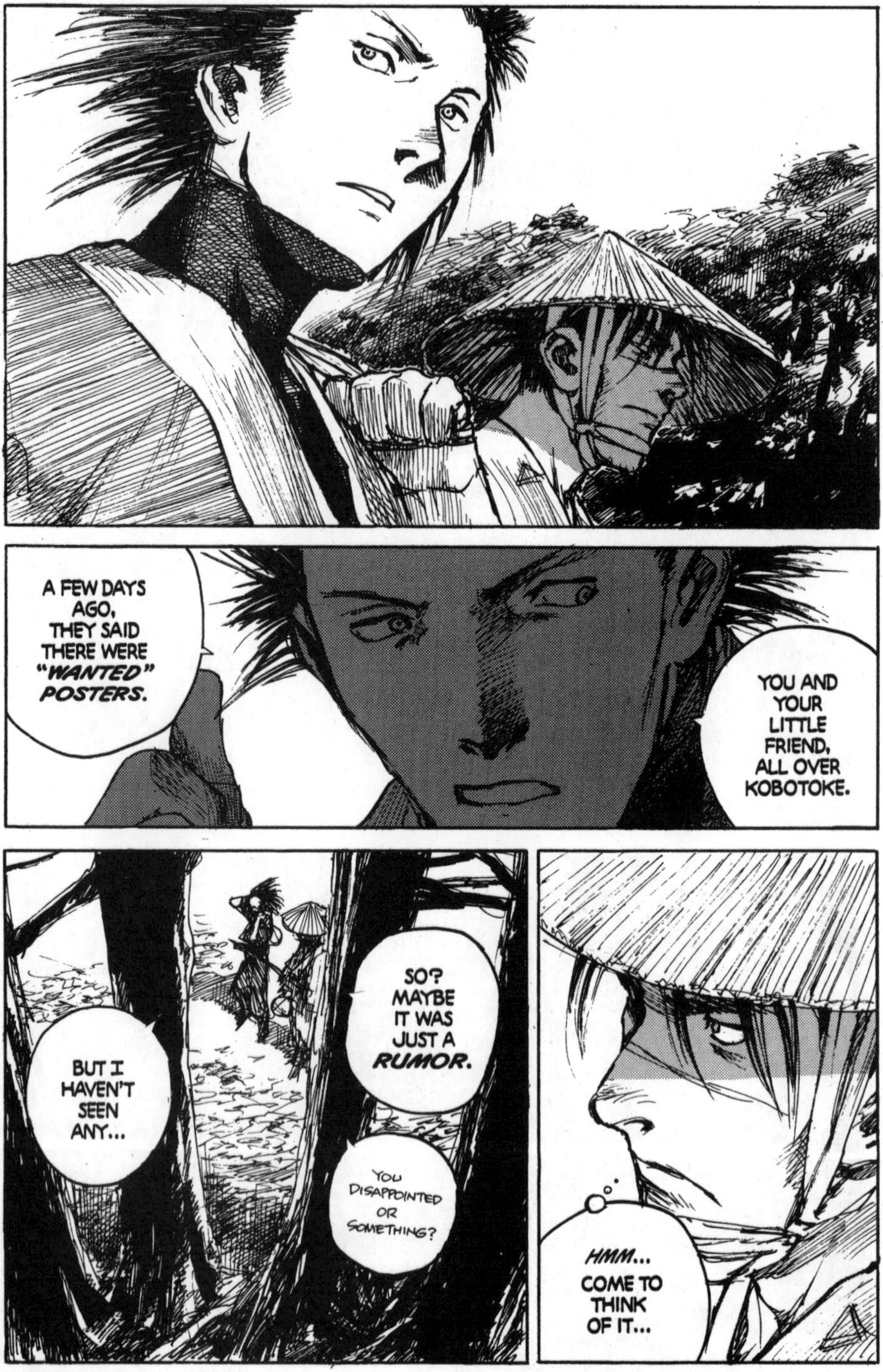
A FEW DAYS AGO, THEY SAID THERE WERE "WANTED" POSTERS.
YOU AND YOUR LITTLE FRIEND, ALL OVER KOBOTOKE.
SO? MAYBE IT WAS JUST A RUMOR.
BUT I HAVEN'T SEEN ANY...
YOU DISAPPOINTED OR SOMETHING?
HMM... COME TO THINK OF IT...

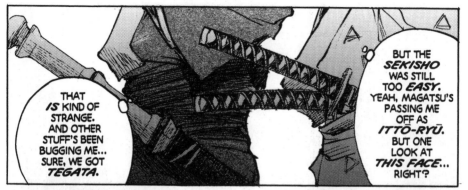

THAT *IS* KIND OF STRANGE. AND OTHER STUFF'S BEEN BUGGING ME... SURE, WE GOT *TEGATA.*

BUT THE *SEKISHO* WAS STILL TOO *EASY.* YEAH, MAGATSU'S PASSING ME OFF AS *ITTŌ-RYŪ.* BUT ONE LOOK AT *THIS FACE...* RIGHT?

SOME-ONE'S PULLING STRINGS.

HMM. MAYBE... IT'S *HER?*

SHE TOLD HER BOSSES I'M A *KENKYAKU* OUT TO KILL ANOTSU?

MAKING UP FOR THE LAST TIME...? DAMN, SHE'S A CUNNING BITCH.

WHEW... WE'VE PUT ON SOME MILES. IF I WALK ALL THE WAY TO *KAGA* WITH YOU...

...I'LL FEEL LIKE A REAL *DUMB-SHIT.*

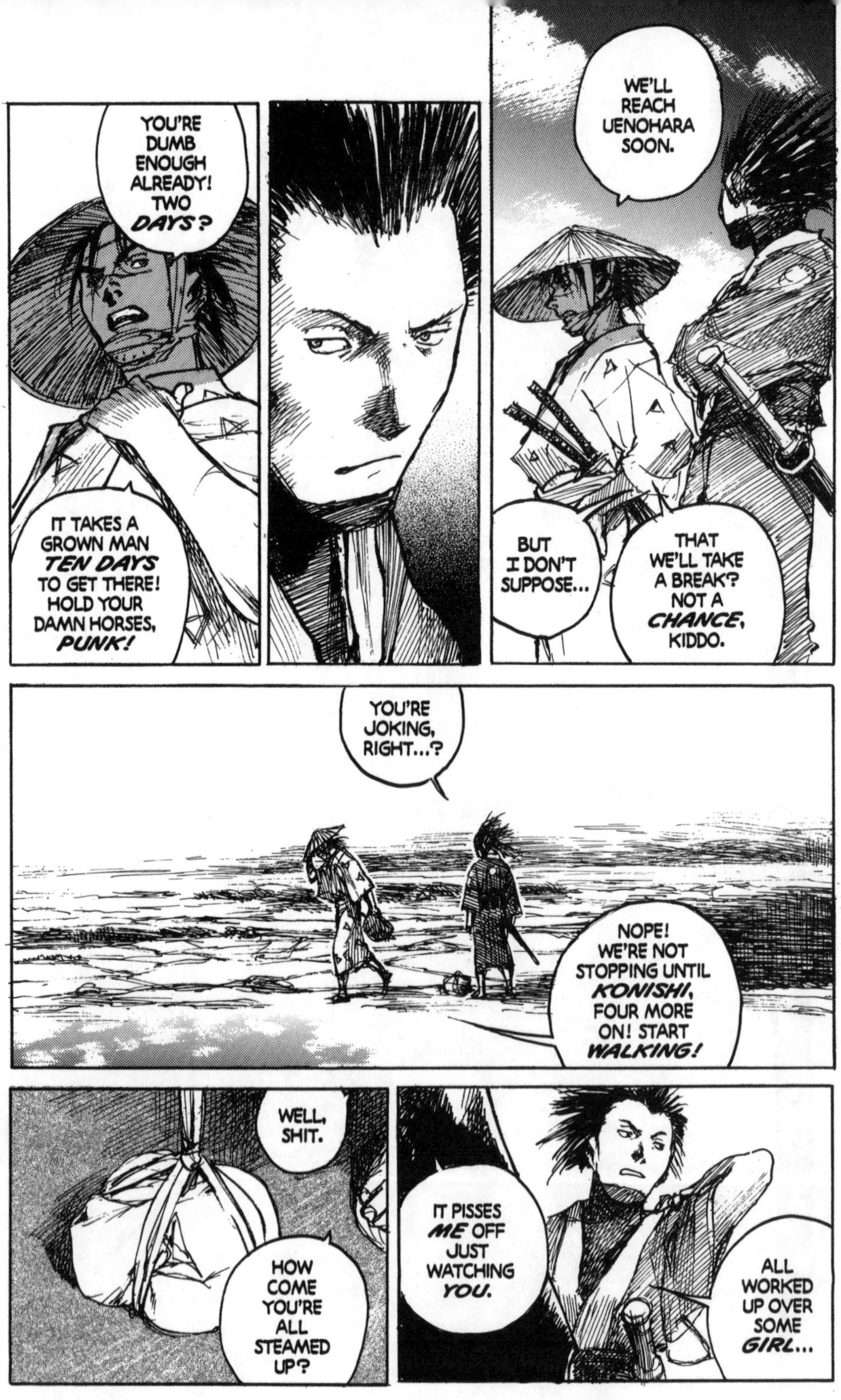
YOU'RE DUMB ENOUGH ALREADY! TWO DAYS?
IT TAKES A GROWN MAN TEN DAYS TO GET THERE! HOLD YOUR DAMN HORSES, PUNK!
WE'LL REACH UENOHARA SOON.
BUT I DON'T SUPPOSE...
THAT WE'LL TAKE A BREAK? NOT A CHANCE, KIDDO.
YOU'RE JOKING, RIGHT...?
NOPE! WE'RE NOT STOPPING UNTIL KONISHI, FOUR MORE ON! START WALKING!
WELL, SHIT.
HOW COME YOU'RE ALL STEAMED UP?
IT PISSES ME OFF JUST WATCHING YOU.
ALL WORKED UP OVER SOME GIRL...

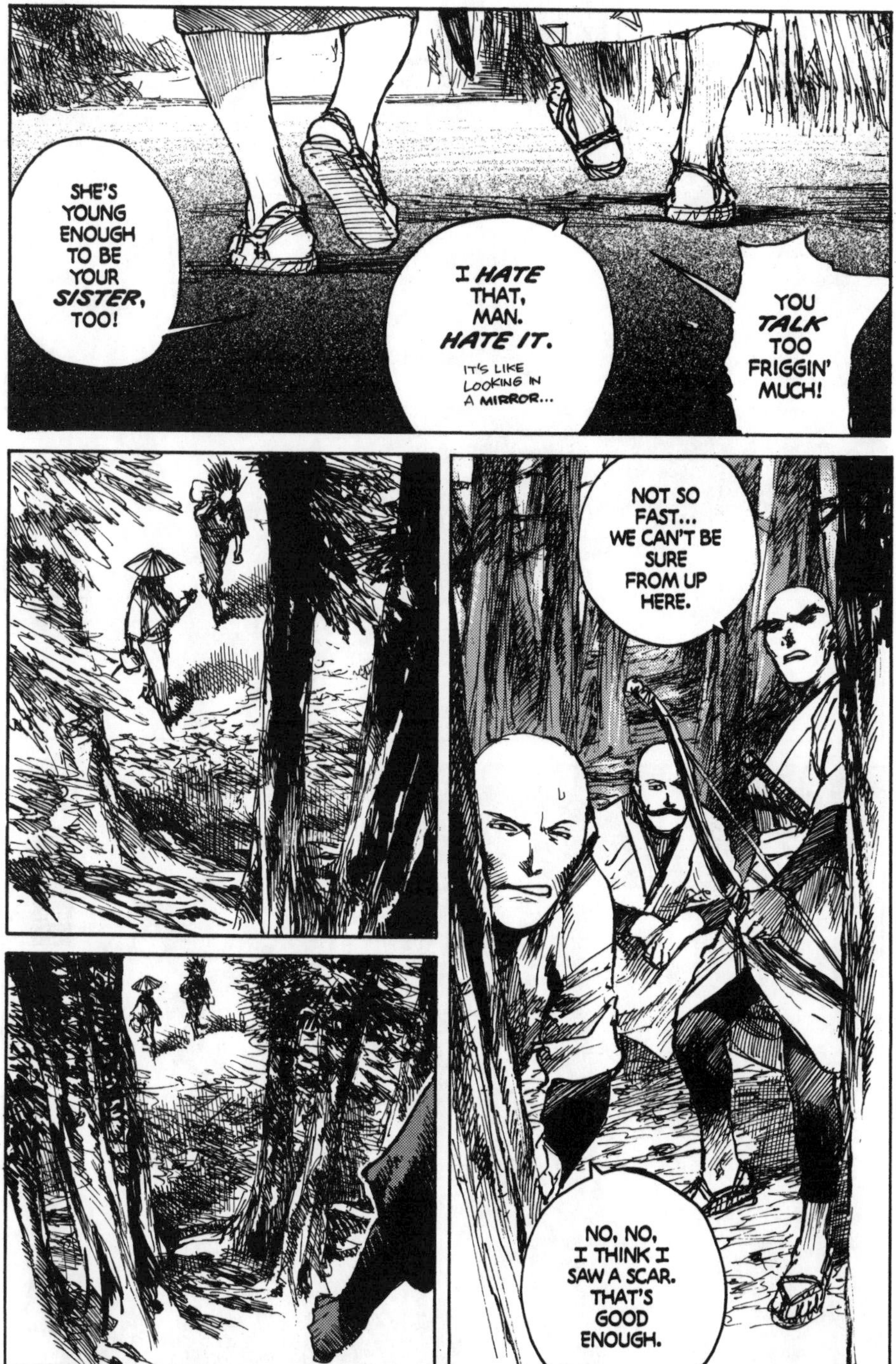
SHE'S YOUNG ENOUGH TO BE YOUR SISTER, TOO!
I HATE THAT, MAN. HATE IT.
IT'S LIKE LOOKING IN A MIRROR...
YOU TALK TOO FRIGGIN' MUCH!
NOT SO FAST... WE CAN'T BE SURE FROM UP HERE.
NO, NO, I THINK I SAW A SCAR. THAT'S GOOD ENOUGH.

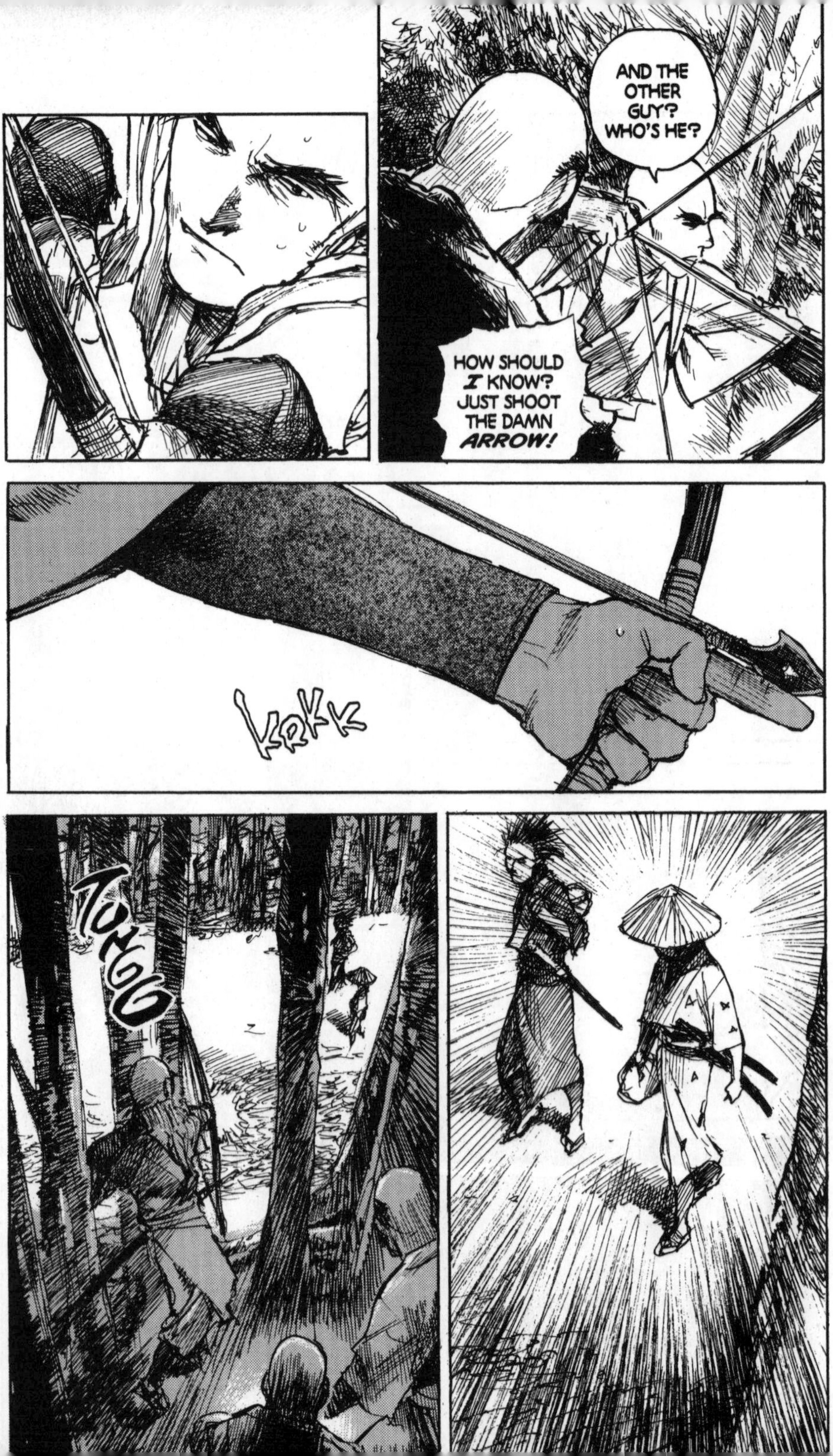
AND THE OTHER GUY? WHO'S HE?
HOW SHOULD I KNOW? JUST SHOOT THE DAMN ARROW!
KRKK
TONGG

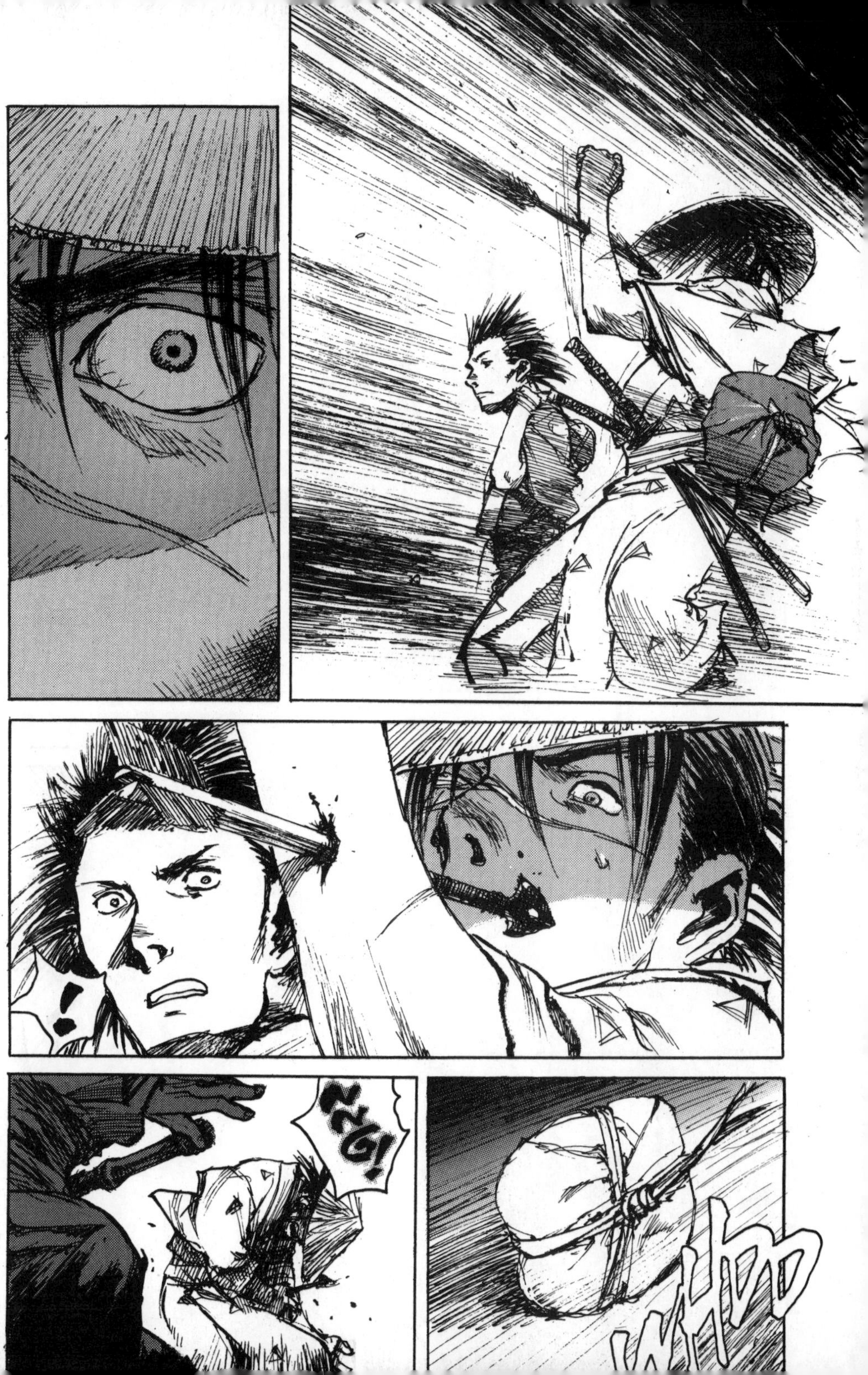
WHUDD

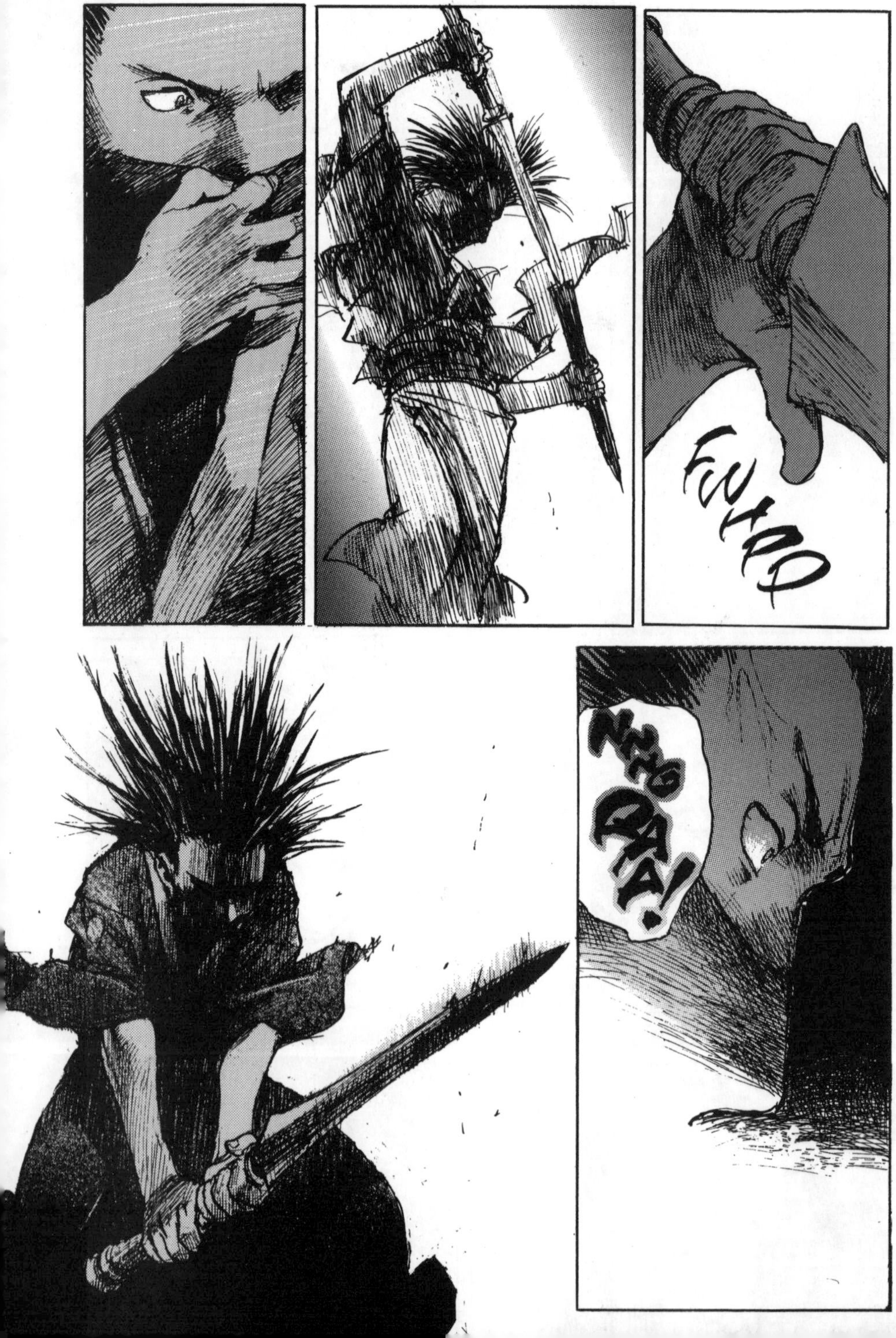
FWIPP
NNG GAA!

STAY RIGHT THERE, YOU *BASTARDS*!!

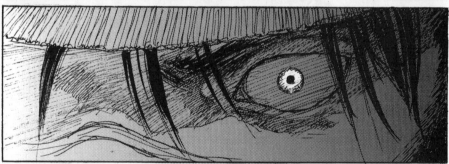

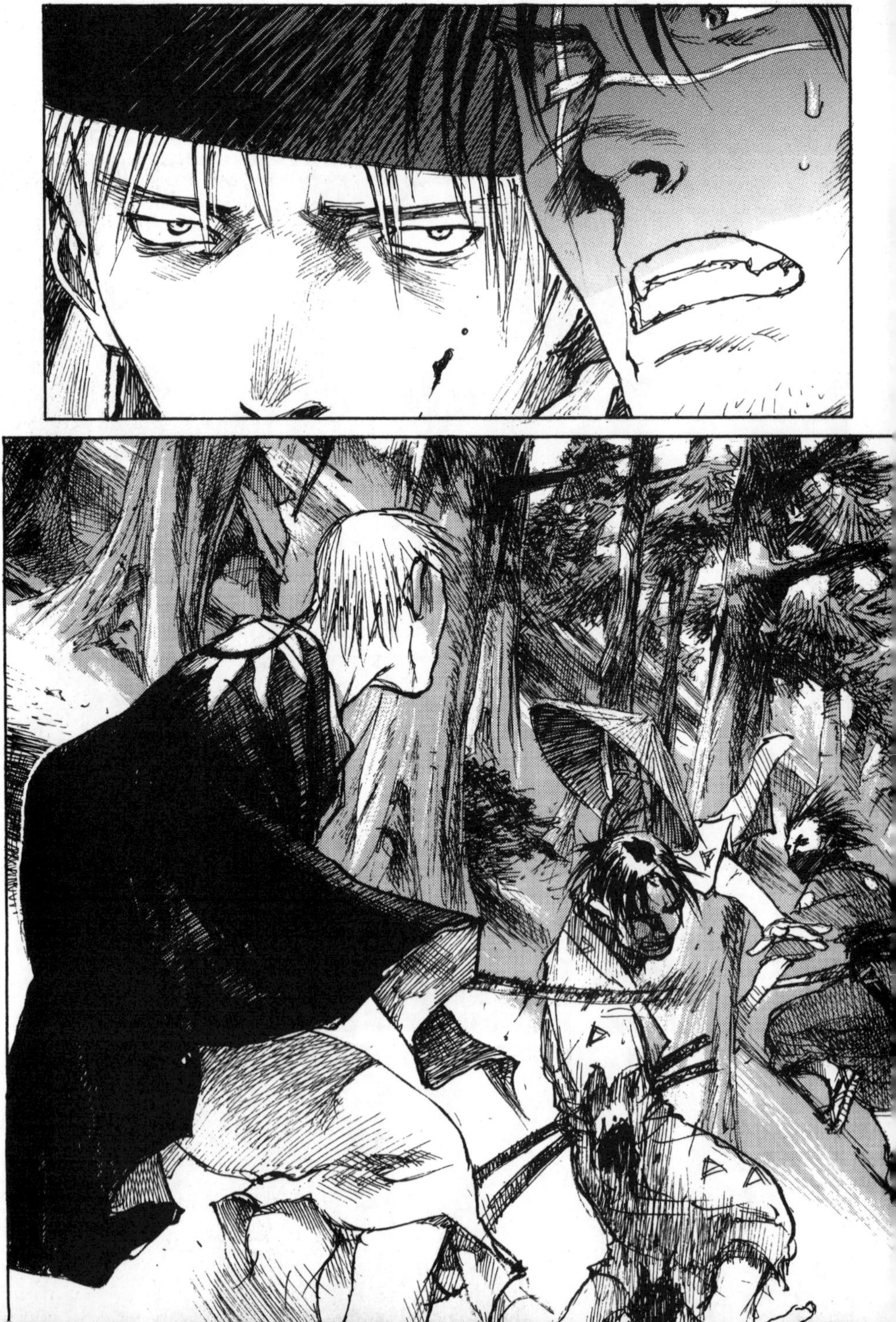

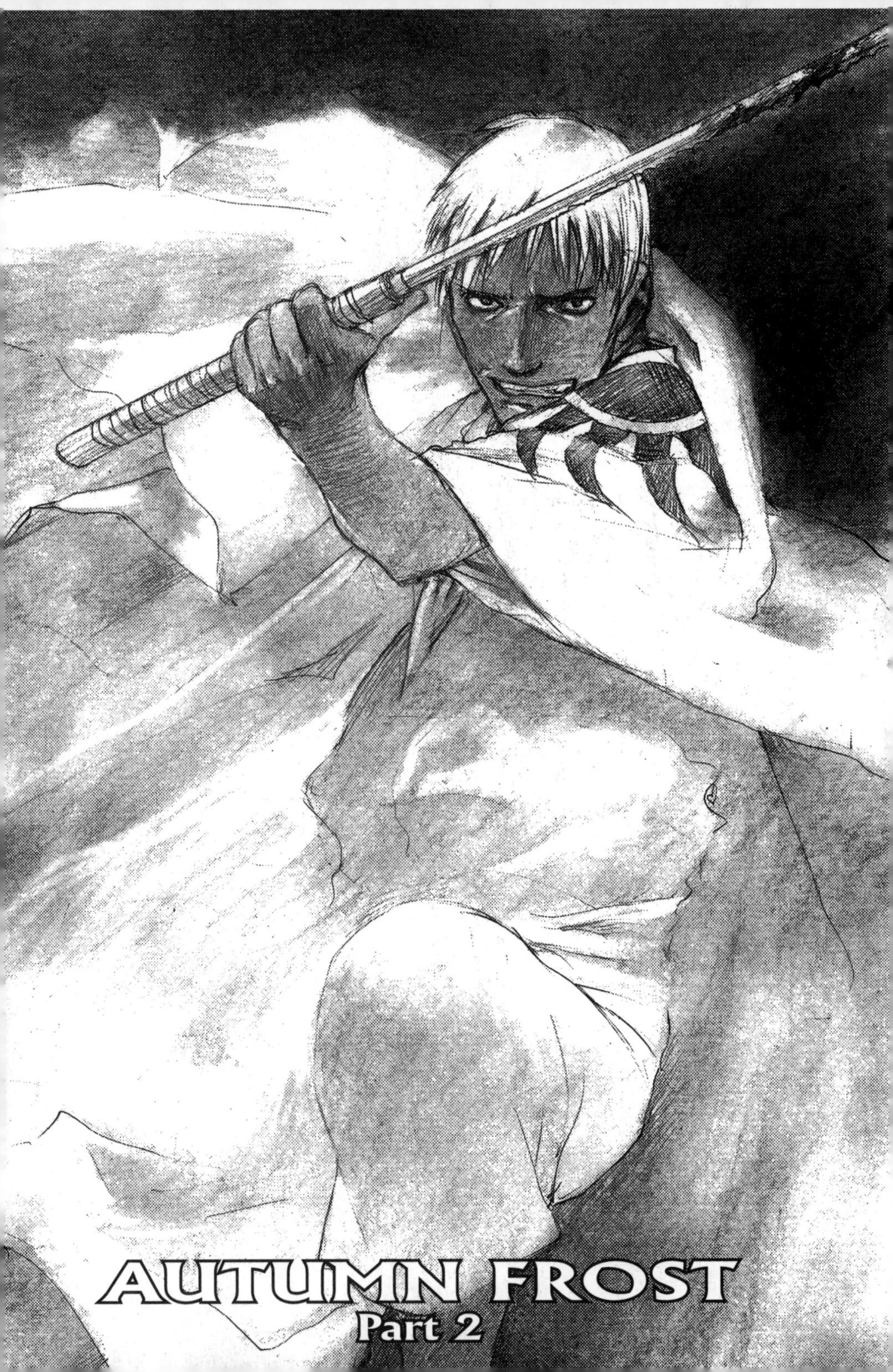
AUTUMN FROST
Part 2

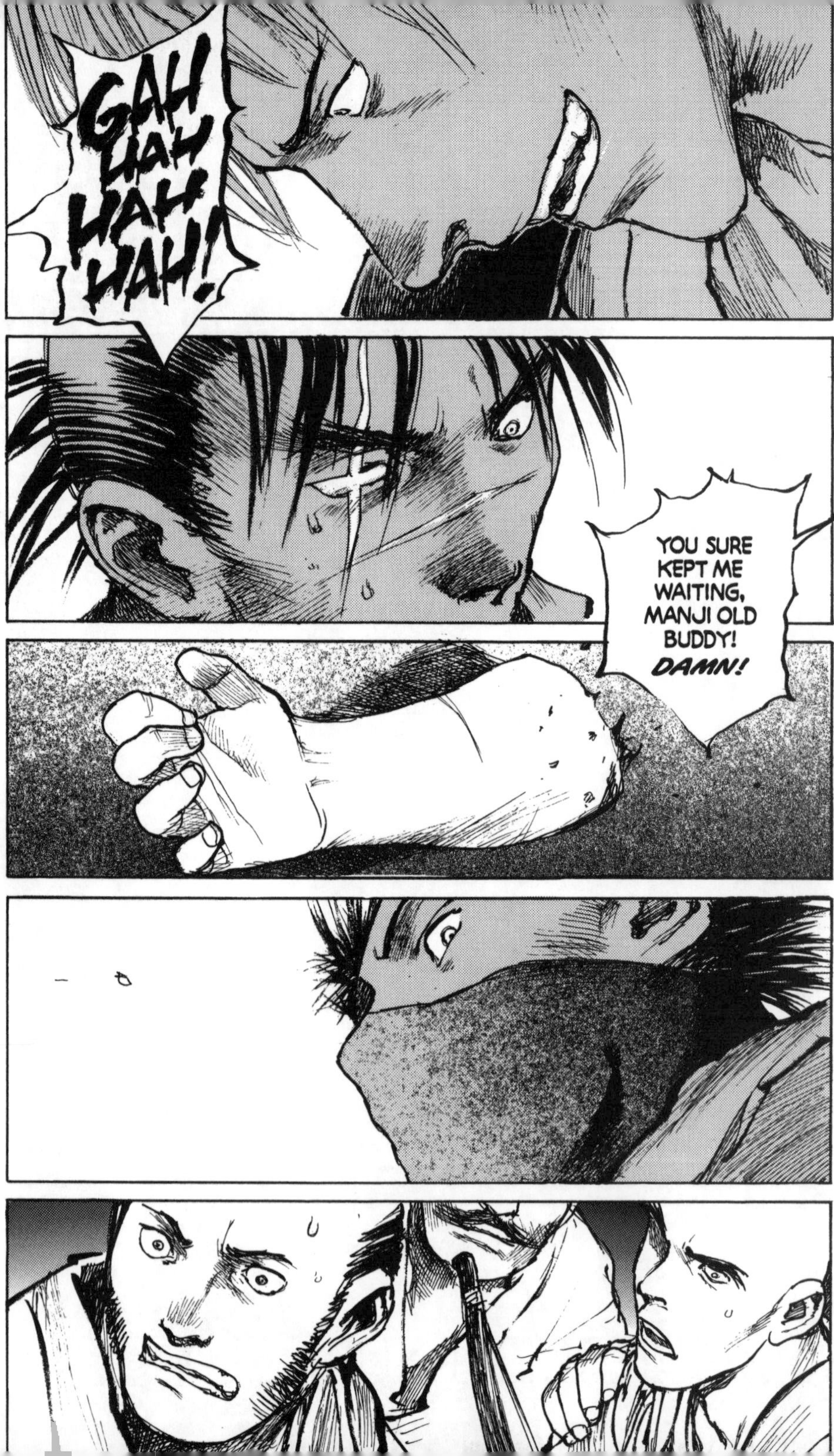
GAH HAH HAH HAH!
YOU SURE KEPT ME WAITING, MANJI OLD BUDDY! DAMN!

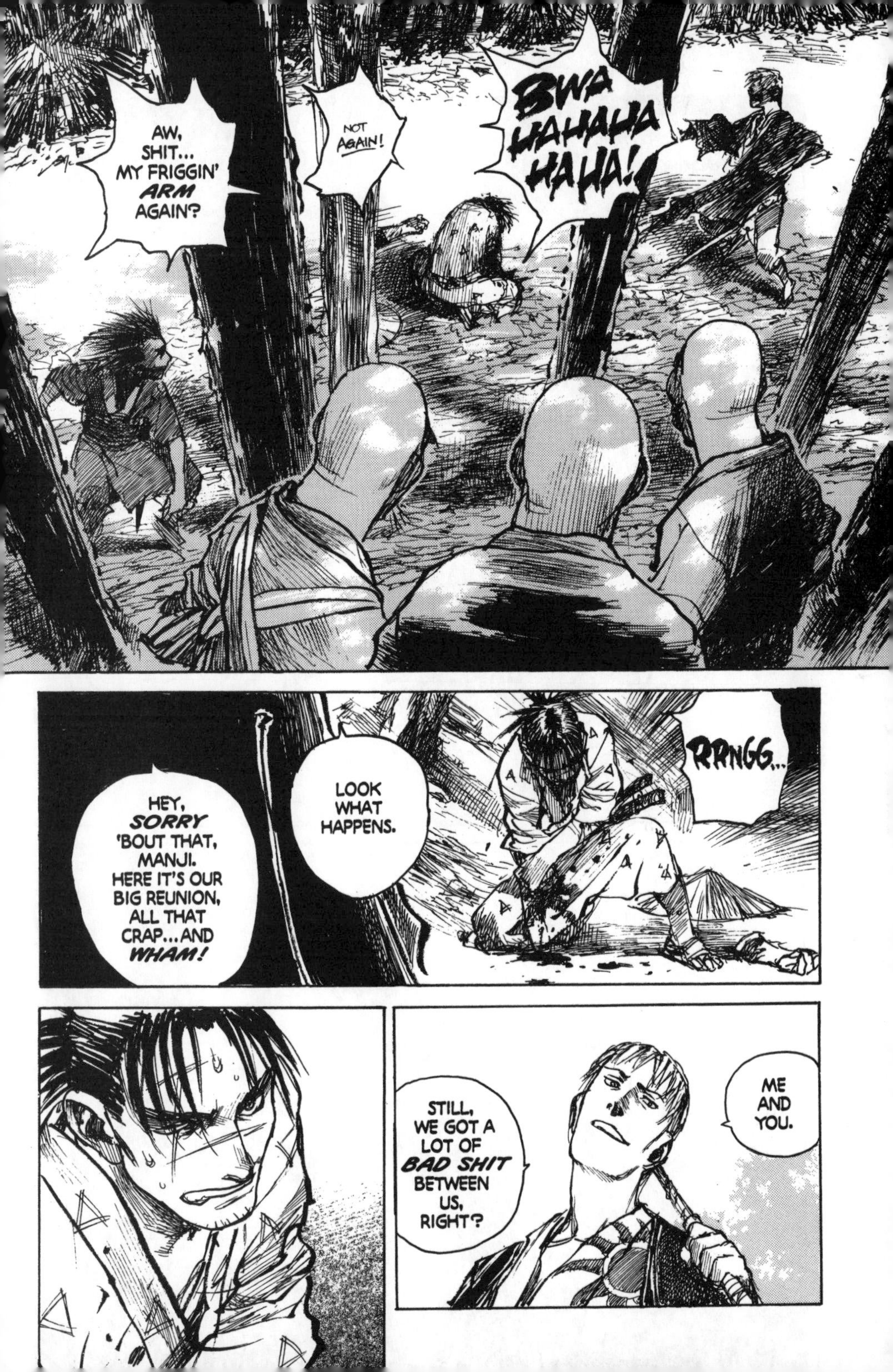
AW, SHIT... MY FRIGGIN' *ARM* AGAIN?
NOT *AGAIN*!
BWA HAHAHA HAHA!
HEY, ***SORRY*** 'BOUT THAT, MANJI. HERE IT'S OUR BIG REUNION, ALL THAT CRAP...AND ***WHAM!***
LOOK WHAT HAPPENS.
RRNGG...
STILL, WE GOT A LOT OF ***BAD SHIT*** BETWEEN US, RIGHT?
ME AND YOU.

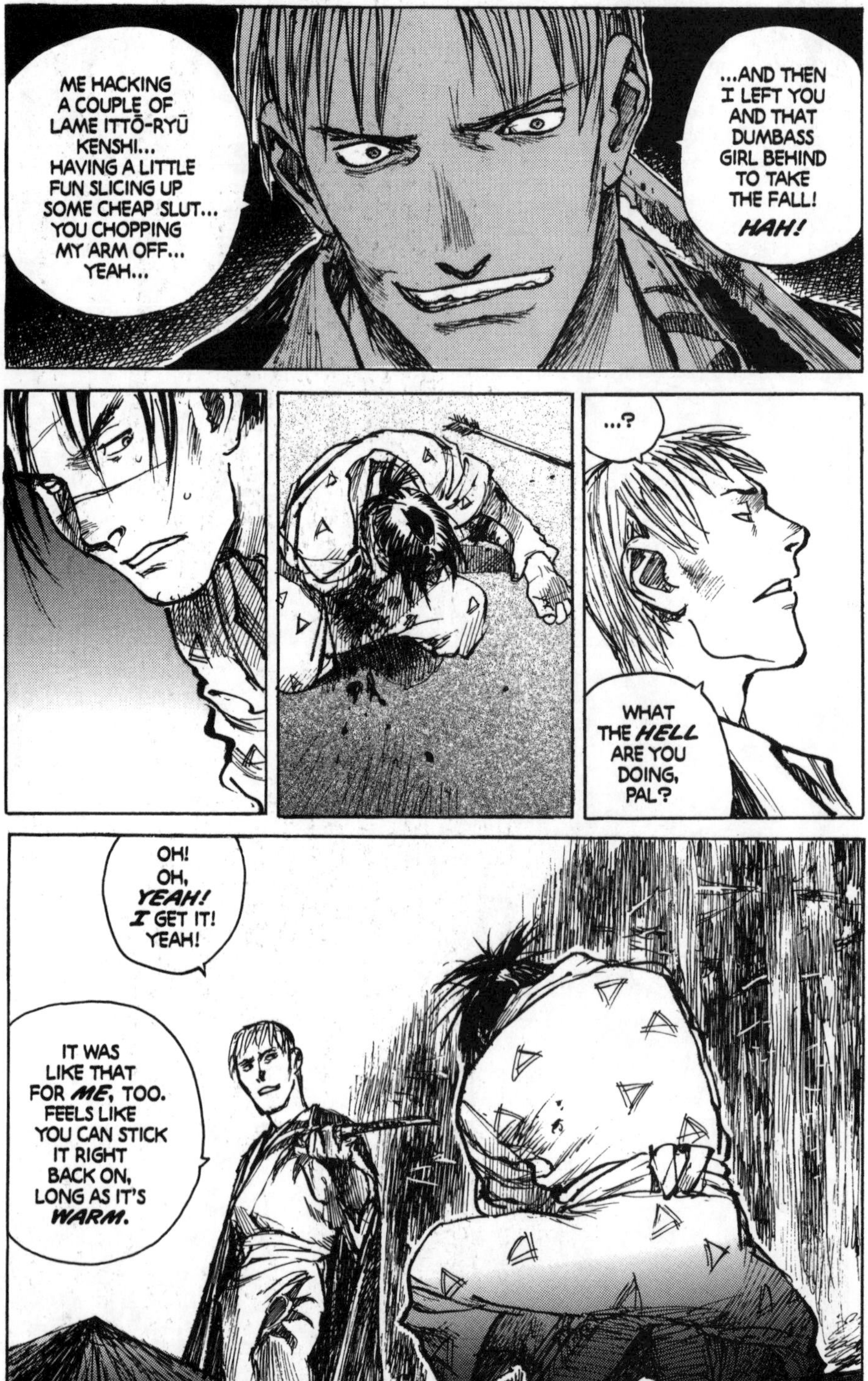
ME HACKING A COUPLE OF LAME ITTŌ-RYŪ KENSHI... HAVING A LITTLE FUN SLICING UP SOME CHEAP SLUT... YOU CHOPPING MY ARM OFF... YEAH...
...AND THEN I LEFT YOU AND THAT DUMBASS GIRL BEHIND TO TAKE THE FALL! HAH!
...?
WHAT THE HELL ARE YOU DOING, PAL?
OH! OH, YEAH! I GET IT! YEAH!
IT WAS LIKE THAT FOR ME, TOO. FEELS LIKE YOU CAN STICK IT RIGHT BACK ON, LONG AS IT'S WARM.

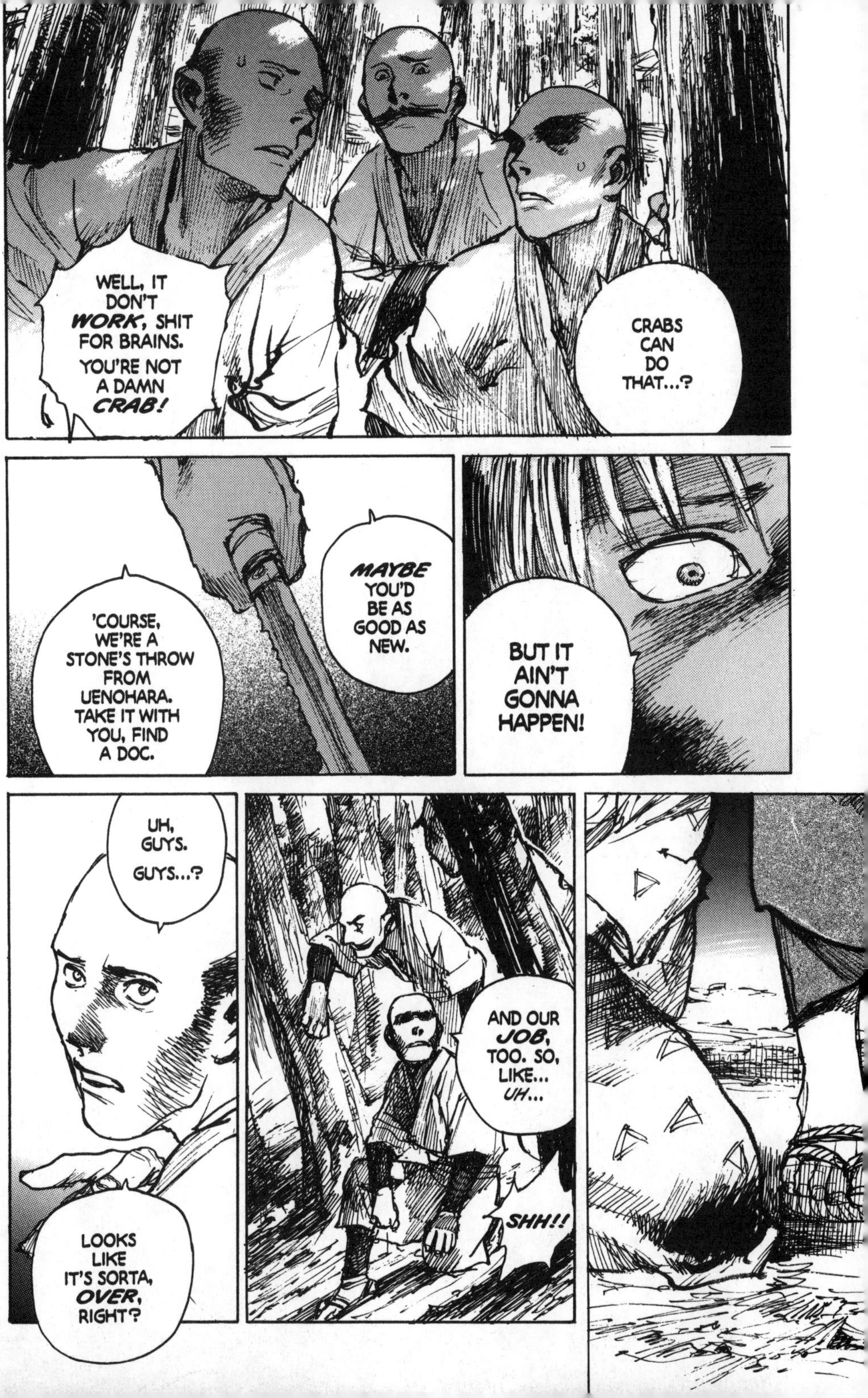
WELL, IT DON'T *WORK*, SHIT FOR BRAINS. YOU'RE NOT A DAMN *CRAB!*
CRABS CAN DO THAT...?
'COURSE, WE'RE A STONE'S THROW FROM UENOHARA. TAKE IT WITH YOU, FIND A DOC.
MAYBE YOU'D BE AS GOOD AS NEW.
BUT IT AIN'T GONNA HAPPEN!
UH, GUYS. GUYS...?
LOOKS LIKE IT'S SORTA, *OVER*, RIGHT?
AND OUR *JOB*, TOO. SO, LIKE... *UH*...
SHH!!

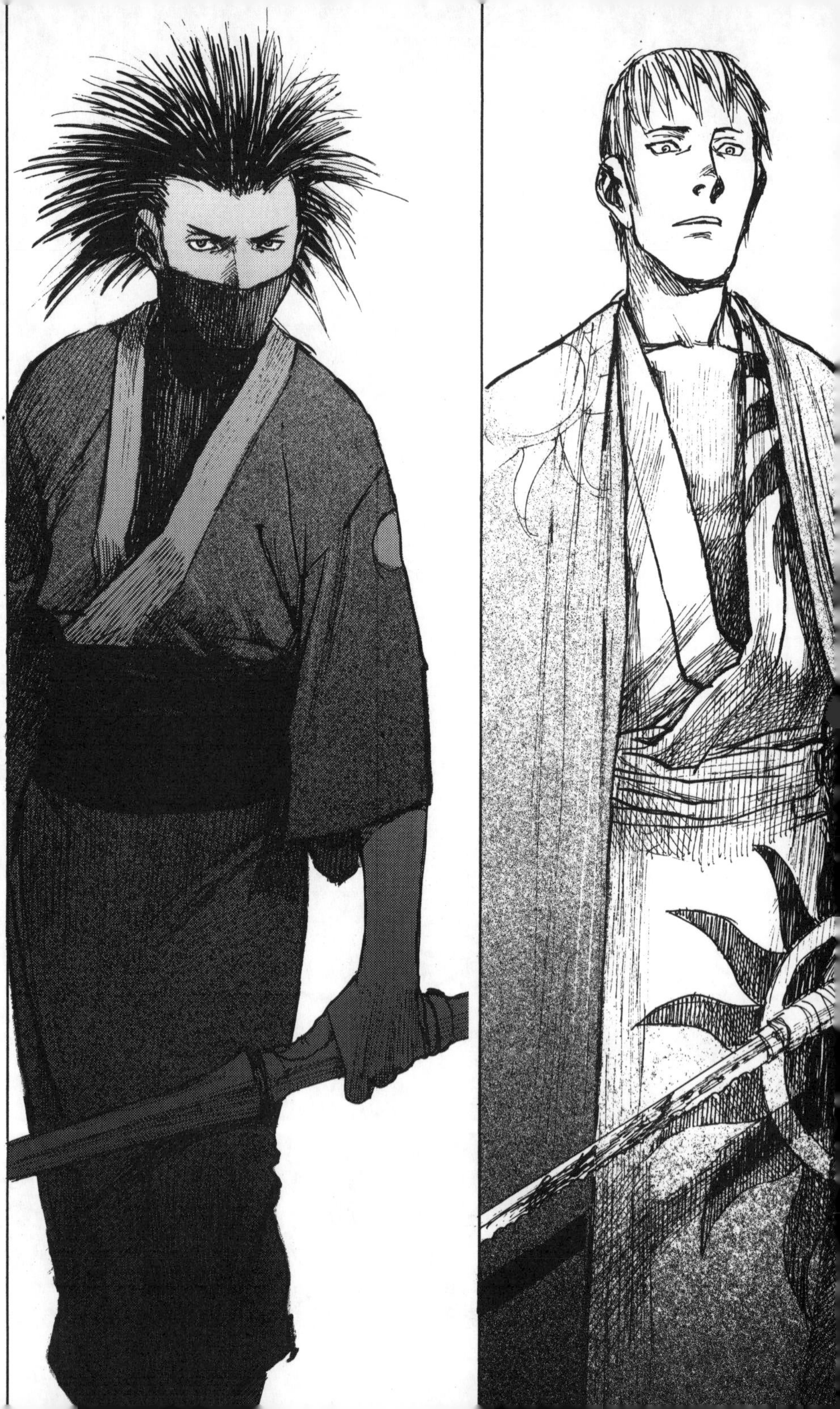

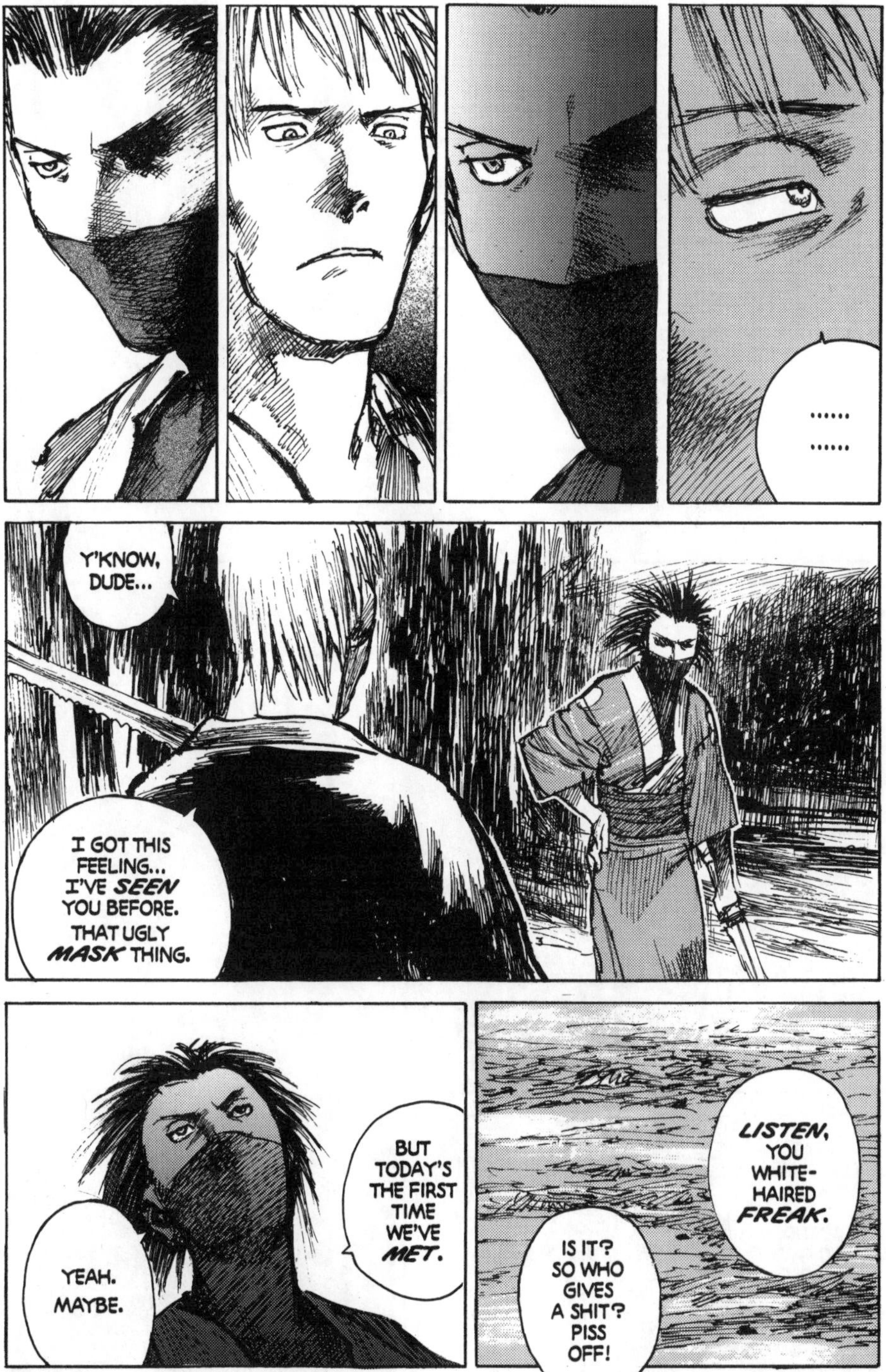
......
......
Y'KNOW, DUDE...
I GOT THIS FEELING... I'VE *SEEN* YOU BEFORE. THAT UGLY ***MASK*** THING.
YEAH. MAYBE.
BUT TODAY'S THE FIRST TIME WE'VE ***MET***.
LISTEN, YOU WHITE-HAIRED ***FREAK***.
IS IT? SO WHO GIVES A SHIT? PISS OFF!

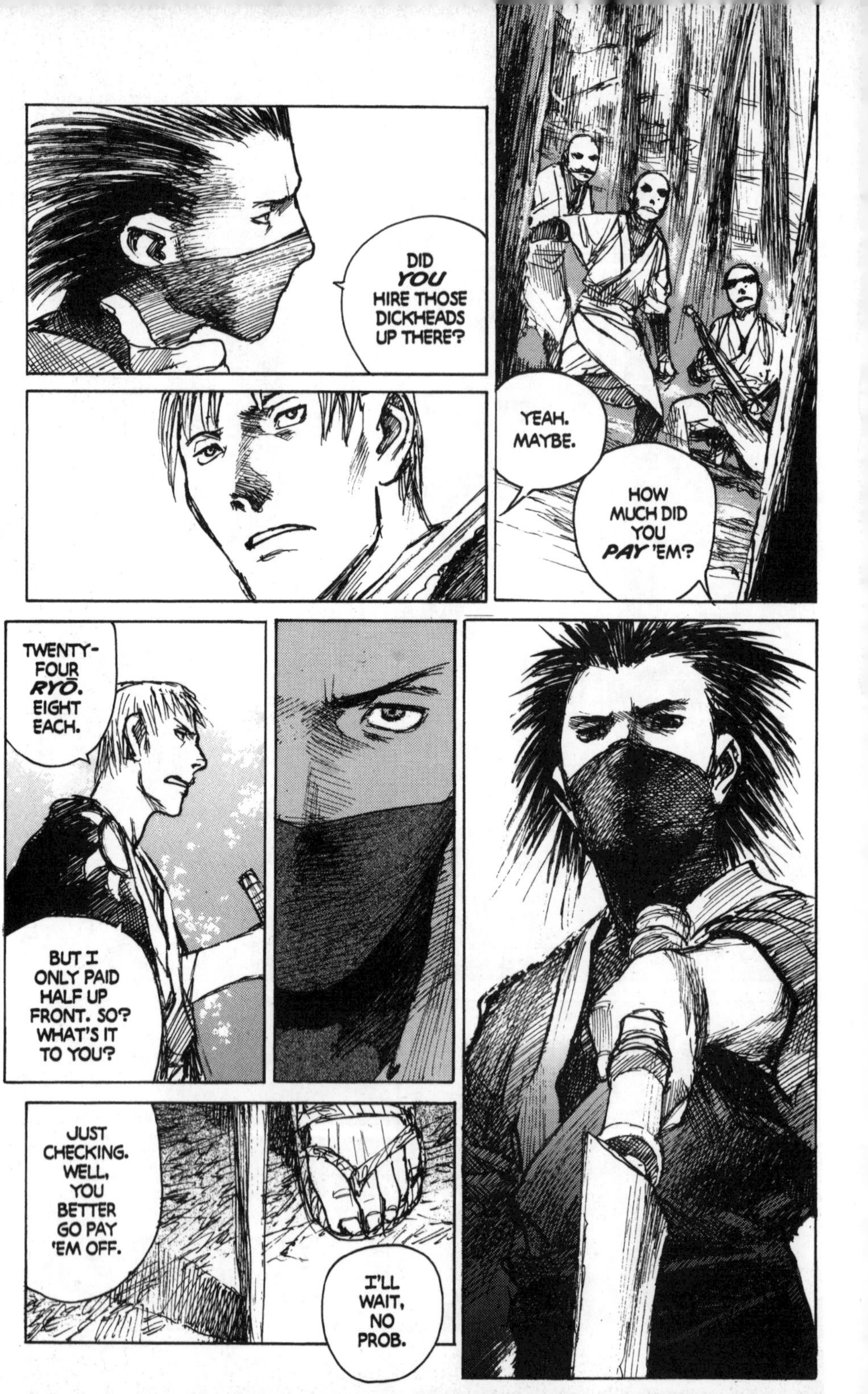
DID *YOU* HIRE THOSE DICKHEADS UP THERE?
YEAH. MAYBE.
HOW MUCH DID YOU *PAY* 'EM?
TWENTY-FOUR *RYŌ*. EIGHT EACH.
BUT I ONLY PAID HALF UP FRONT. SO? WHAT'S IT TO YOU?
JUST CHECKING. WELL, YOU BETTER GO PAY 'EM OFF.
I'LL WAIT, NO PROB.

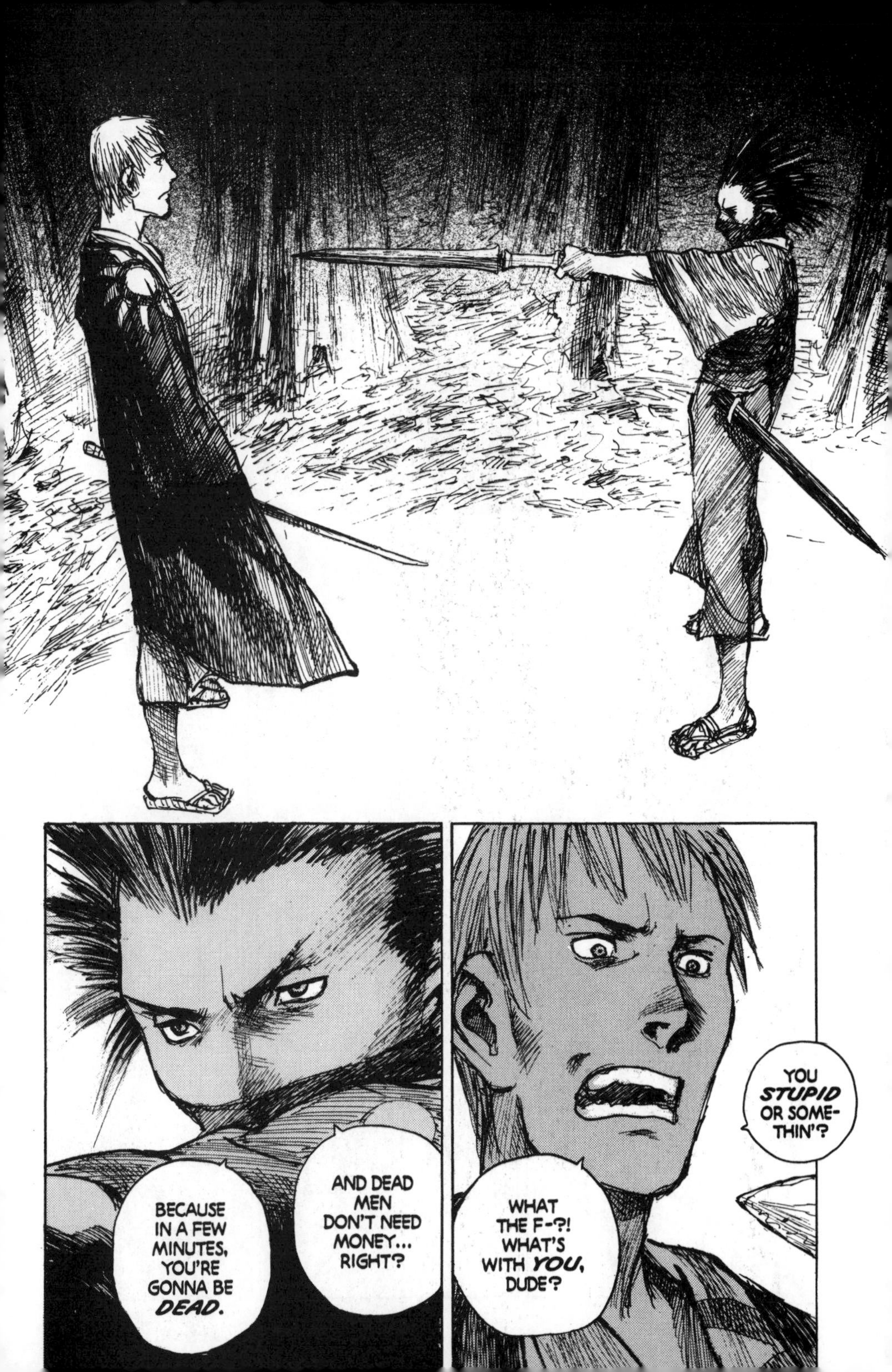
BECAUSE IN A FEW MINUTES, YOU'RE GONNA BE *DEAD*.
AND DEAD MEN DON'T NEED MONEY... RIGHT?
WHAT THE F-?! WHAT'S WITH *YOU*, DUDE?
YOU *STUPID* OR SOME-THIN'?

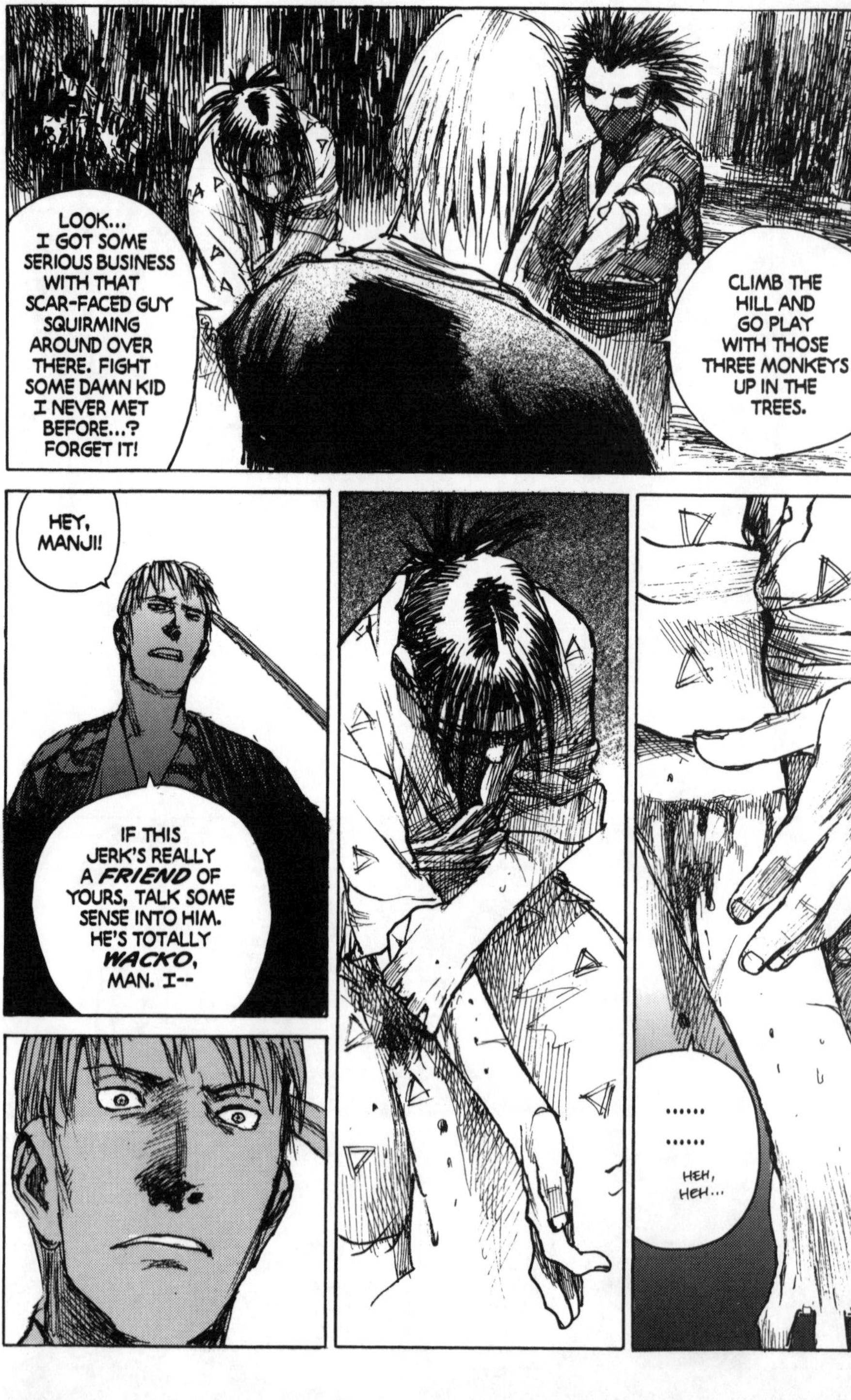
LOOK... I GOT SOME SERIOUS BUSINESS WITH THAT SCAR-FACED GUY SQUIRMING AROUND OVER THERE. FIGHT SOME DAMN KID I NEVER MET BEFORE...? FORGET IT!
CLIMB THE HILL AND GO PLAY WITH THOSE THREE MONKEYS UP IN THE TREES.
HEY, MANJI!
IF THIS JERK'S REALLY A *FRIEND* OF YOURS, TALK SOME SENSE INTO HIM. HE'S TOTALLY *WACKO*, MAN. I--
......
......
HEH, HEH...

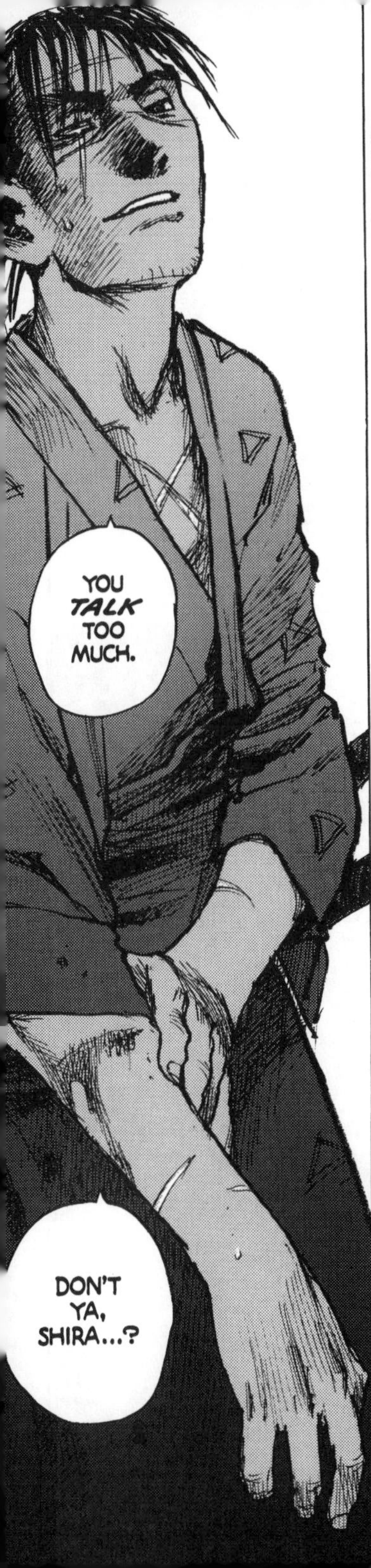
YOU *TALK* TOO MUCH.
DON'T YA, SHIRA...?

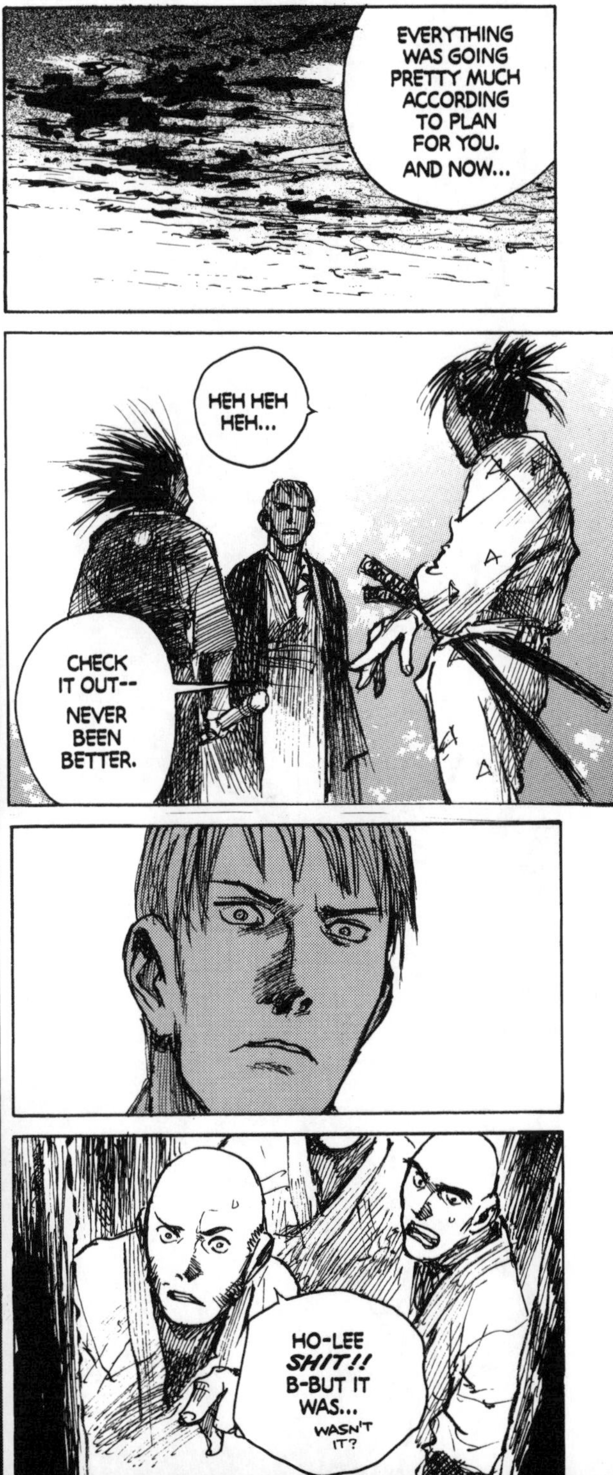
EVERYTHING WAS GOING PRETTY MUCH ACCORDING TO PLAN FOR YOU. AND NOW...
HEH HEH HEH...
CHECK IT OUT-- NEVER BEEN BETTER.
HO-LEE *SHIT!!* B-BUT IT WAS... WASN'T IT?

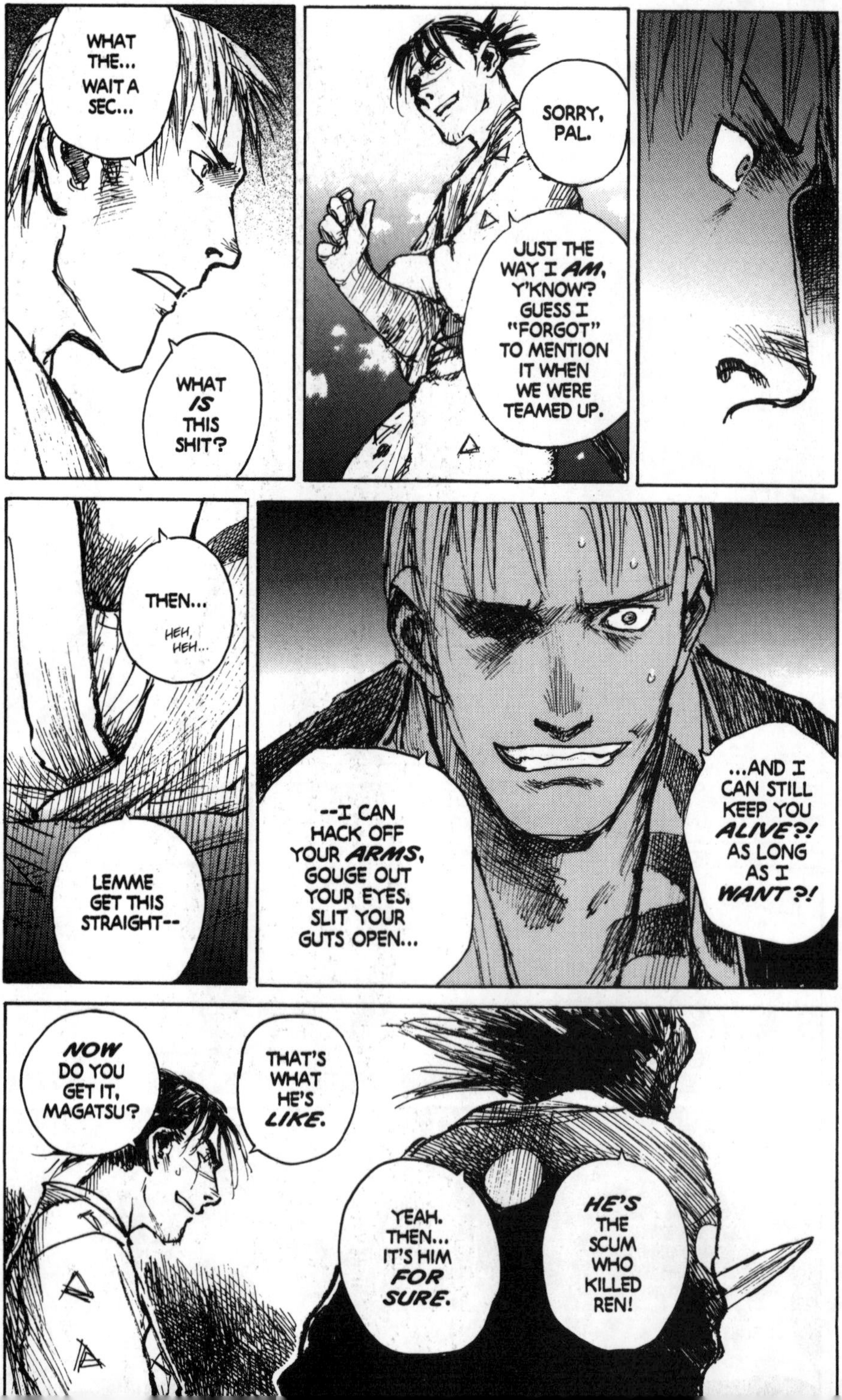
WHAT THE... WAIT A SEC...
WHAT IS THIS SHIT?
SORRY, PAL.
JUST THE WAY I AM, Y'KNOW? GUESS I "FORGOT" TO MENTION IT WHEN WE WERE TEAMED UP.
THEN... HEH, HEH...
LEMME GET THIS STRAIGHT--
--I CAN HACK OFF YOUR ARMS, GOUGE OUT YOUR EYES, SLIT YOUR GUTS OPEN...
...AND I CAN STILL KEEP YOU ALIVE?! AS LONG AS I WANT?!
NOW DO YOU GET IT, MAGATSU?
THAT'S WHAT HE'S LIKE.
YEAH. THEN... IT'S HIM FOR SURE.
HE'S THE SCUM WHO KILLED REN!

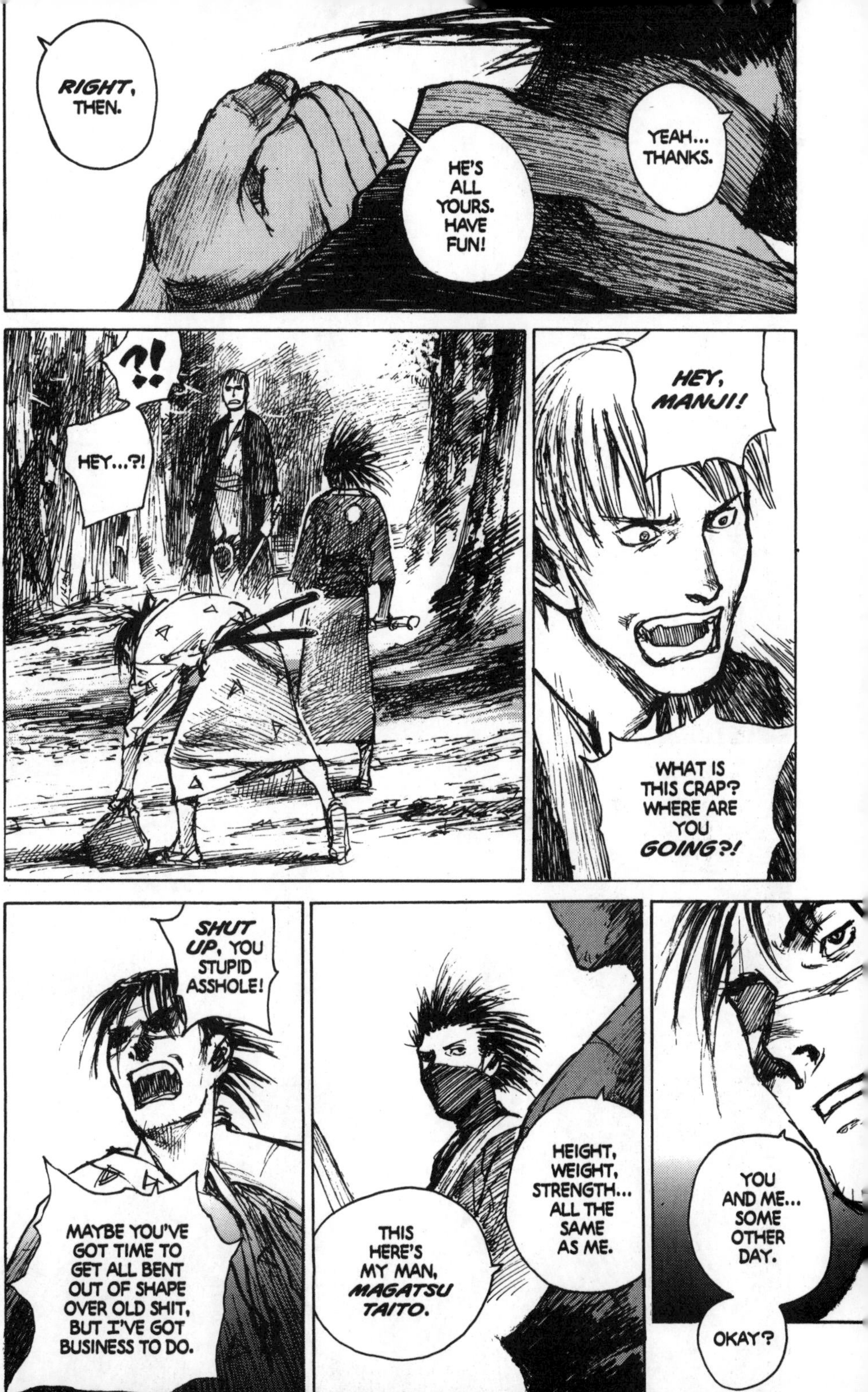
RIGHT, THEN.
HE'S ALL YOURS. HAVE FUN!
YEAH... THANKS.
?!
HEY...?!
HEY, MANJI!
WHAT IS THIS CRAP? WHERE ARE YOU GOING?!
SHUT UP, YOU STUPID ASSHOLE!
MAYBE YOU'VE GOT TIME TO GET ALL BENT OUT OF SHAPE OVER OLD SHIT, BUT I'VE GOT BUSINESS TO DO.
THIS HERE'S MY MAN, MAGATSU TAITO.
HEIGHT, WEIGHT, STRENGTH... ALL THE SAME AS ME.
YOU AND ME... SOME OTHER DAY.
OKAY?

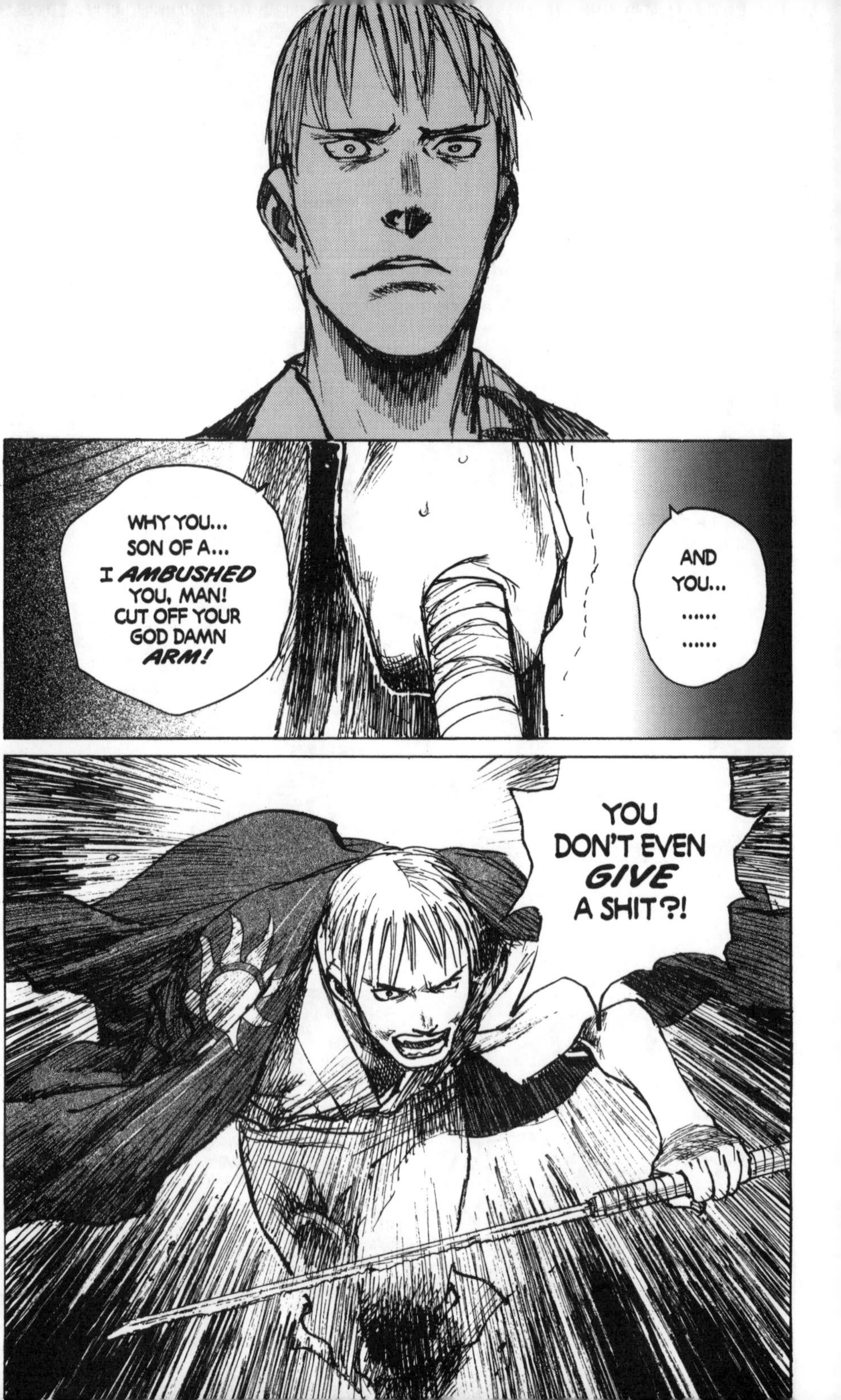
WHY YOU... SON OF A... I AMBUSHED YOU, MAN! CUT OFF YOUR GOD DAMN ARM!
AND YOU... ....
YOU DON'T EVEN GIVE A SHIT?!

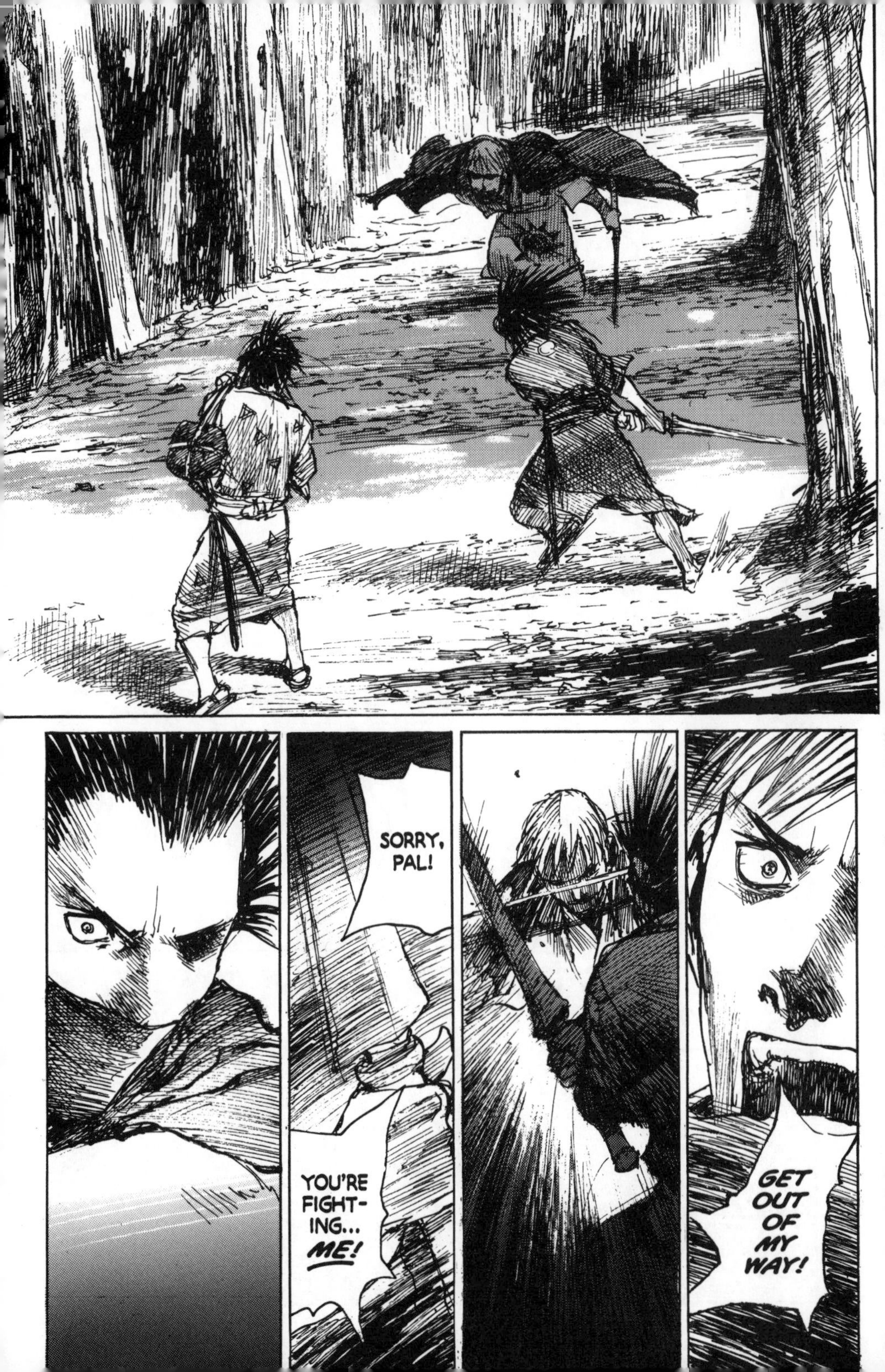
SORRY, PAL!
YOU'RE FIGHT-ING... ME!
GET OUT OF MY WAY!

KANGG

HEH.

DIE, YOU--

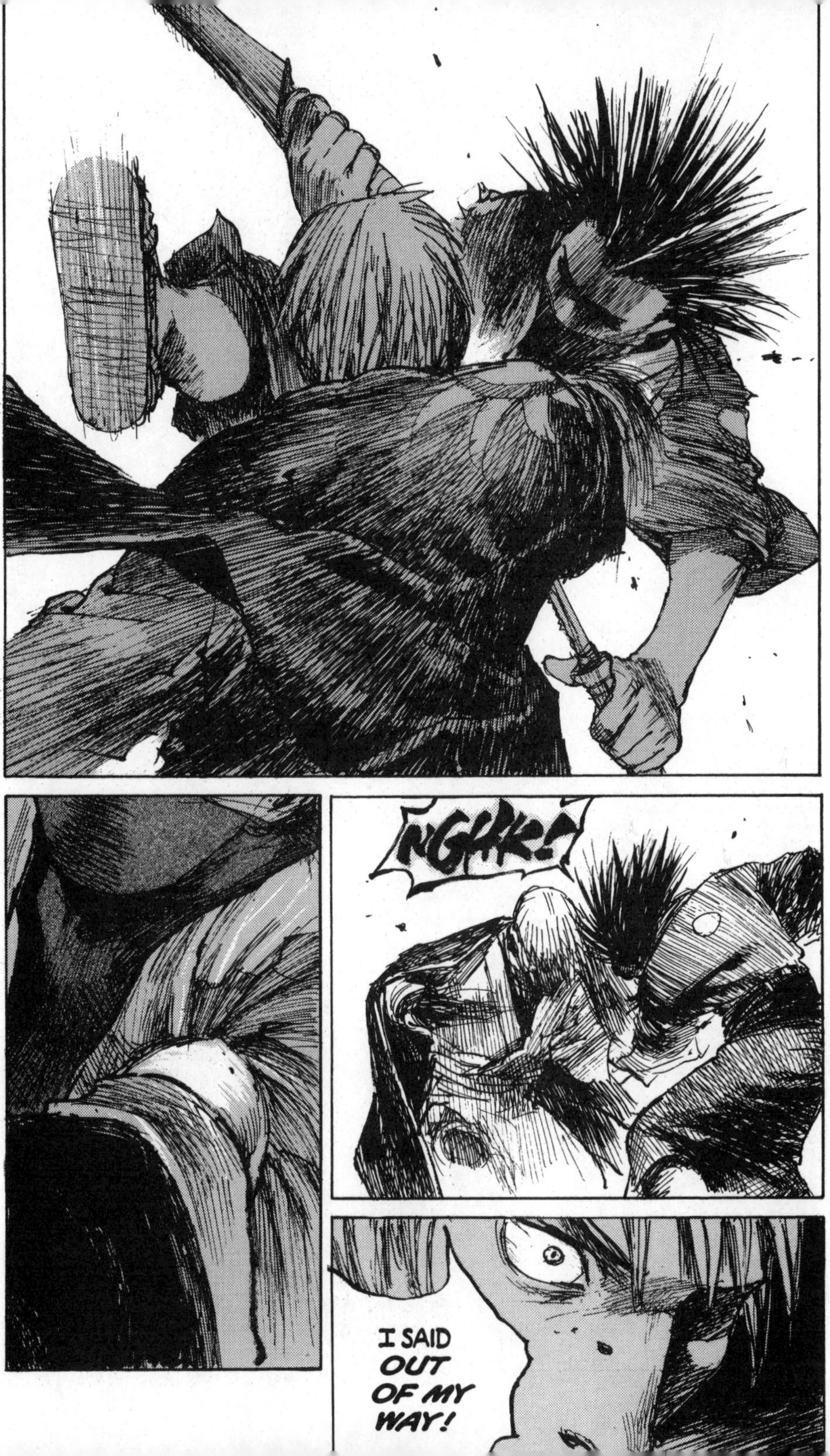
NGAK!
I SAID *OUT OF MY WAY!*

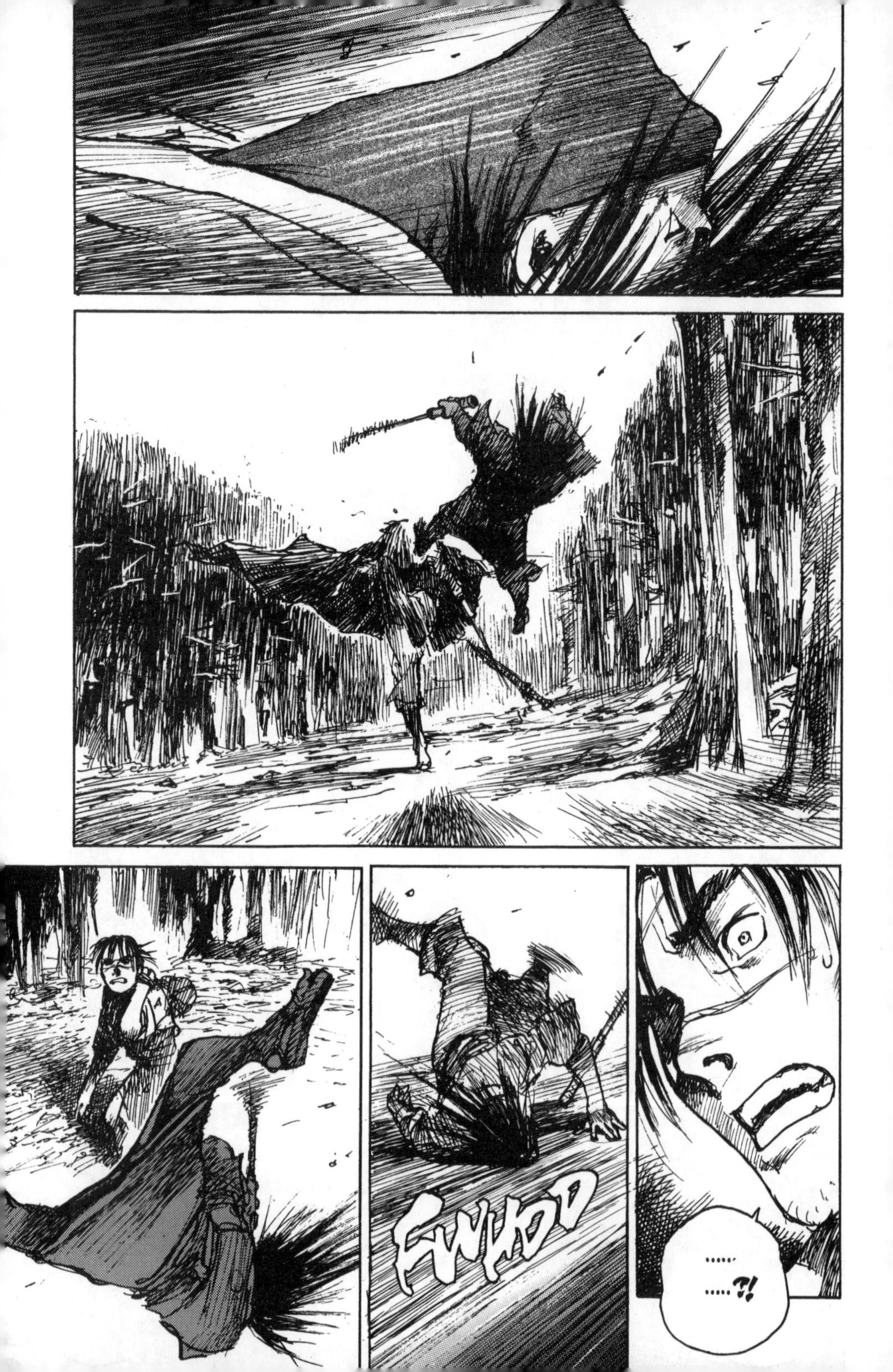
FWUDD
......,
......?!

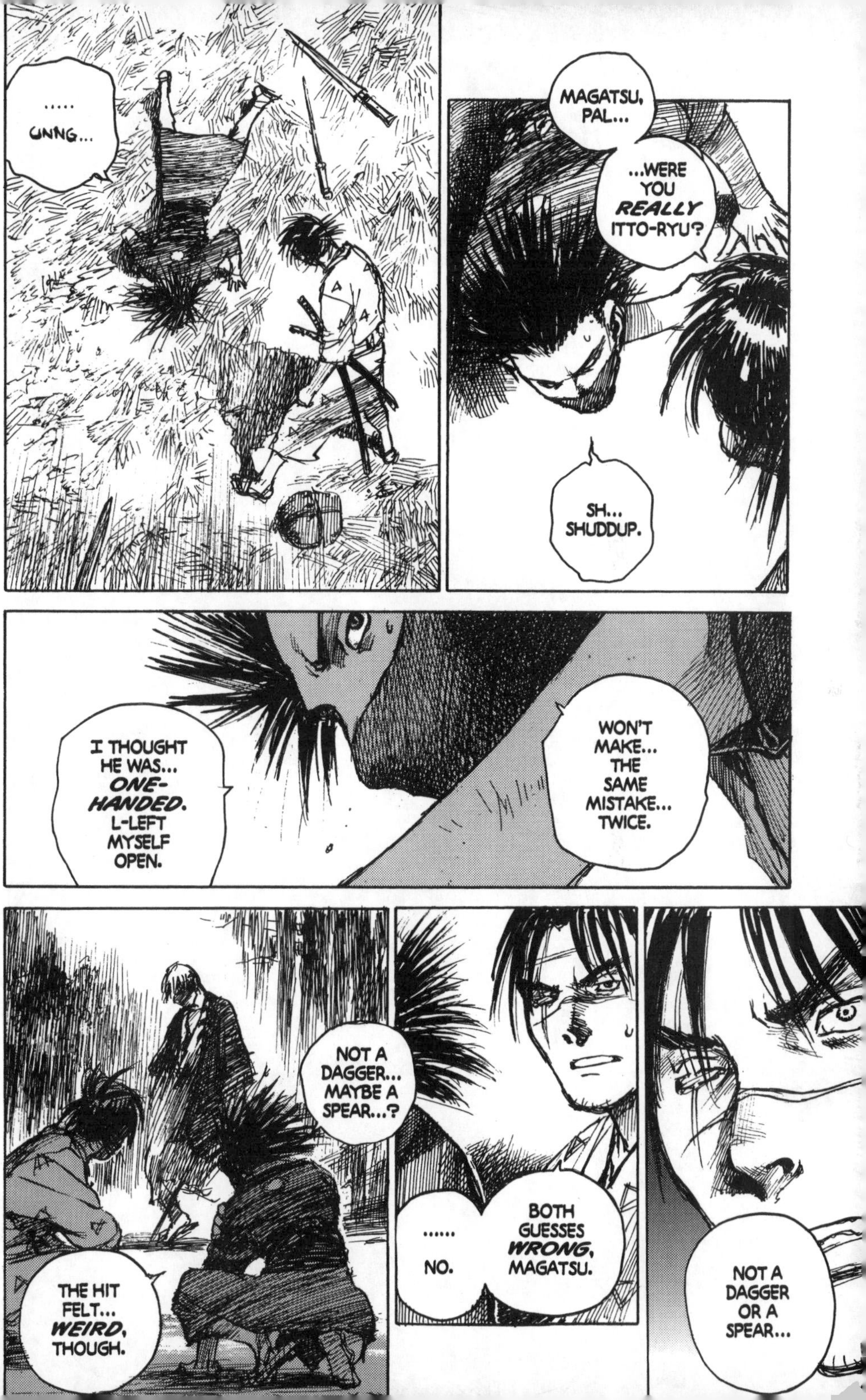

.....
UNNG...
MAGATSU, PAL...
...WERE YOU *REALLY* ITTO-RYU?
SH... SHUDDUP.
I THOUGHT HE WAS... *ONE-HANDED*. L-LEFT MYSELF OPEN.
WON'T MAKE... THE SAME MISTAKE... TWICE.
NOT A DAGGER... MAYBE A SPEAR...?
THE HIT FELT... *WEIRD*, THOUGH.
......
NO.
BOTH GUESSES *WRONG*, MAGATSU.
NOT A DAGGER OR A SPEAR...

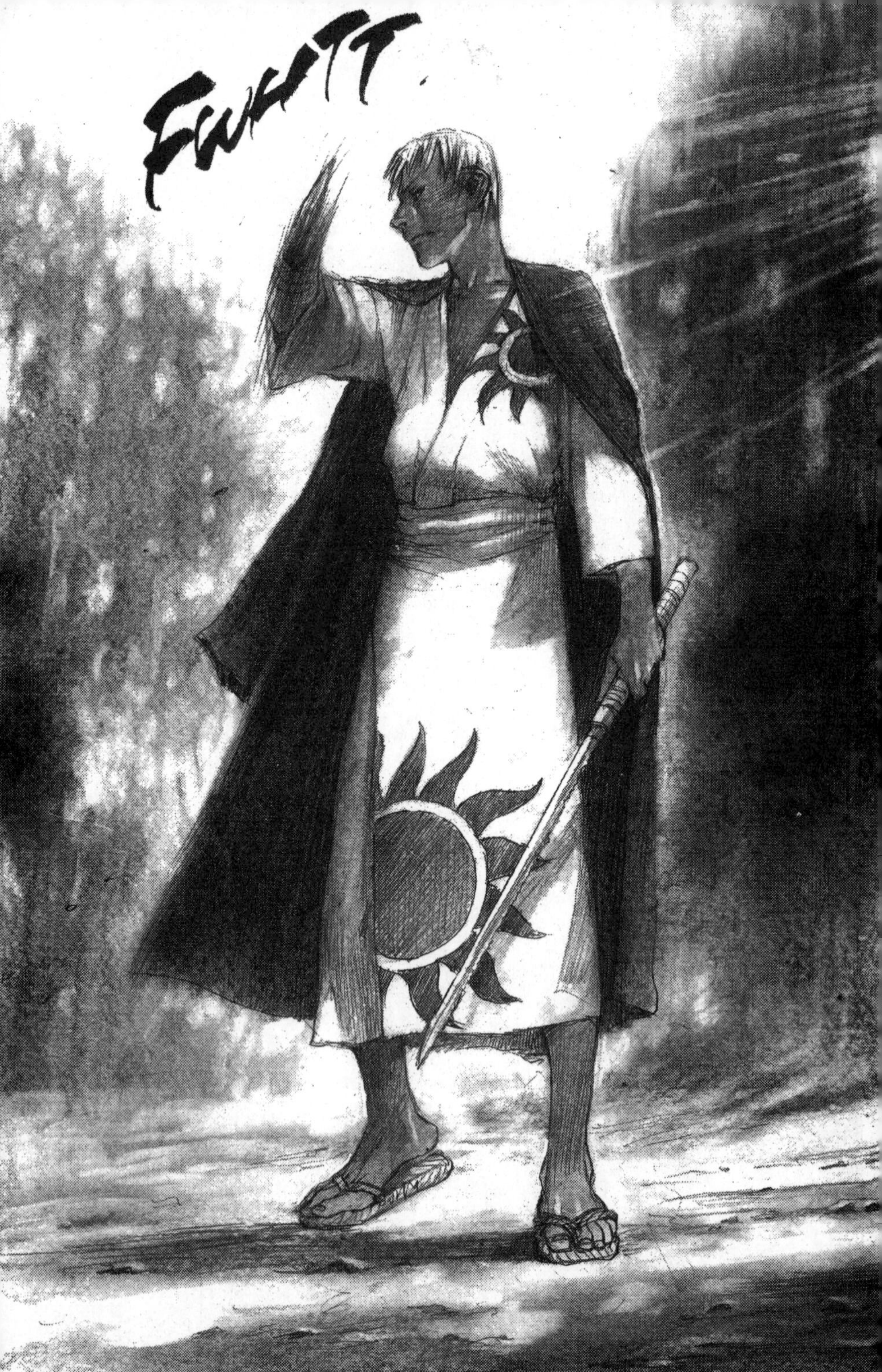
FWHTT

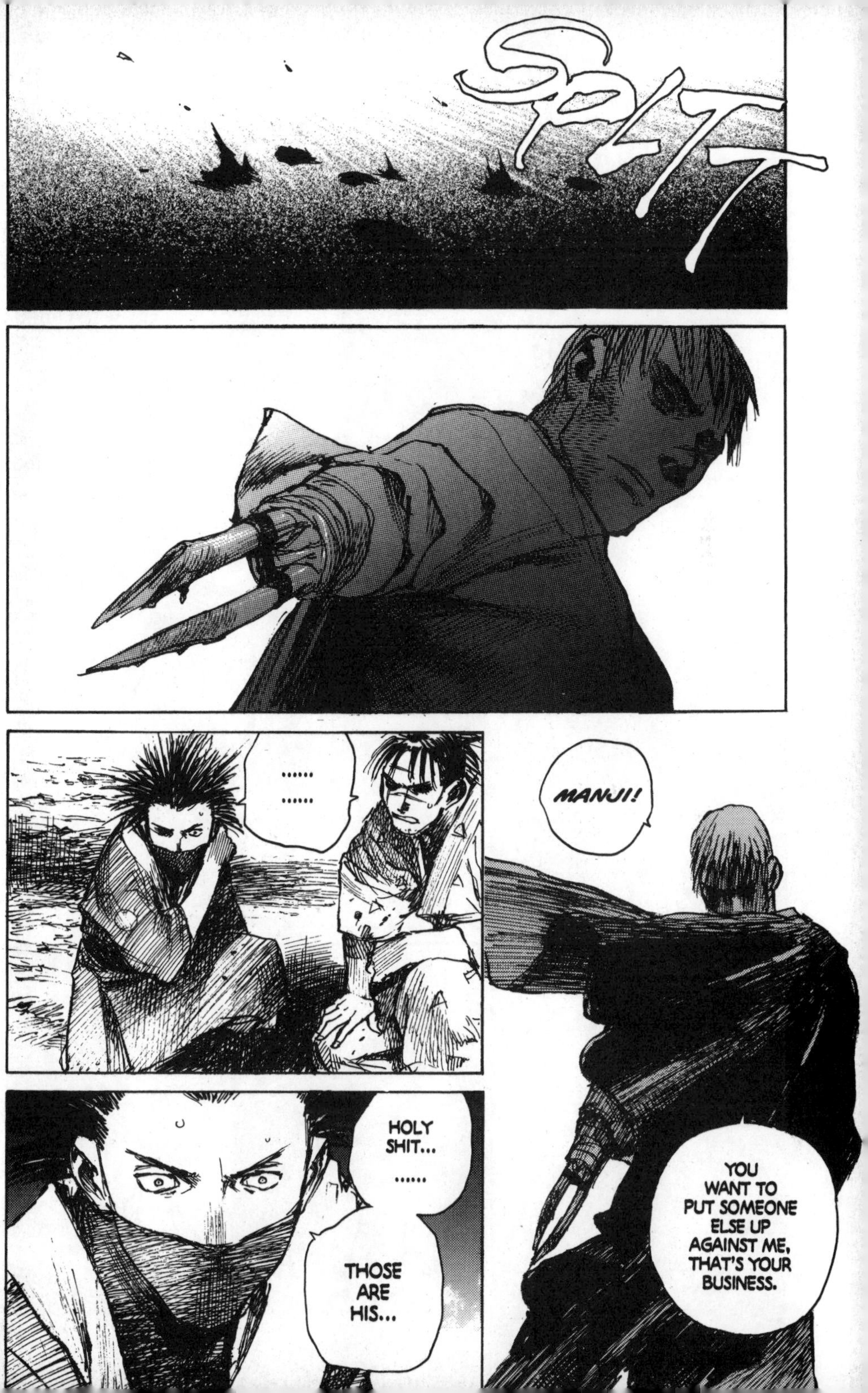
SPLIT
......
......
HOLY SHIT...
......
THOSE ARE HIS...
MANJI!
YOU WANT TO PUT SOMEONE ELSE UP AGAINST ME, THAT'S YOUR BUSINESS.

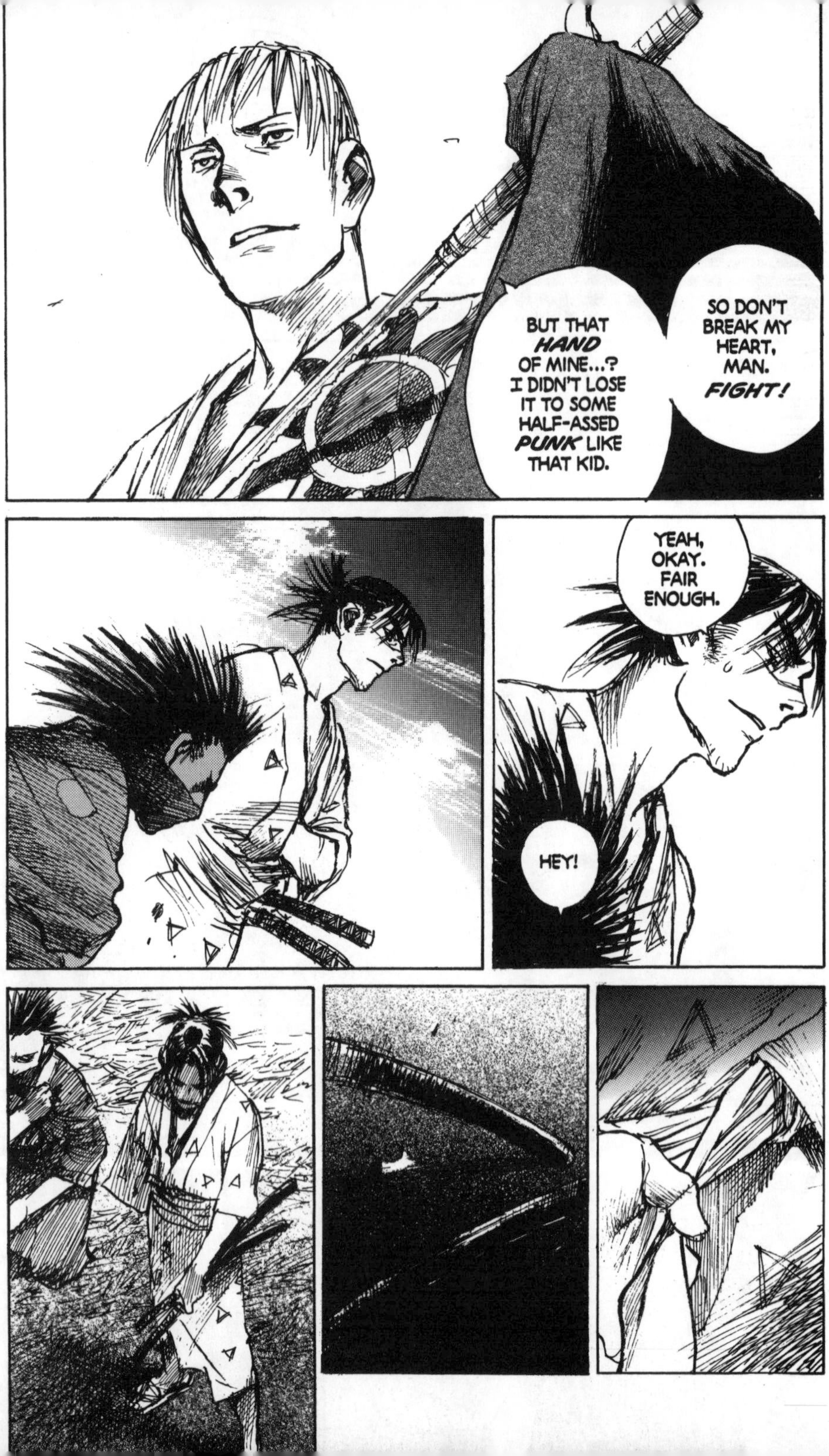
BUT THAT HAND OF MINE...? I DIDN'T LOSE IT TO SOME HALF-ASSED PUNK LIKE THAT KID.
SO DON'T BREAK MY HEART, MAN. FIGHT!
YEAH, OKAY. FAIR ENOUGH.
HEY!

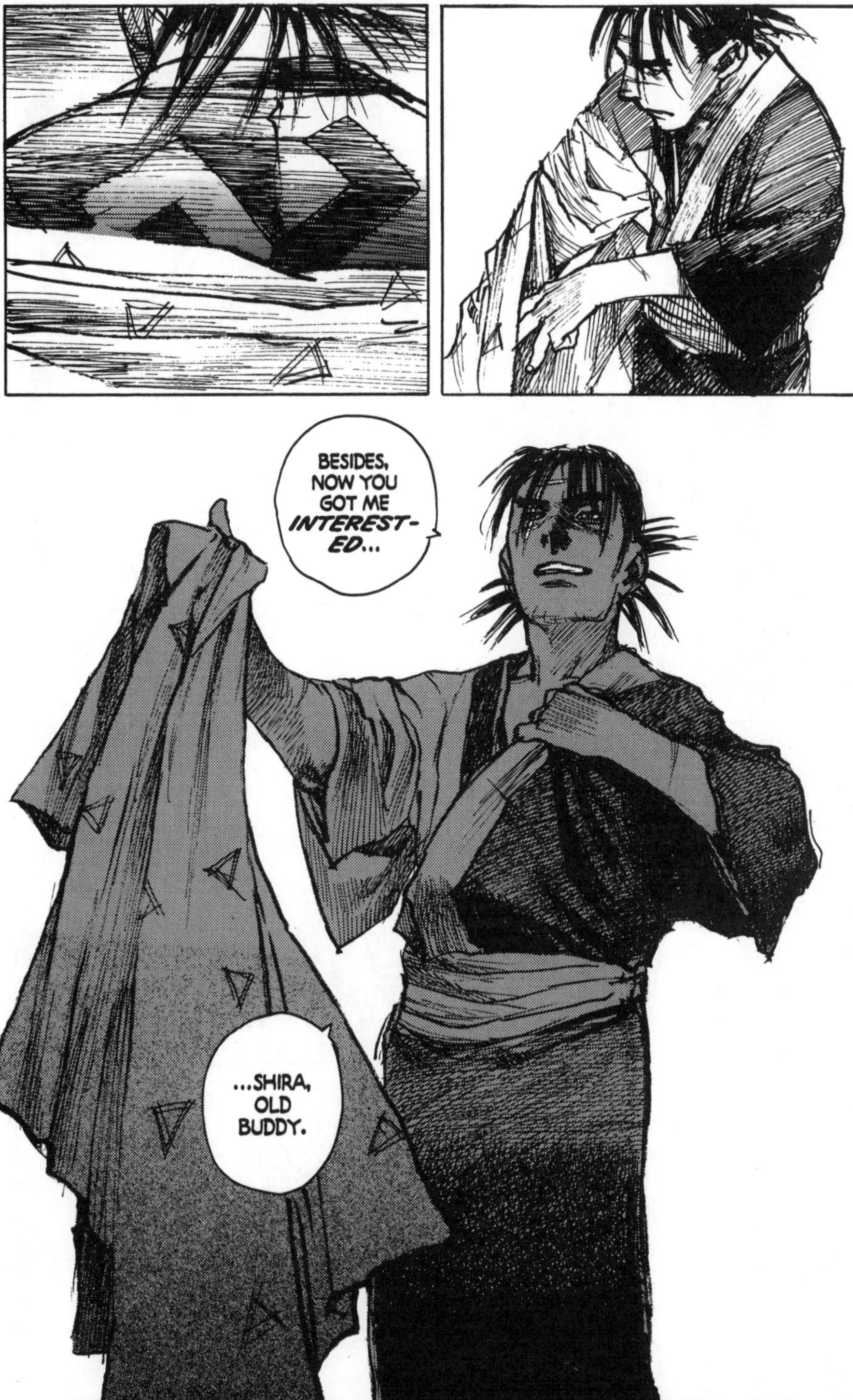
BESIDES, NOW YOU GOT ME *INTEREST-ED...*
...SHIRA, OLD BUDDY.

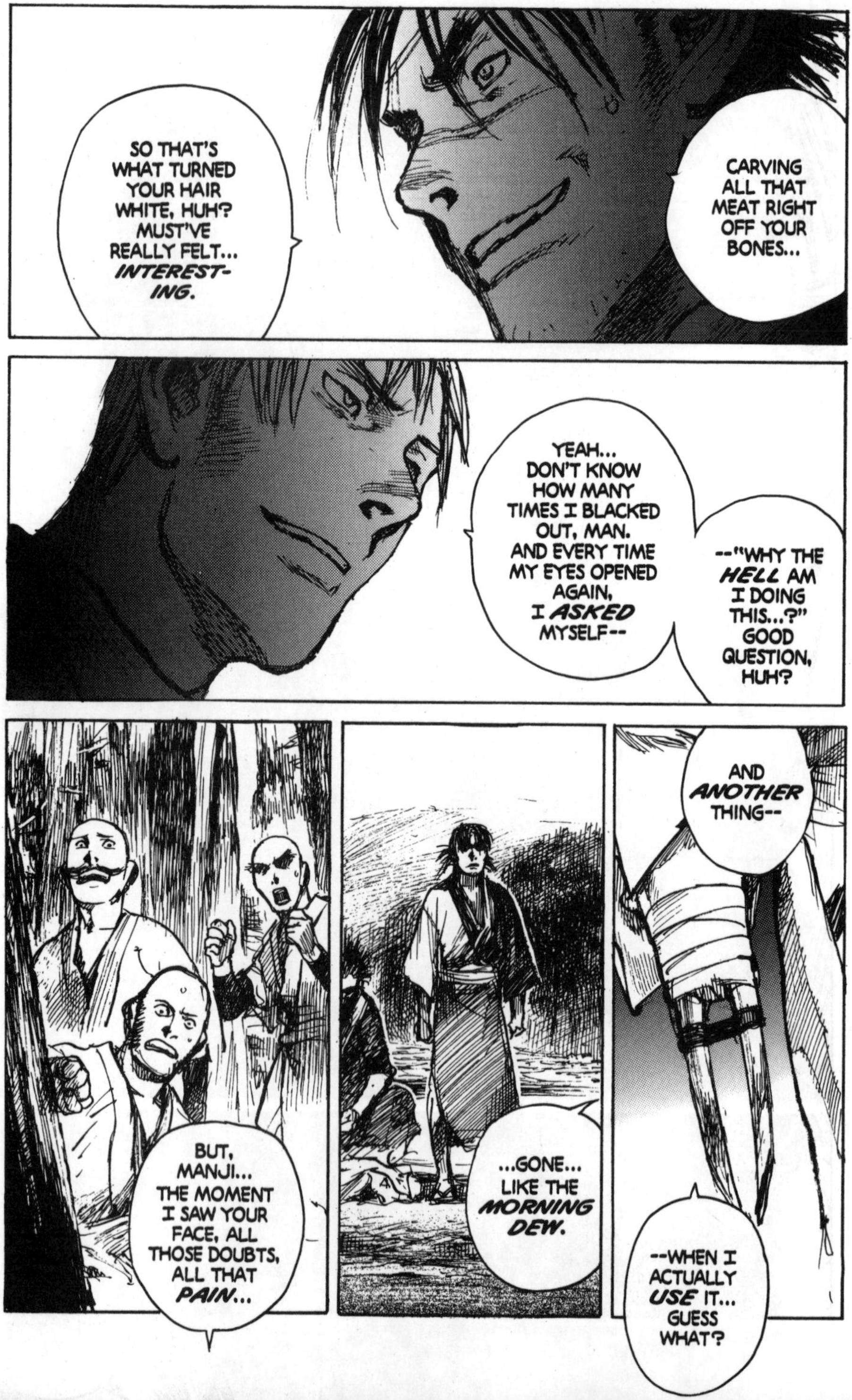
SO THAT'S WHAT TURNED YOUR HAIR WHITE, HUH? MUST'VE REALLY FELT... *INTERESTING*.
CARVING ALL THAT MEAT RIGHT OFF YOUR BONES...
YEAH... DON'T KNOW HOW MANY TIMES I BLACKED OUT, MAN. AND EVERY TIME MY EYES OPENED AGAIN, I *ASKED* MYSELF--
--"WHY THE *HELL* AM I DOING THIS...?" GOOD QUESTION, HUH?
BUT, MANJI... THE MOMENT I SAW YOUR FACE, ALL THOSE DOUBTS, ALL THAT *PAIN*...
...GONE... LIKE THE *MORNING DEW*.
AND *ANOTHER* THING--
--WHEN I ACTUALLY *USE* IT... GUESS WHAT?

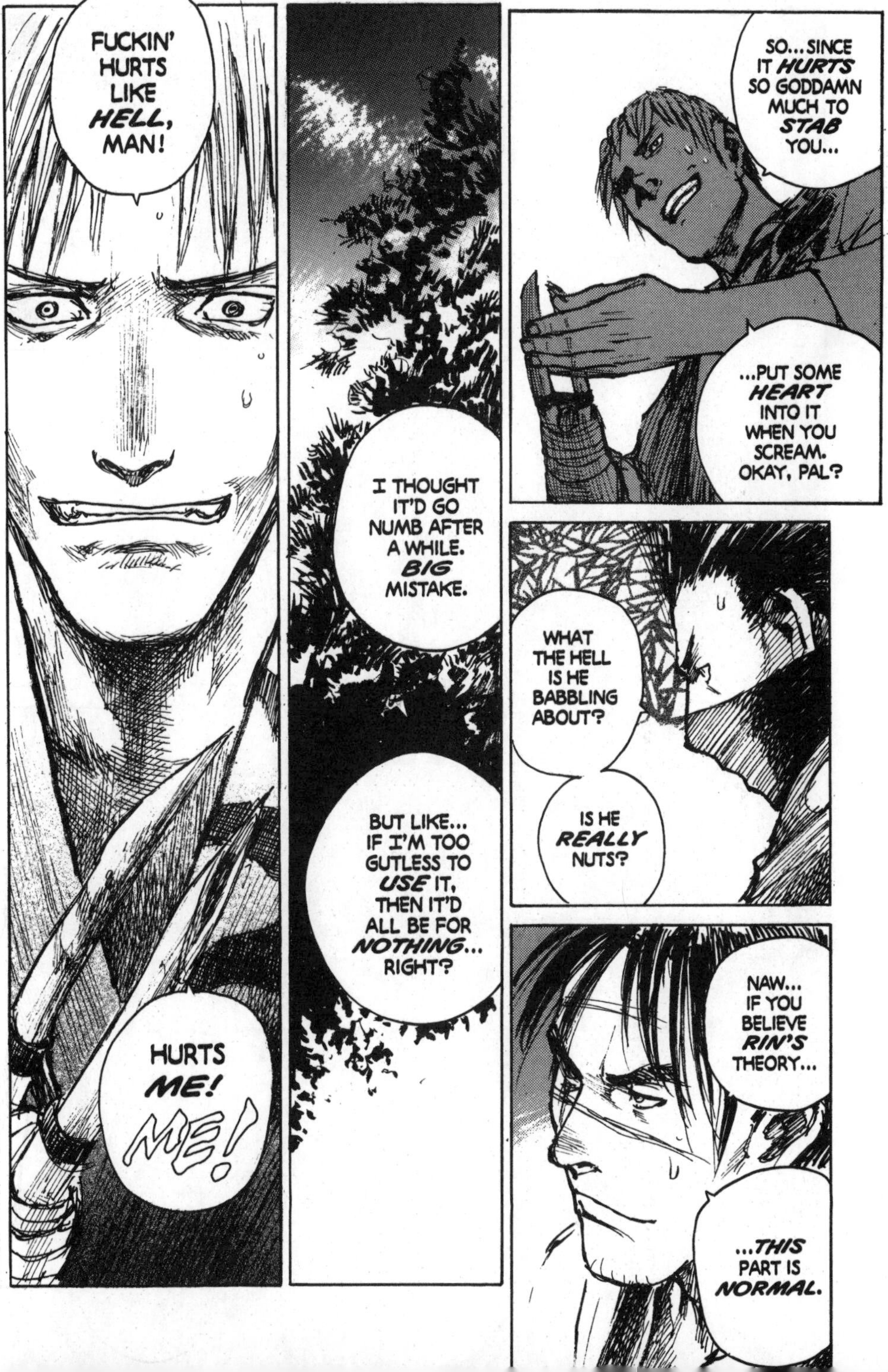
FUCKIN' HURTS LIKE HELL, MAN!
HURTS ME!
ME!
I THOUGHT IT'D GO NUMB AFTER A WHILE. BIG MISTAKE.
BUT LIKE... IF I'M TOO GUTLESS TO USE IT, THEN IT'D ALL BE FOR NOTHING... RIGHT?
SO... SINCE IT HURTS SO GODDAMN MUCH TO STAB YOU...
...PUT SOME HEART INTO IT WHEN YOU SCREAM. OKAY, PAL?
WHAT THE HELL IS HE BABBLING ABOUT?
IS HE REALLY NUTS?
NAW... IF YOU BELIEVE RIN'S THEORY...
...THIS PART IS NORMAL.

STILL... IT'S ALWAYS NICE TO FEEL *WANTED*... KNOW WHAT I MEAN?

ANYWAY...

NOW I *CAN'T* LEAVE YOU TO SOMEONE ELSE.

YOU'RE THE *REAL DEAL*, SHIRA.

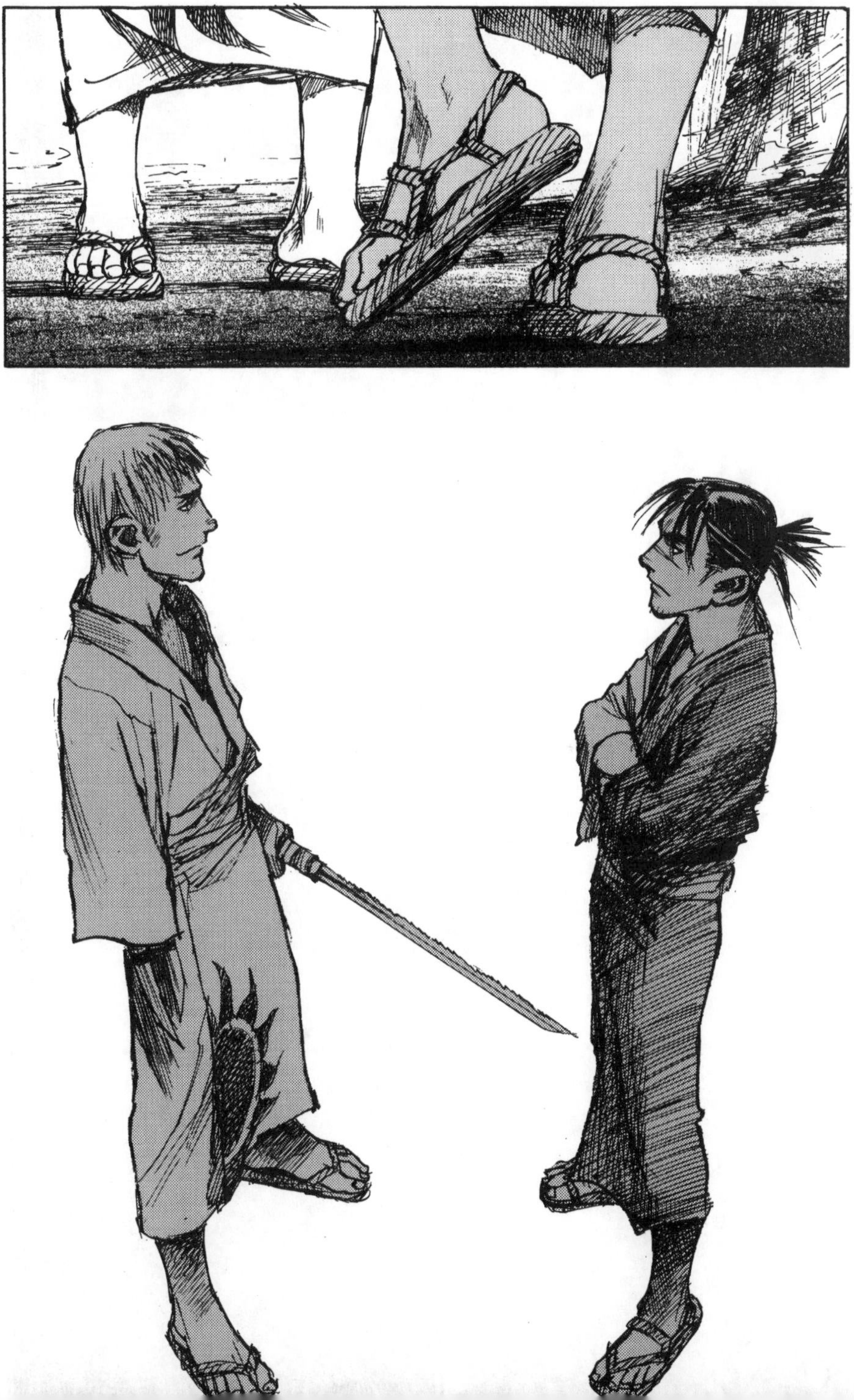

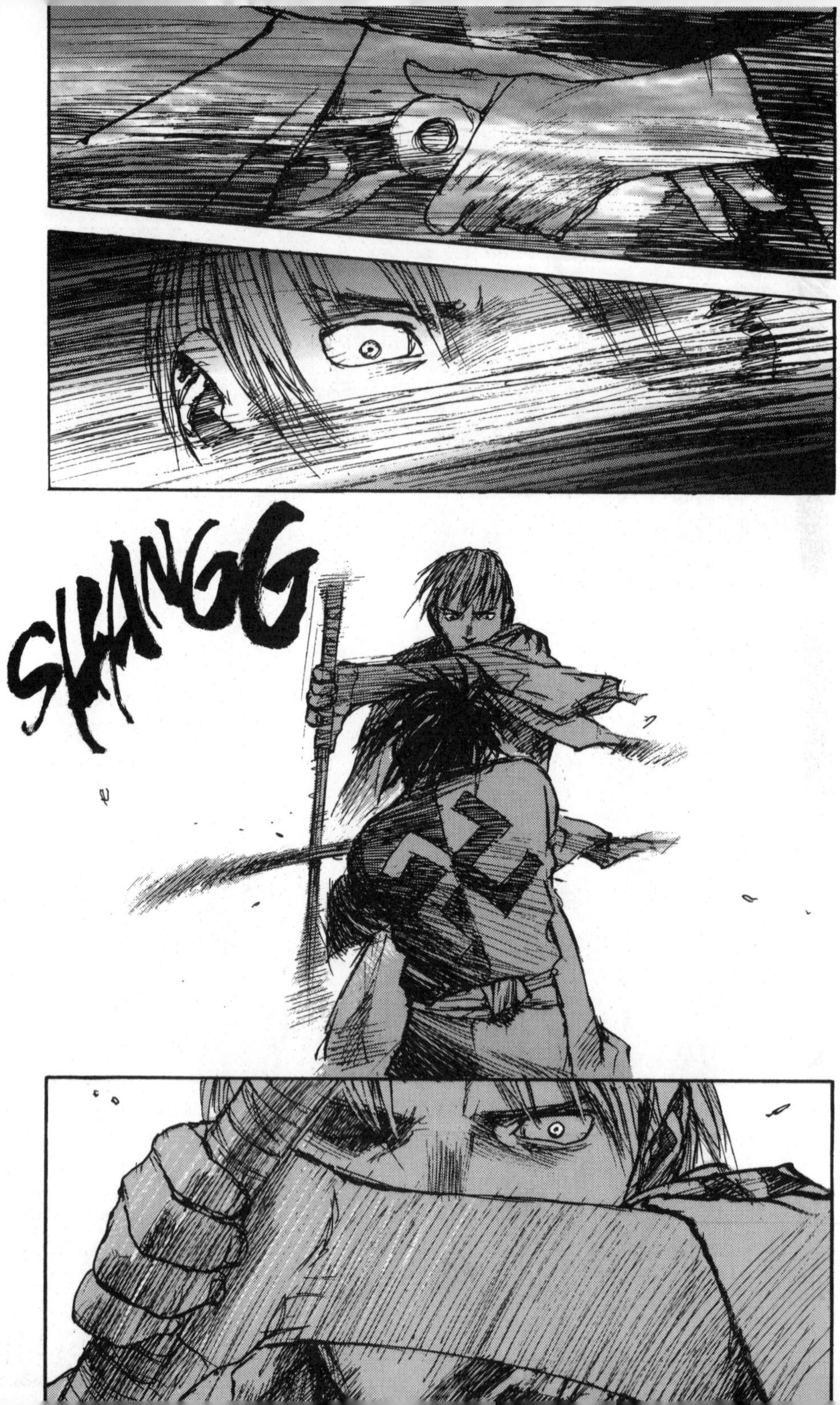
SHANGG

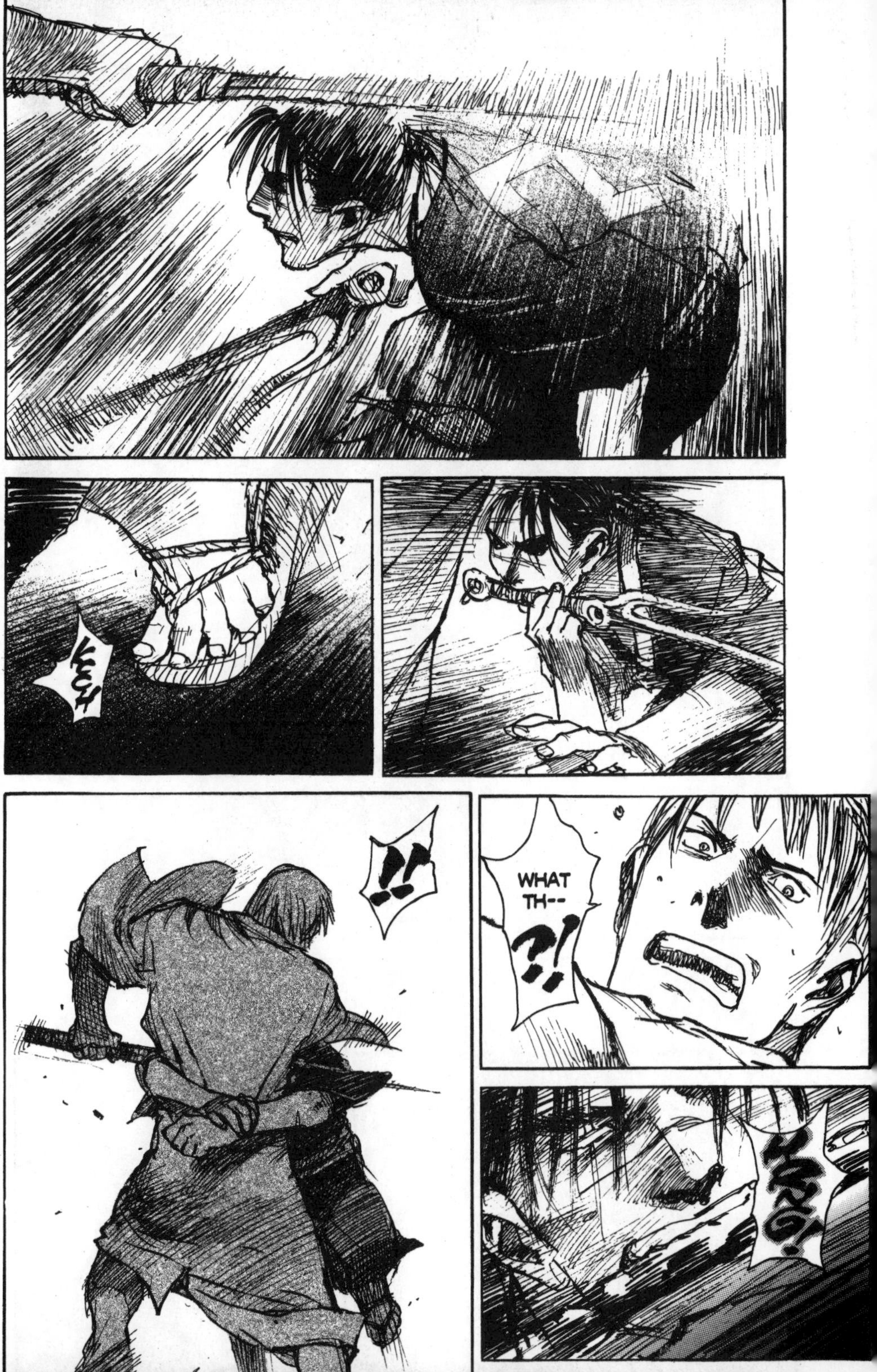
KUCH
!!
WHAT TH-- ?!
HRNG!

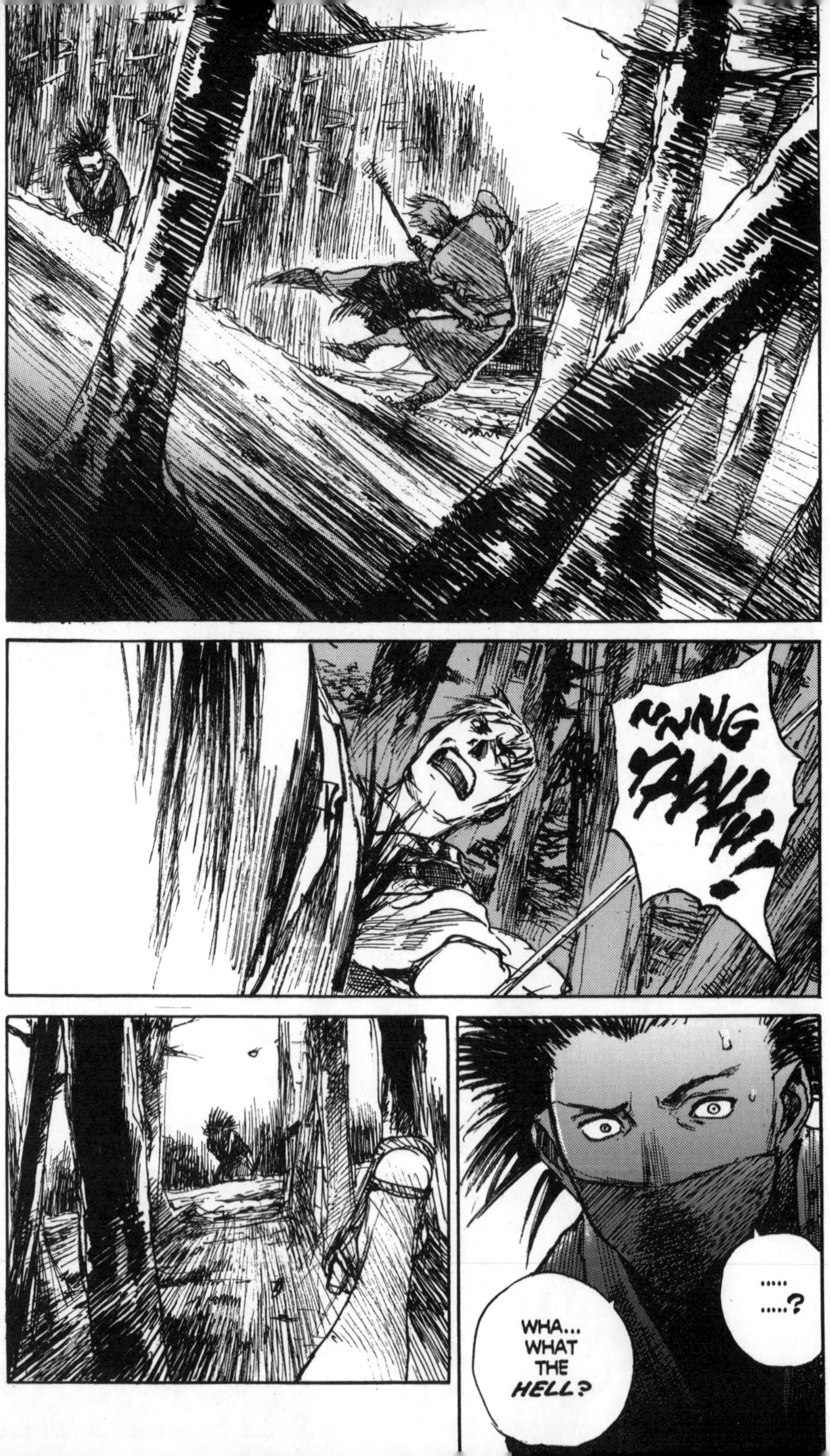
NNNG YAAAH!
WHA... WHAT THE HELL?
.....
.....?

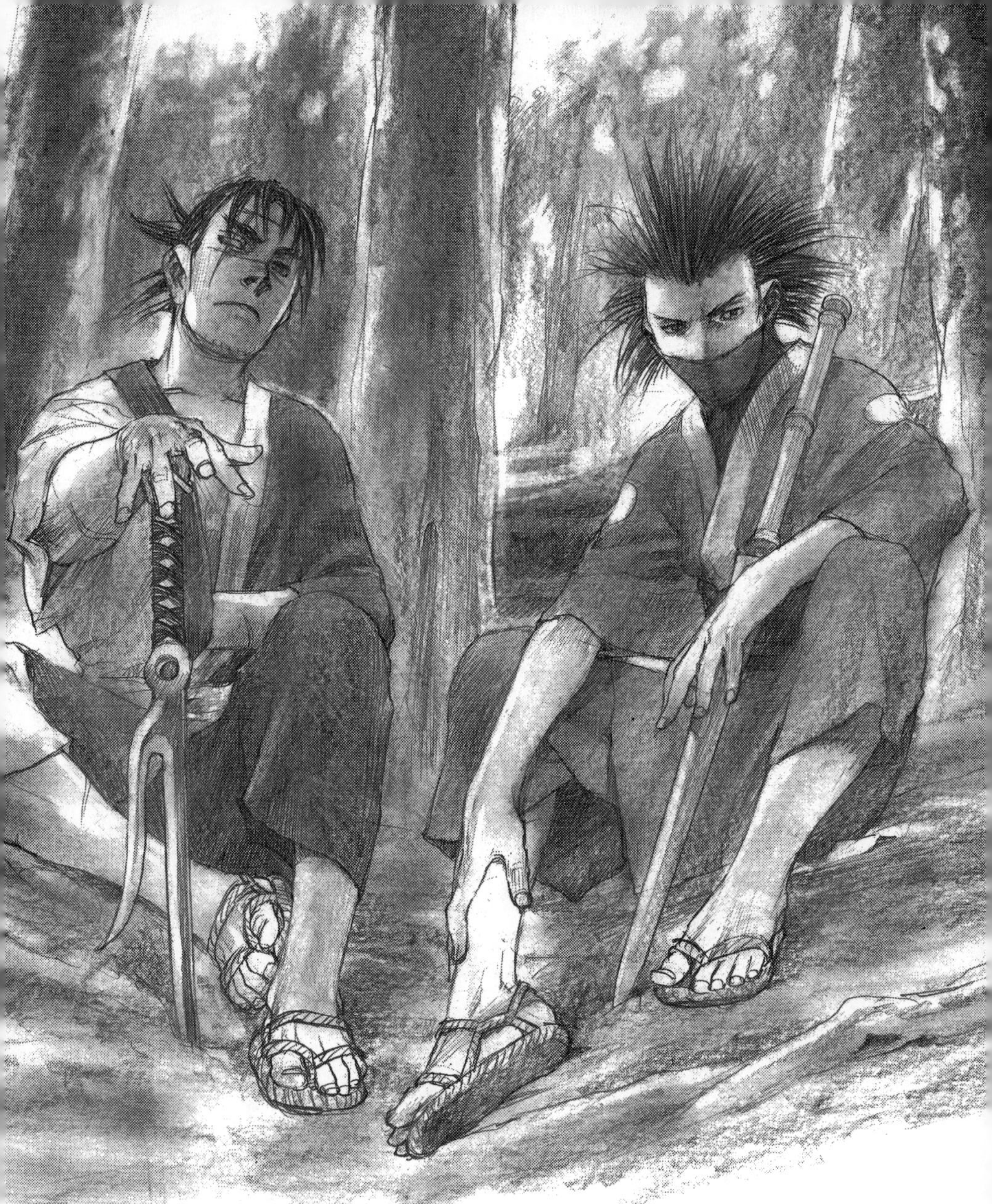

AUTUMN FROST
Part 3

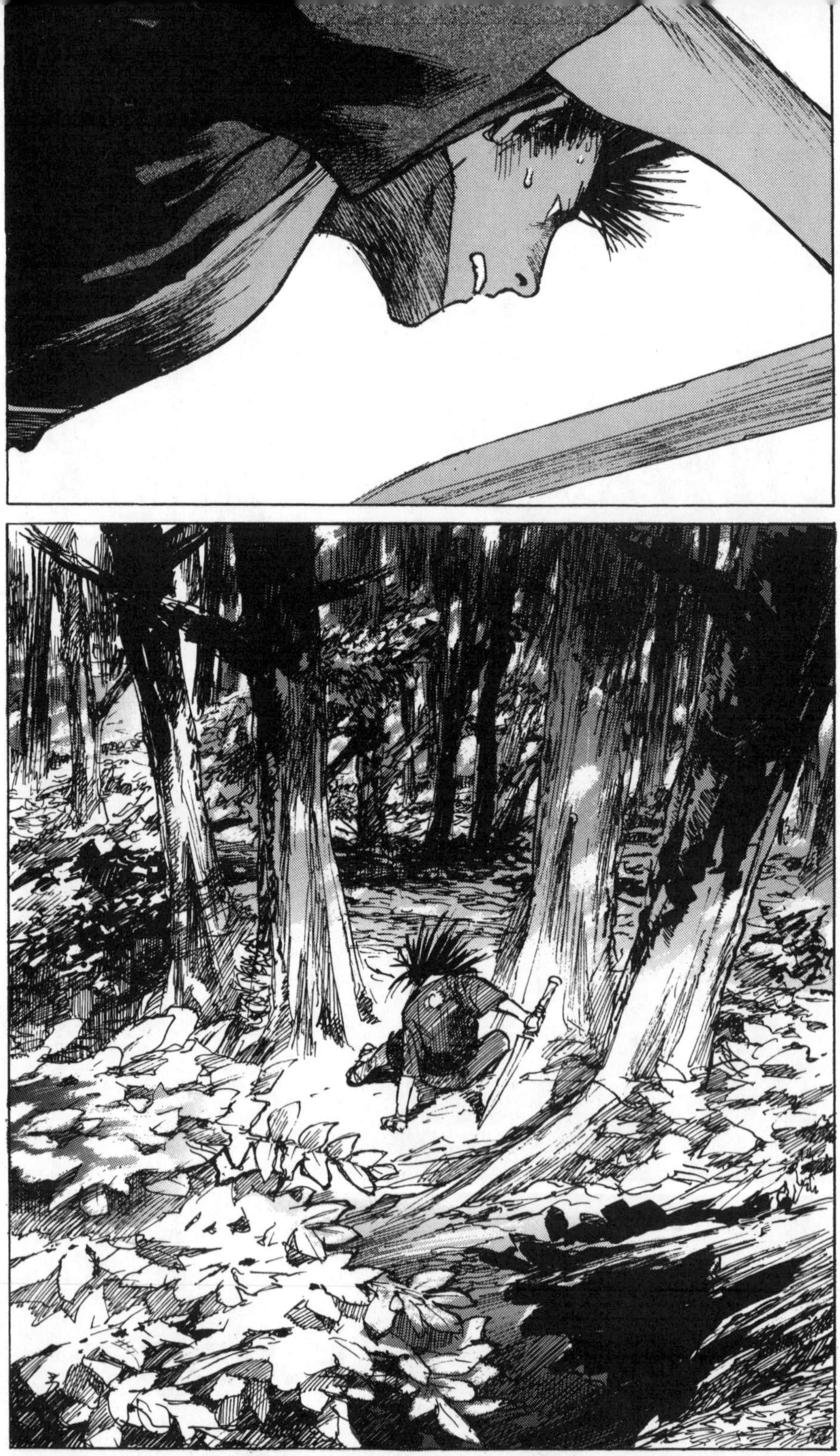

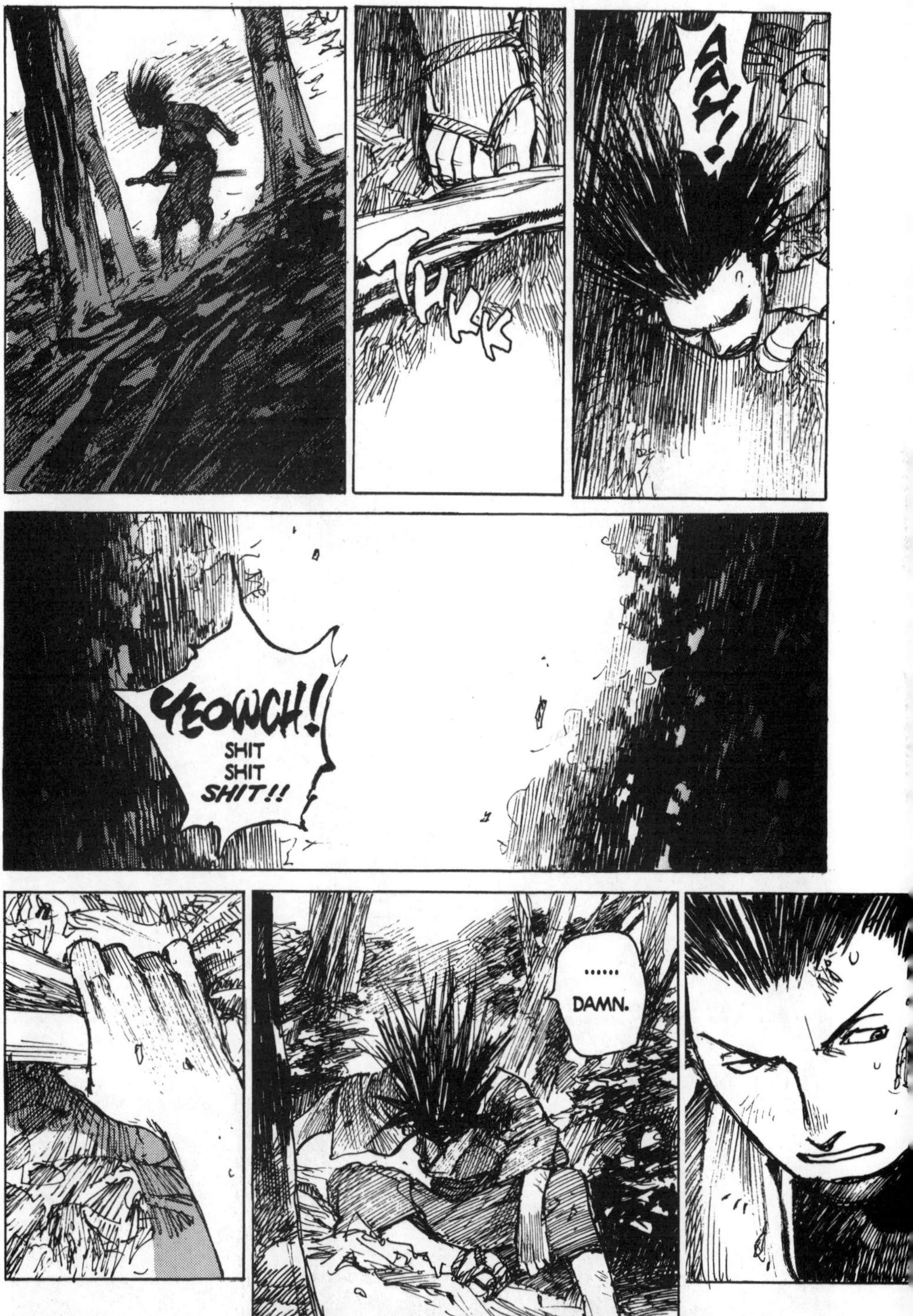
THKK
AAH!
YEOWCH!
SHIT
SHIT
SHIT!!
......
DAMN.

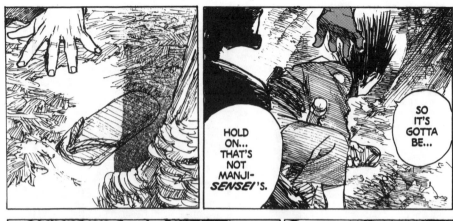

HOLD ON... THAT'S NOT MANJI-*SENSEI*'S.

SO IT'S GOTTA BE...

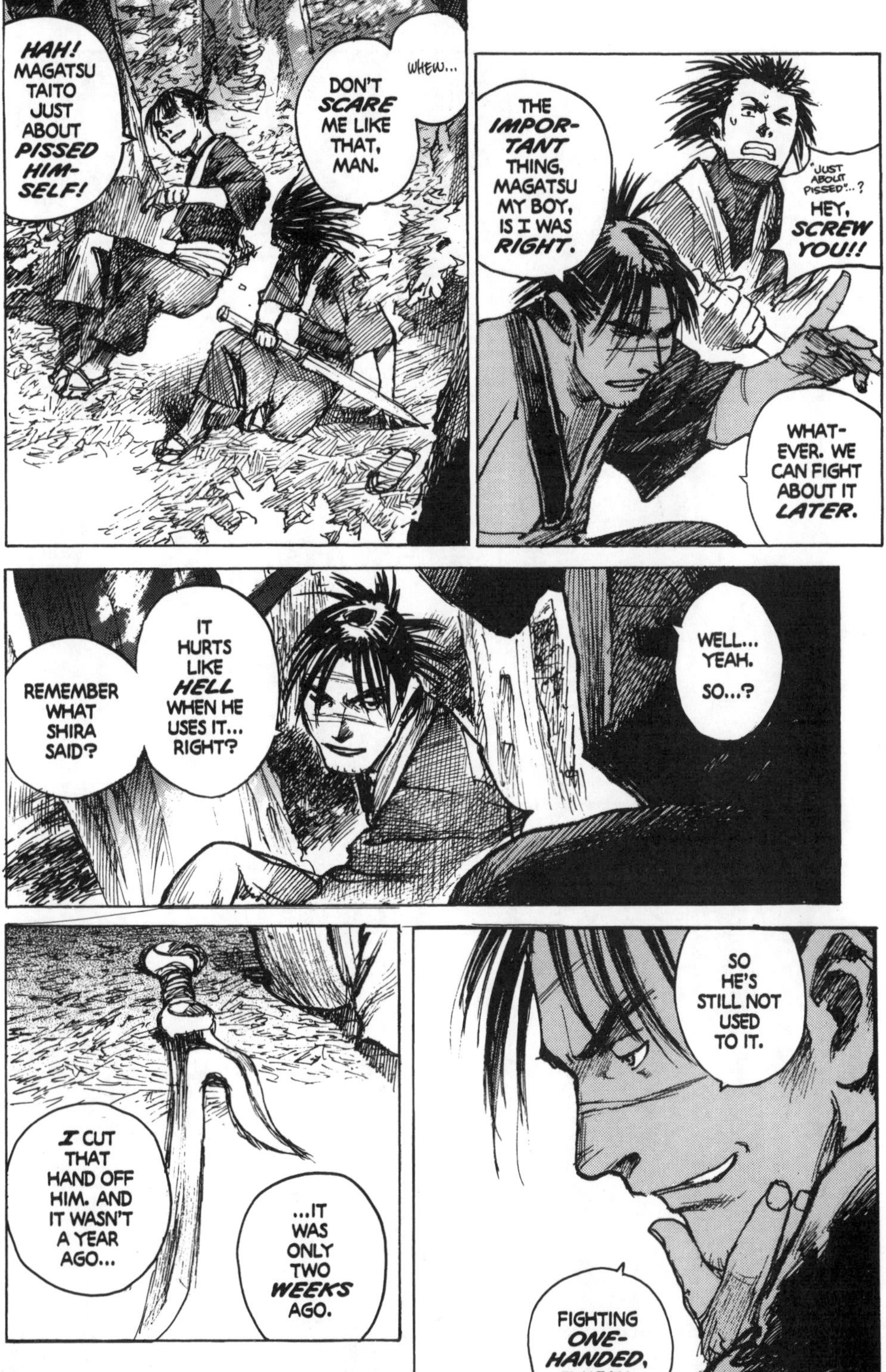
HAH! MAGATSU TAITO JUST ABOUT PISSED HIMSELF!
DON'T SCARE ME LIKE THAT, MAN.
WHEW...
THE IMPORTANT THING, MAGATSU MY BOY, IS I WAS RIGHT.
"JUST ABOUT PISSED"...? HEY, SCREW YOU!!
WHATEVER. WE CAN FIGHT ABOUT IT LATER.
REMEMBER WHAT SHIRA SAID?
IT HURTS LIKE HELL WHEN HE USES IT... RIGHT?
WELL... YEAH.
SO...?
I CUT THAT HAND OFF HIM. AND IT WASN'T A YEAR AGO...
...IT WAS ONLY TWO WEEKS AGO.
SO HE'S STILL NOT USED TO IT.
FIGHTING ONE-HANDED, I MEAN.

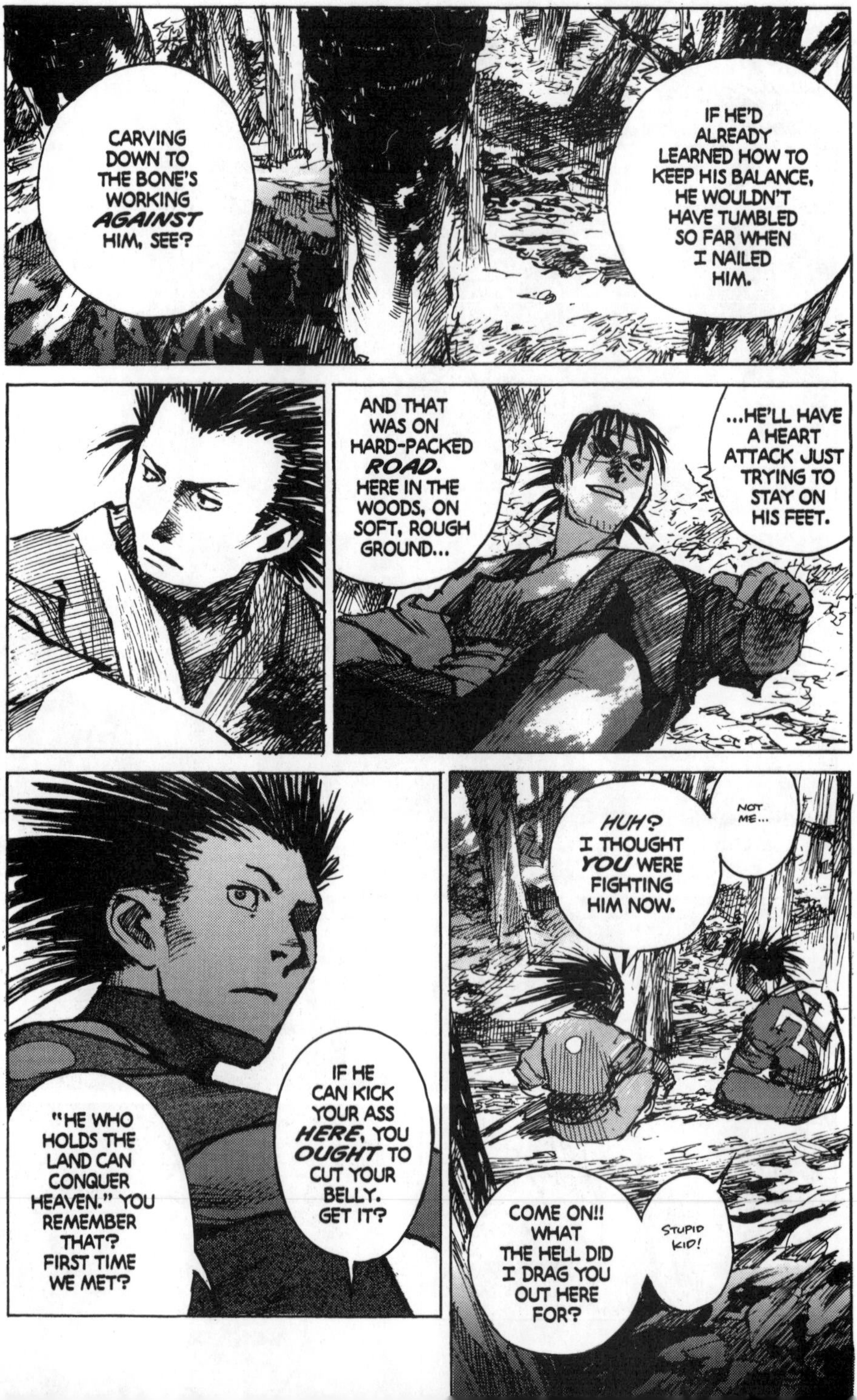

CARVING DOWN TO THE BONE'S WORKING AGAINST HIM, SEE?
IF HE'D ALREADY LEARNED HOW TO KEEP HIS BALANCE, HE WOULDN'T HAVE TUMBLED SO FAR WHEN I NAILED HIM.
AND THAT WAS ON HARD-PACKED ROAD. HERE IN THE WOODS, ON SOFT, ROUGH GROUND...
...HE'LL HAVE A HEART ATTACK JUST TRYING TO STAY ON HIS FEET.
"HE WHO HOLDS THE LAND CAN CONQUER HEAVEN." YOU REMEMBER THAT? FIRST TIME WE MET?
IF HE CAN KICK YOUR ASS HERE, YOU OUGHT TO CUT YOUR BELLY. GET IT?
HUH? I THOUGHT YOU WERE FIGHTING HIM NOW.
NOT ME...
COME ON!! WHAT THE HELL DID I DRAG YOU OUT HERE FOR?
STUPID KID!

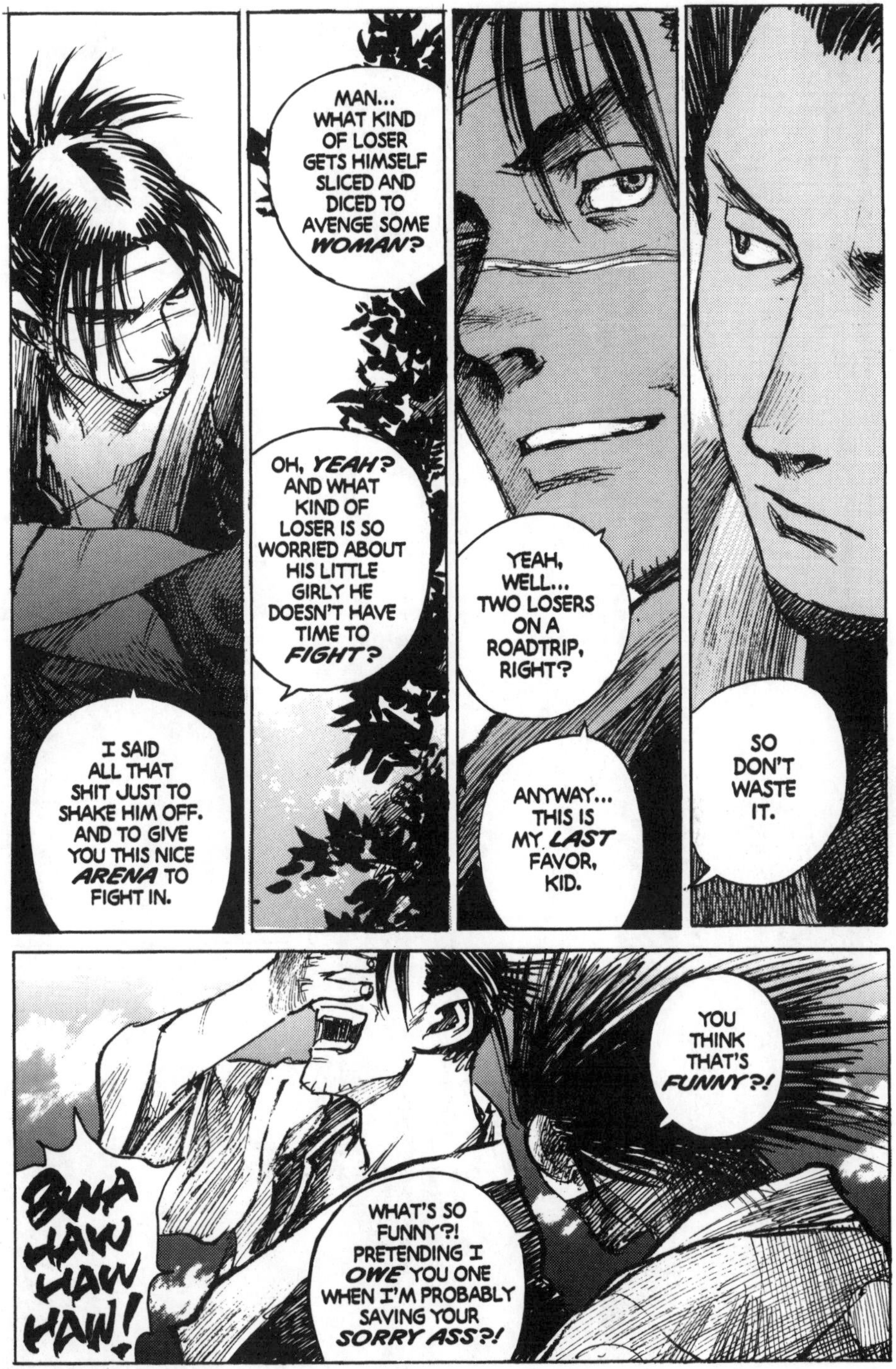
MAN... WHAT KIND OF LOSER GETS HIMSELF SLICED AND DICED TO AVENGE SOME WOMAN?
OH, YEAH? AND WHAT KIND OF LOSER IS SO WORRIED ABOUT HIS LITTLE GIRLY HE DOESN'T HAVE TIME TO FIGHT?
I SAID ALL THAT SHIT JUST TO SHAKE HIM OFF. AND TO GIVE YOU THIS NICE ARENA TO FIGHT IN.
YEAH, WELL... TWO LOSERS ON A ROADTRIP, RIGHT?
ANYWAY... THIS IS MY LAST FAVOR, KID.
SO DON'T WASTE IT.
BWAHAW HAW HAW!
YOU THINK THAT'S FUNNY?!
WHAT'S SO FUNNY?! PRETENDING I OWE YOU ONE WHEN I'M PROBABLY SAVING YOUR SORRY ASS?!

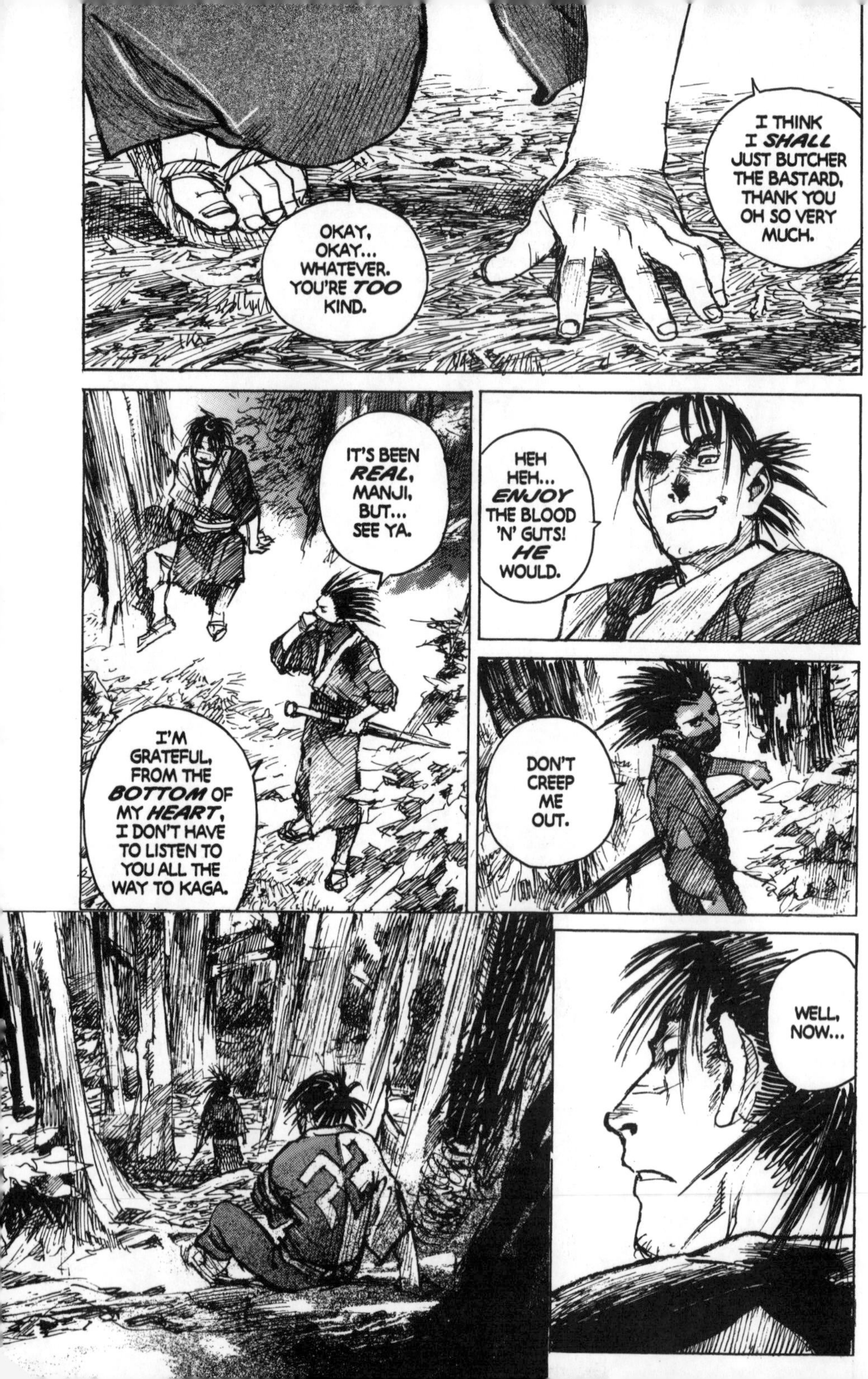
I THINK I SHALL JUST BUTCHER THE BASTARD, THANK YOU OH SO VERY MUCH.
OKAY, OKAY... WHATEVER. YOU'RE TOO KIND.
IT'S BEEN REAL, MANJI, BUT... SEE YA.
I'M GRATEFUL, FROM THE BOTTOM OF MY HEART, I DON'T HAVE TO LISTEN TO YOU ALL THE WAY TO KAGA.
HEH HEH... ENJOY THE BLOOD 'N' GUTS! HE WOULD.
DON'T CREEP ME OUT.
WELL, NOW...

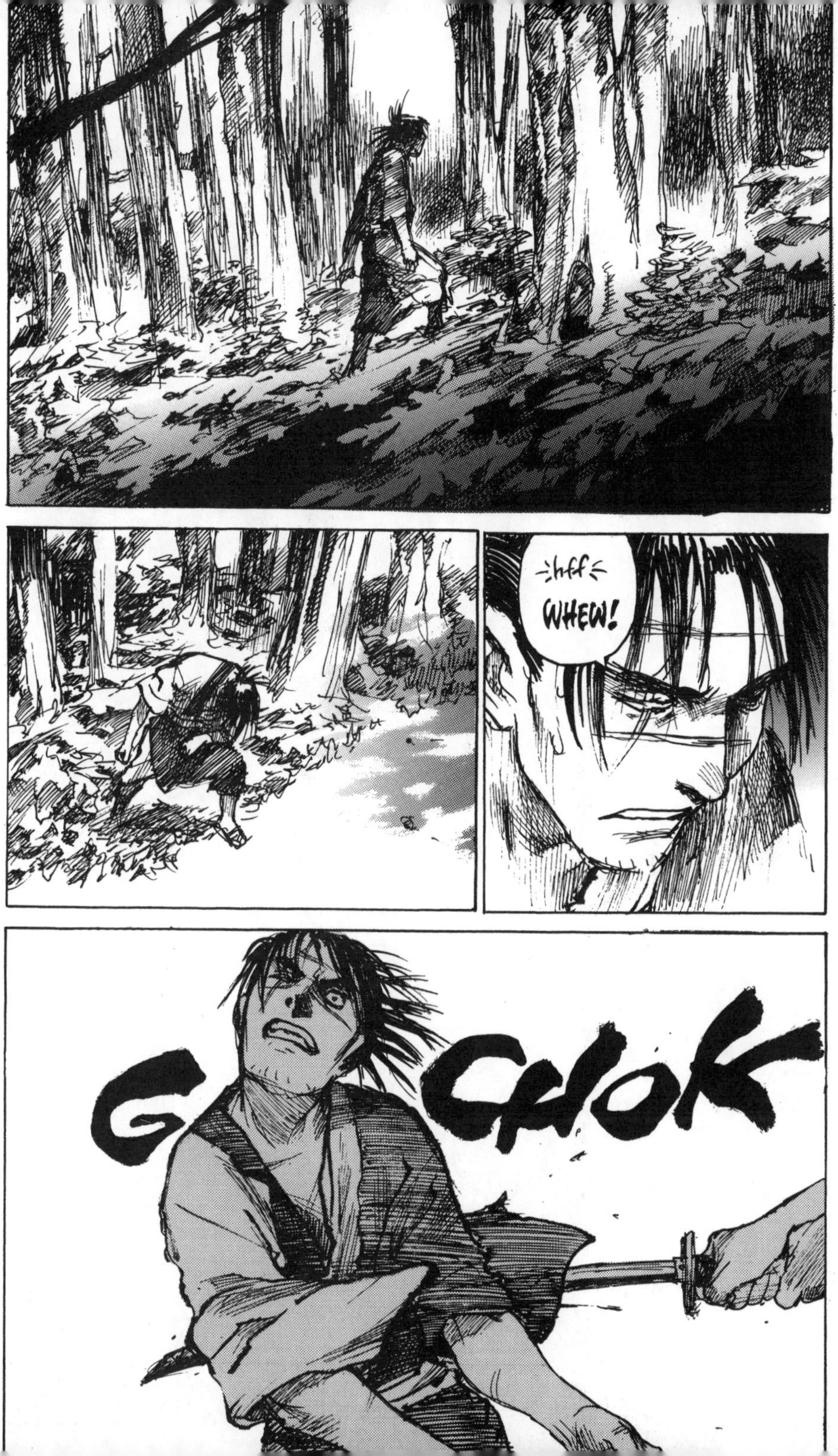
hff
WHEW!
G CHOK

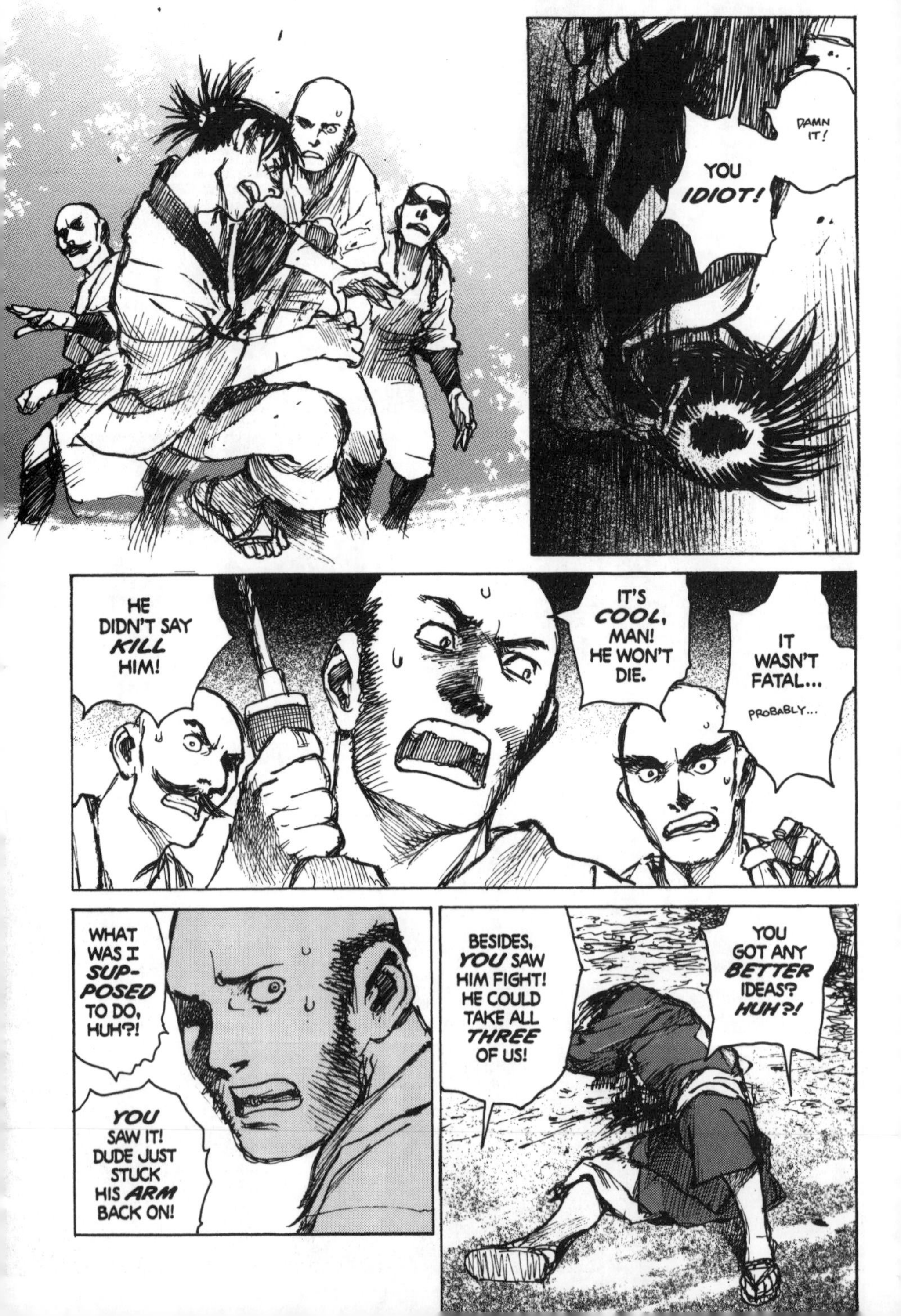
YOU *IDIOT!*
DAMN IT!
HE DIDN'T SAY *KILL* HIM!
IT'S *COOL*, MAN! HE WON'T DIE.
IT WASN'T FATAL...
PROBABLY...
WHAT WAS I *SUP-POSED* TO DO, HUH?!
YOU SAW IT! DUDE JUST STUCK HIS *ARM* BACK ON!
BESIDES, *YOU* SAW HIM FIGHT! HE COULD TAKE ALL *THREE* OF US!
YOU GOT ANY *BETTER* IDEAS? *HUH?!*

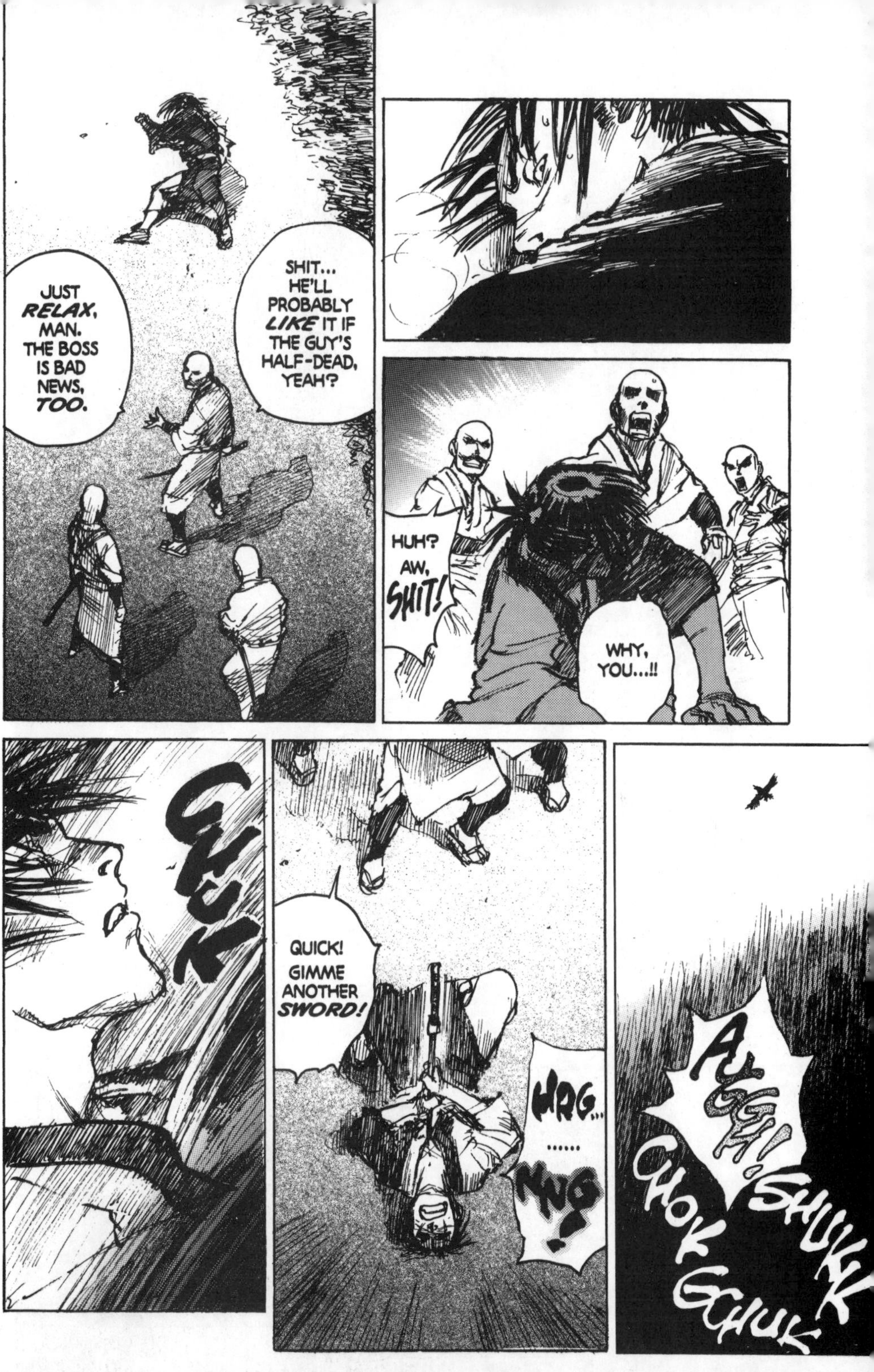
JUST *RELAX*, MAN. THE BOSS IS BAD NEWS, *TOO*.
SHIT... HE'LL PROBABLY *LIKE* IT IF THE GUY'S HALF-DEAD, YEAH?
HUH? AW, SHIT!
WHY, YOU...!!
GLUK
QUICK! GIMME ANOTHER *SWORD*!
HRG... ...... NNG!
AUGGH!
SHUKK
CHOK GCHUK

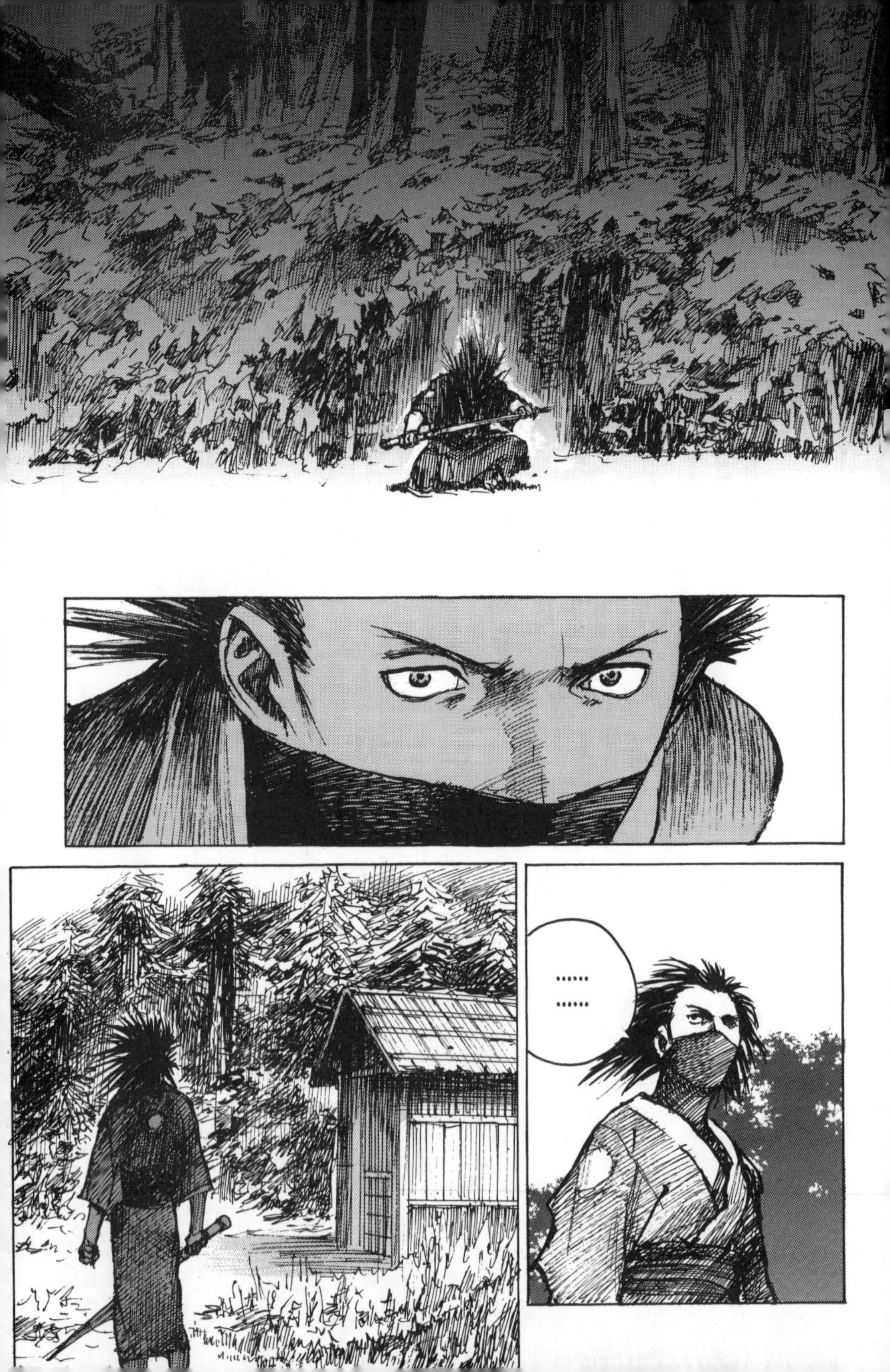
......
......

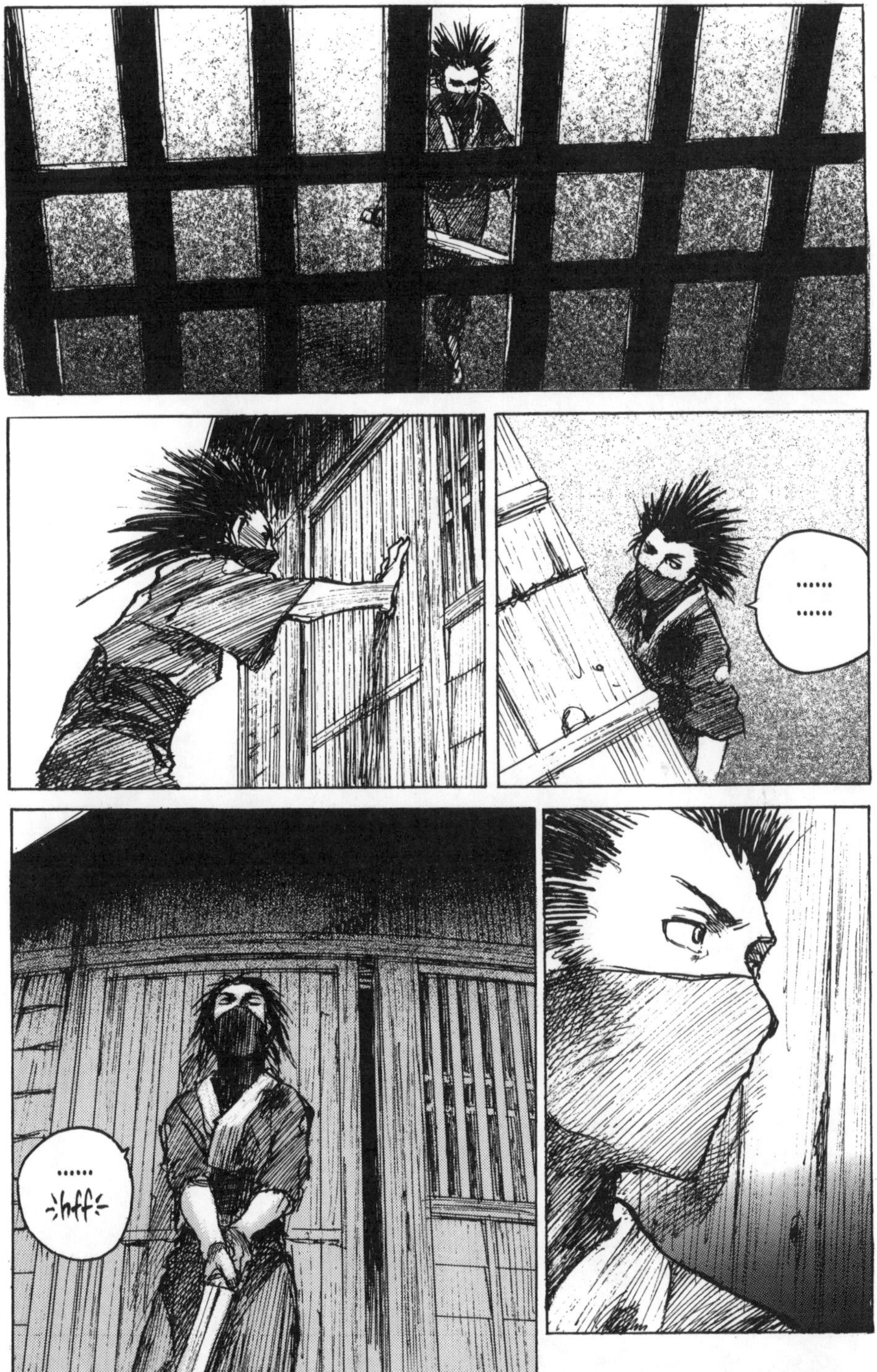

......
......
......
hff

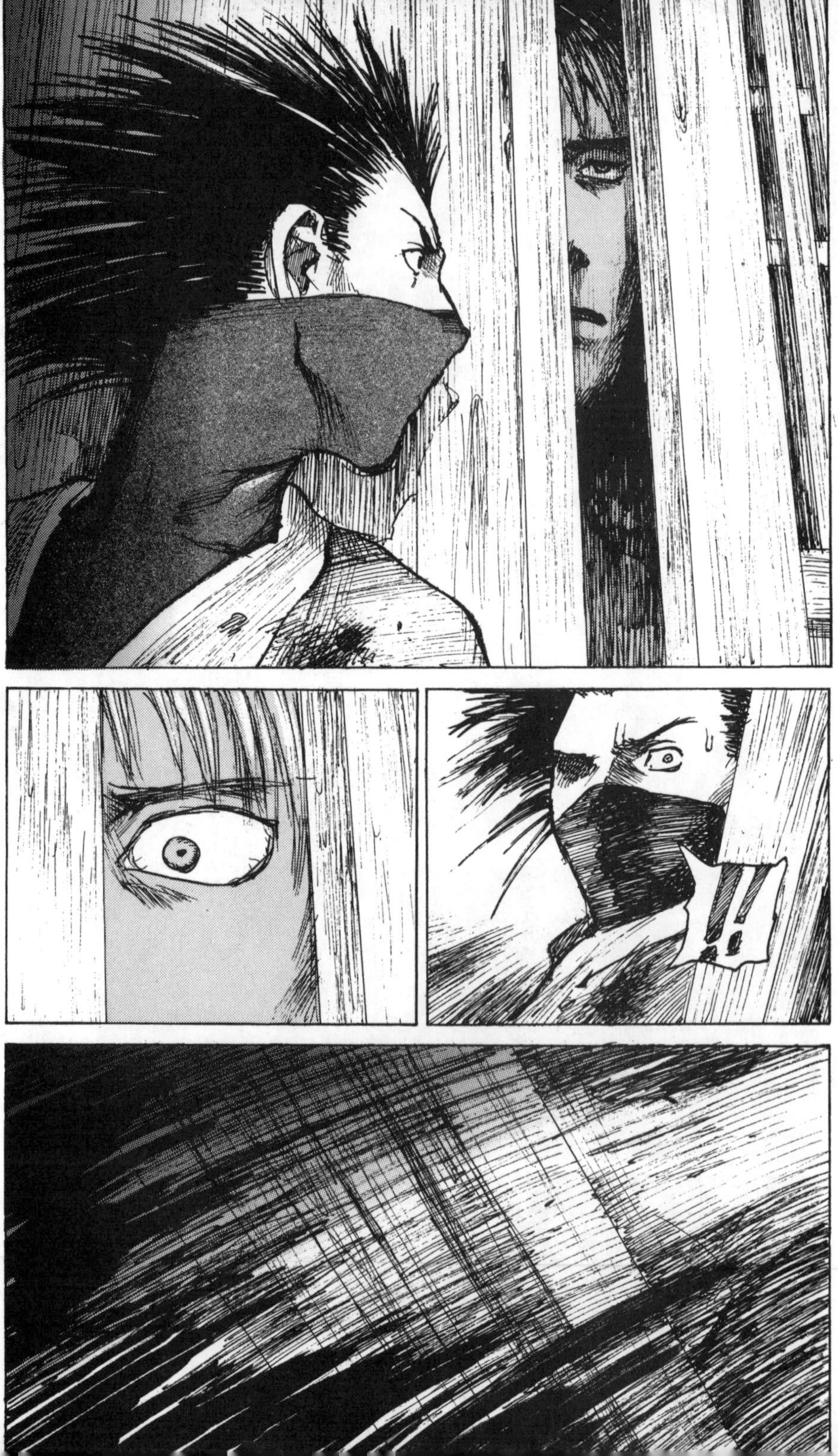
!

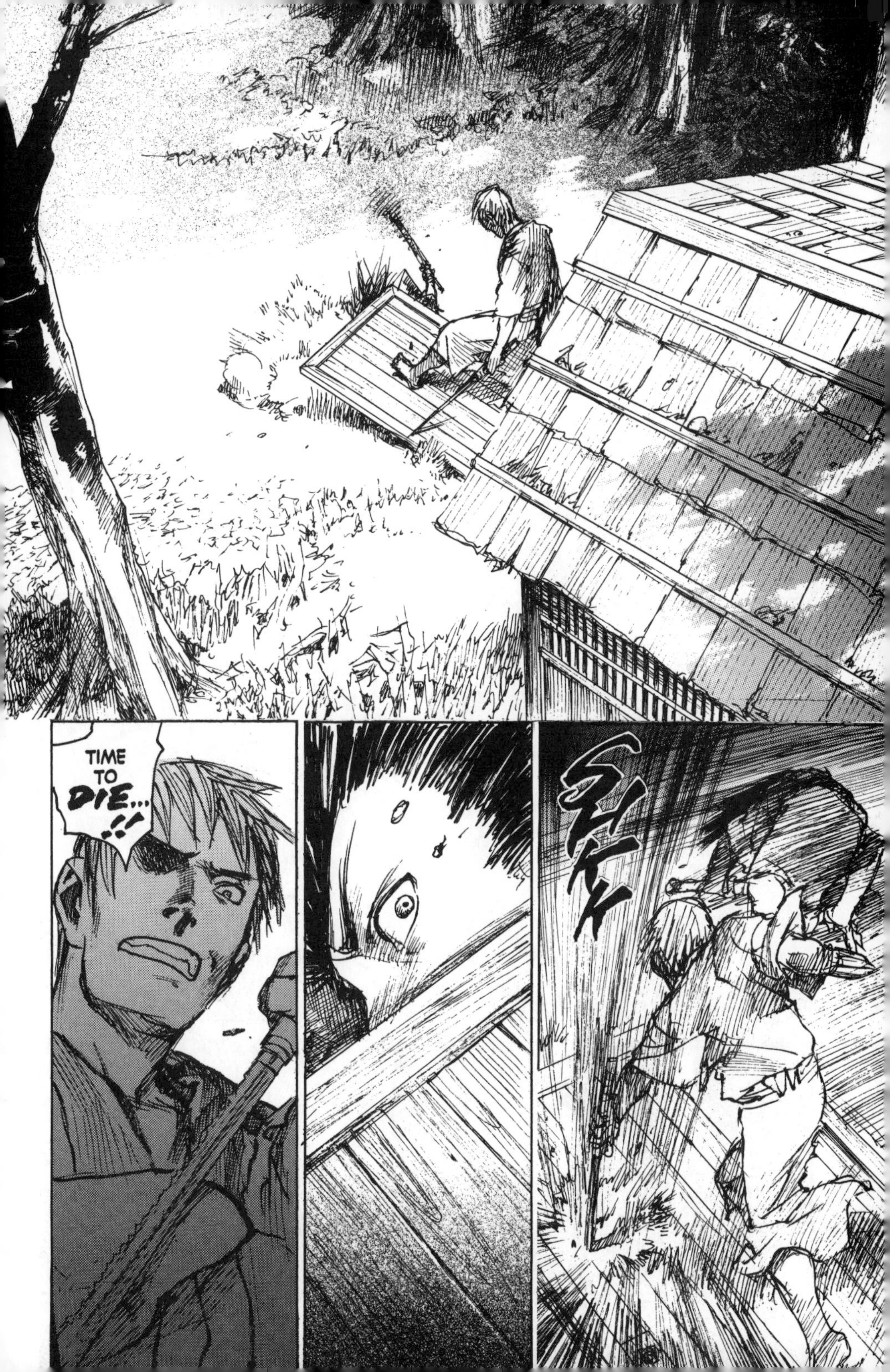
TIME TO DIE...!!
SHKK

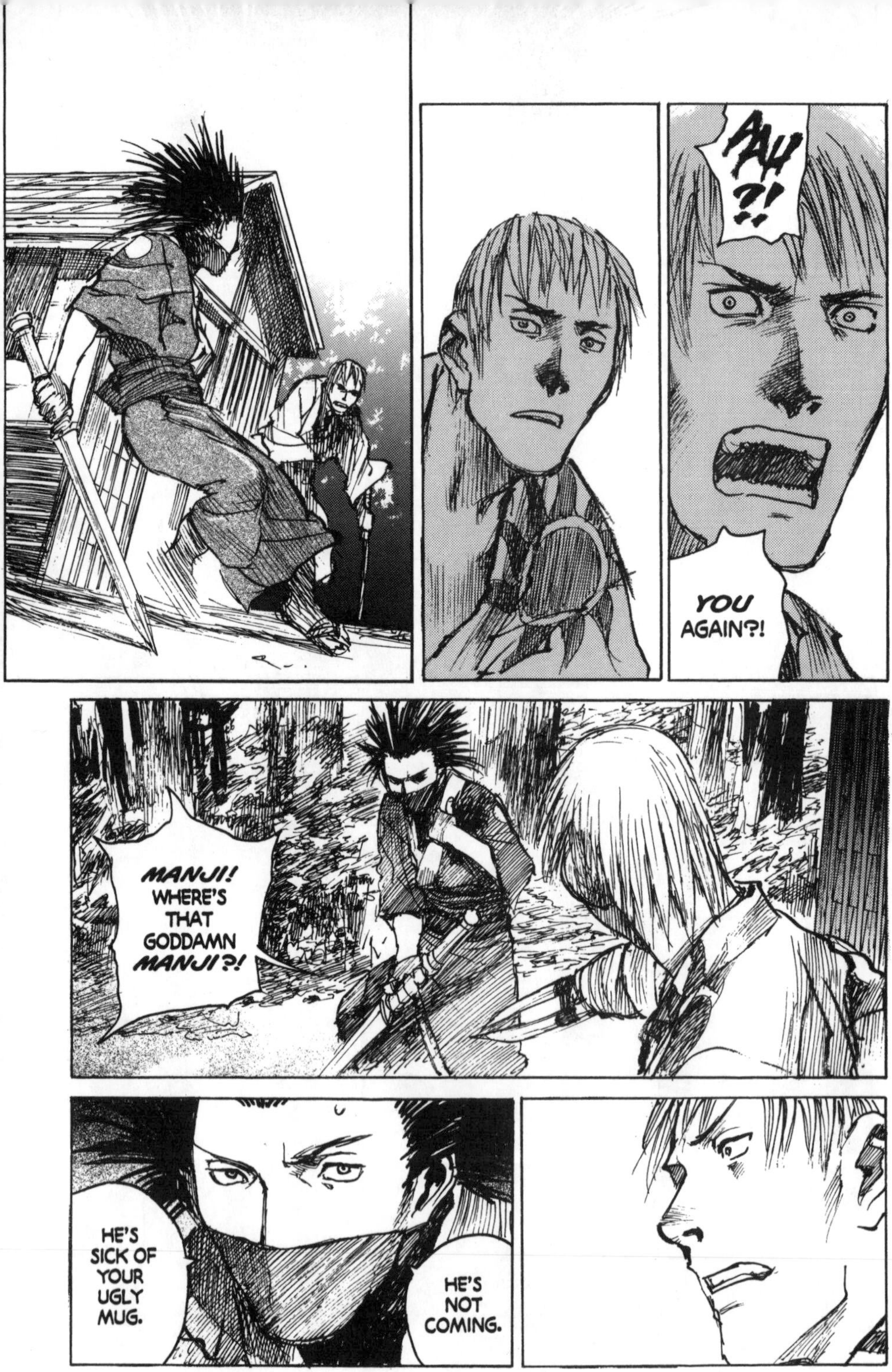
AAH ?!!
YOU AGAIN?!
MANJI! WHERE'S THAT GODDAMN MANJI?!
HE'S SICK OF YOUR UGLY MUG.
HE'S NOT COMING.

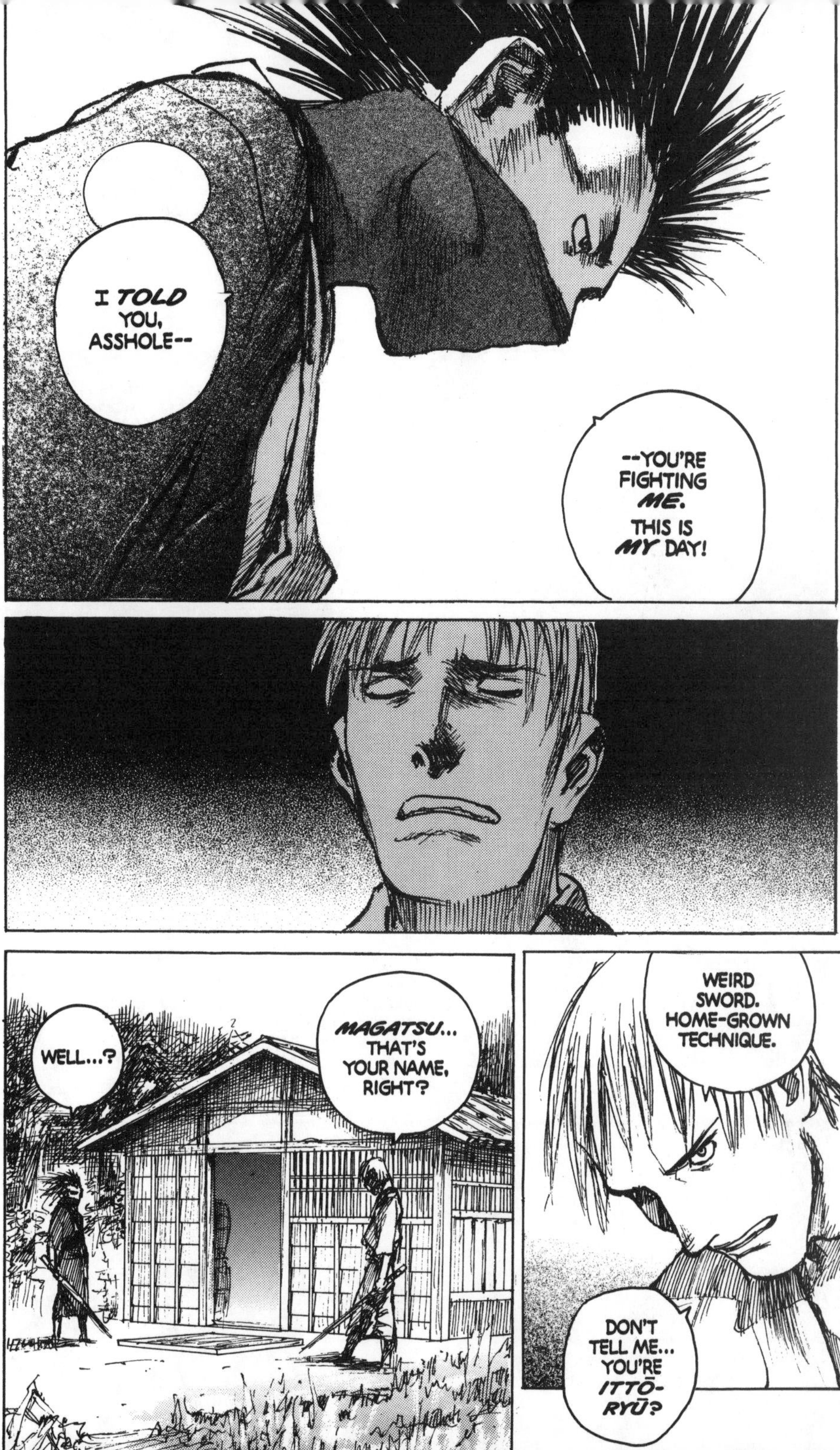
I *TOLD* YOU, ASSHOLE--
--YOU'RE FIGHTING *ME.* THIS IS *MY* DAY!
WELL...?
MAGATSU... THAT'S YOUR NAME, RIGHT?
WEIRD SWORD. HOME-GROWN TECHNIQUE.
DON'T TELL ME... YOU'RE *ITTŌ-RYŪ?*

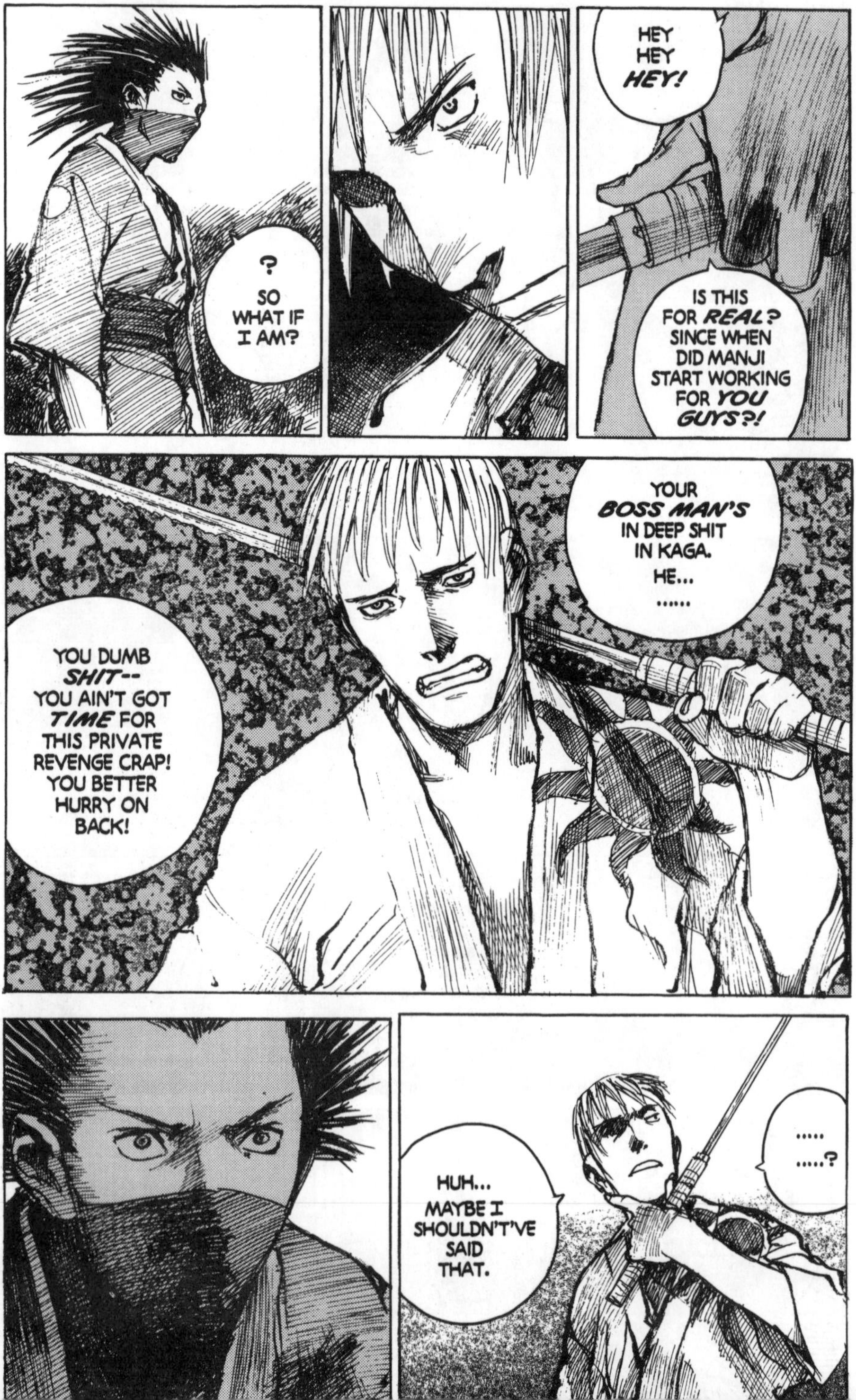
?
SO WHAT IF I AM?
HEY HEY HEY!
IS THIS FOR REAL? SINCE WHEN DID MANJI START WORKING FOR YOU GUYS?!
YOUR BOSS MAN'S IN DEEP SHIT IN KAGA. HE... ......
YOU DUMB SHIT-- YOU AIN'T GOT TIME FOR THIS PRIVATE REVENGE CRAP! YOU BETTER HURRY ON BACK!
HUH... MAYBE I SHOULDN'T'VE SAID THAT.
....?

HEY!

WHAT'S GOING ON IN KAGA?! *TELL* ME!

HEH, HEH... NOT TOO *CLASSY*, BEGGING FOR HANDOUTS. RIGHT, PAL?

YOU WANT TO SEE "WHAT'S GOING ON IN KAGA"...?

GO FIND OUT FOR *YOUR-SELF*.

AND LET *MANJI* DEAL WITH *ME*. YEAH?

HRM... THOSE THREE *STOOGES*...

...THEY BETTER BE DOING THEIR DAMN *JOB*.

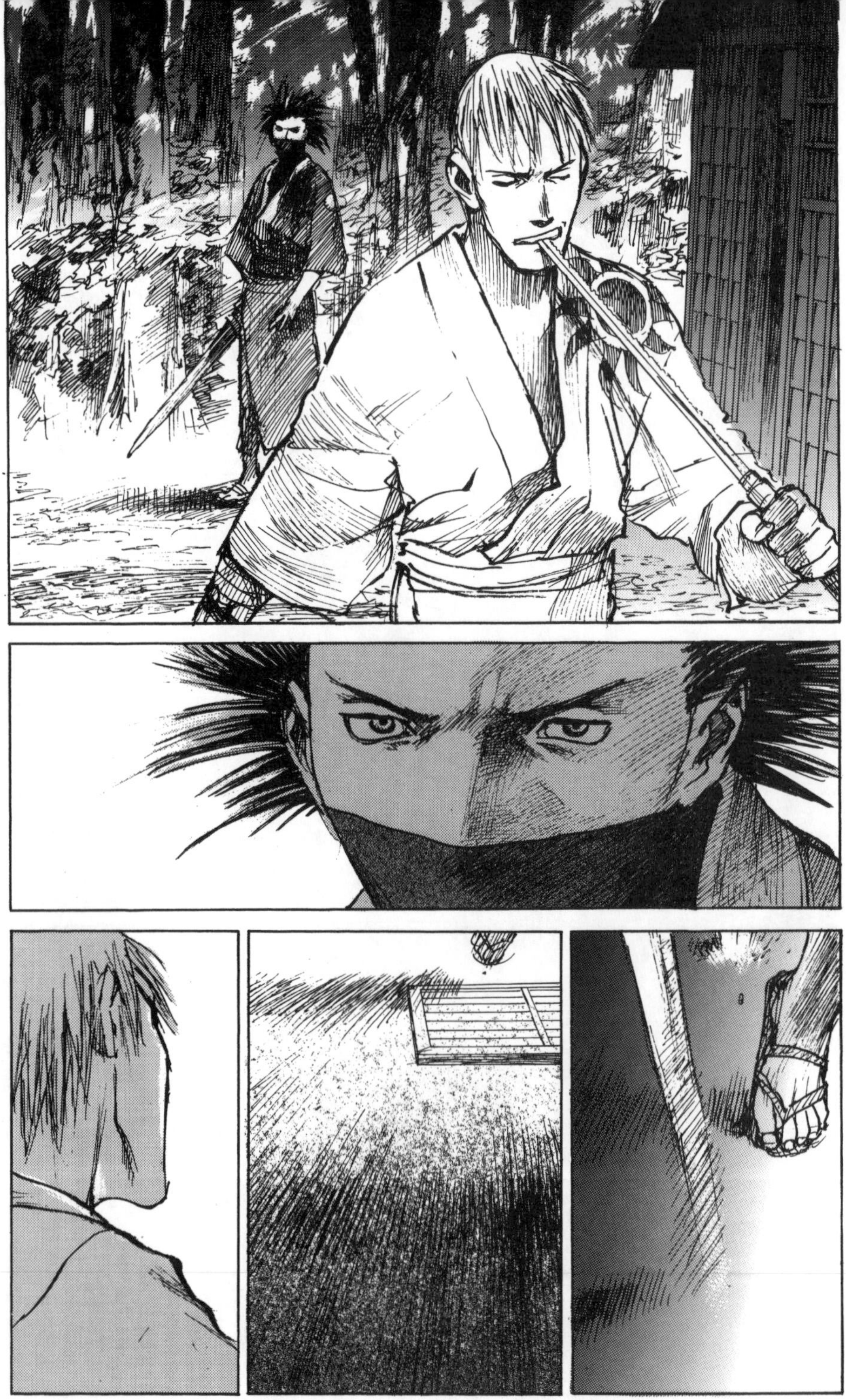

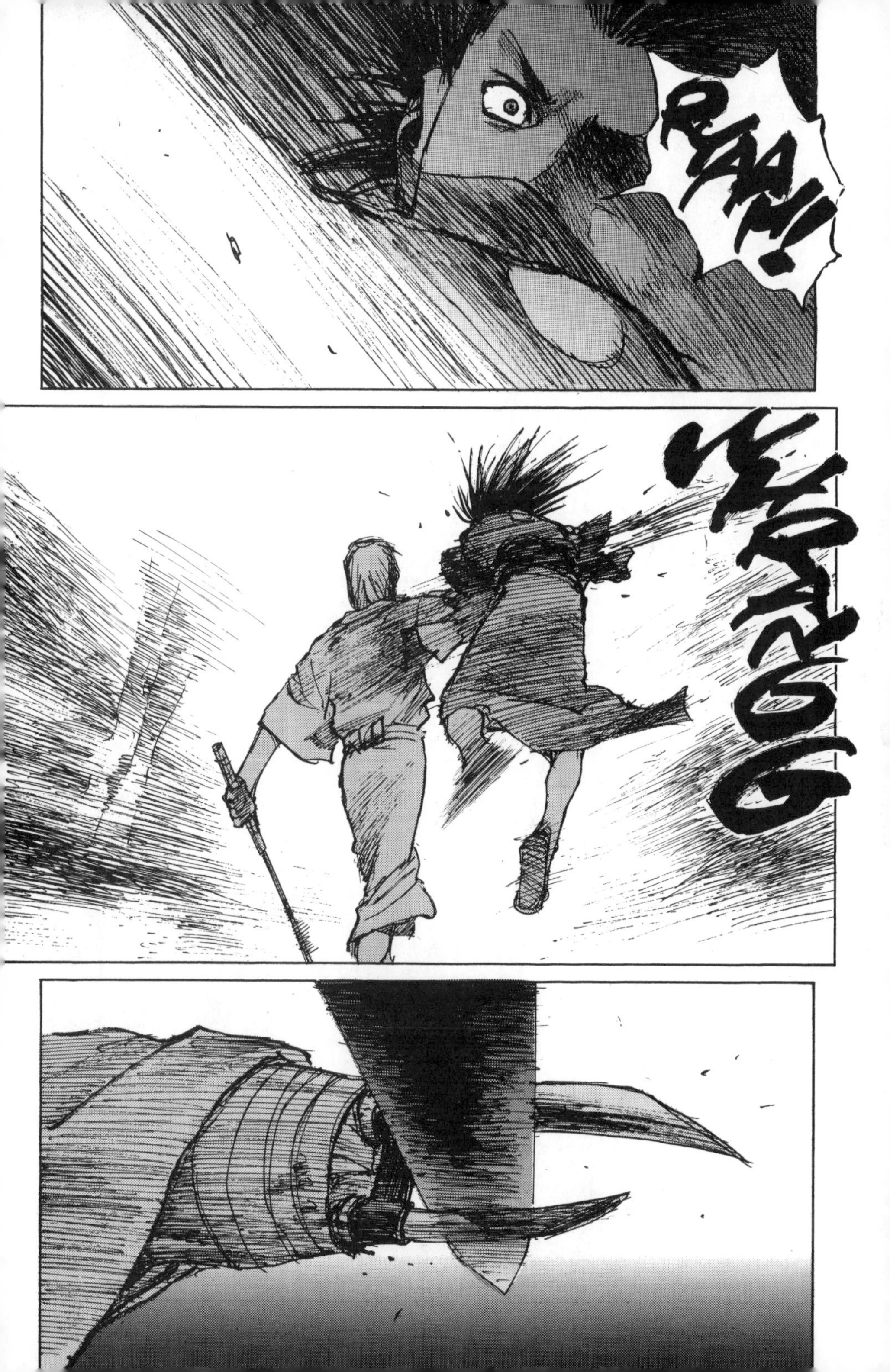
RAAH!

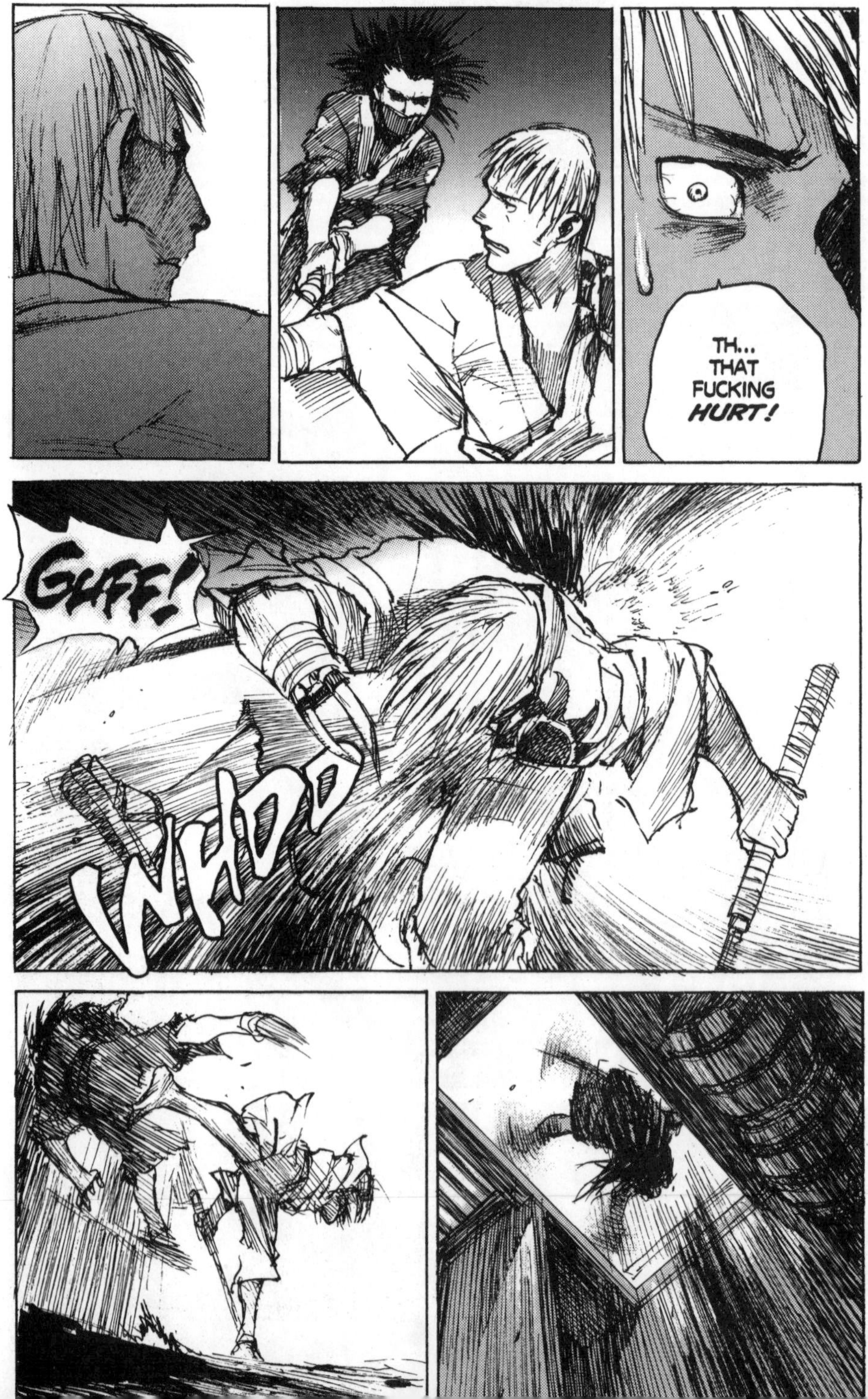
TH...
THAT
FUCKING
HURT!
GUFF!
WHOO

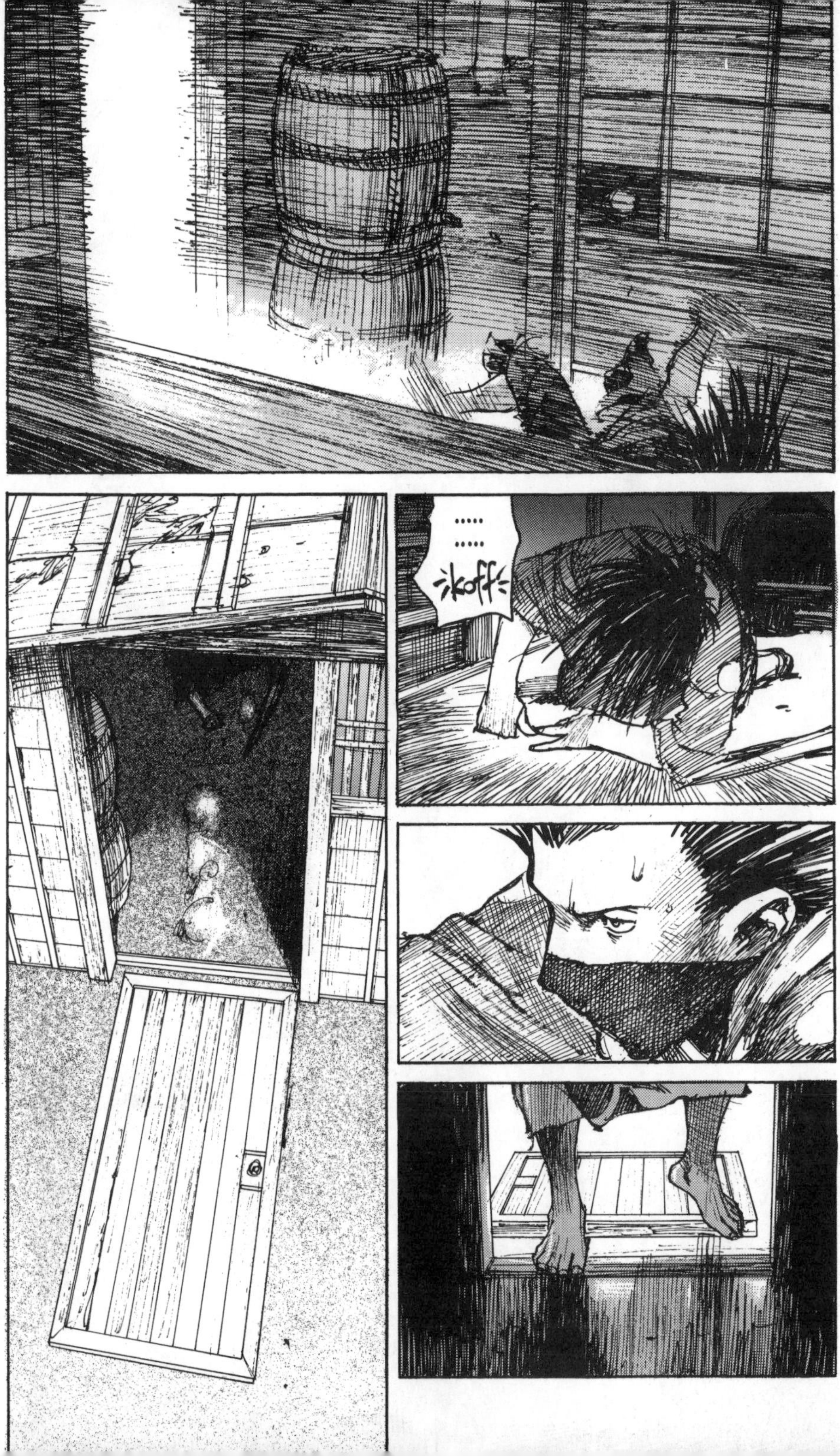

......
......
koff

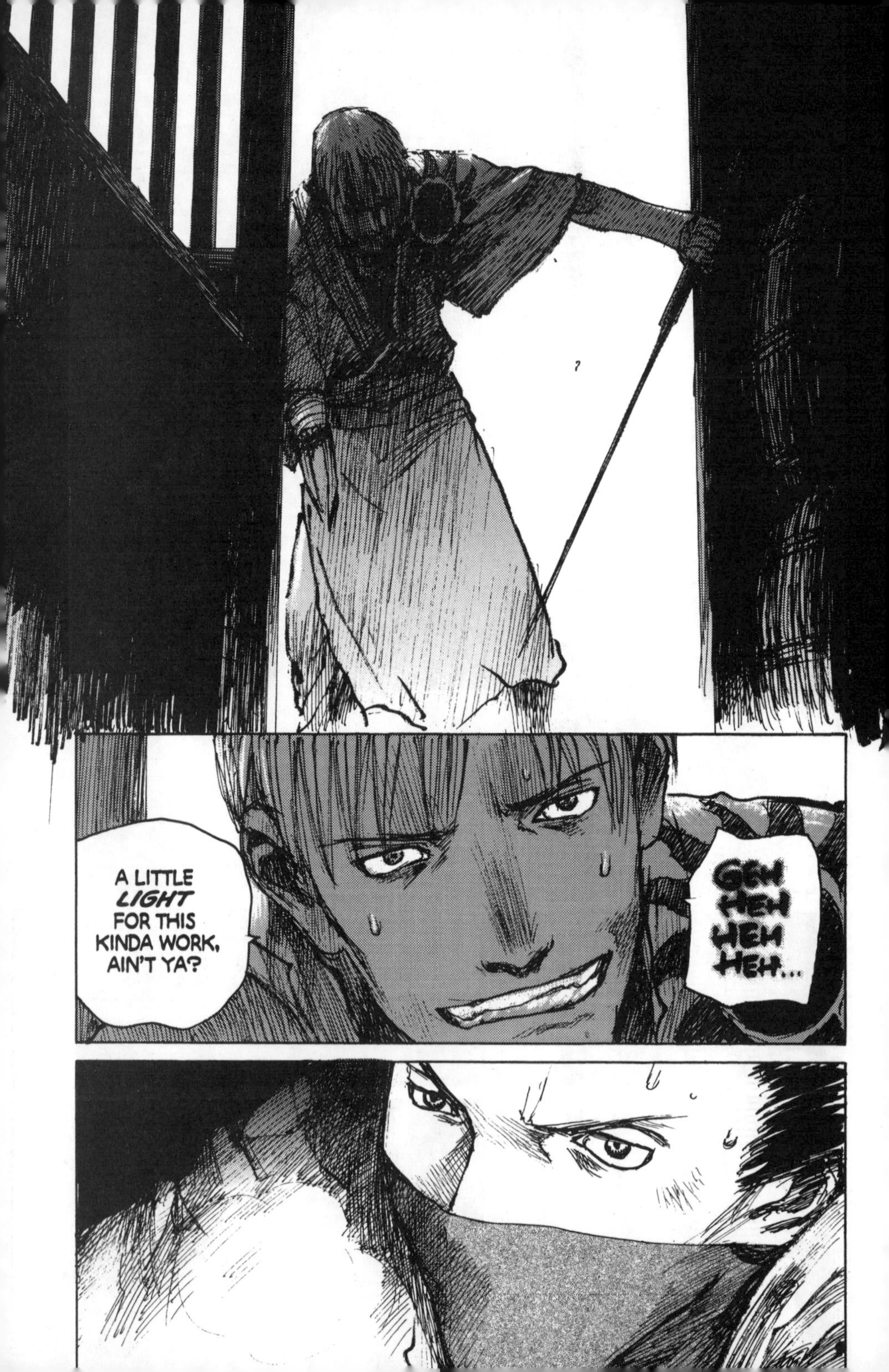
A LITTLE *LIGHT* FOR THIS KINDA WORK, AIN'T YA?
GEH HEH HEH HEH...

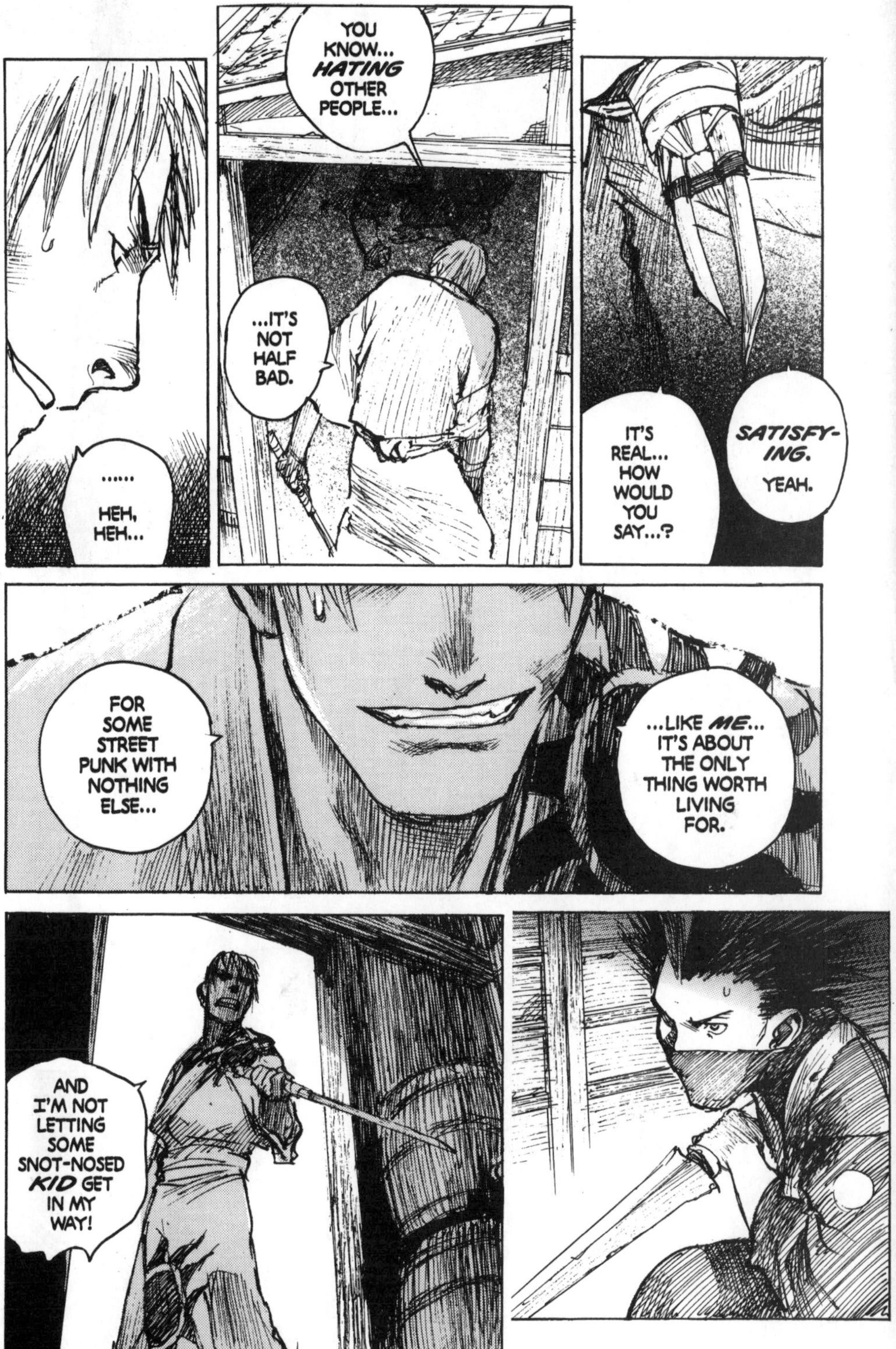
......
HEH, HEH...
YOU KNOW... HATING OTHER PEOPLE...
...IT'S NOT HALF BAD.
IT'S REAL... HOW WOULD YOU SAY...?
SATISFY-ING. YEAH.
FOR SOME STREET PUNK WITH NOTHING ELSE...
...LIKE ME... IT'S ABOUT THE ONLY THING WORTH LIVING FOR.
AND I'M NOT LETTING SOME SNOT-NOSED KID GET IN MY WAY!

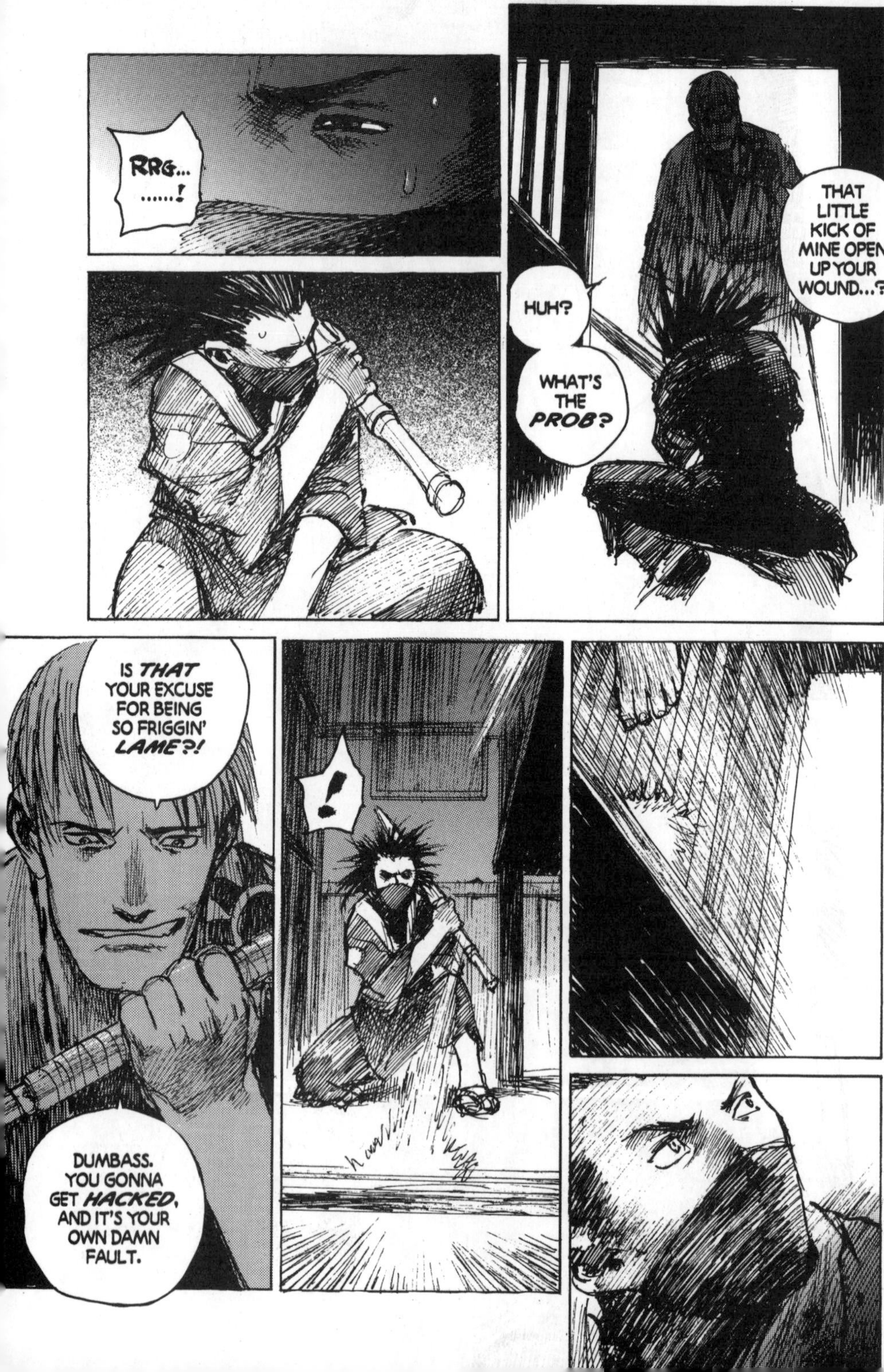
RRG... ......!
HUH?
WHAT'S THE PROB?
THAT LITTLE KICK OF MINE OPEN UP YOUR WOUND...?
IS THAT YOUR EXCUSE FOR BEING SO FRIGGIN' LAME?!
DUMBASS. YOU GONNA GET HACKED, AND IT'S YOUR OWN DAMN FAULT.
!

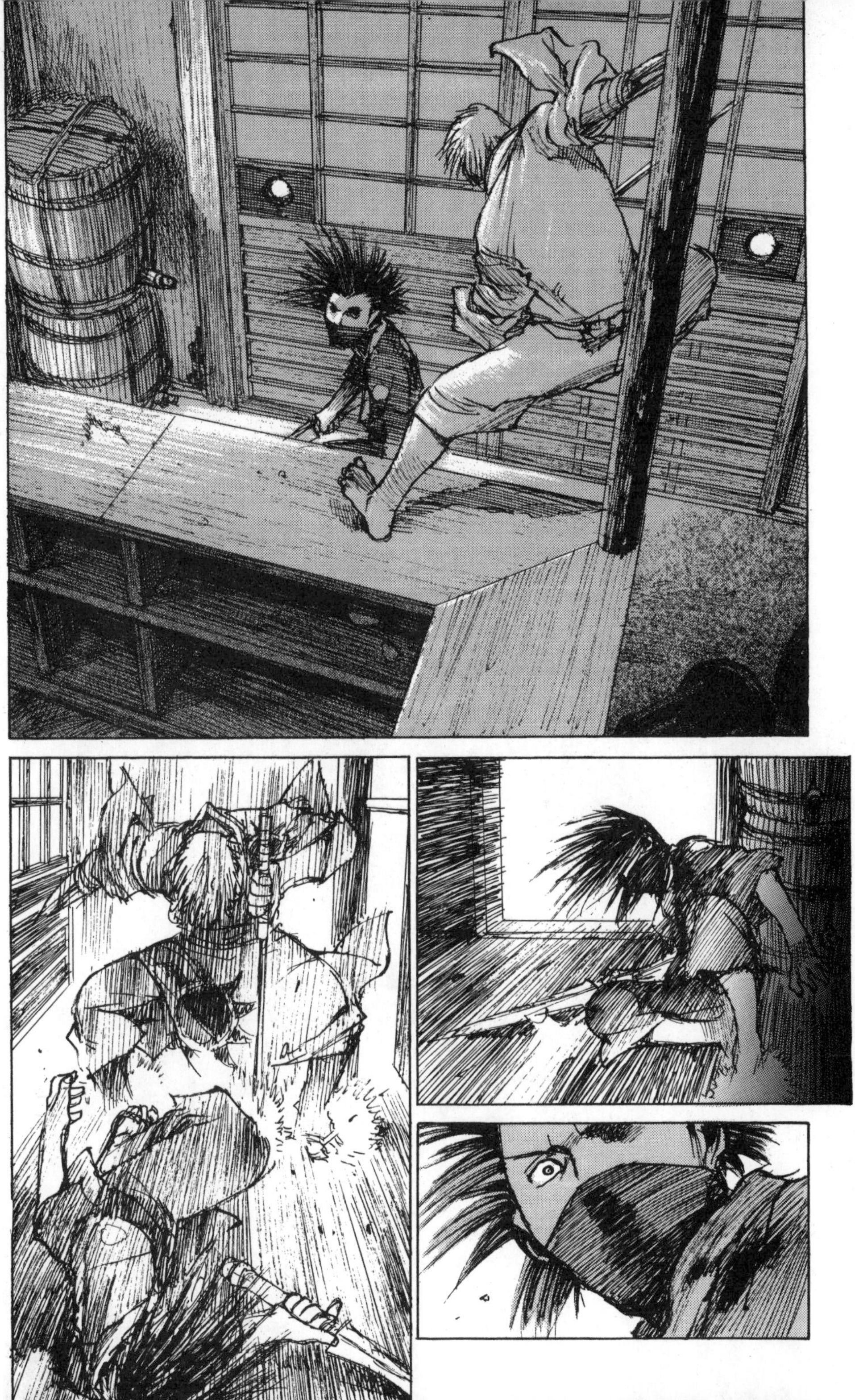

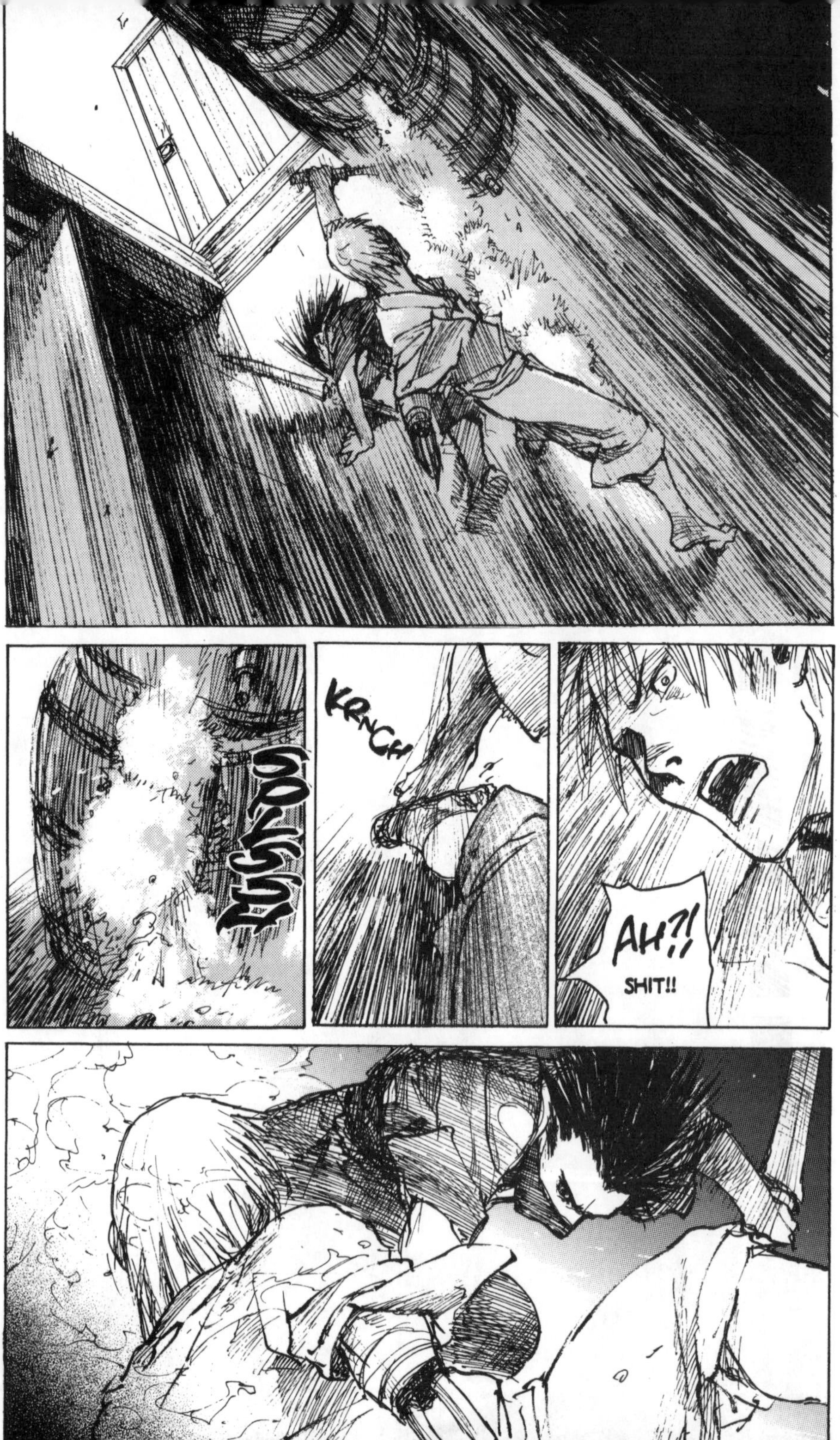
KRNCH
AH?!
SHIT!!

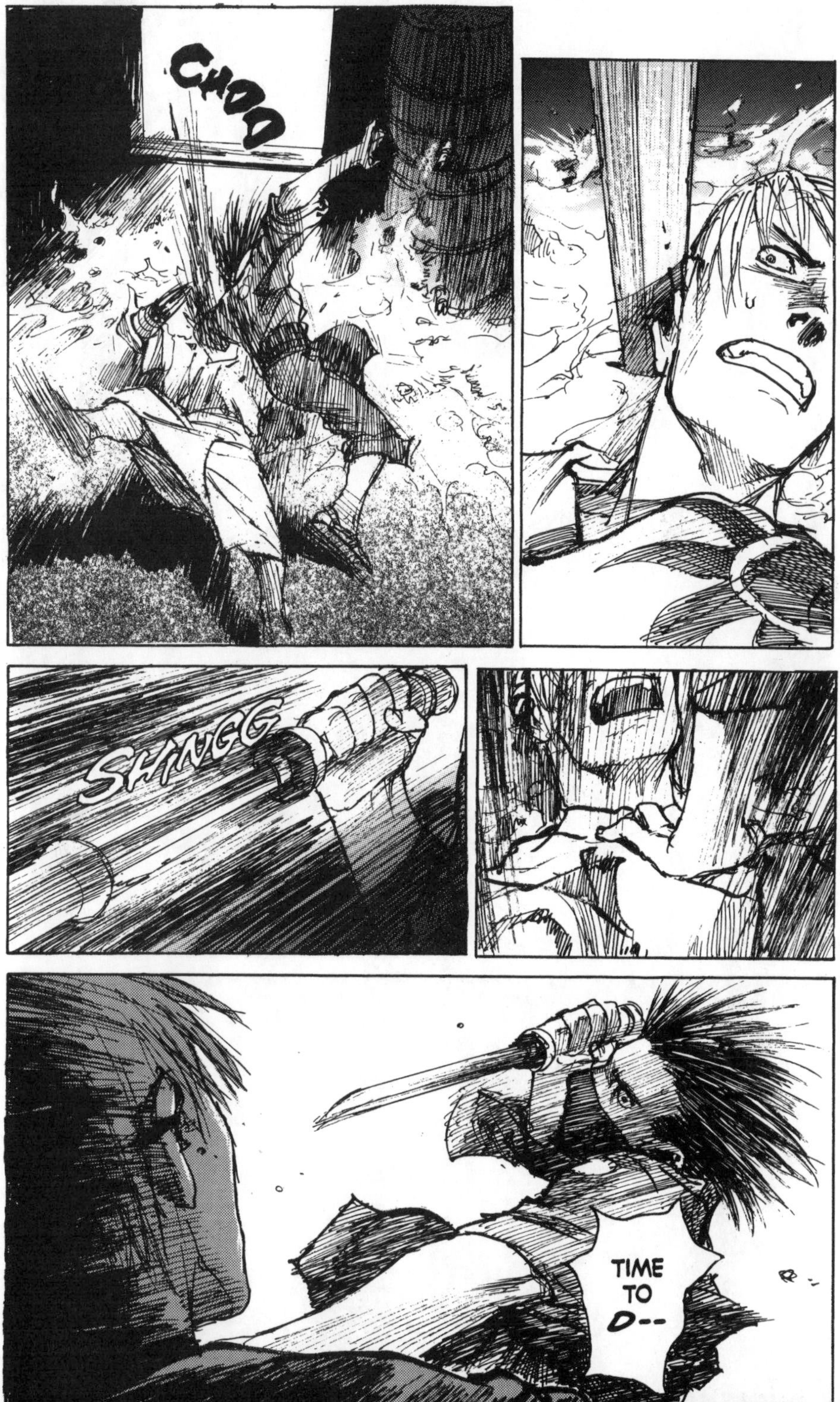
CHOO
SHINGG
TIME TO D--

KRAK

FDD

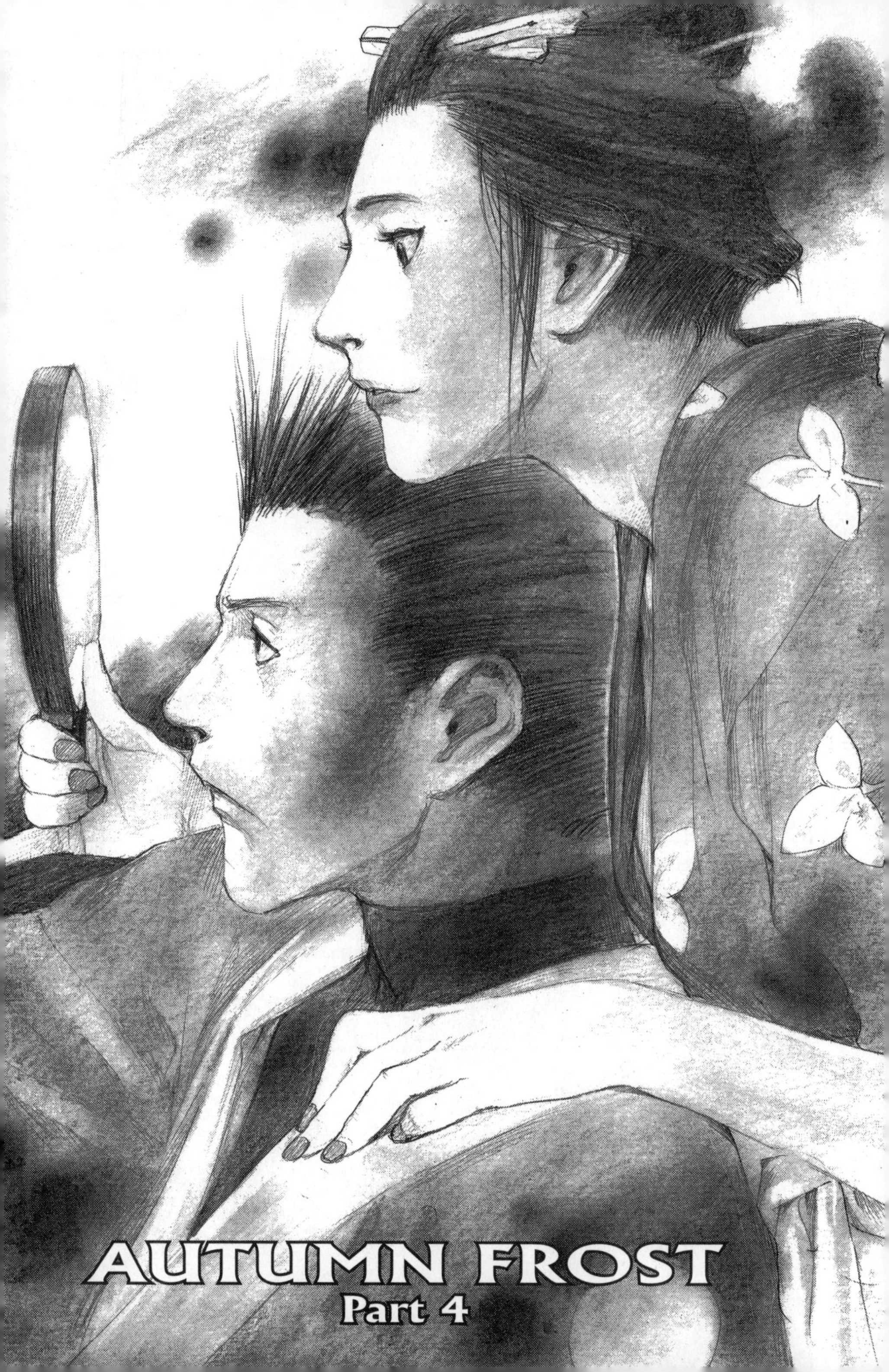
AUTUMN FROST
Part 4

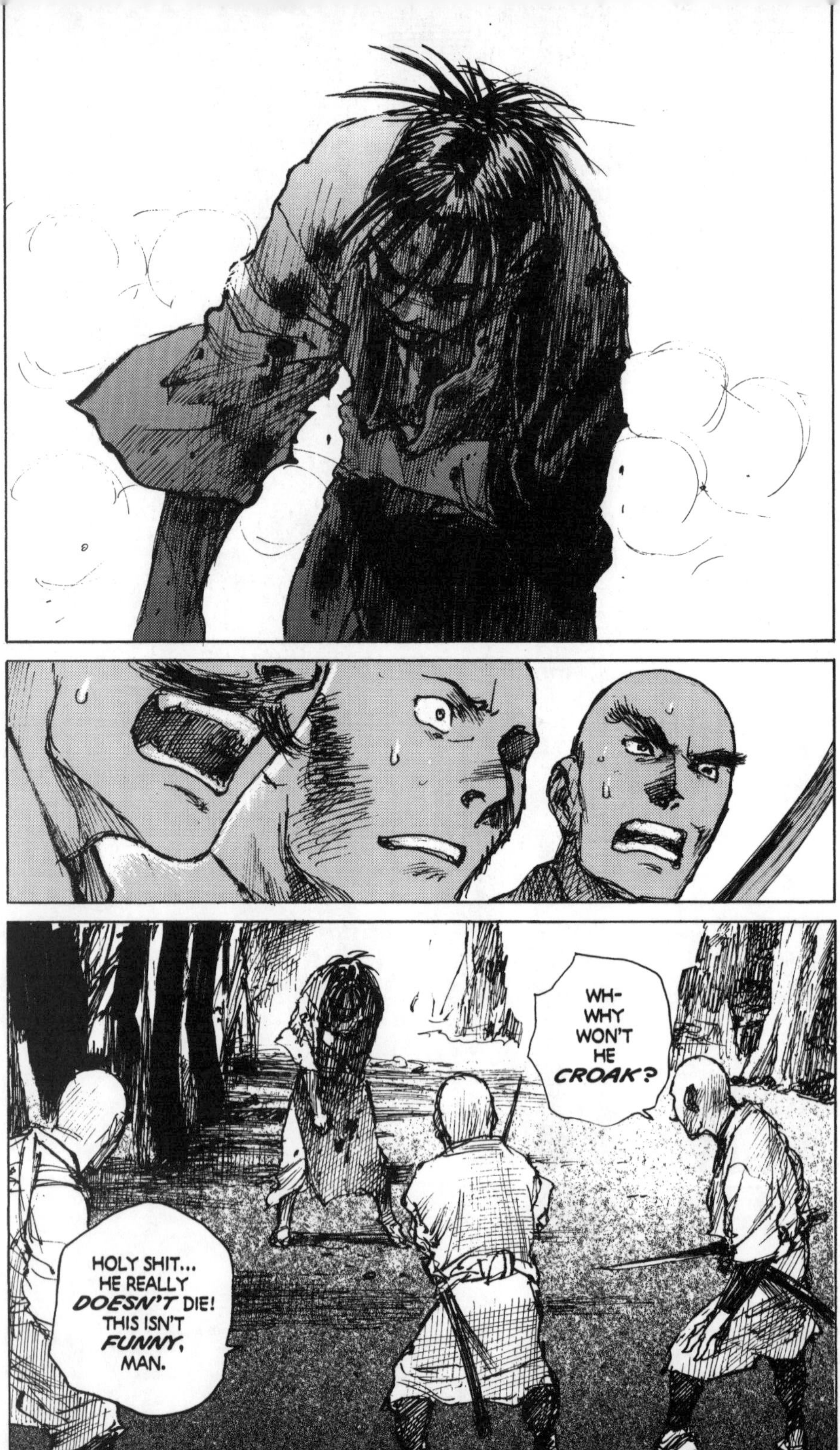
WH- WHY WON'T HE CROAK?
HOLY SHIT... HE REALLY DOESN'T DIE! THIS ISN'T FUNNY, MAN.

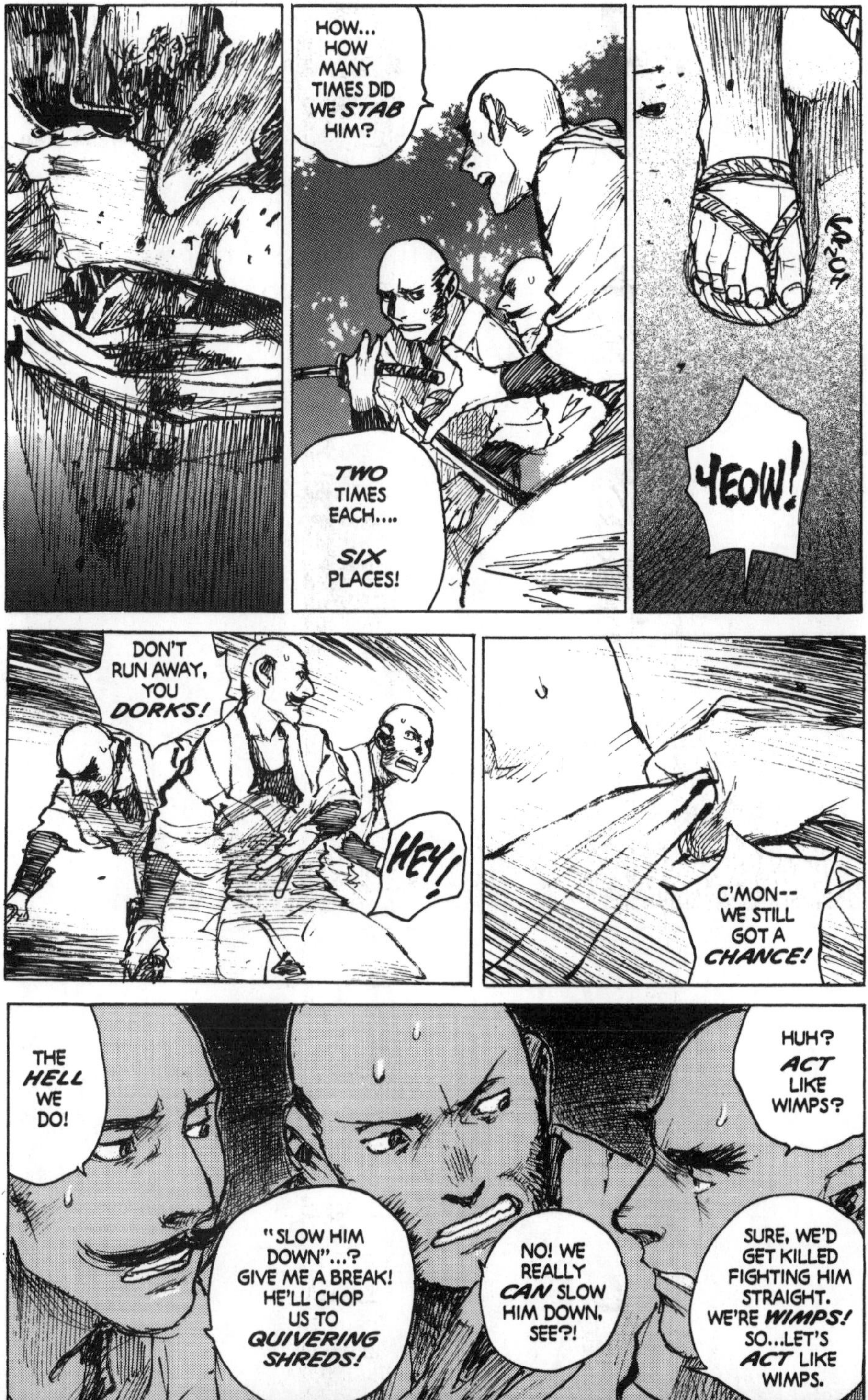

HOW... HOW MANY TIMES DID WE STAB HIM?
TWO TIMES EACH.... SIX PLACES!
YEOW!
DON'T RUN AWAY, YOU DORKS!
HEY!
C'MON-- WE STILL GOT A CHANCE!
THE HELL WE DO!
"SLOW HIM DOWN"...? GIVE ME A BREAK! HE'LL CHOP US TO QUIVERING SHREDS!
NO! WE REALLY CAN SLOW HIM DOWN, SEE?!
HUH? ACT LIKE WIMPS?
SURE, WE'D GET KILLED FIGHTING HIM STRAIGHT. WE'RE WIMPS! SO...LET'S ACT LIKE WIMPS.

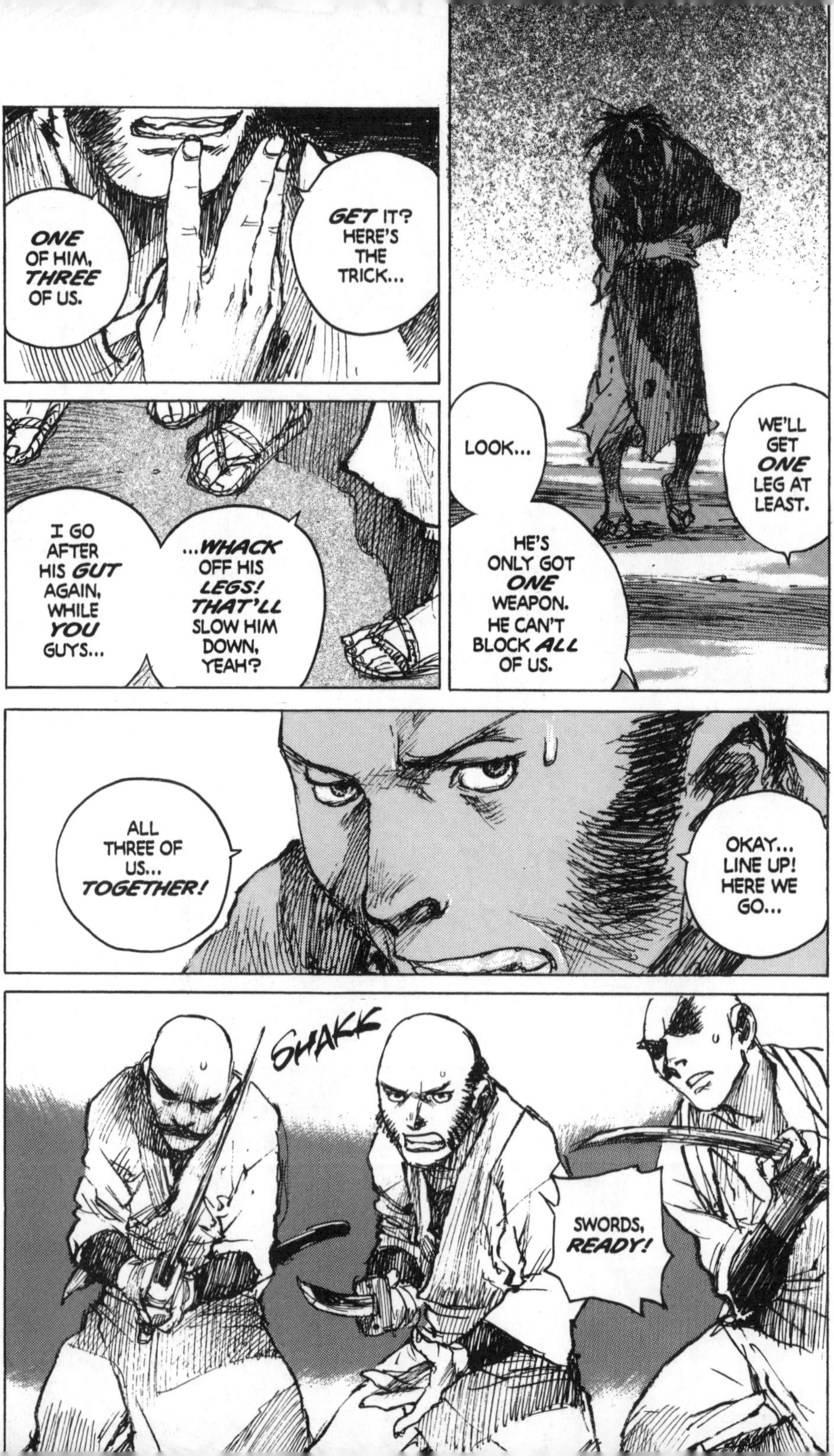

ONE OF HIM, THREE OF US.
GET IT? HERE'S THE TRICK...
I GO AFTER HIS GUT AGAIN, WHILE YOU GUYS...
...WHACK OFF HIS LEGS! THAT'LL SLOW HIM DOWN, YEAH?
LOOK...
HE'S ONLY GOT ONE WEAPON. HE CAN'T BLOCK ALL OF US.
WE'LL GET ONE LEG AT LEAST.
ALL THREE OF US... TOGETHER!
OKAY... LINE UP! HERE WE GO...
SHAKK
SWORDS, READY!

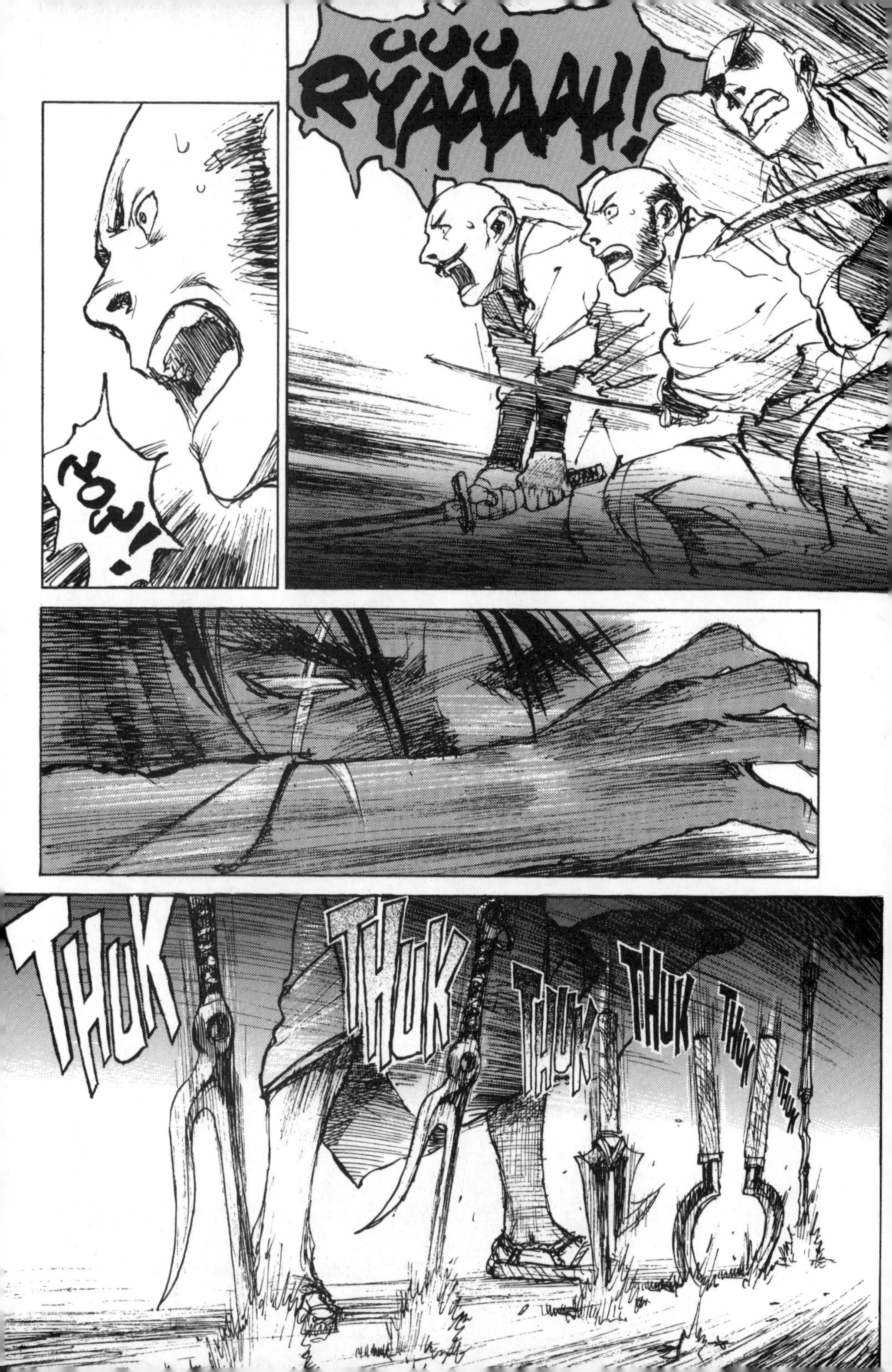
NOW!
UUU
RYAAAAH!
THUK
THUK
THUK
THUK
THUK
THUK

CRK!

WH... WHAT TH--?!

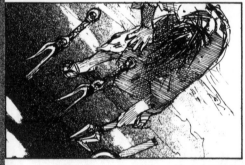

AW, SHIT!!

:koff:

...... HEY.

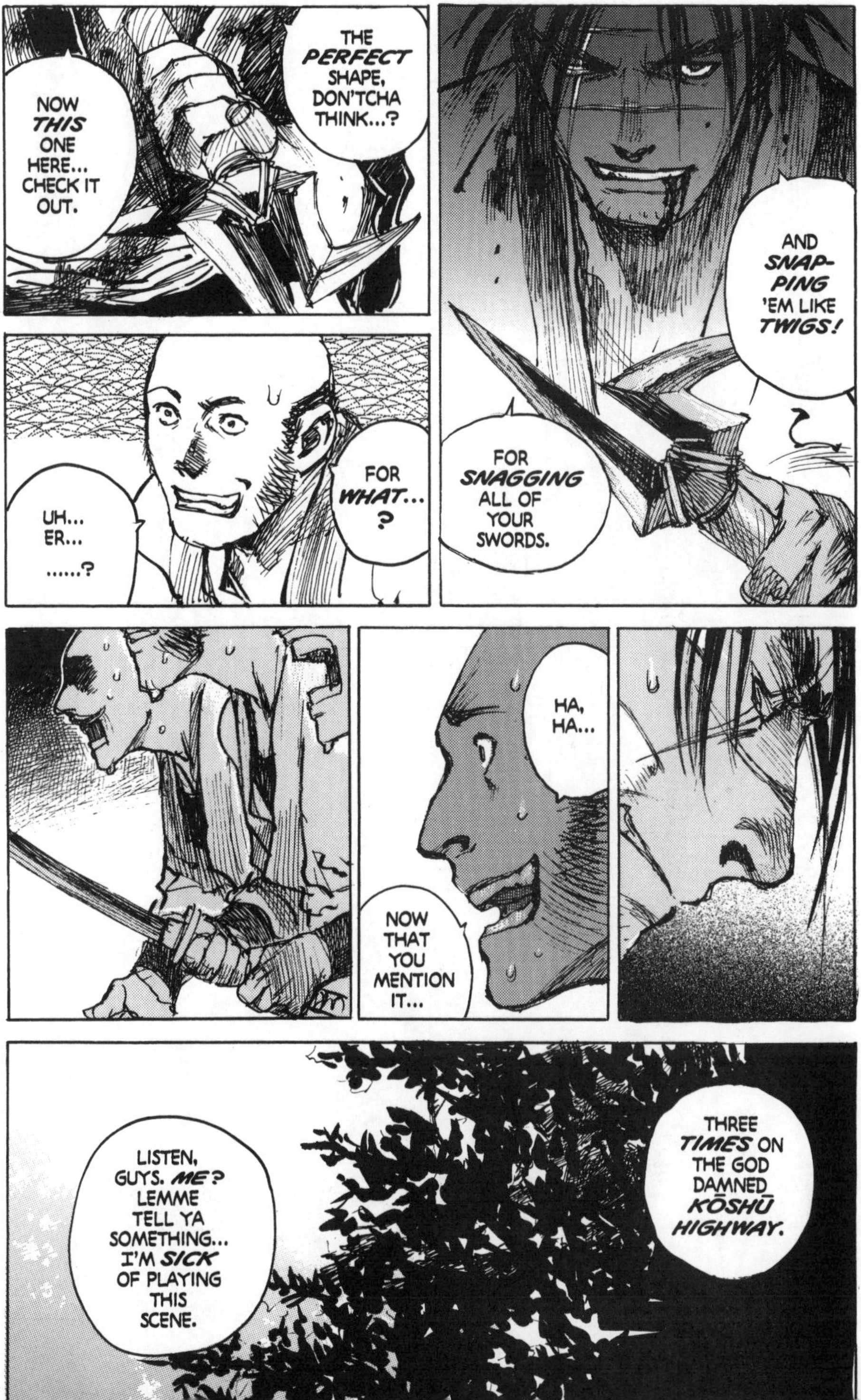
NOW *THIS* ONE HERE... CHECK IT OUT.
THE *PERFECT* SHAPE, DON'TCHA THINK...?
FOR *SNAGGING* ALL OF YOUR SWORDS.
AND *SNAPPING* 'EM LIKE *TWIGS!*
UH... ER... ......?
FOR *WHAT*...?
HA, HA...
NOW THAT YOU MENTION IT...
LISTEN, GUYS. *ME?* LEMME TELL YA SOMETHING... I'M *SICK* OF PLAYING THIS SCENE.
THREE *TIMES* ON THE GOD DAMNED *KŌSHŪ HIGHWAY.*

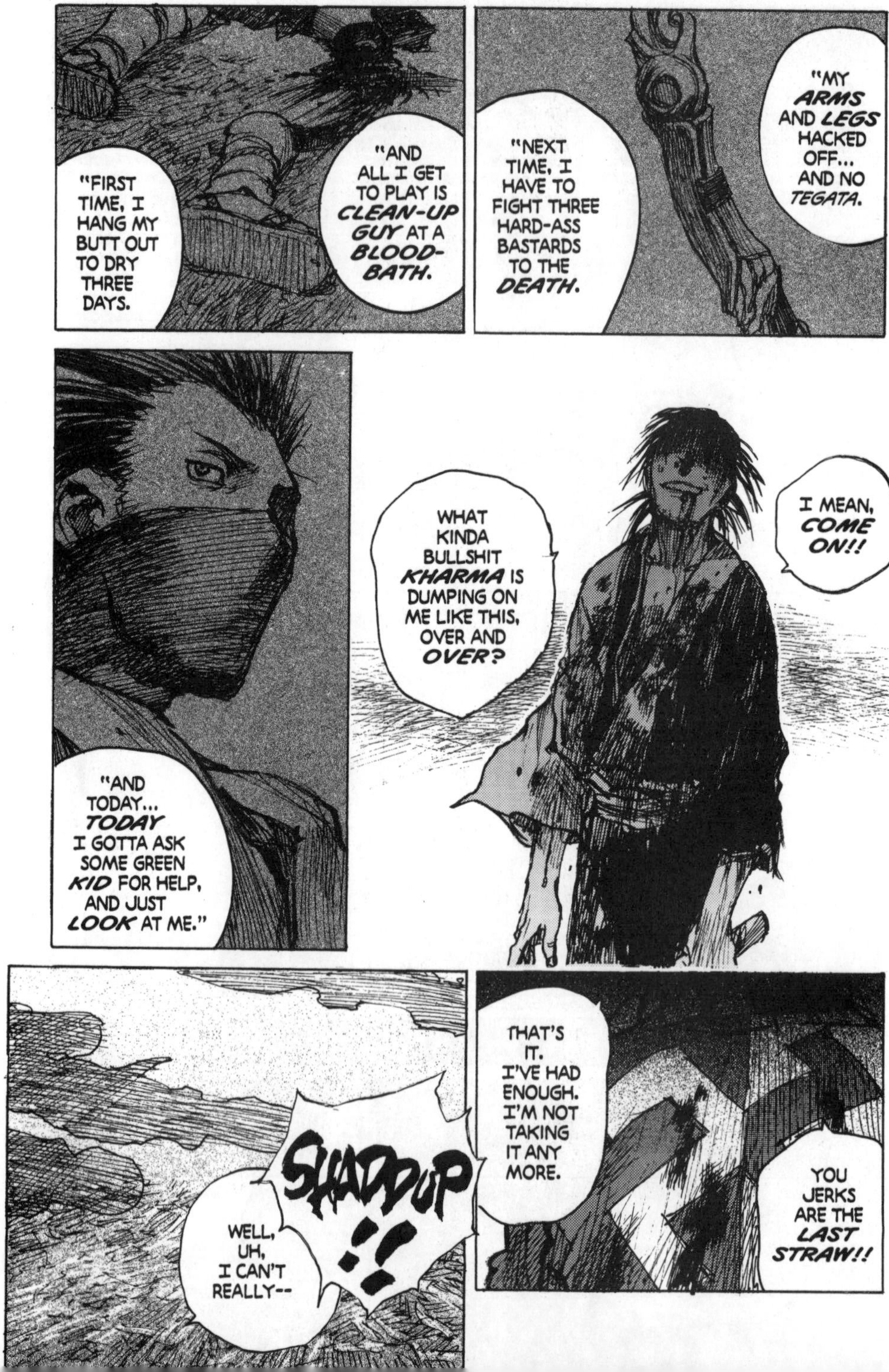
"FIRST TIME, I HANG MY BUTT OUT TO DRY THREE DAYS.
"AND ALL I GET TO PLAY IS *CLEAN-UP GUY* AT A *BLOOD-BATH*.
"NEXT TIME, I HAVE TO FIGHT THREE HARD-ASS BASTARDS TO THE *DEATH*.
"MY *ARMS* AND *LEGS* HACKED OFF... AND NO *TEGATA*.
"AND TODAY... *TODAY* I GOTTA ASK SOME GREEN *KID* FOR HELP, AND JUST *LOOK* AT ME."
WHAT KINDA BULLSHIT *KHARMA* IS DUMPING ON ME LIKE THIS, OVER AND *OVER?*
I MEAN, *COME ON!!*
WELL, UH, I CAN'T REALLY--
SHADDUP!!
THAT'S IT. I'VE HAD ENOUGH. I'M NOT TAKING IT ANY MORE.
YOU JERKS ARE THE *LAST STRAW!!*

I'LL KILL YOU ALL!!

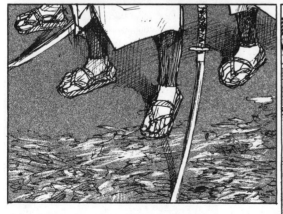

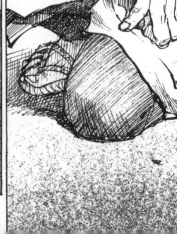

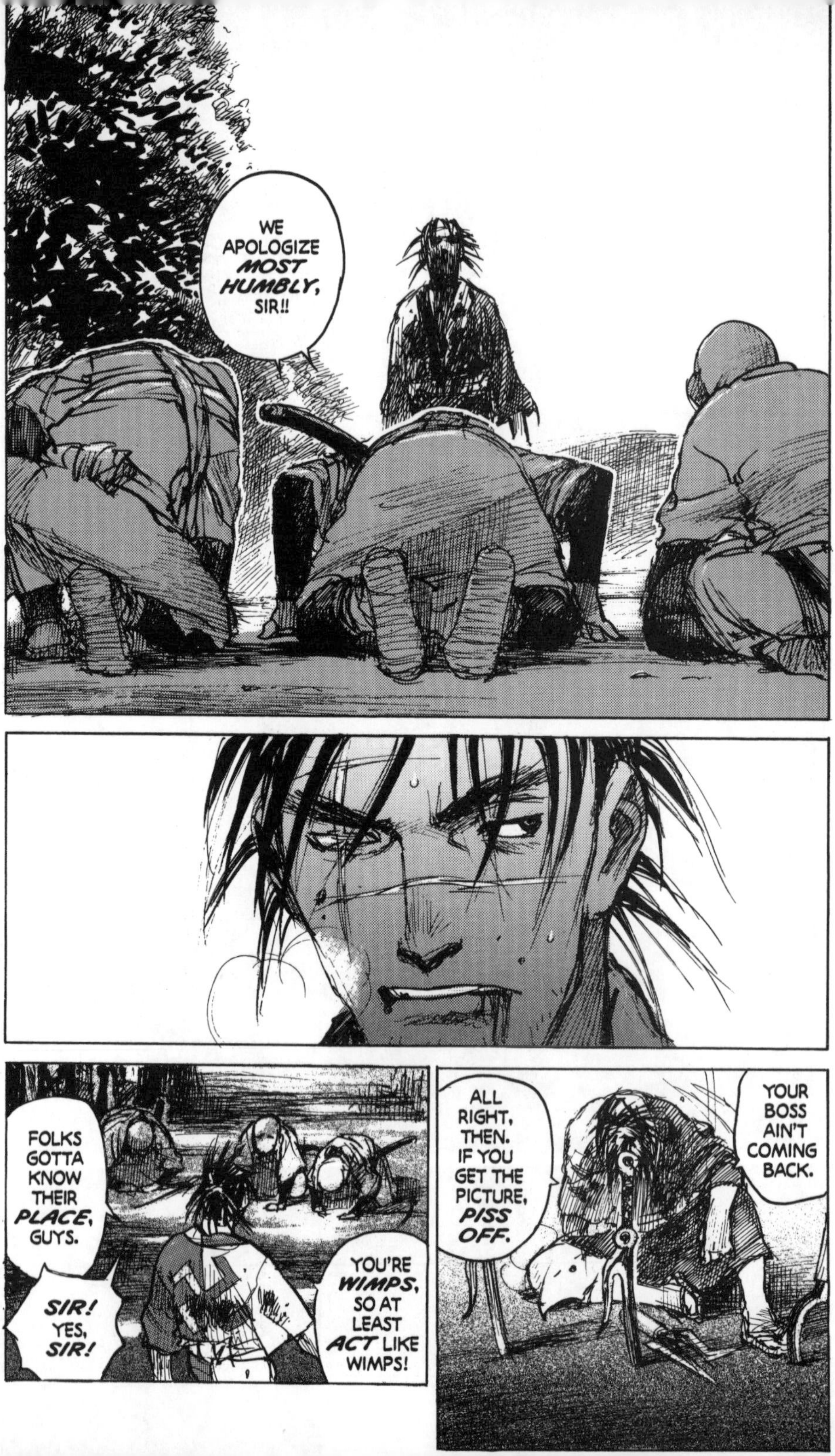
WE APOLOGIZE MOST HUMBLY, SIR!!
FOLKS GOTTA KNOW THEIR PLACE, GUYS.
SIR! YES, SIR!
YOU'RE WIMPS, SO AT LEAST ACT LIKE WIMPS!
ALL RIGHT, THEN. IF YOU GET THE PICTURE, PISS OFF.
YOUR BOSS AIN'T COMING BACK.

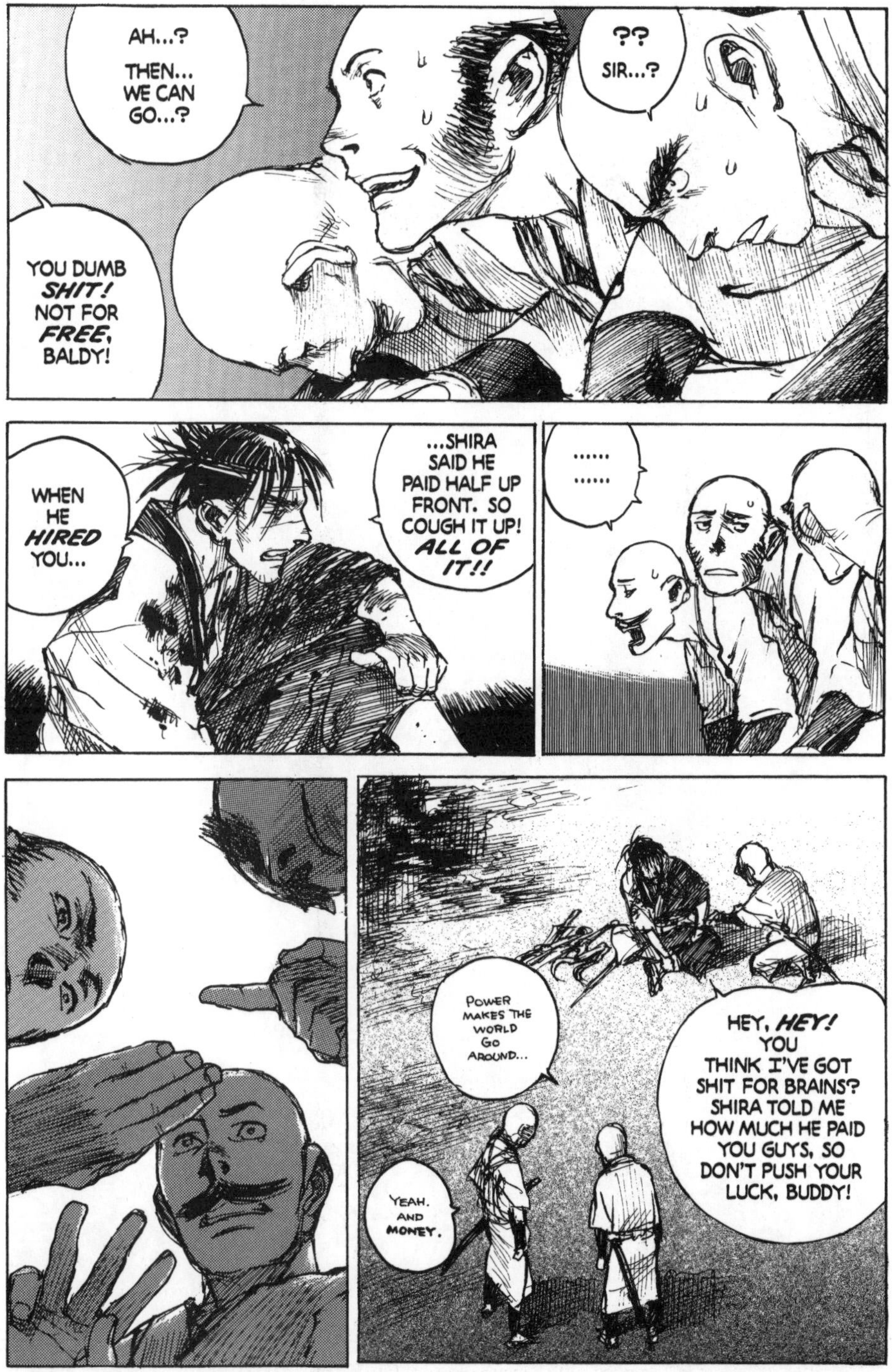
AH...? THEN... WE CAN GO...?
?? SIR...?
YOU DUMB SHIT! NOT FOR FREE, BALDY!
WHEN HE HIRED YOU...
...SHIRA SAID HE PAID HALF UP FRONT. SO COUGH IT UP! ALL OF IT!!
....
POWER MAKES THE WORLD GO AROUND...
HEY, HEY! YOU THINK I'VE GOT SHIT FOR BRAINS? SHIRA TOLD ME HOW MUCH HE PAID YOU GUYS, SO DON'T PUSH YOUR LUCK, BUDDY!
YEAH. AND MONEY.

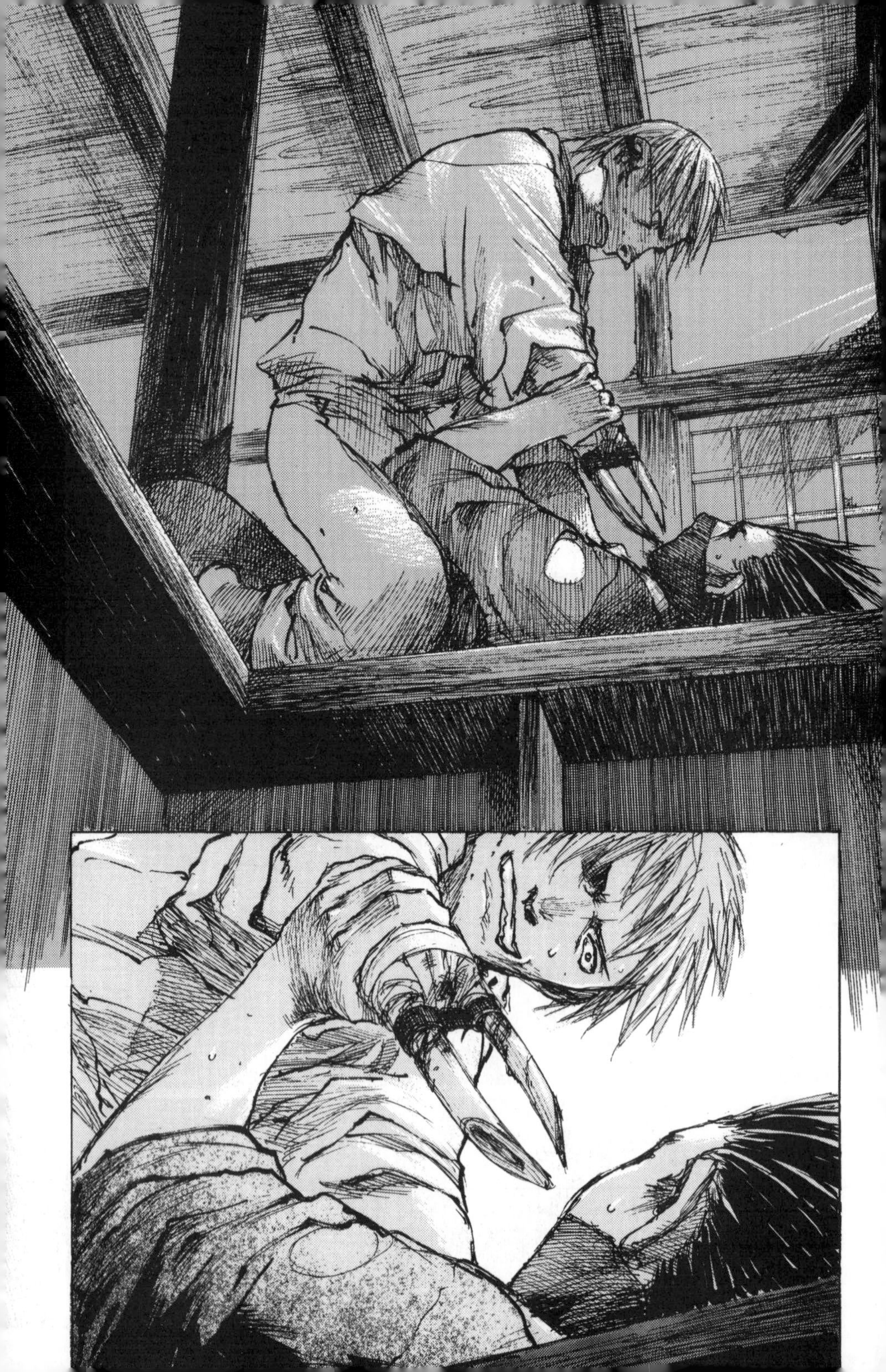

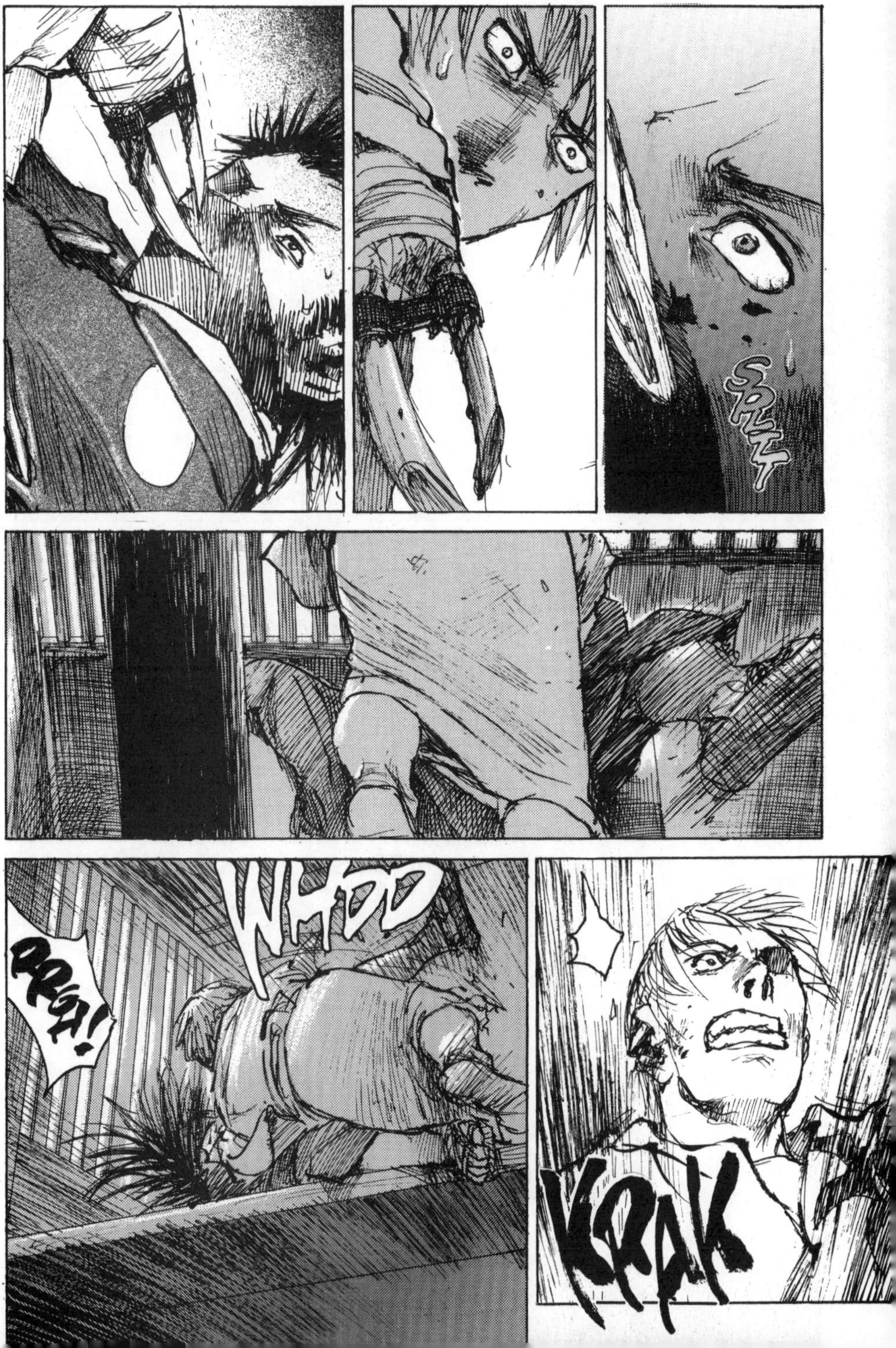
SPLLT
WHDD
DOSH!
KRAK

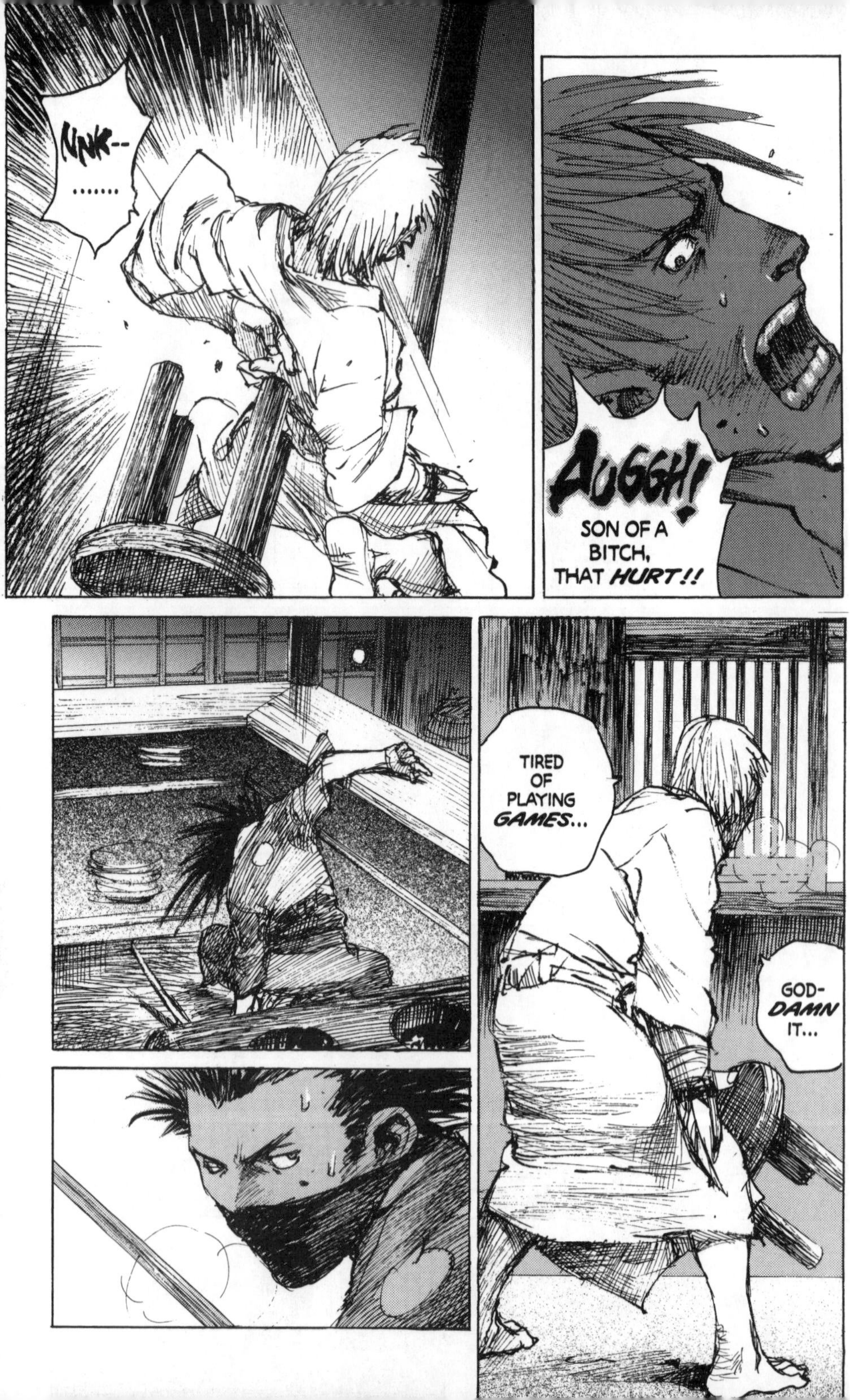
NNK--
....
AUGGH!
SON OF A BITCH, THAT HURT!!
TIRED OF PLAYING GAMES...
GOD-DAMN IT...

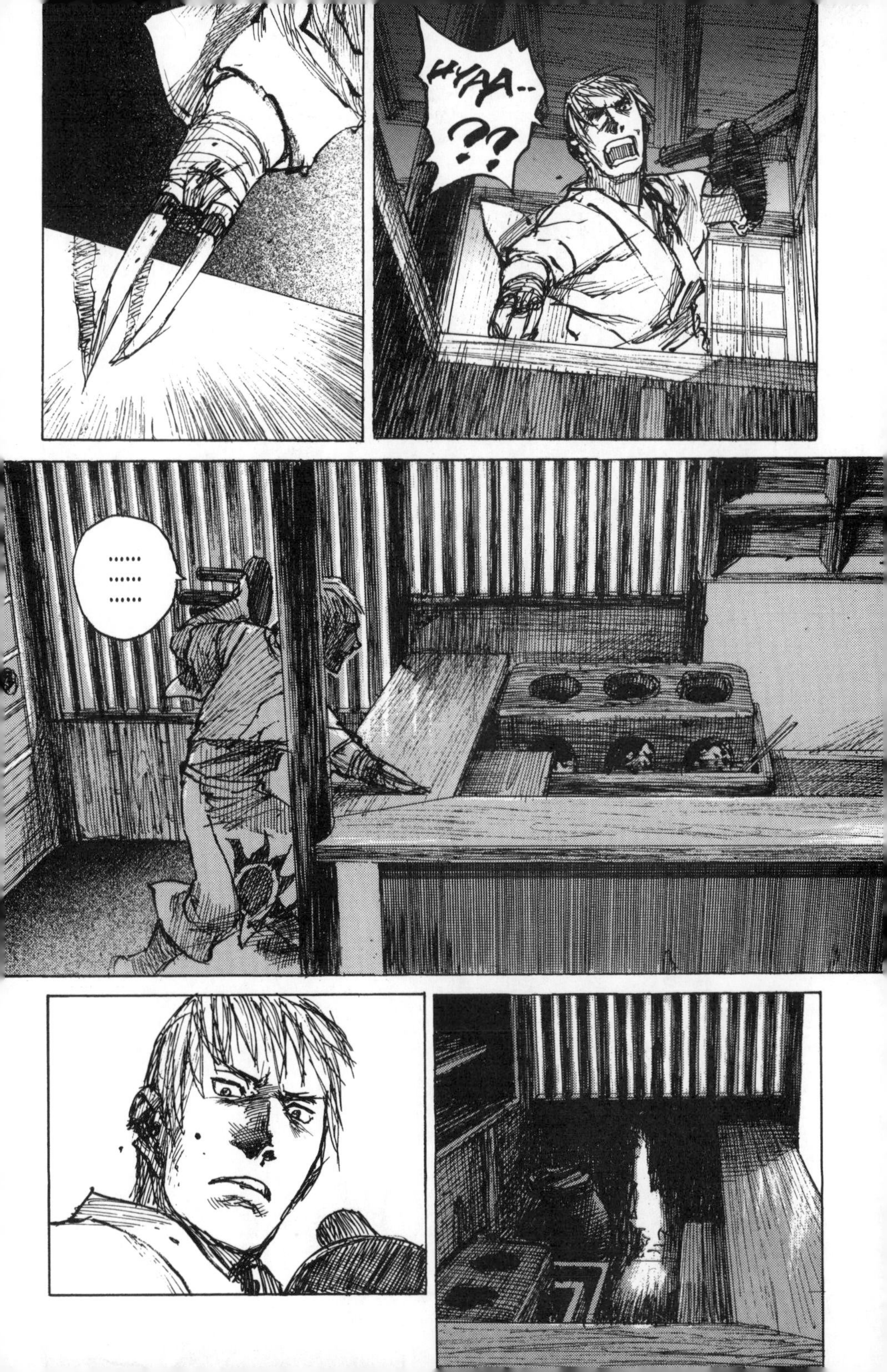
HYAA--
??
......
......
......

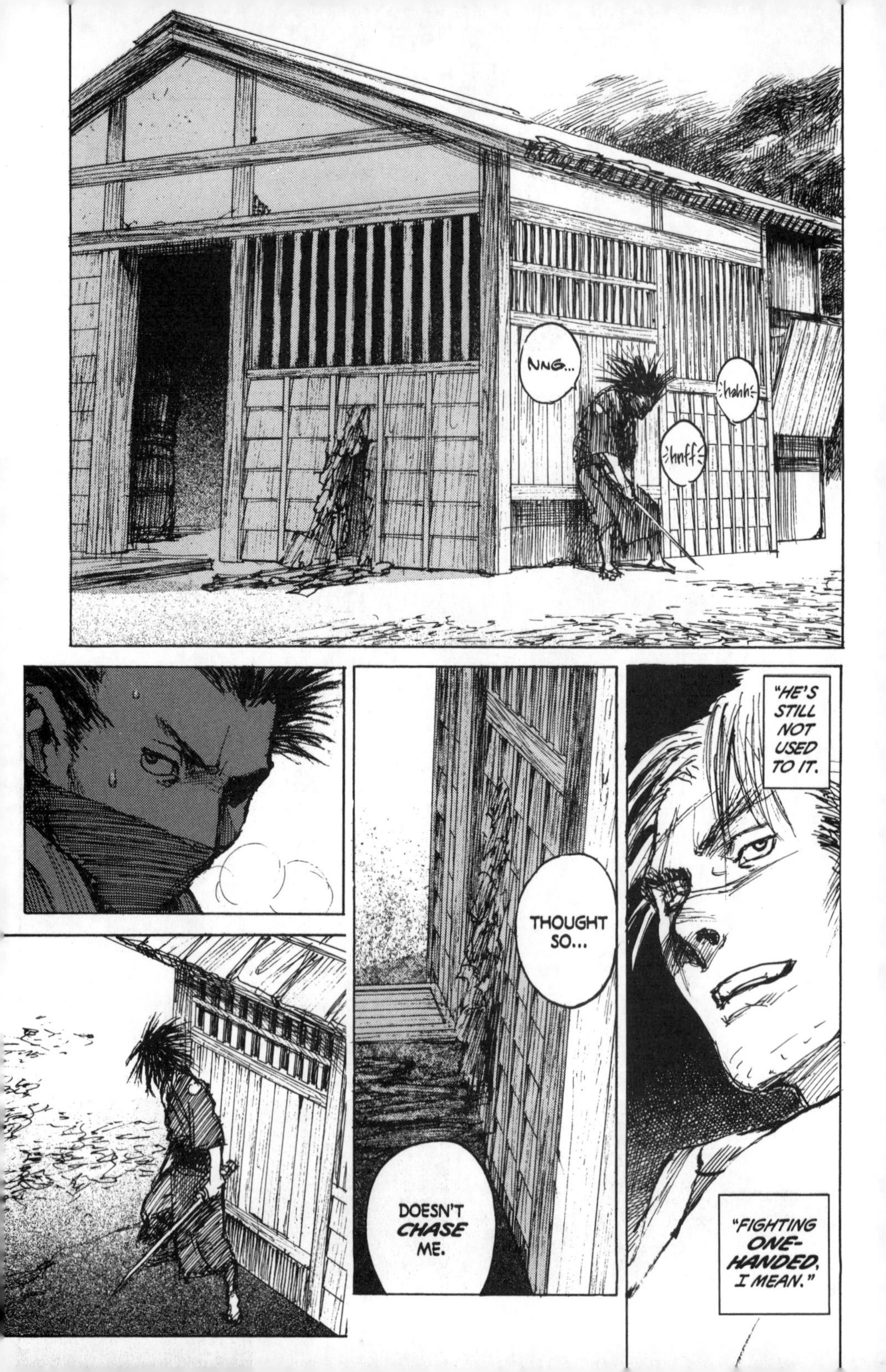
NNG...
hahh
hnff
THOUGHT SO...
DOESN'T *CHASE* ME.
"HE'S STILL NOT USED TO IT.
"FIGHTING *ONE-HANDED*, I MEAN."

THE ENEMY'S NOT ALWAYS AS DUMB AS YOU THINK...

...MANJI, OLD BUDDY, OLD PAL.

HE DAMN WELL *NOTICED* HE'S GOT A PROBLEM...

...AND FIGURED OUT HE CAN'T FIGHT WELL IN THE FOREST.

WELL, SO BE IT.

IF IT'S THE HUT, IT'S THE *HUT*.

I'M SMALLER. MAYBE I'LL HAVE AN EDGE.

JUST YOU WAIT, SHIRA.

WE'LL SEE WHO LAUGHS LAST--

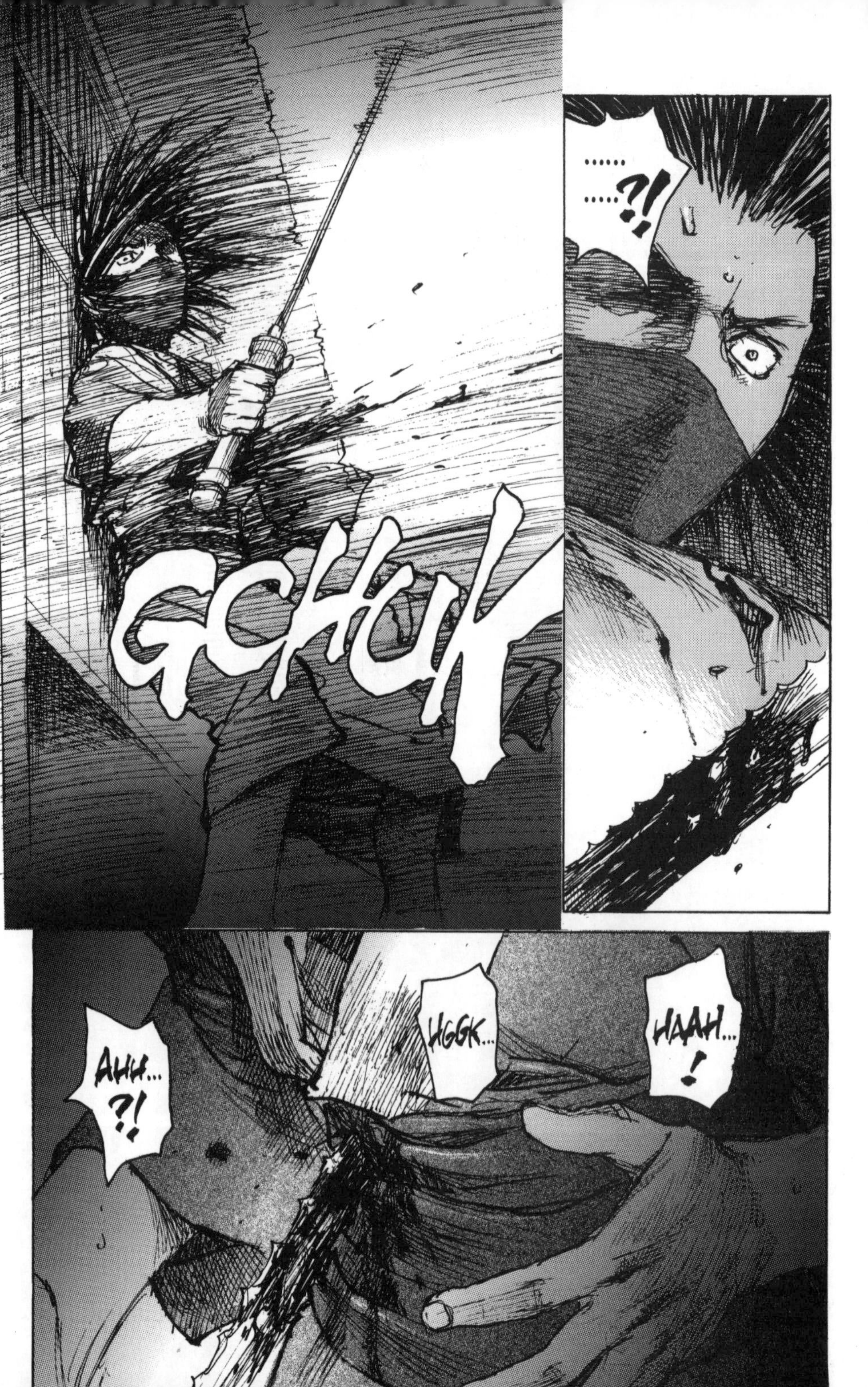
GCHUK
......
......?!
AHH...
?!
HGGK...
HAAH...
!

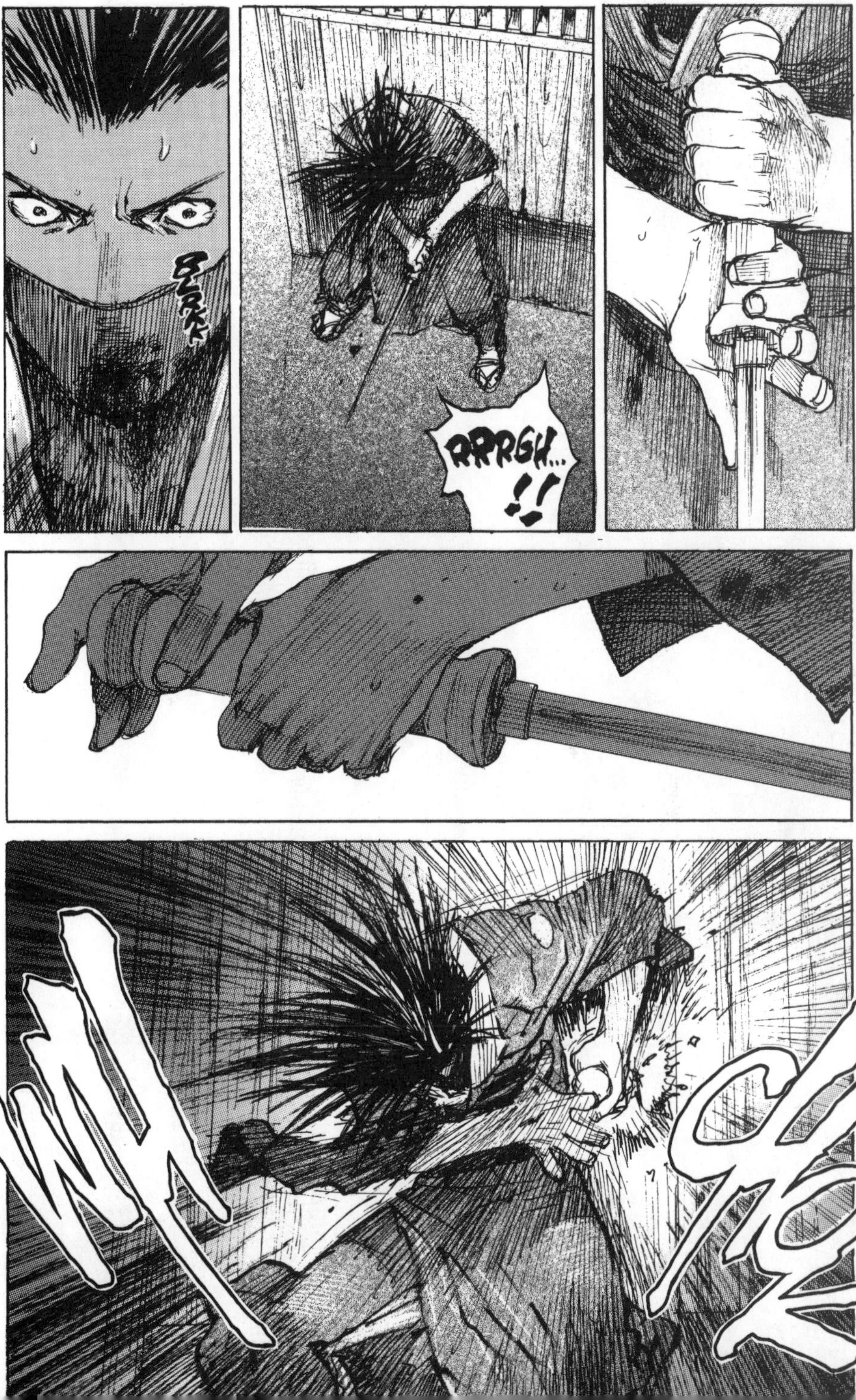
BLRKK
RRRGH... !!

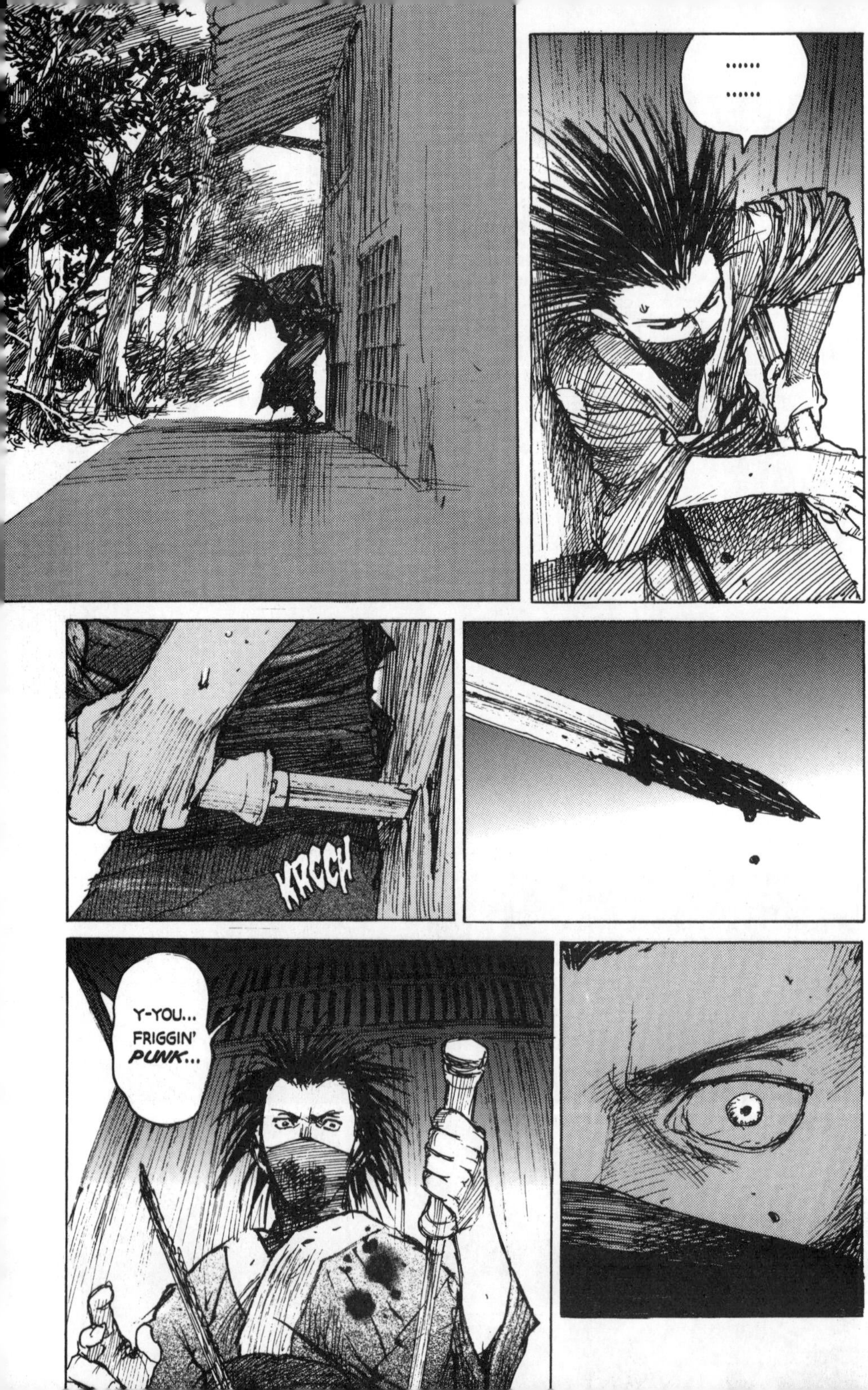

......
......
KRCCH
Y-YOU... FRIGGIN' PUNK...

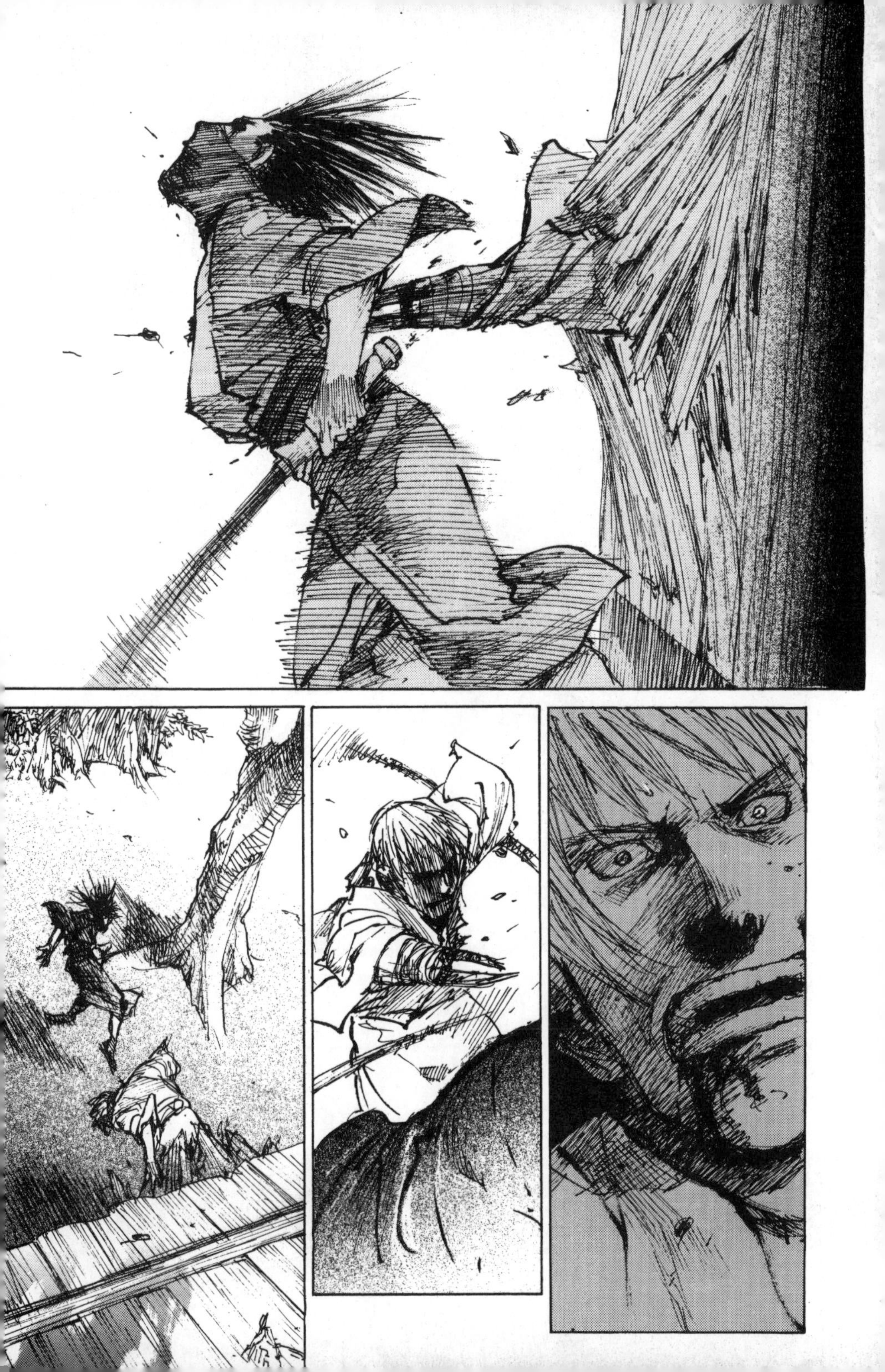

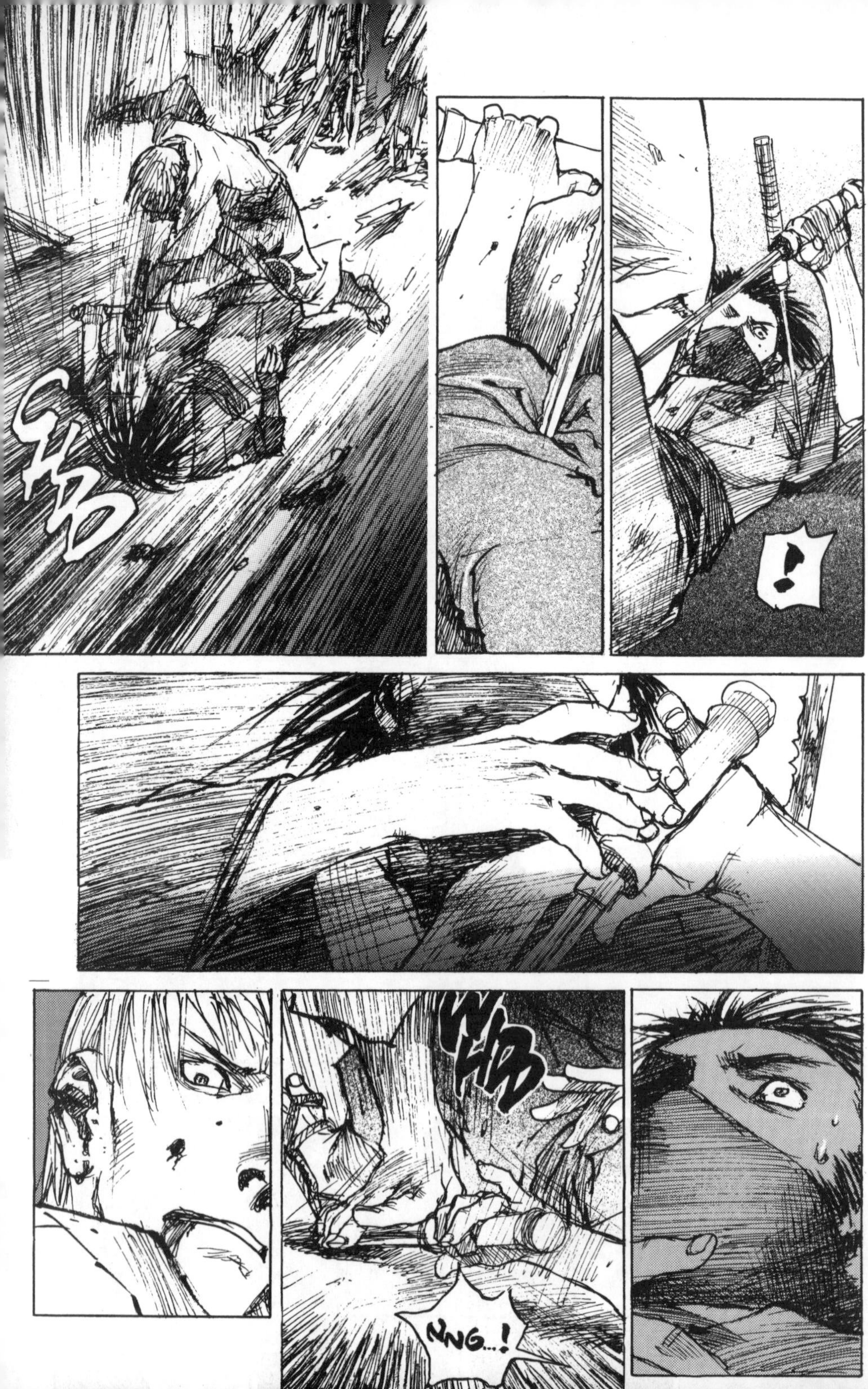
CHD
!
WHD
NNG...!

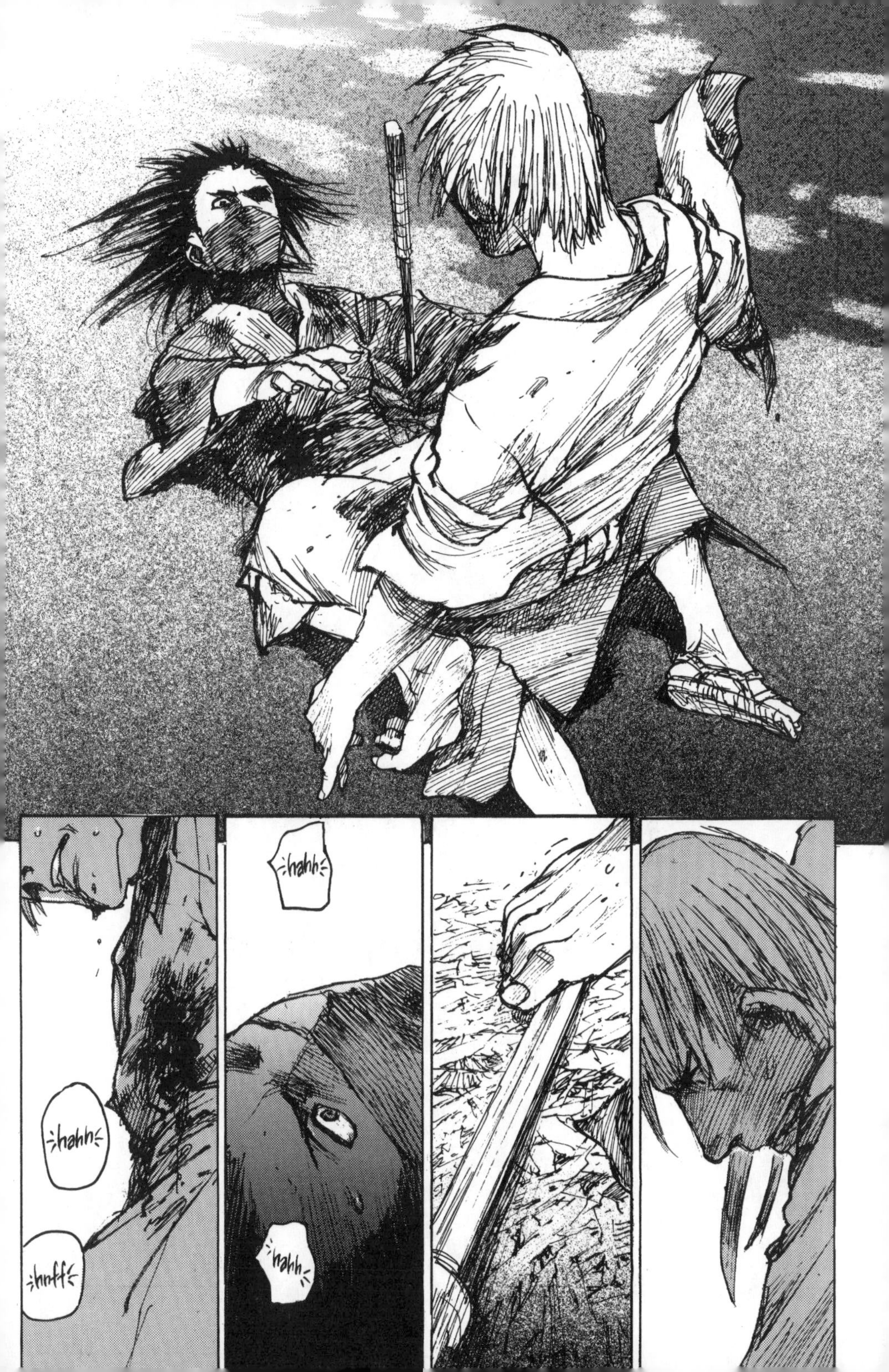
hahh
hnff
hahh
hahh

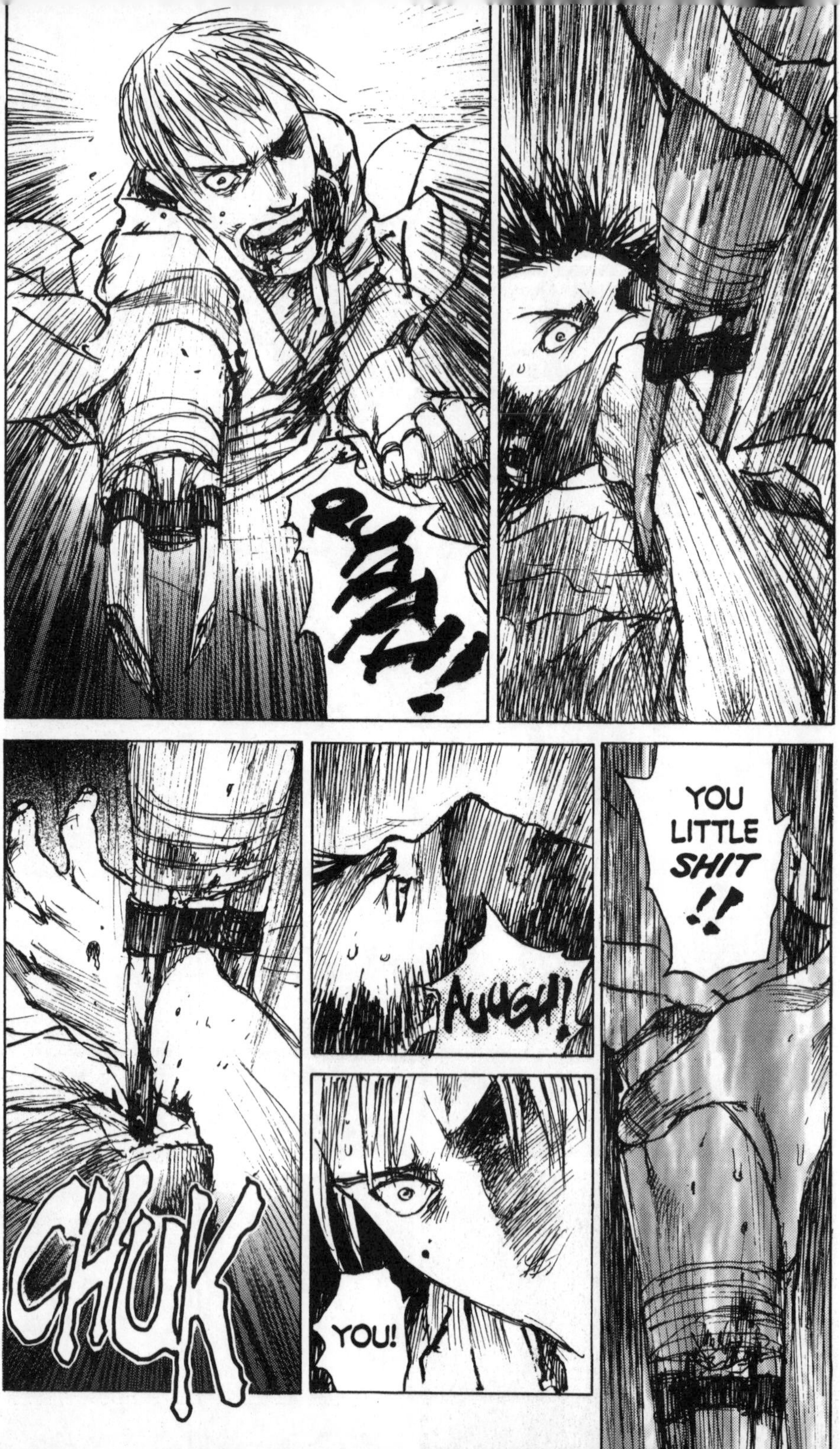
CHUK
AUUGH!
YOU!
YOU LITTLE SHIT!!

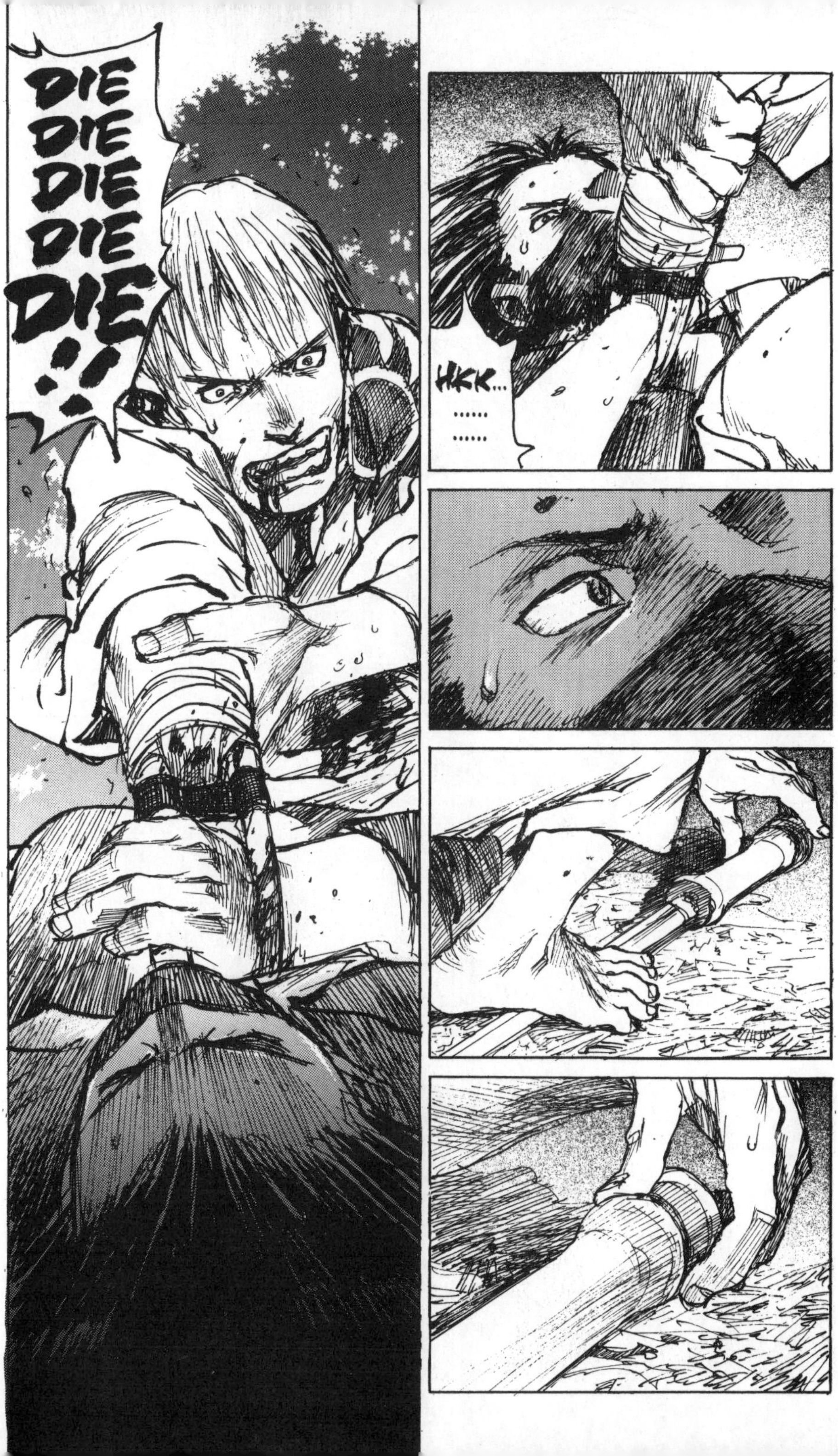
DIE DIE DIE DIE DIE !!
HKK...
......
......

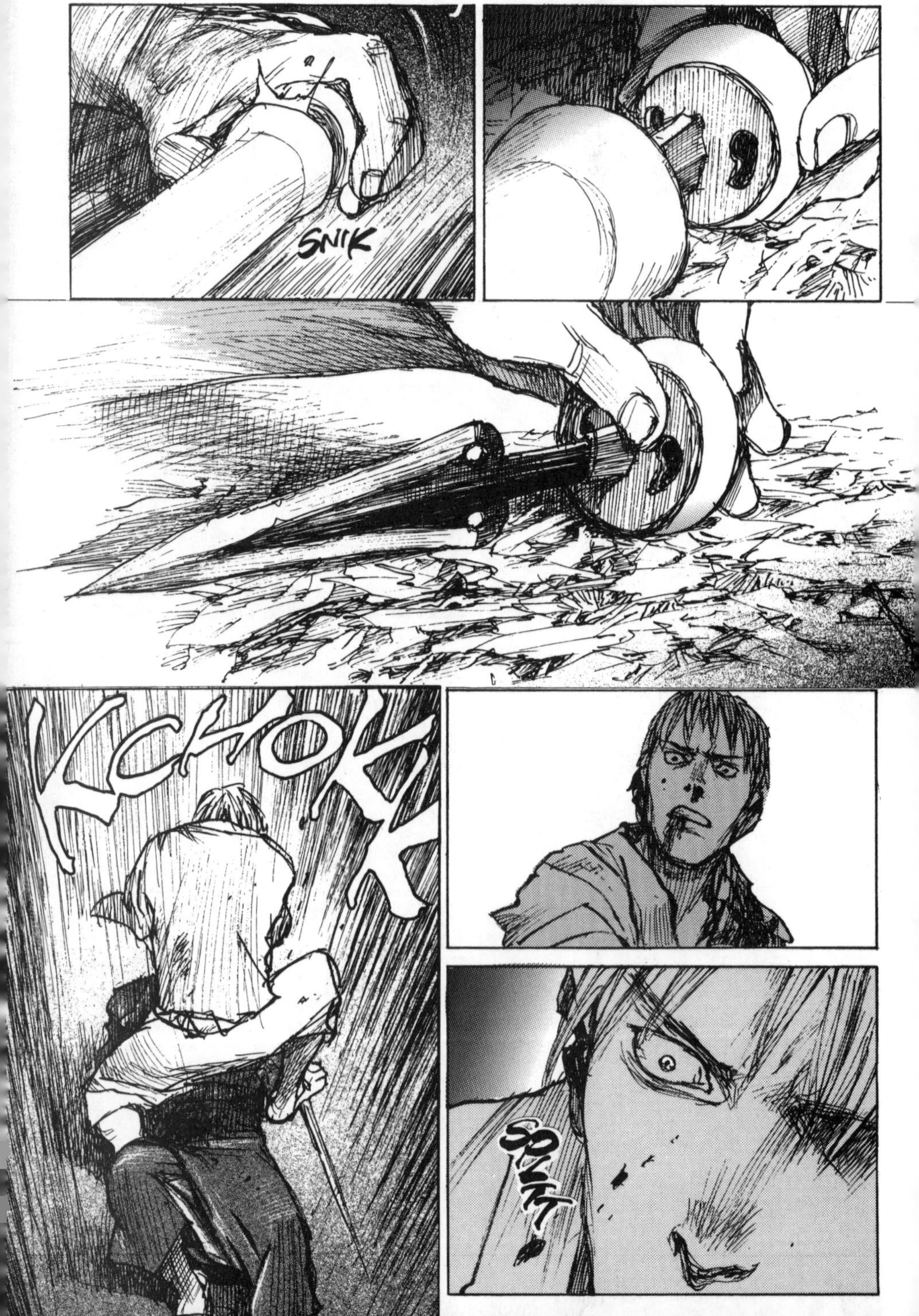
SNIK
KCHOK
SPLKT

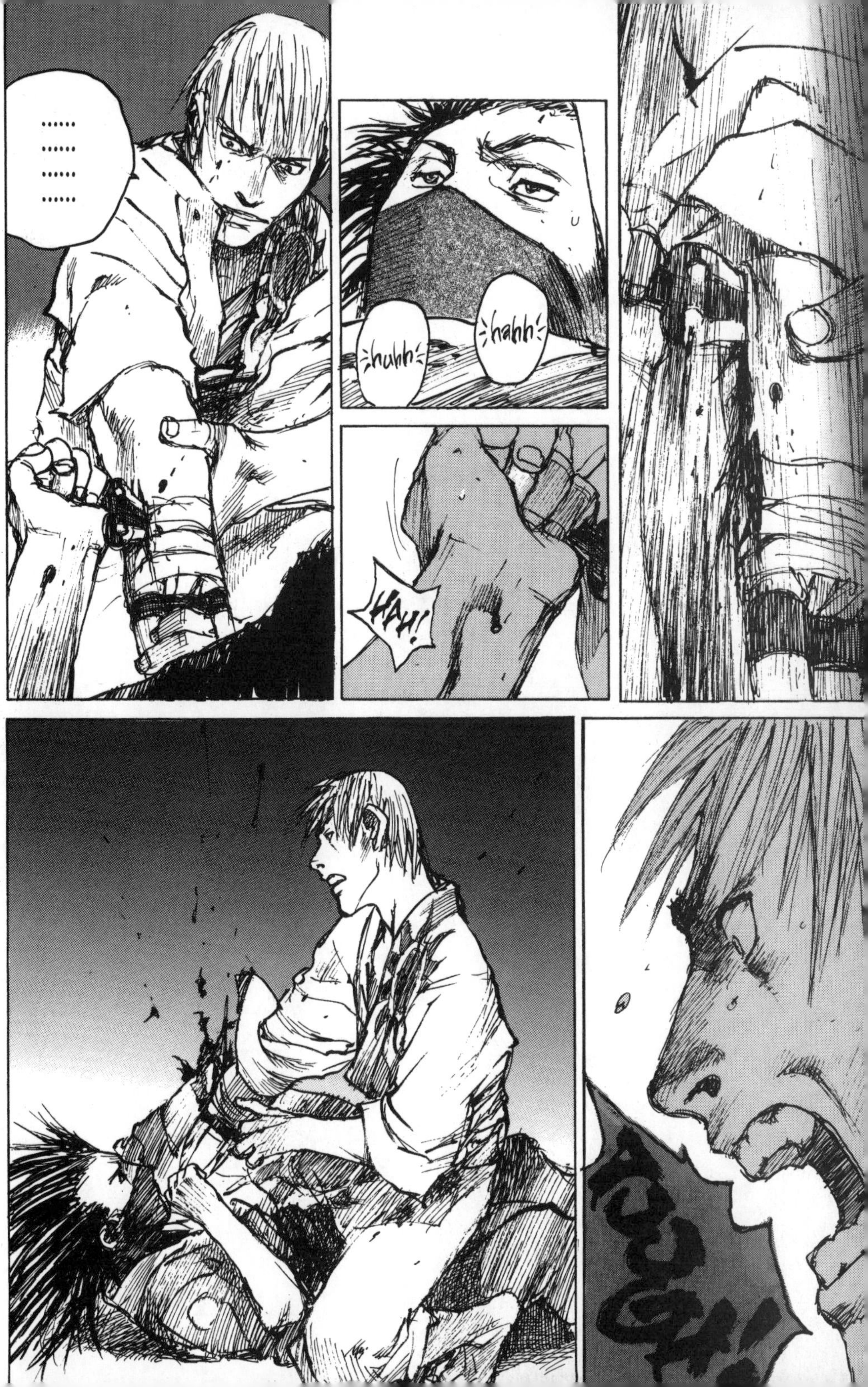
......
......
......
......
huhh
hahh
HAH!
AUGH!!

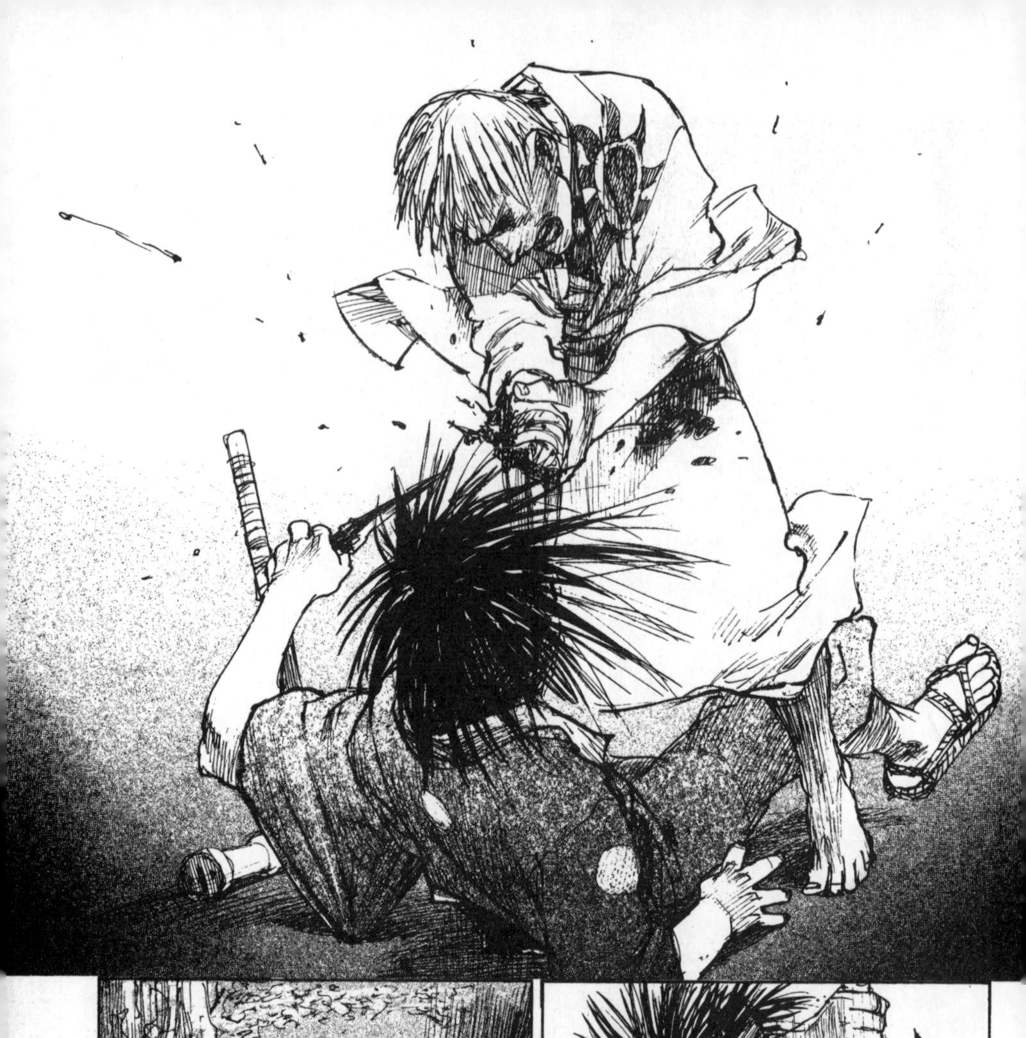
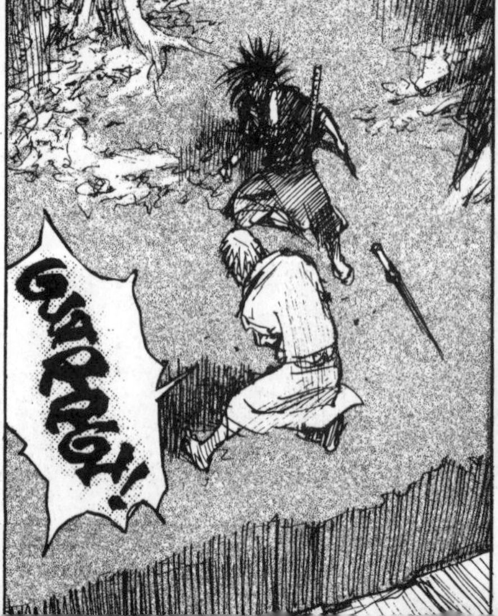
GUURRGH!
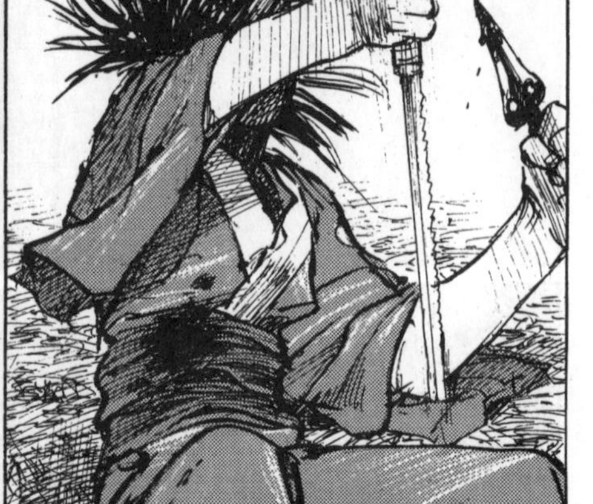

YOU...
YOU...

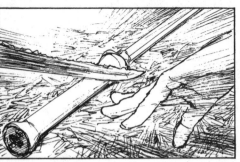

IS *THIS* IT...?

THE SWORD THAT SLICED OPEN O-REN'S *BREAST*?

IT MUST HAVE BEEN *SOFT*... SO EASY TO *CUT*...

THE FLESH OF A YOUNG *WOMAN*...

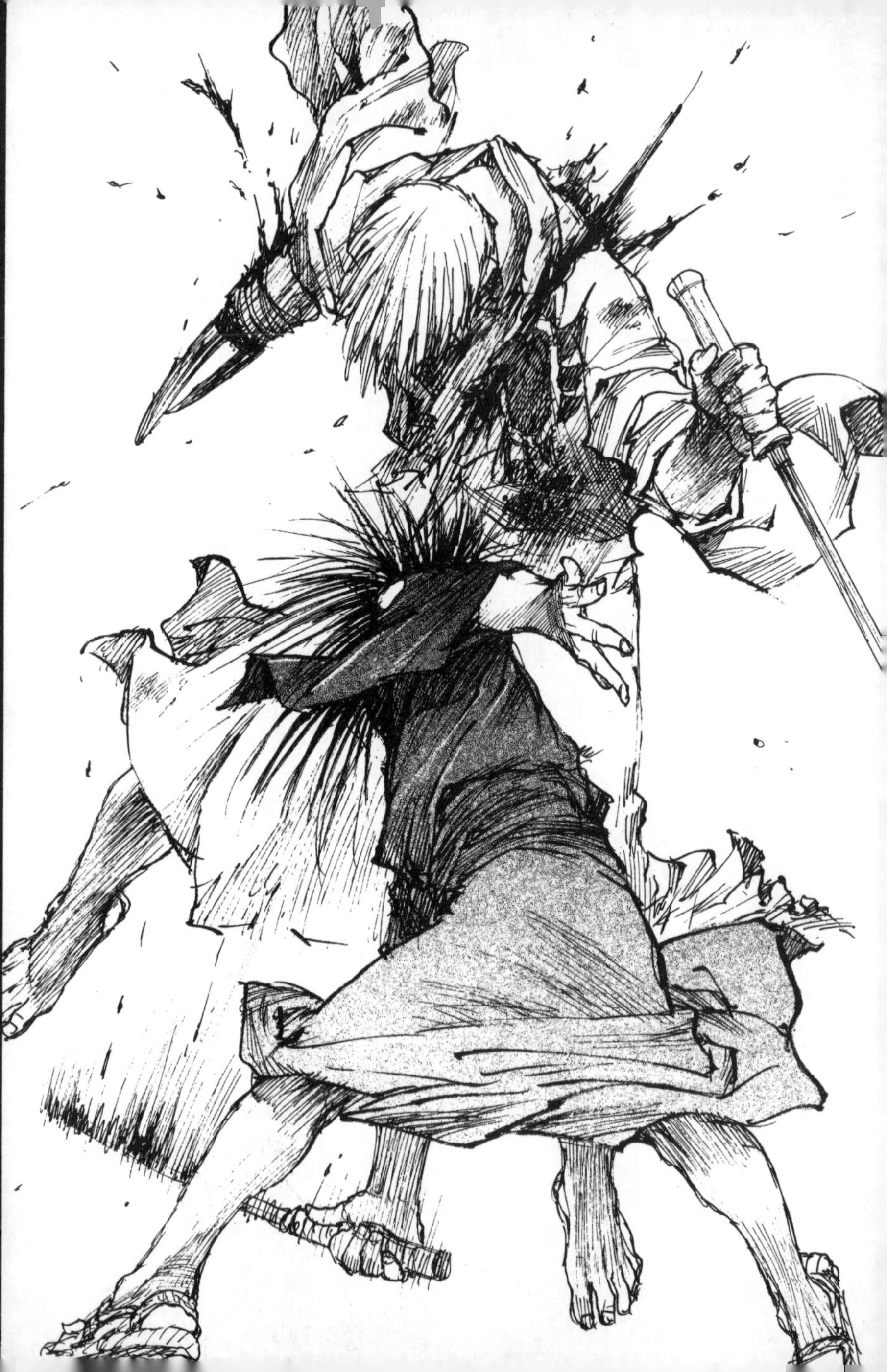

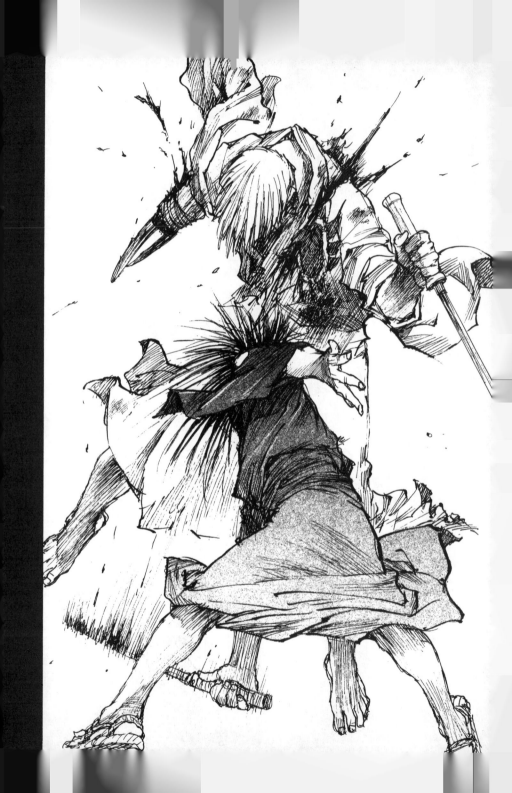

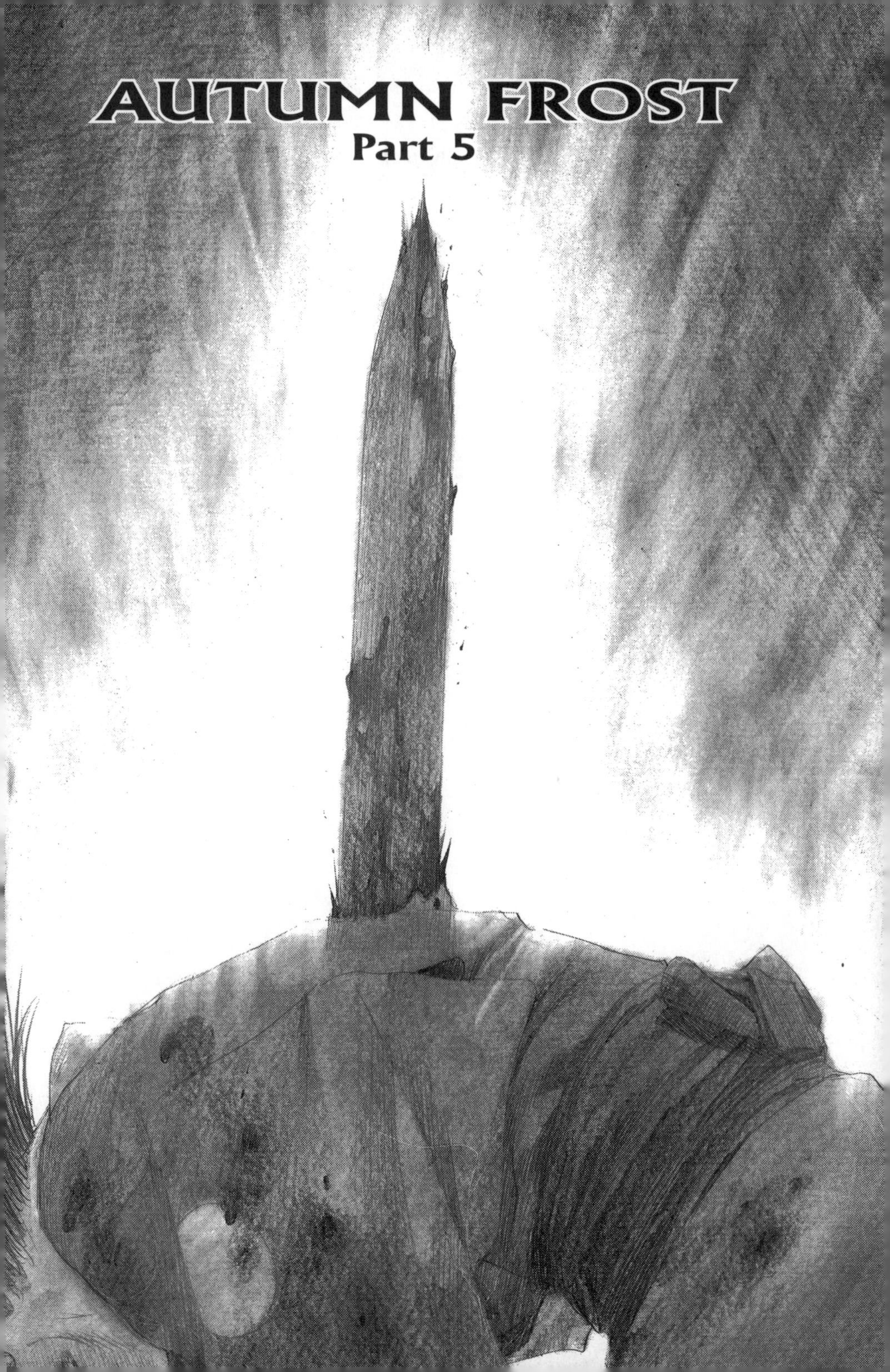
AUTUMN FROST
Part 5

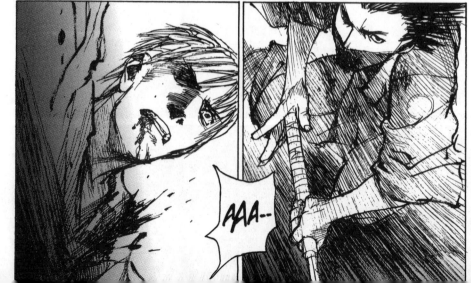

AAA--

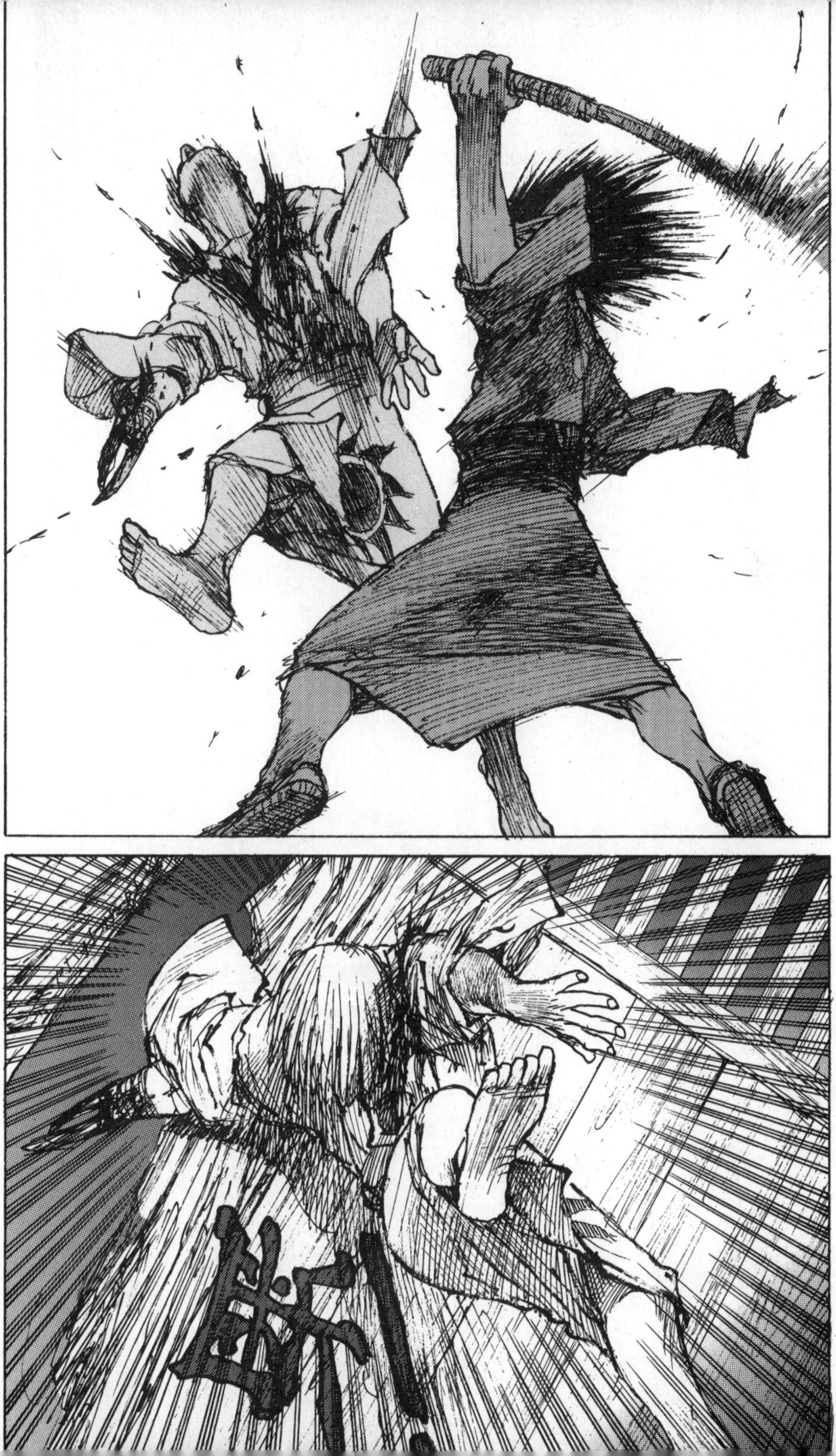
斬

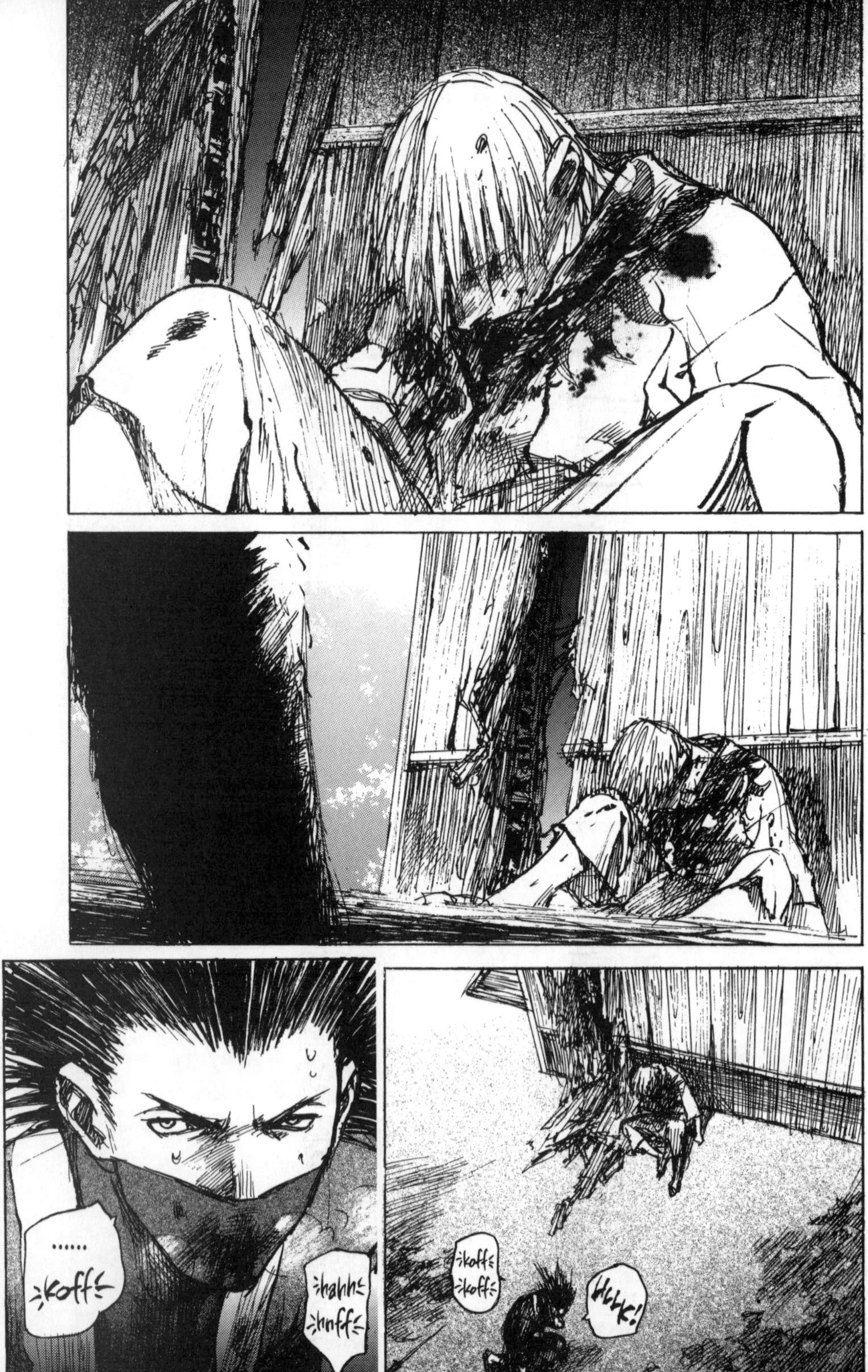

......
koff
hahh
hnff
koff
koff
HULK!

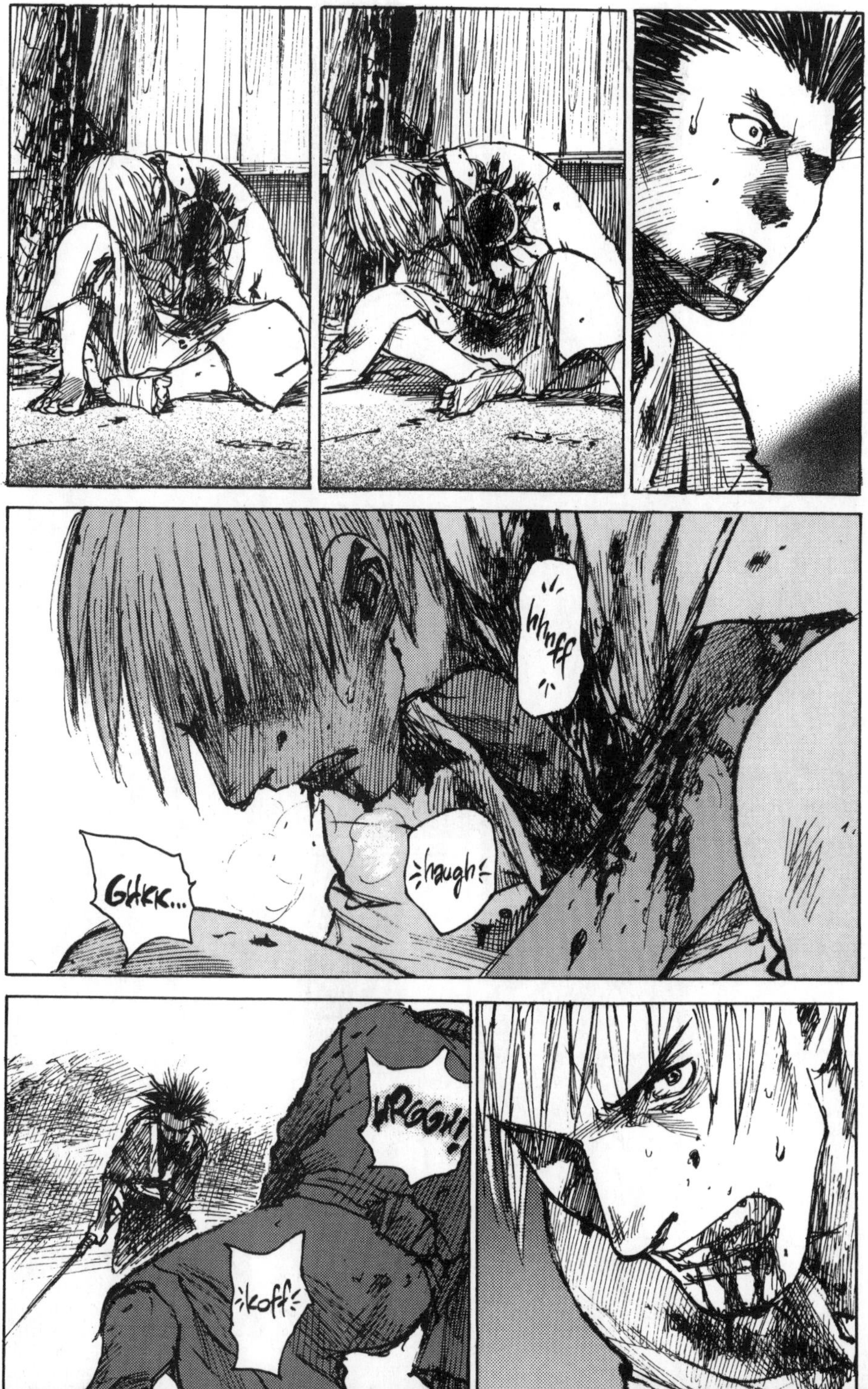
hhnff
haugh
GHKK...
URGGH!!
koff

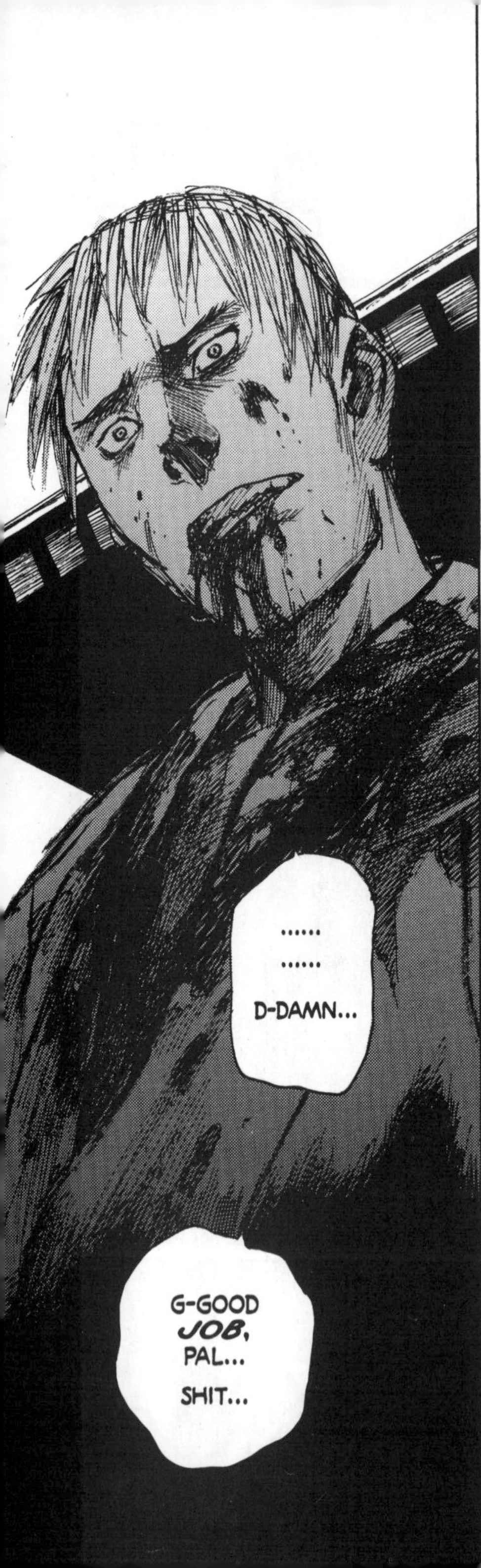
.... D-DAMN...
G-GOOD JOB, PAL... SHIT...

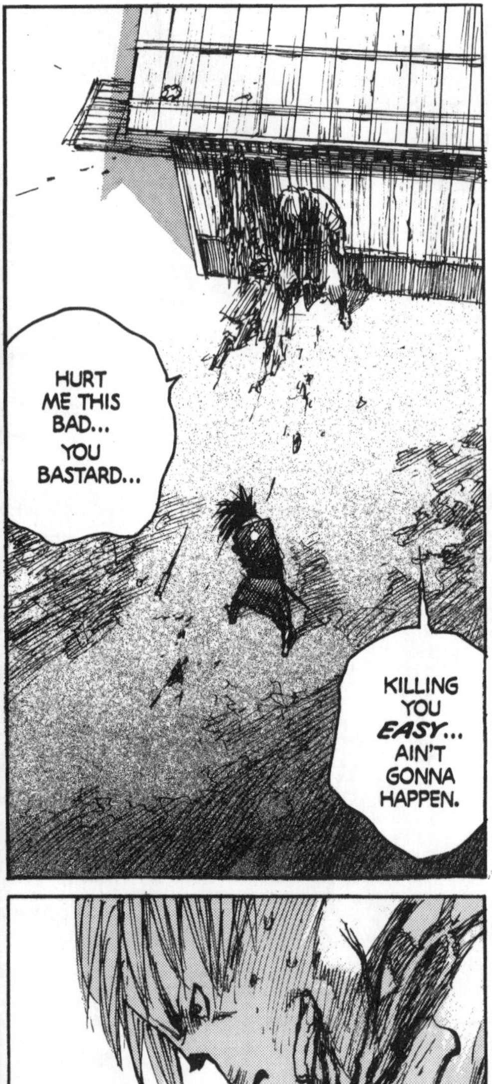
HURT ME THIS BAD... YOU BASTARD...
KILLING YOU EASY... AIN'T GONNA HAPPEN.

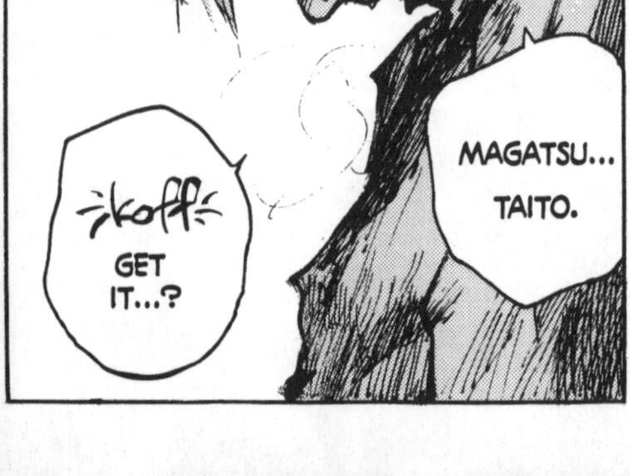
koff GET IT...?
MAGATSU... TAITO.

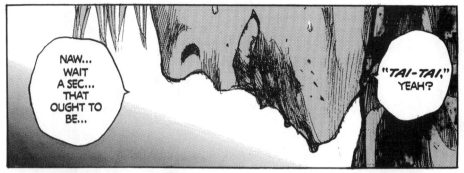

NAW... WAIT A SEC... THAT OUGHT TO BE...

"*TAI-TAI,*" YEAH?

?!!

≈pteh≈

......

Y-YOU *SCUM!*

HEH! SCORED WITH *THAT* ONE, DIDN'T I?

?? YOU DIDN'T KNOW FOR SURE...?

NOT UNTIL NOW. SO...THAT *WAS* YOUR LITTLE SWEETIE.

TOO *SKINNY,* BUT AN OKAY PIECE OF ASS.

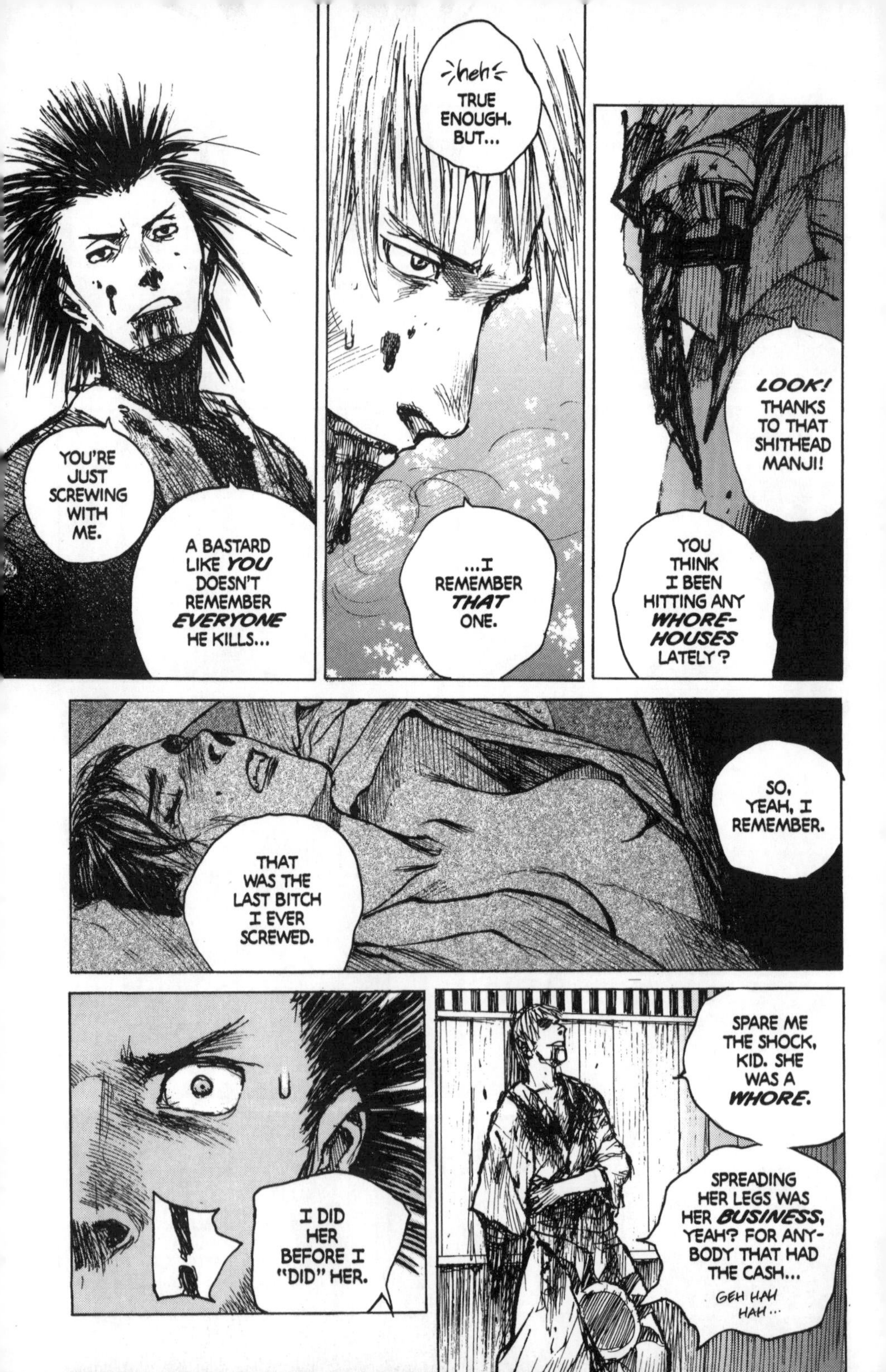
YOU'RE JUST SCREWING WITH ME.
A BASTARD LIKE *YOU* DOESN'T REMEMBER *EVERYONE* HE KILLS...
heh
TRUE ENOUGH. BUT...
...I REMEMBER *THAT* ONE.
LOOK! THANKS TO THAT SHITHEAD MANJI!
YOU THINK I BEEN HITTING ANY *WHORE-HOUSES* LATELY?
SO, YEAH, I REMEMBER.
THAT WAS THE LAST BITCH I EVER SCREWED.
I DID HER BEFORE I "DID" HER.
SPARE ME THE SHOCK, KID. SHE WAS A *WHORE*.
SPREADING HER LEGS WAS HER *BUSINESS*, YEAH? FOR ANY-BODY THAT HAD THE CASH...
GEH HAH HAH...

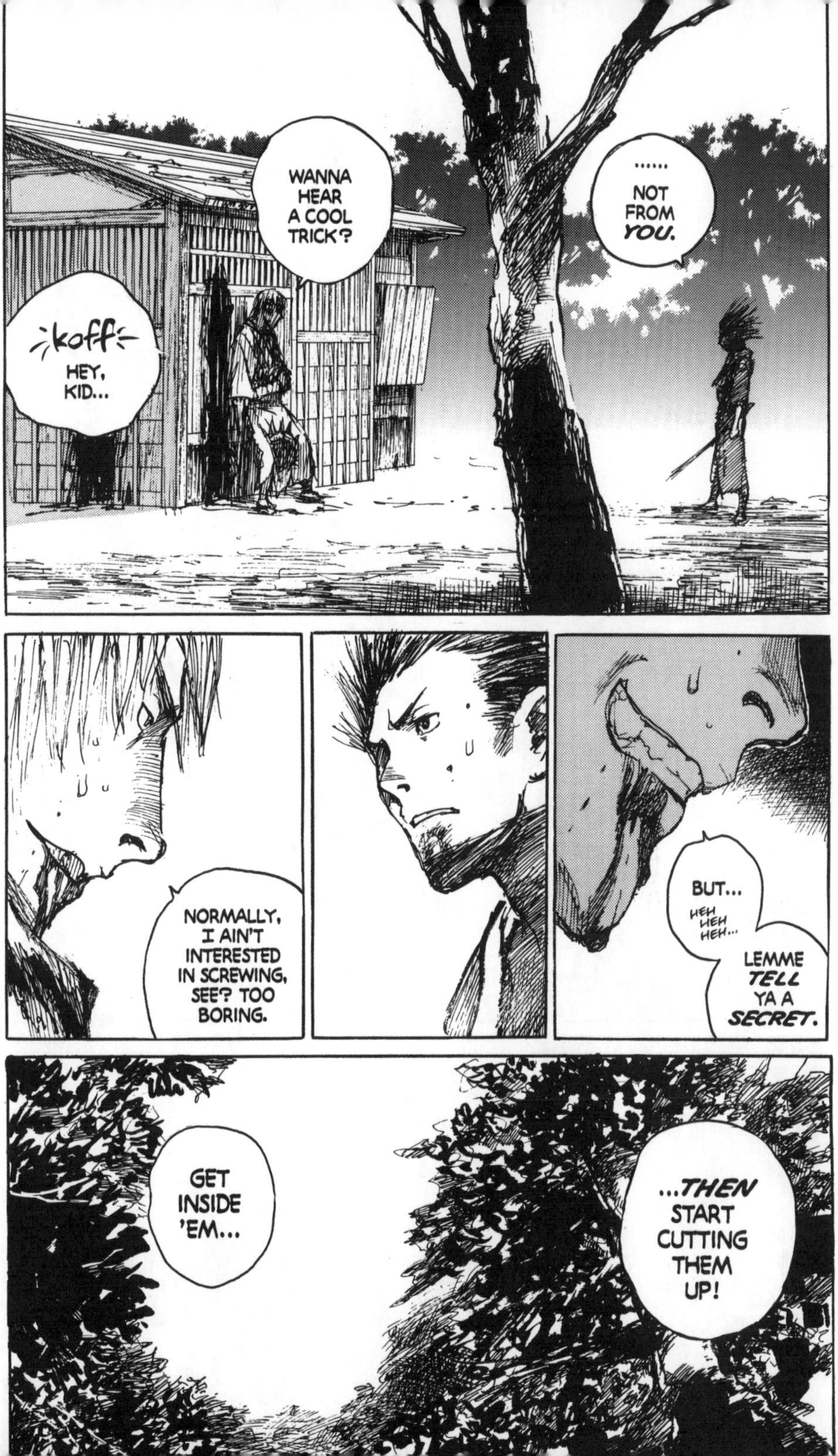
koff
HEY, KID...
WANNA HEAR A COOL TRICK?
...... NOT FROM YOU.
NORMALLY, I AIN'T INTERESTED IN SCREWING, SEE? TOO BORING.
BUT...
HEH HEH HEH...
LEMME TELL YA A SECRET.
GET INSIDE 'EM...
...THEN START CUTTING THEM UP!

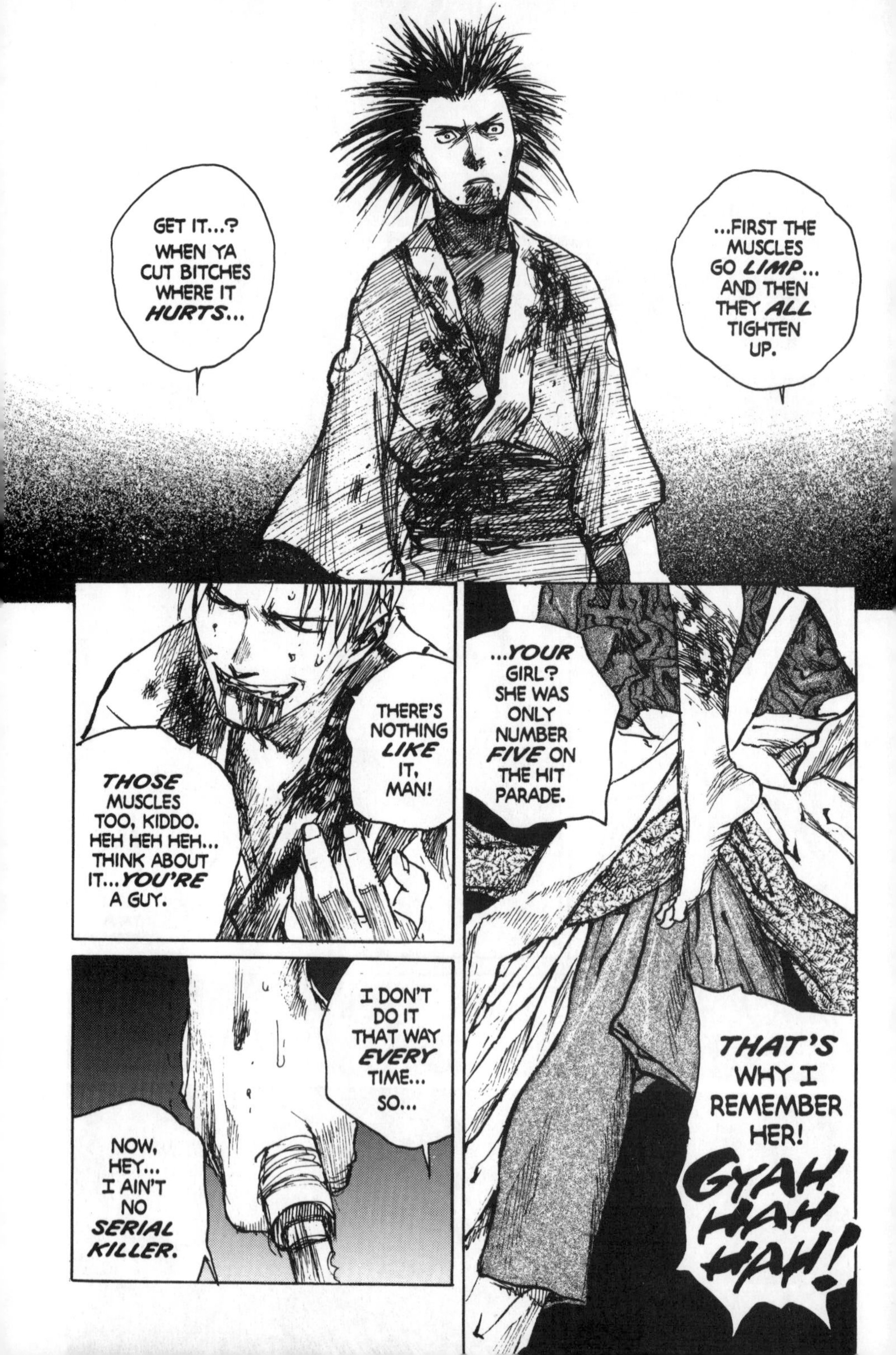
GET IT...? WHEN YA CUT BITCHES WHERE IT *HURTS*...
...FIRST THE MUSCLES GO *LIMP*... AND THEN THEY *ALL* TIGHTEN UP.
THERE'S NOTHING *LIKE* IT, MAN!
THOSE MUSCLES TOO, KIDDO. HEH HEH HEH... THINK ABOUT IT...*YOU'RE* A GUY.
I DON'T DO IT THAT WAY *EVERY* TIME... SO...
NOW, HEY... I AIN'T NO *SERIAL KILLER*.
...*YOUR* GIRL? SHE WAS ONLY NUMBER *FIVE* ON THE HIT PARADE.
THAT'S WHY I REMEMBER HER!
GYAH HAH HAH!

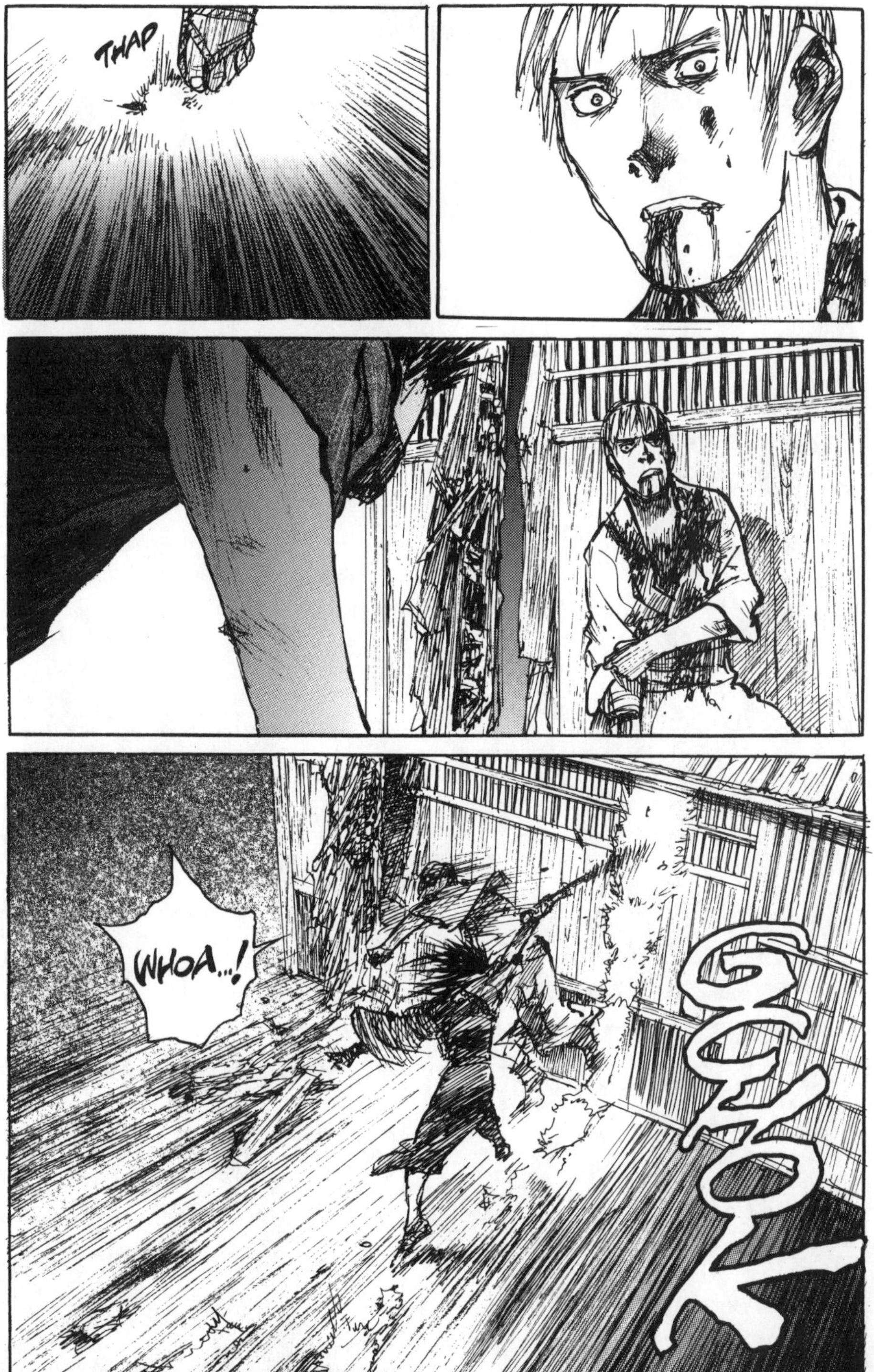
THAP
WHOA...!
GONK

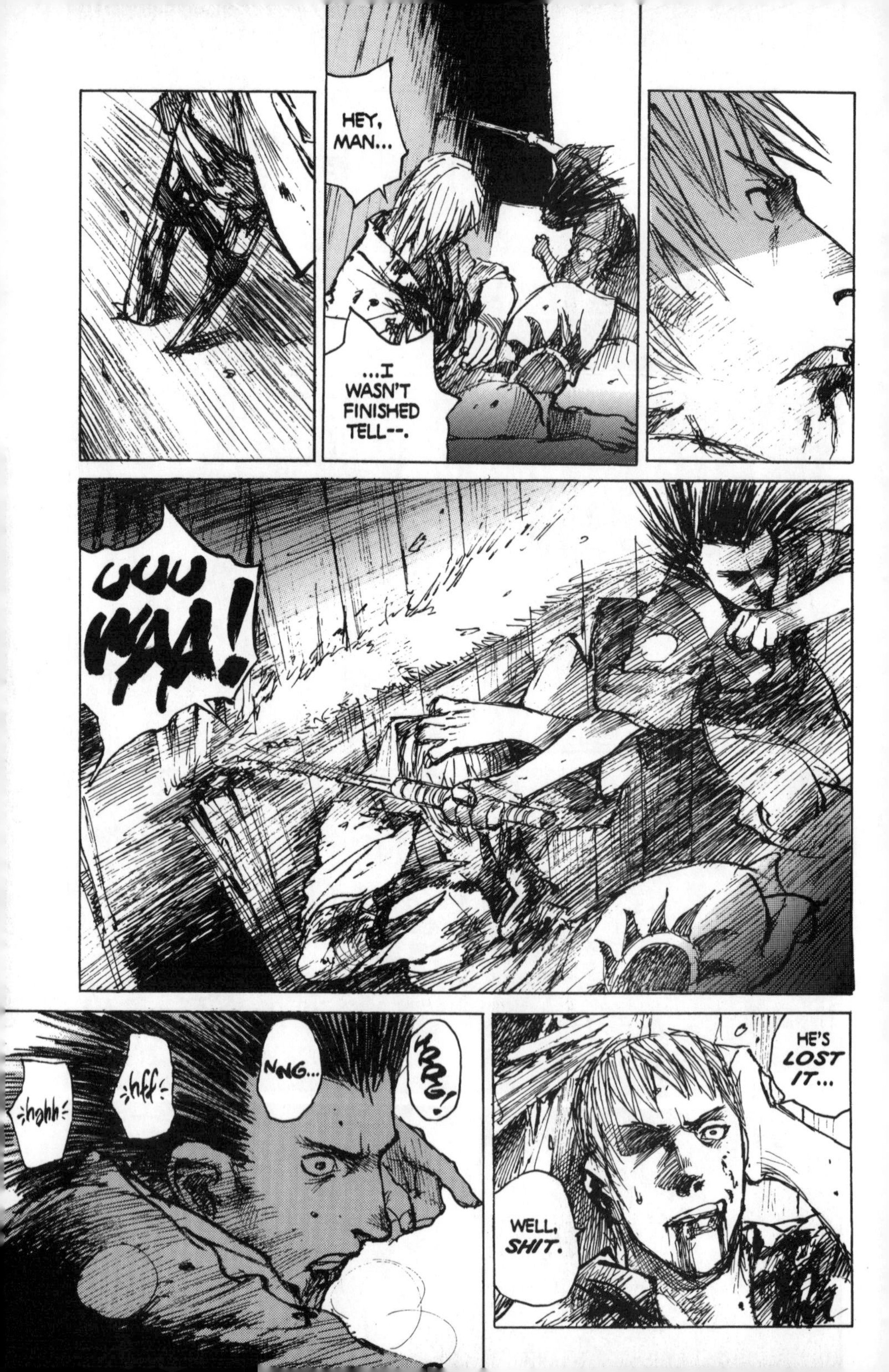
HEY, MAN...
...I WASN'T FINISHED TELL--.
UUU WAA!
hghh
hff
NNG...
UOOG!
HE'S LOST IT...
WELL, SHIT.

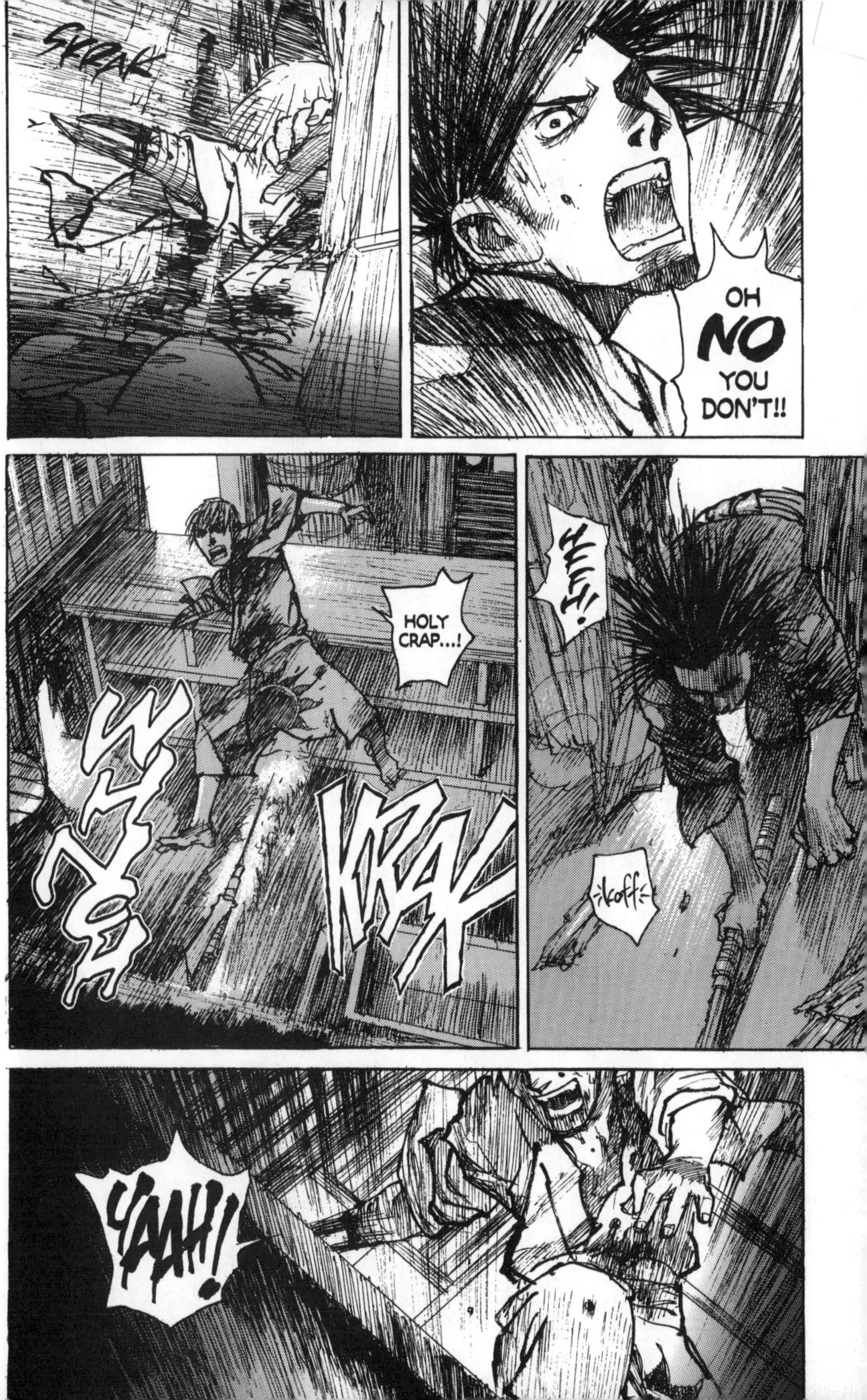
SKRONK
OH NO YOU DON'T!!
HOLY CRAP...!
KRAK
koff
YAAH!

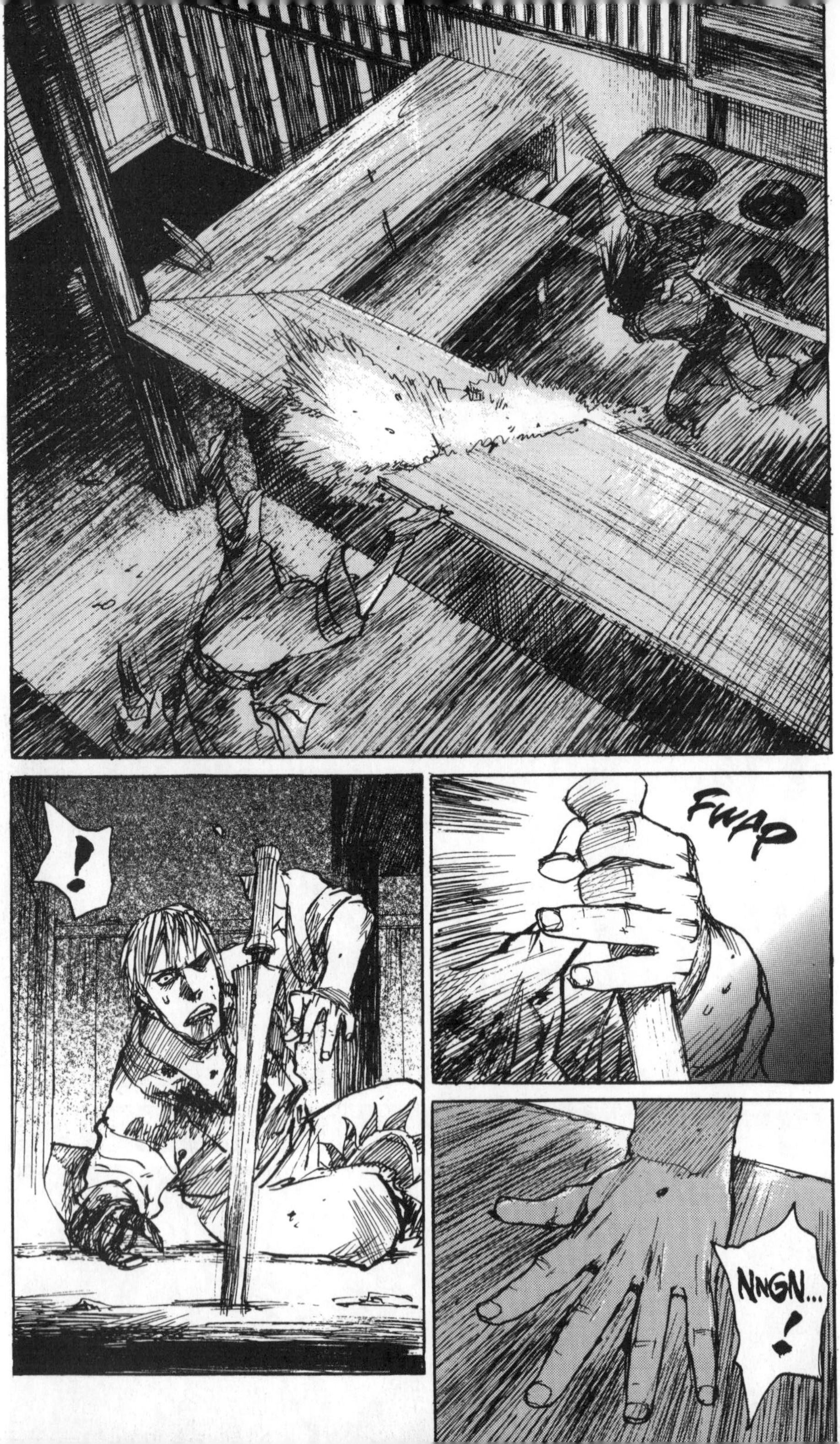
!
FWAP
NNGN... !

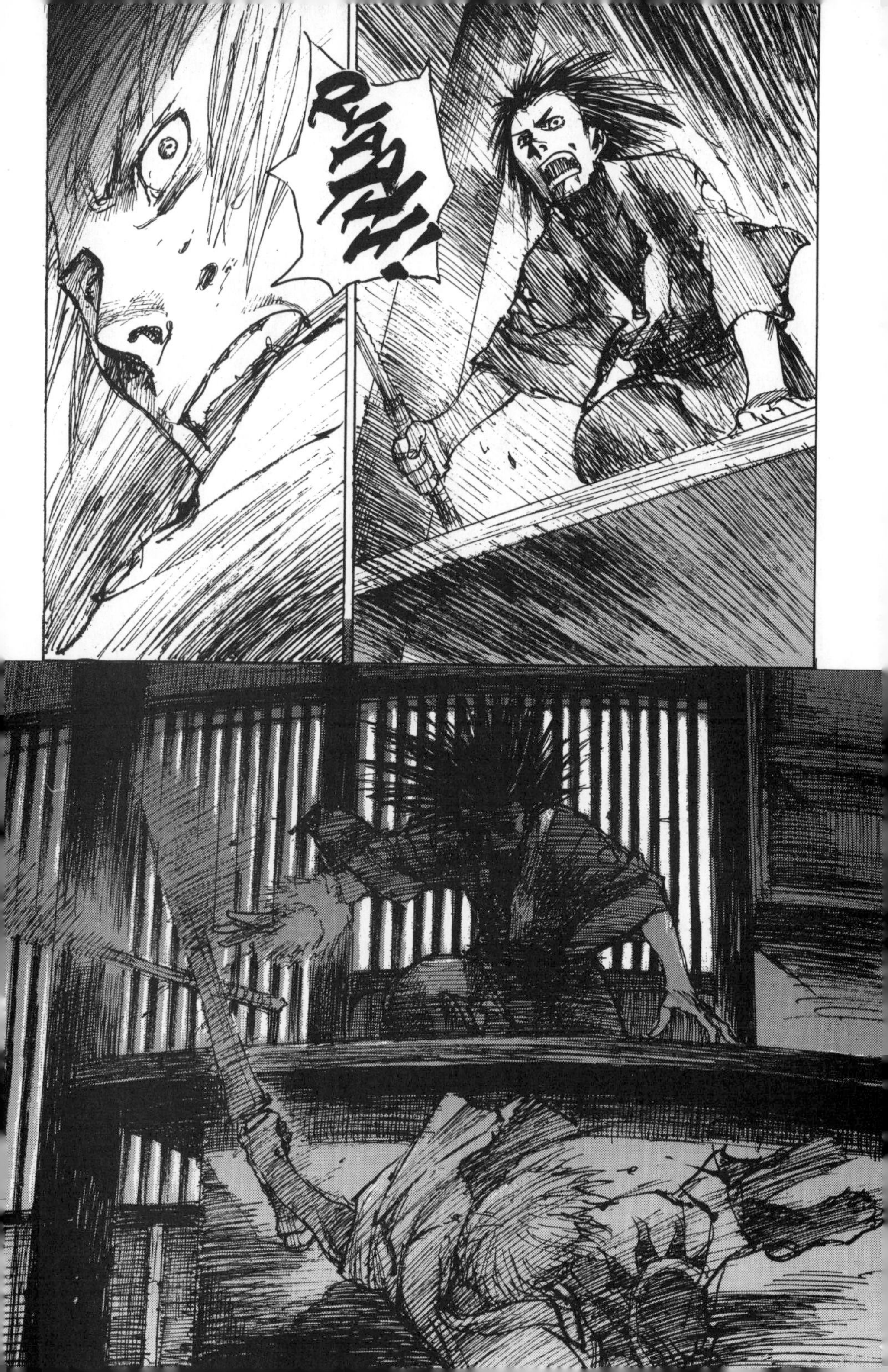
RWAAHH!!

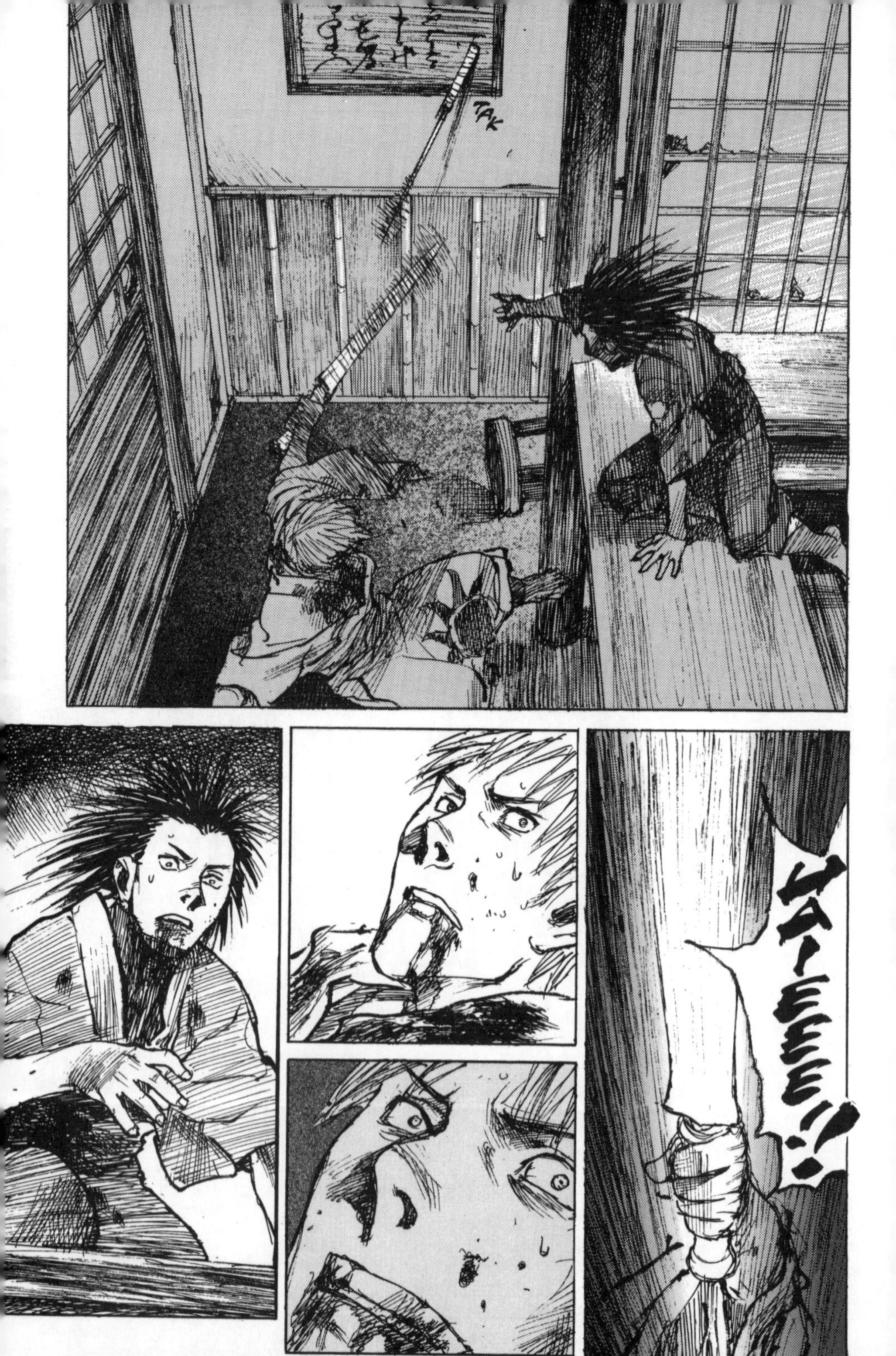
TAK
WAIEEEE!!

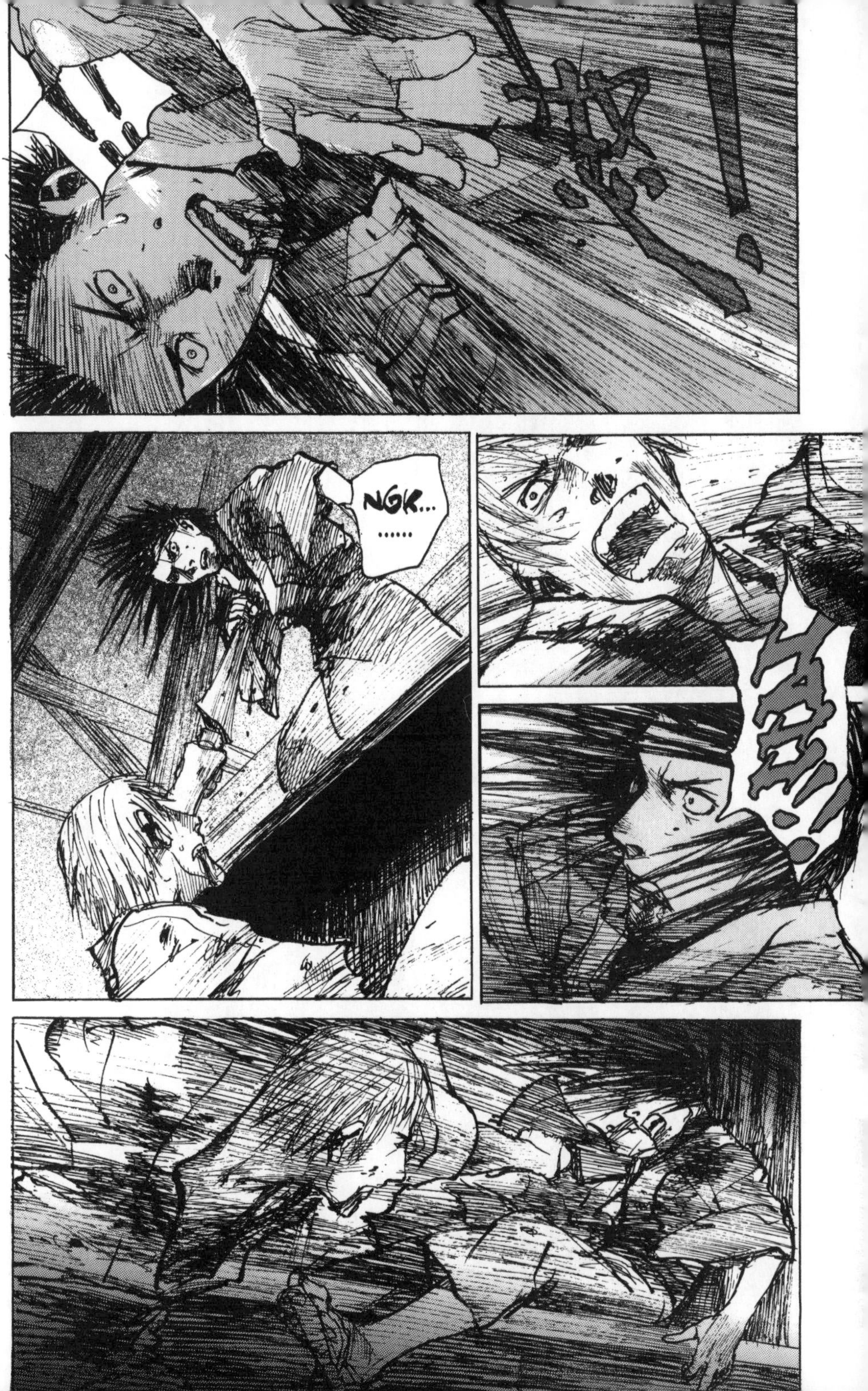
NGK...
......

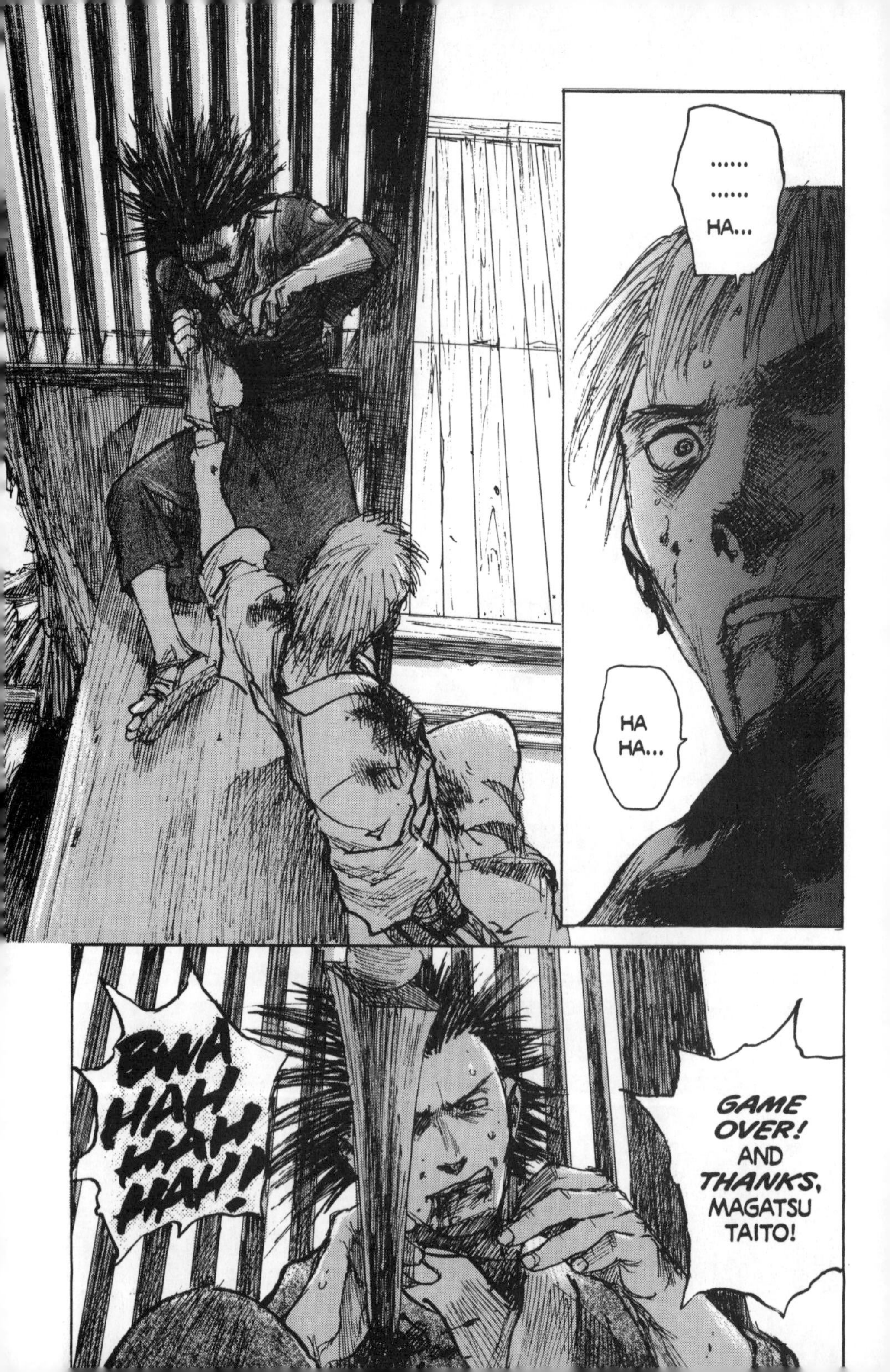
......
......
HA...
HA HA...
BWA HAH HAH HAH!
GAME OVER! AND THANKS, MAGATSU TAITO!

NO, REALLY! I *OWE YOU*, BUDDY!

FORGETTING YOU LEFT *THIS THING* LYING AROUND... *GOOD ONE*, KID!

.... UNNG...

AWW, DON'T LOOK SO *SAD*.

YOU'RE GONNA MEET YOUR LITTLE CUTIE, YEAH?

I'M *SUCH* A BAD GUY... TWO LI'L LOVE-BIRDS...

SHOULDN'T HAVE TORN YOU APART.

BUT THAT'S OVER *NOW!*

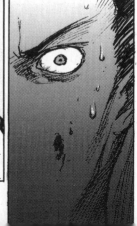

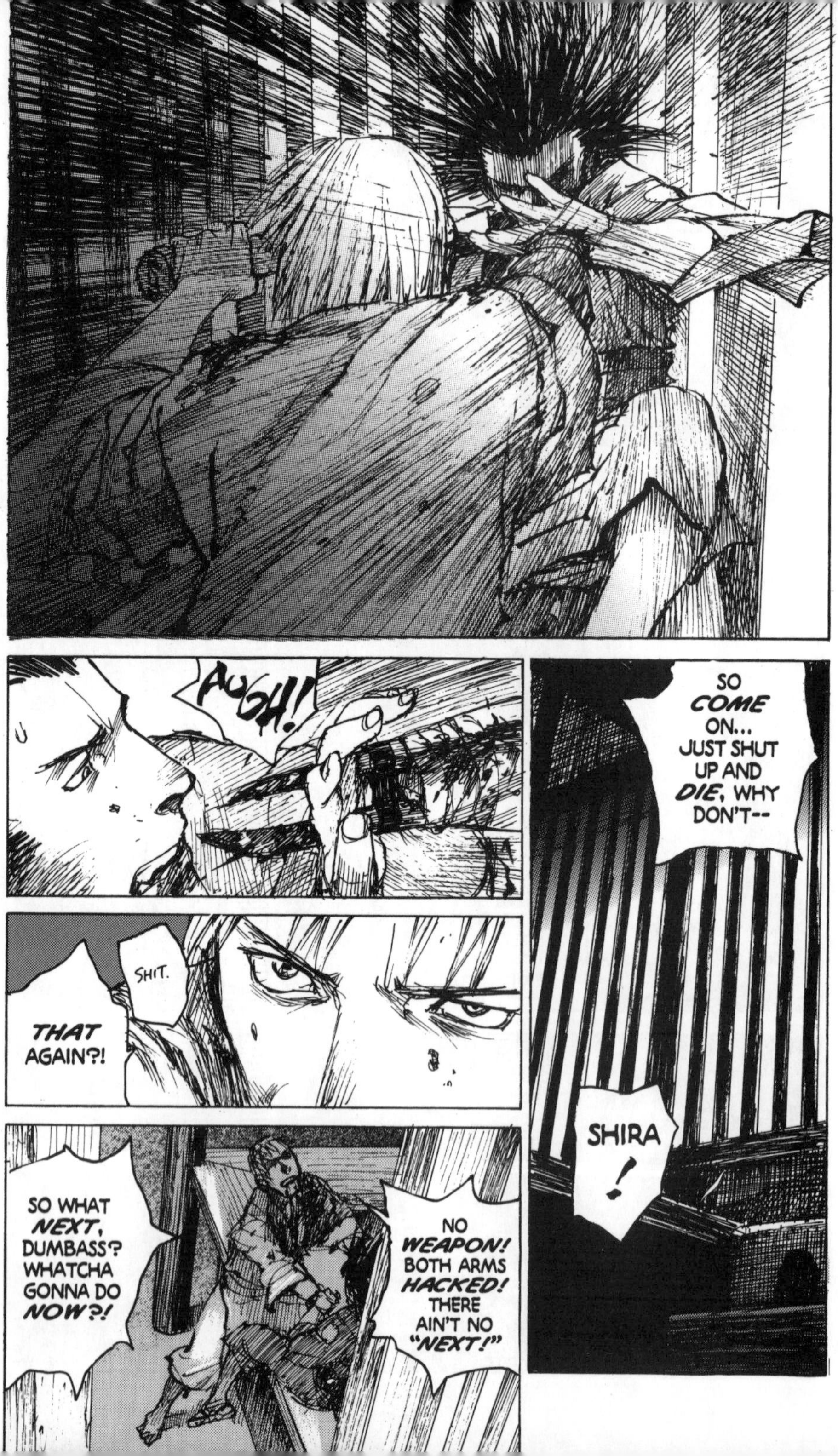
AUGH!
SHIT.
THAT AGAIN?!
SO WHAT NEXT, DUMBASS? WHATCHA GONNA DO NOW?!
NO WEAPON! BOTH ARMS HACKED! THERE AIN'T NO "NEXT!"
SO COME ON... JUST SHUT UP AND DIE, WHY DON'T--
SHIRA!

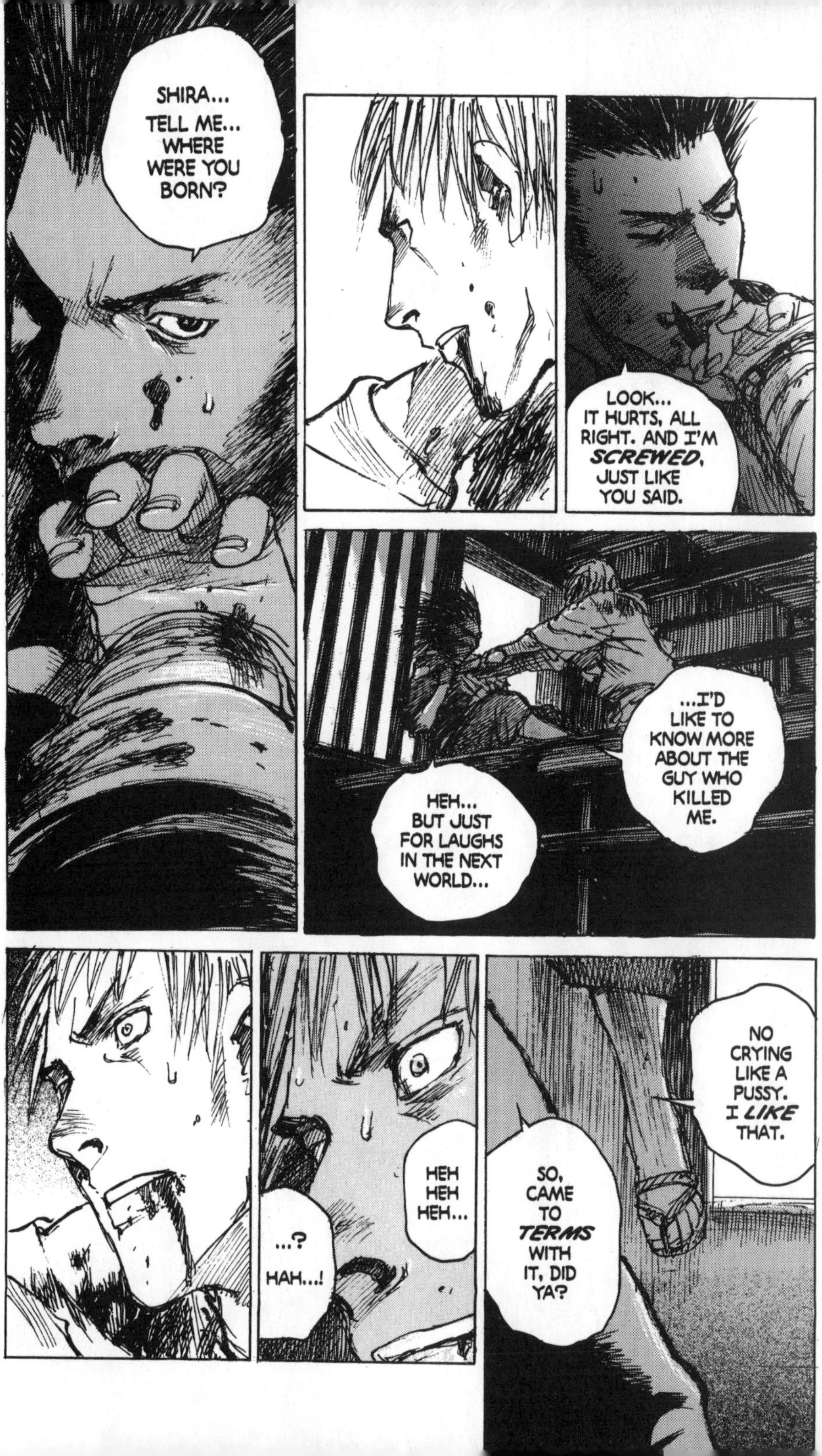
SHIRA... TELL ME... WHERE WERE YOU BORN?
LOOK... IT HURTS, ALL RIGHT. AND I'M *SCREWED*, JUST LIKE YOU SAID.
HEH... BUT JUST FOR LAUGHS IN THE NEXT WORLD...
...I'D LIKE TO KNOW MORE ABOUT THE GUY WHO KILLED ME.
...?
HAH...!
HEH HEH HEH...
SO, CAME TO *TERMS* WITH IT, DID YA?
NO CRYING LIKE A PUSSY. I *LIKE* THAT.

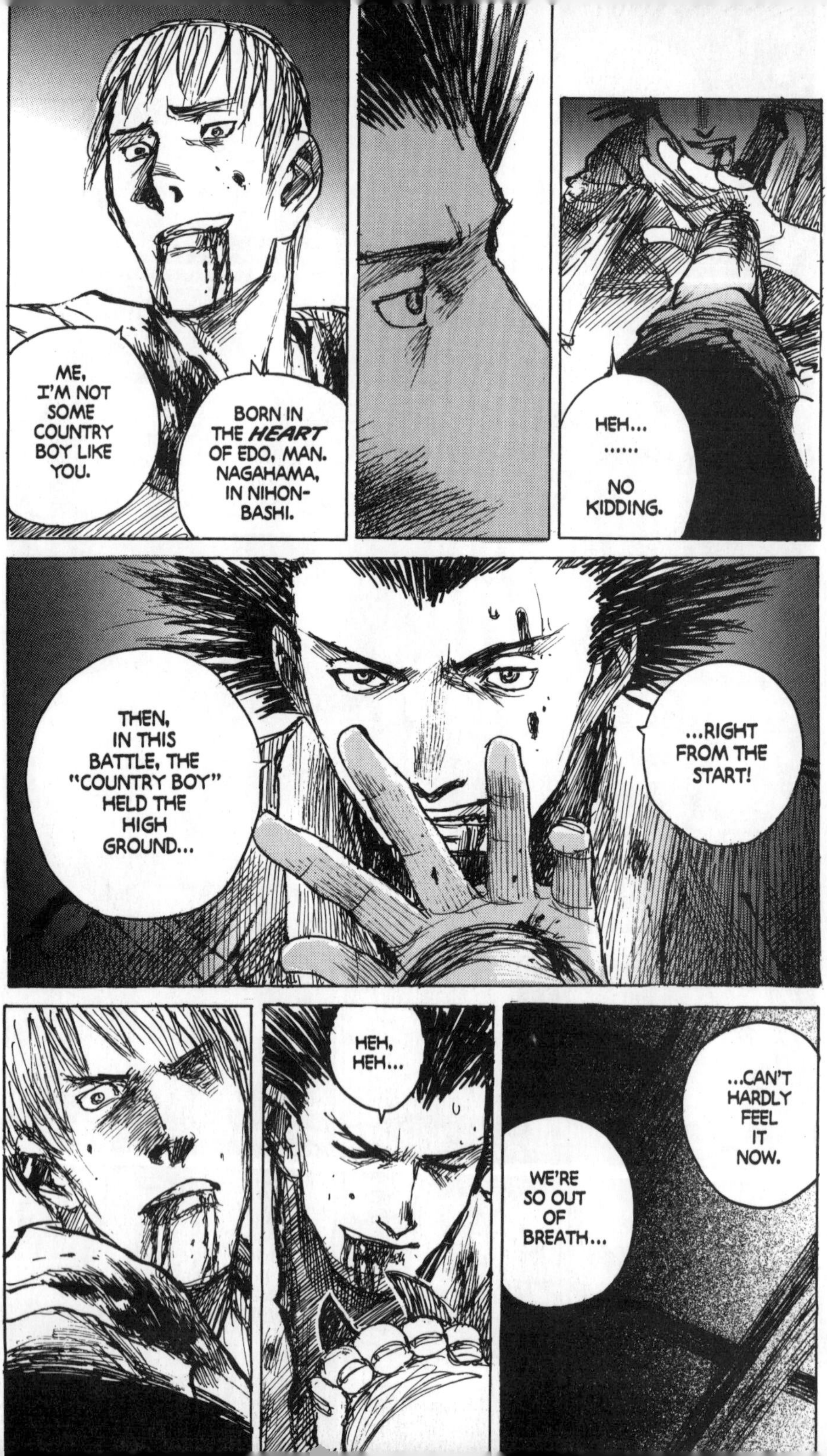
ME, I'M NOT SOME COUNTRY BOY LIKE YOU.
BORN IN THE ***HEART*** OF EDO, MAN. NAGAHAMA, IN NIHON-BASHI.
HEH... ...... NO KIDDING.
THEN, IN THIS BATTLE, THE "COUNTRY BOY" HELD THE HIGH GROUND...
...RIGHT FROM THE START!
HEH, HEH...
WE'RE SO OUT OF BREATH...
...CAN'T HARDLY FEEL IT NOW.

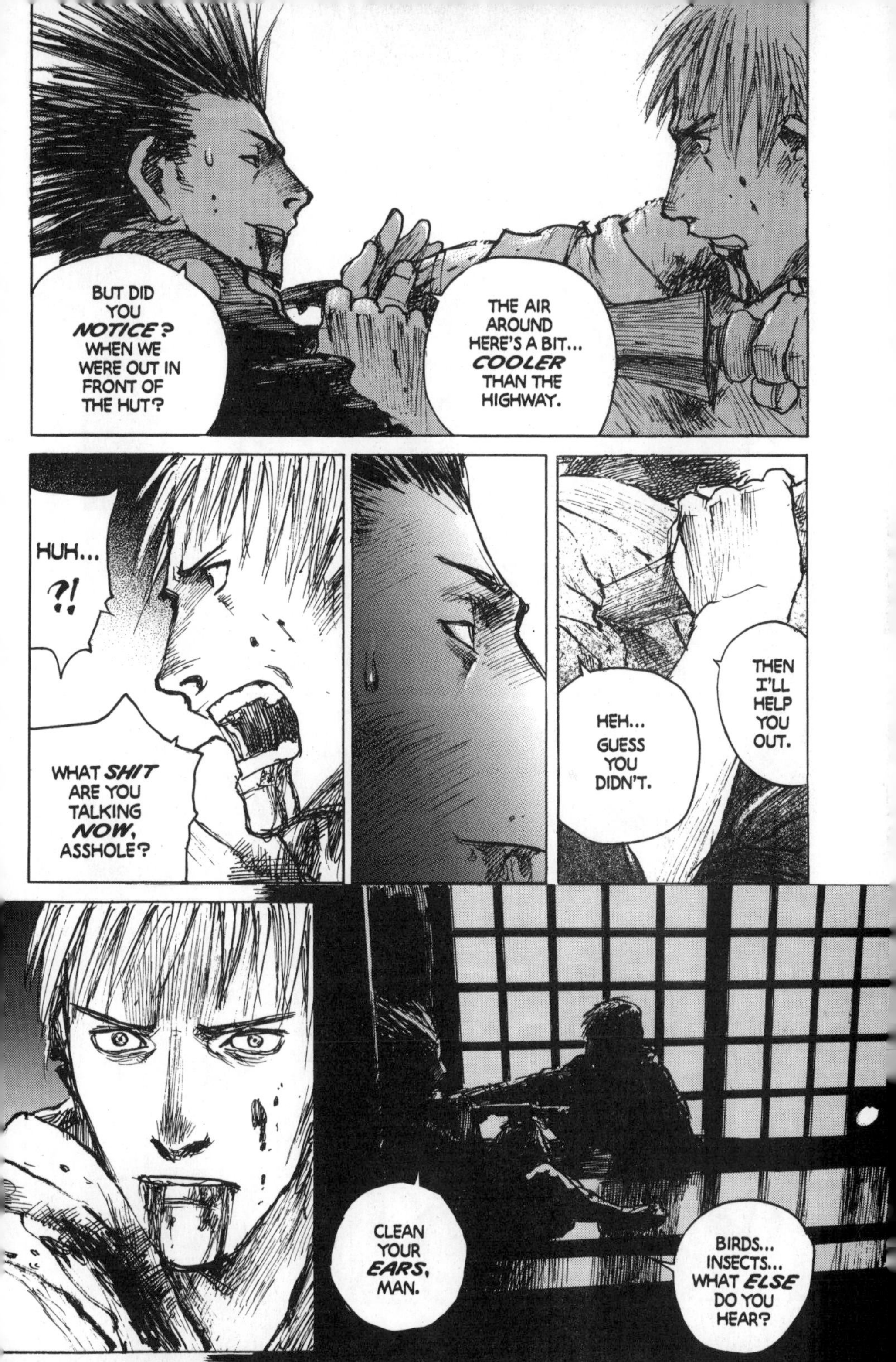
BUT DID YOU NOTICE? WHEN WE WERE OUT IN FRONT OF THE HUT?
THE AIR AROUND HERE'S A BIT... COOLER THAN THE HIGHWAY.
HUH...
?!
WHAT SHIT ARE YOU TALKING NOW, ASSHOLE?
HEH... GUESS YOU DIDN'T.
THEN I'LL HELP YOU OUT.
CLEAN YOUR EARS, MAN.
BIRDS... INSECTS... WHAT ELSE DO YOU HEAR?

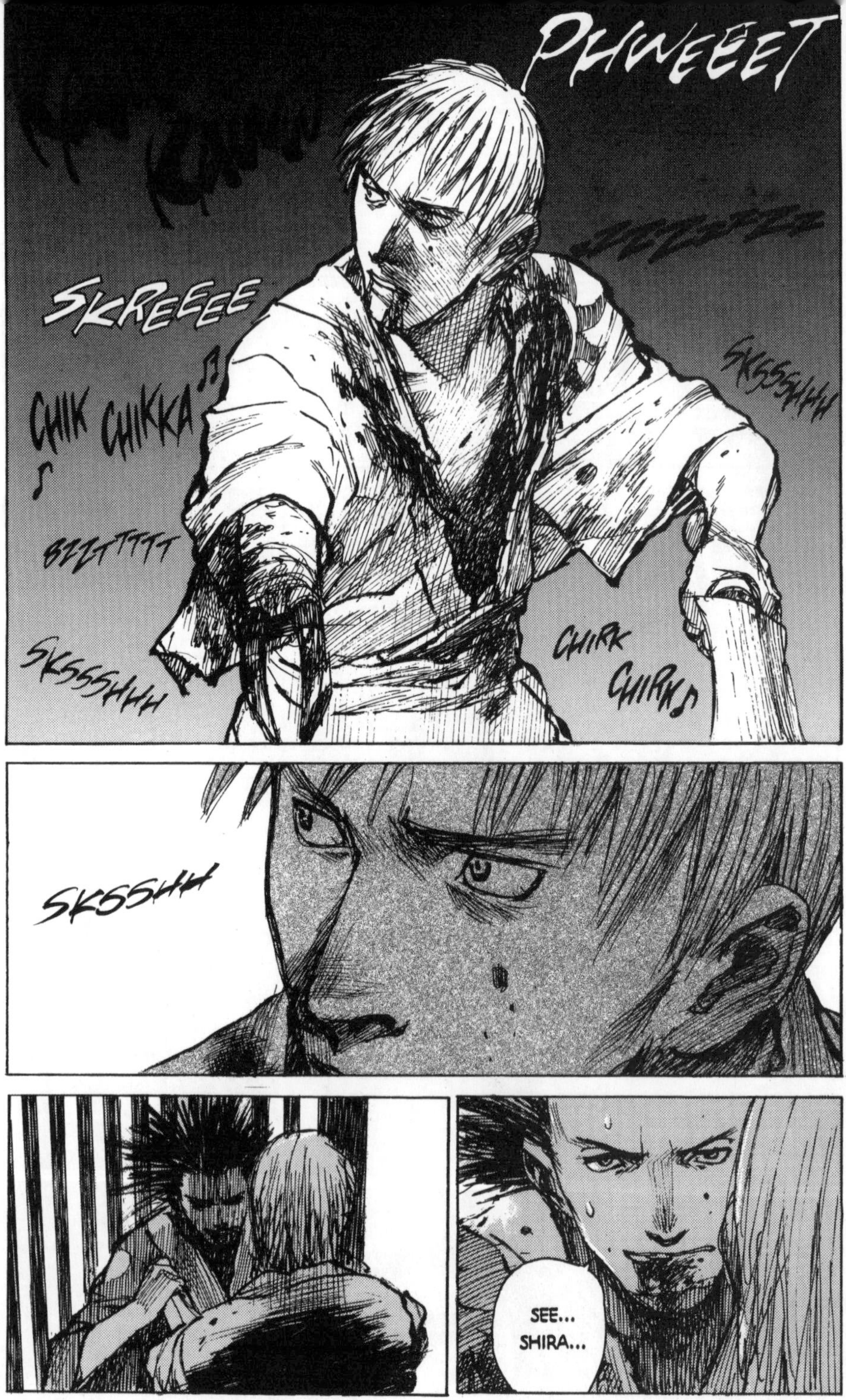
PHWEEET
SKREEEEE
SKSSSHHH
CHIK CHIKKA
BZZZTTTTT
CHIRK CHIRK
SKSSSHHH
SKSSHH
SEE...
SHIRA...

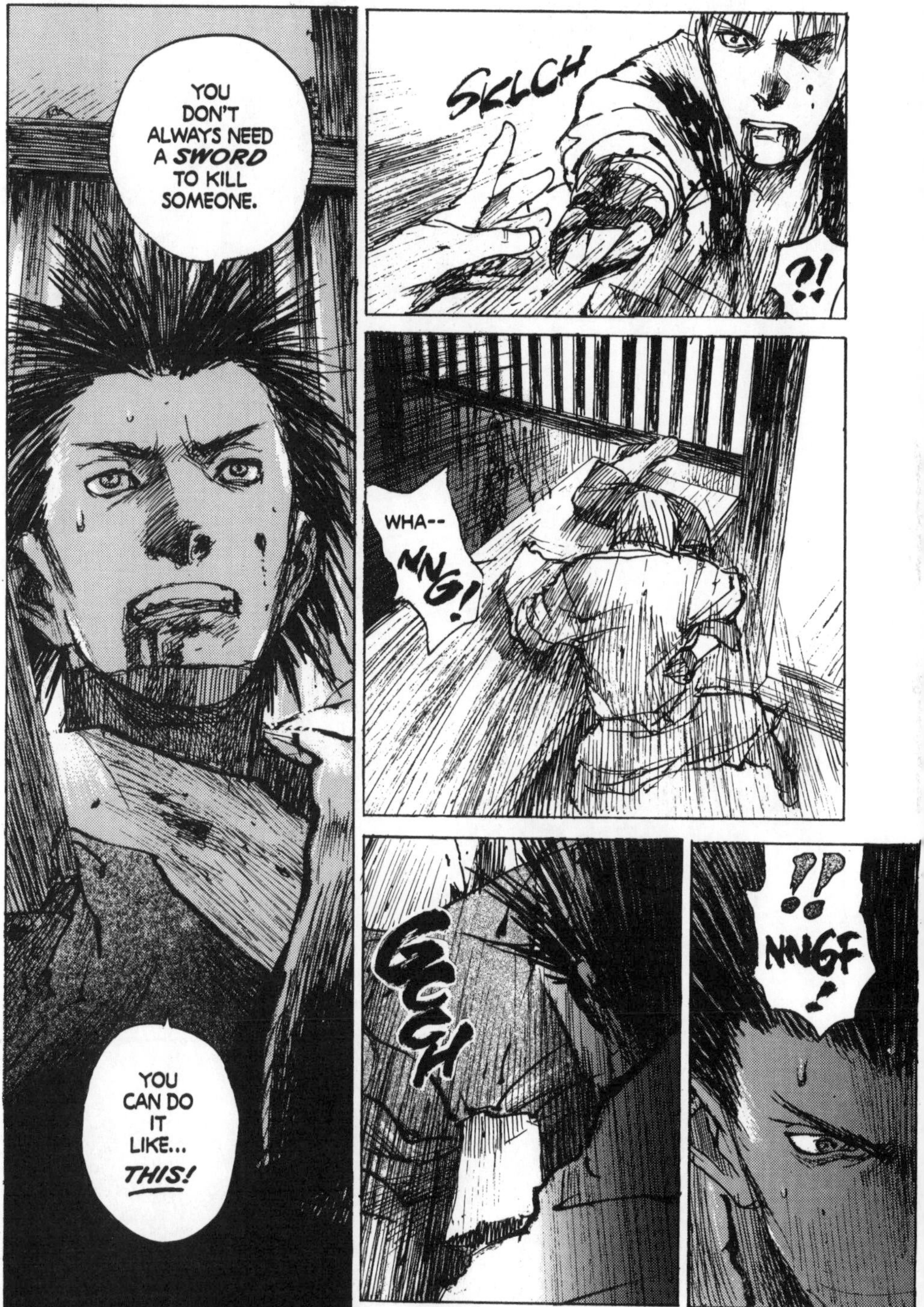
YOU DON'T ALWAYS NEED A SWORD TO KILL SOMEONE.
YOU CAN DO IT LIKE... THIS!
SKLCH
?!
WHA--
NNG!
GGGH
!!
NNGF!

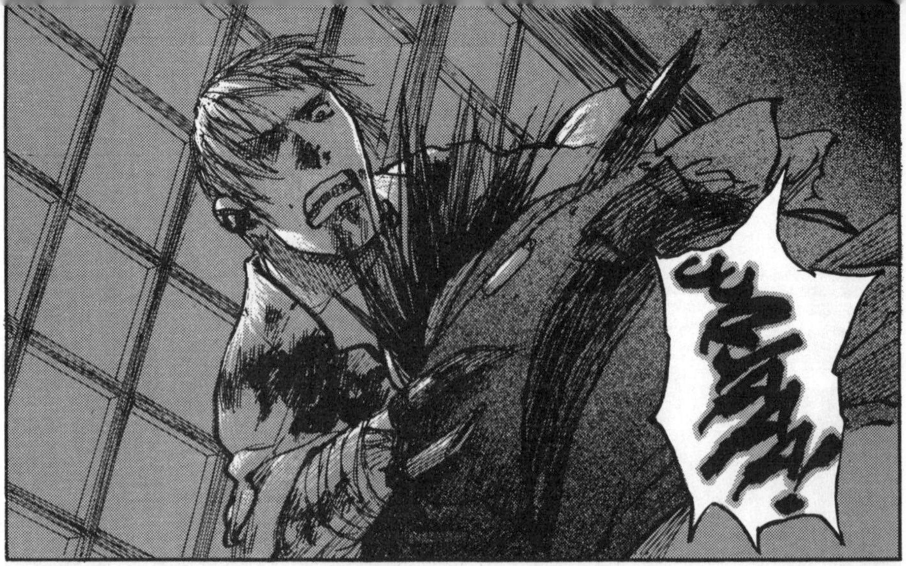

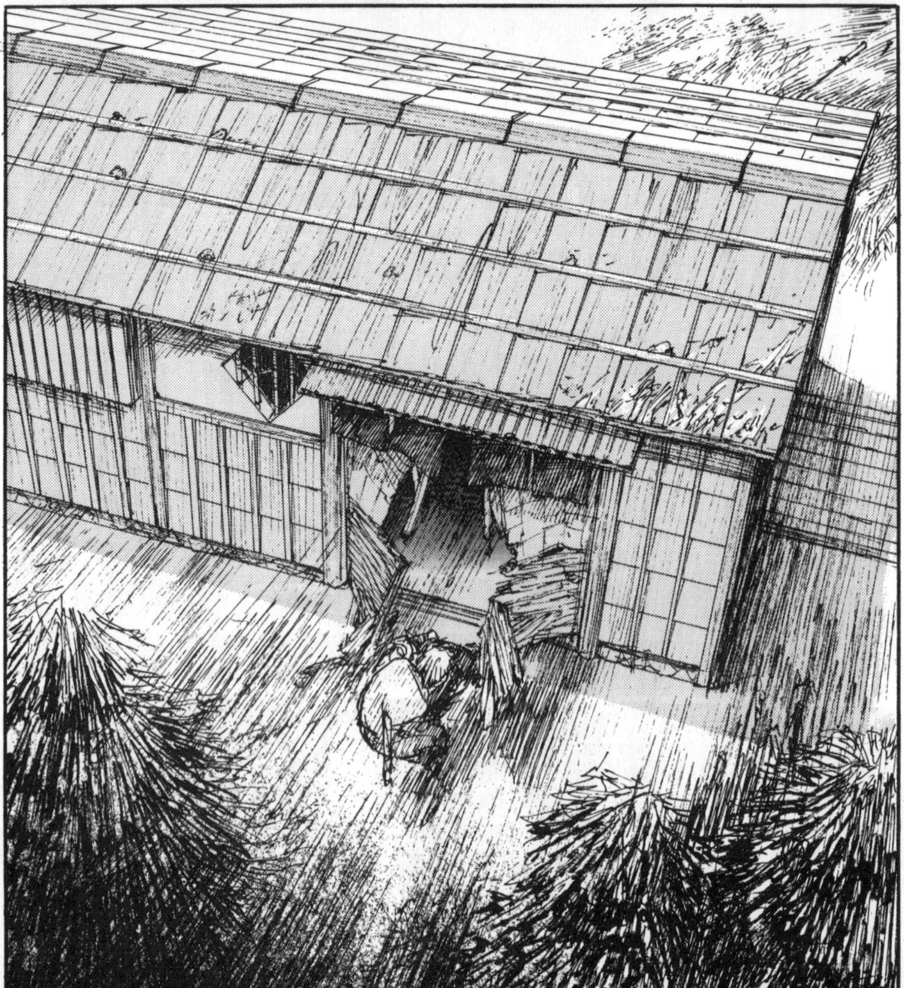

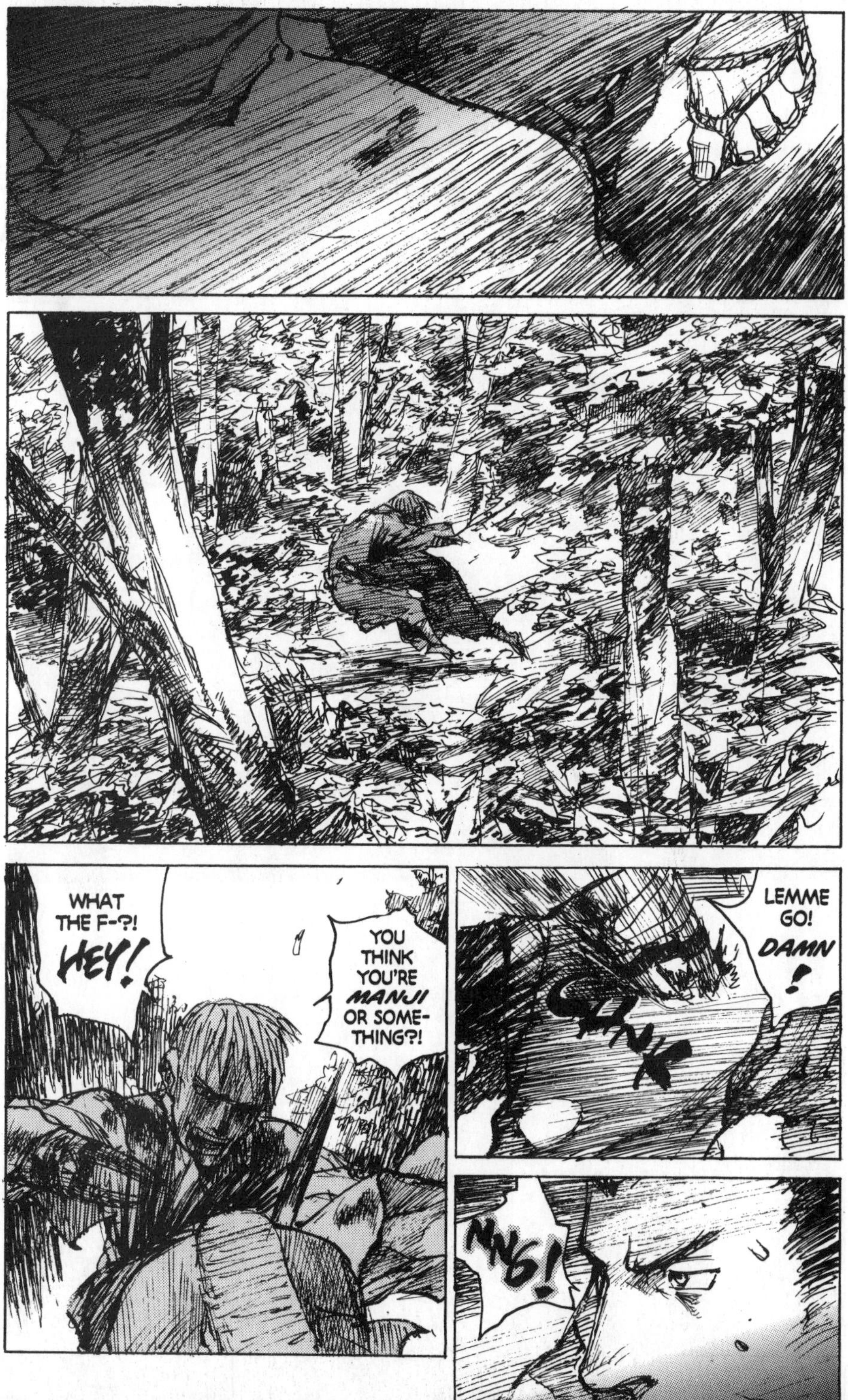
WHAT THE F-?! HEY!
YOU THINK YOU'RE *MANJI* OR SOME-THING?!
LEMME GO! *DAMN*!
CLINK
MNG!

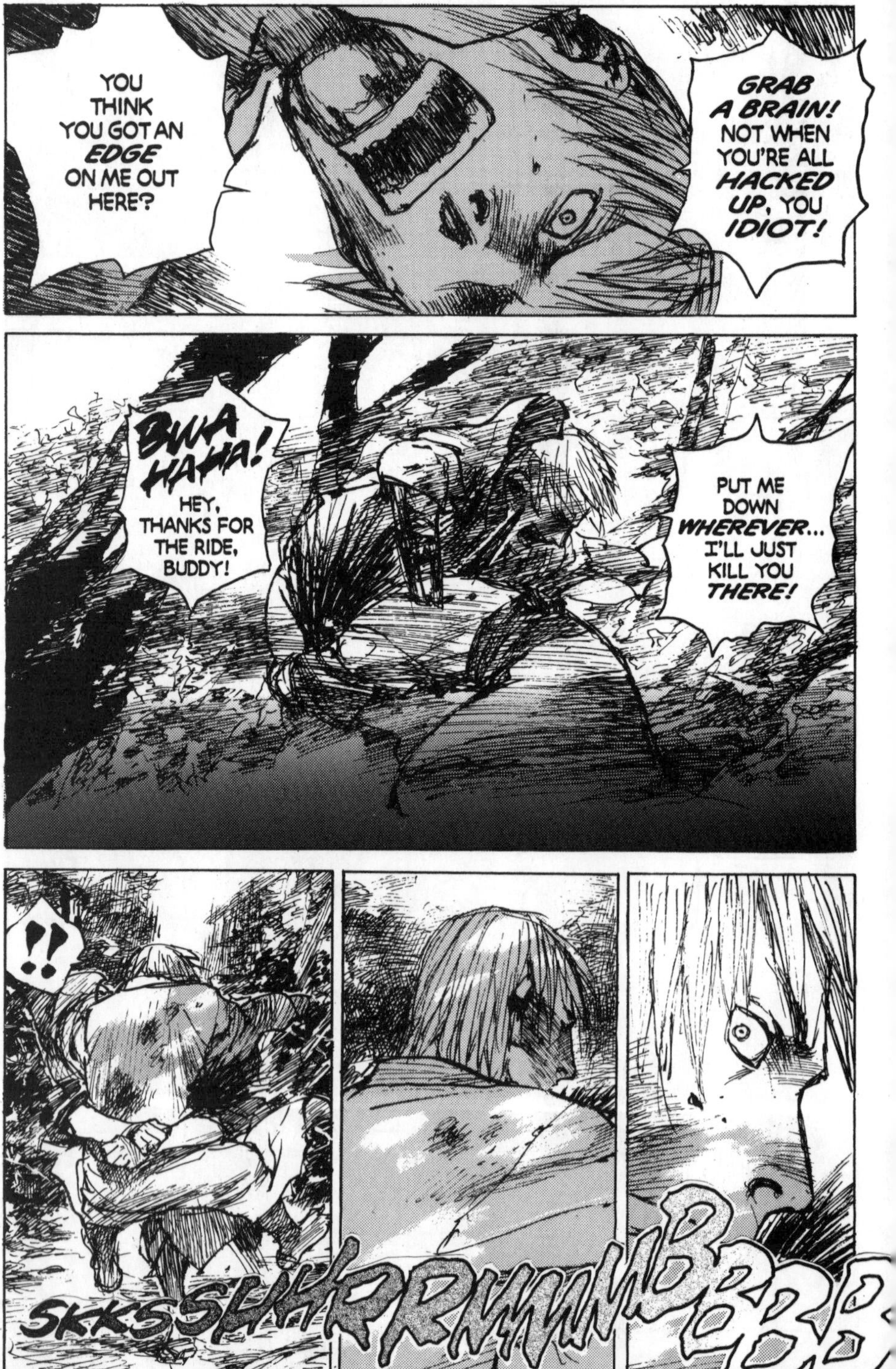
YOU THINK YOU GOT AN *EDGE* ON ME OUT HERE?
GRAB A BRAIN! NOT WHEN YOU'RE ALL *HACKED UP*, YOU *IDIOT!*
BWA HAHA! HEY, THANKS FOR THE RIDE, BUDDY!
PUT ME DOWN *WHEREVER*... I'LL JUST KILL YOU *THERE!*
!!
SKKS SHHRRMMMMBBBBB

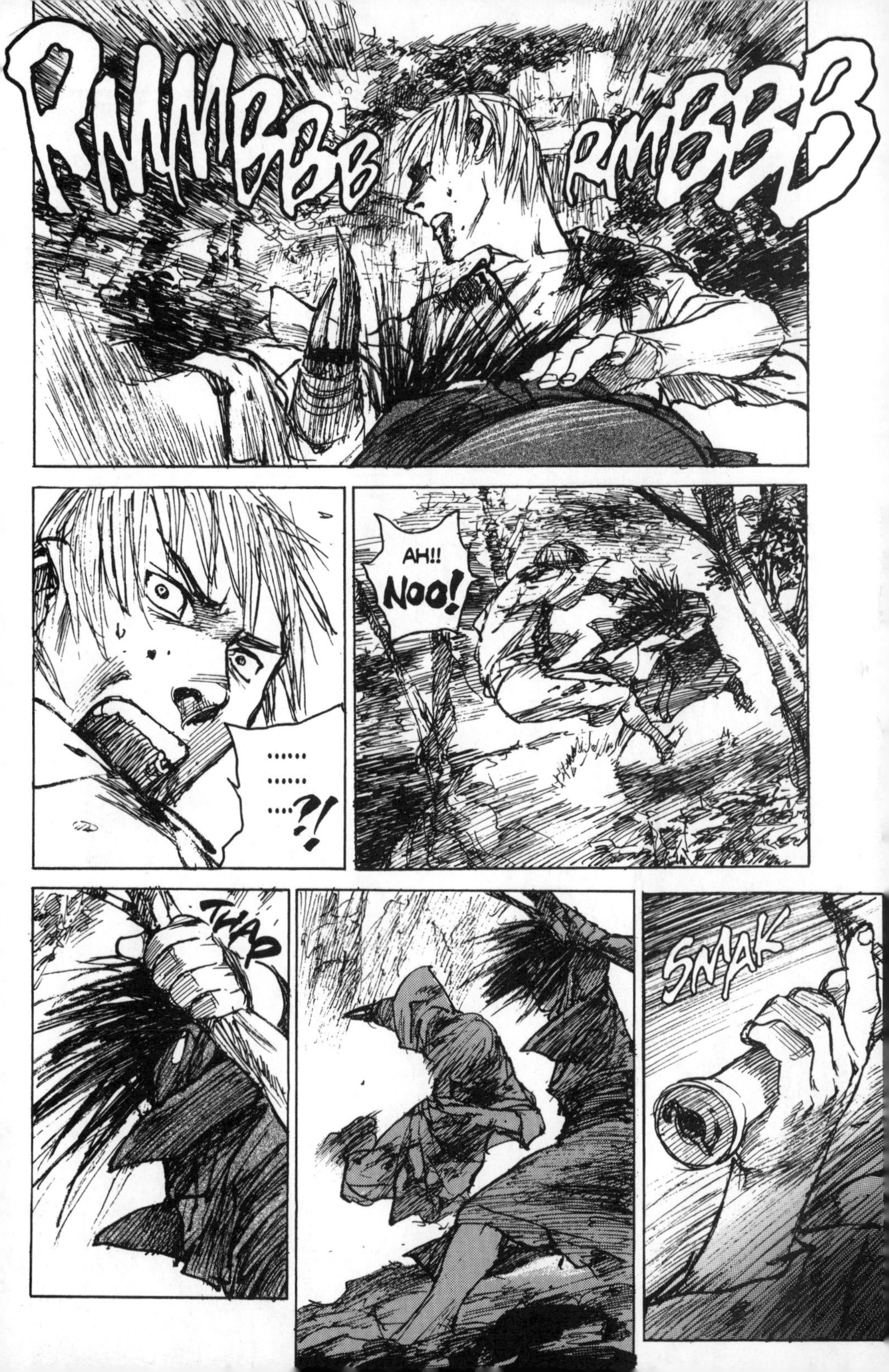
RMMBBB
RMBBBB
......
......
....?!
AH!!
NOO!
THAP
SNAK

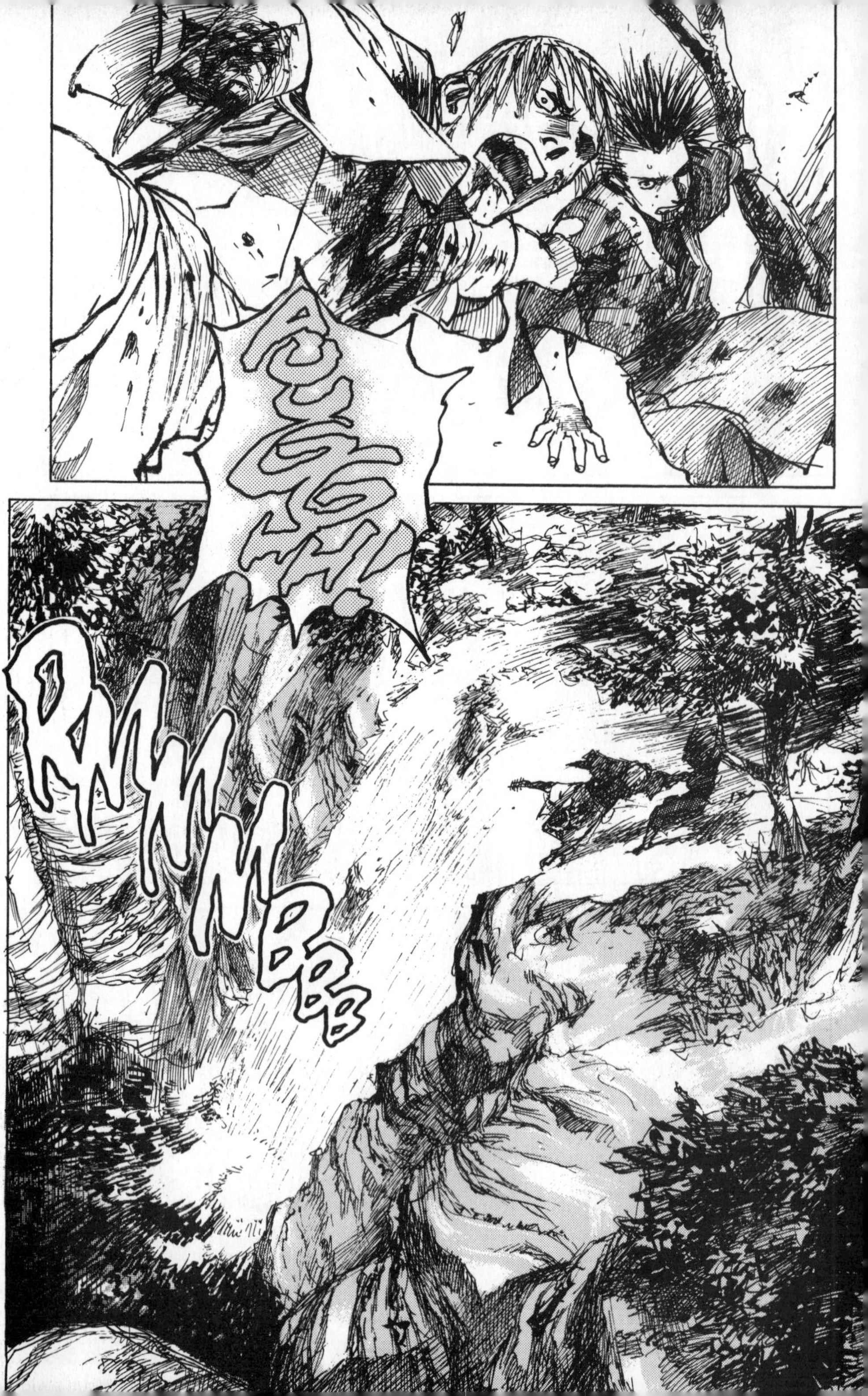
AUGGH!
RMMMBBB

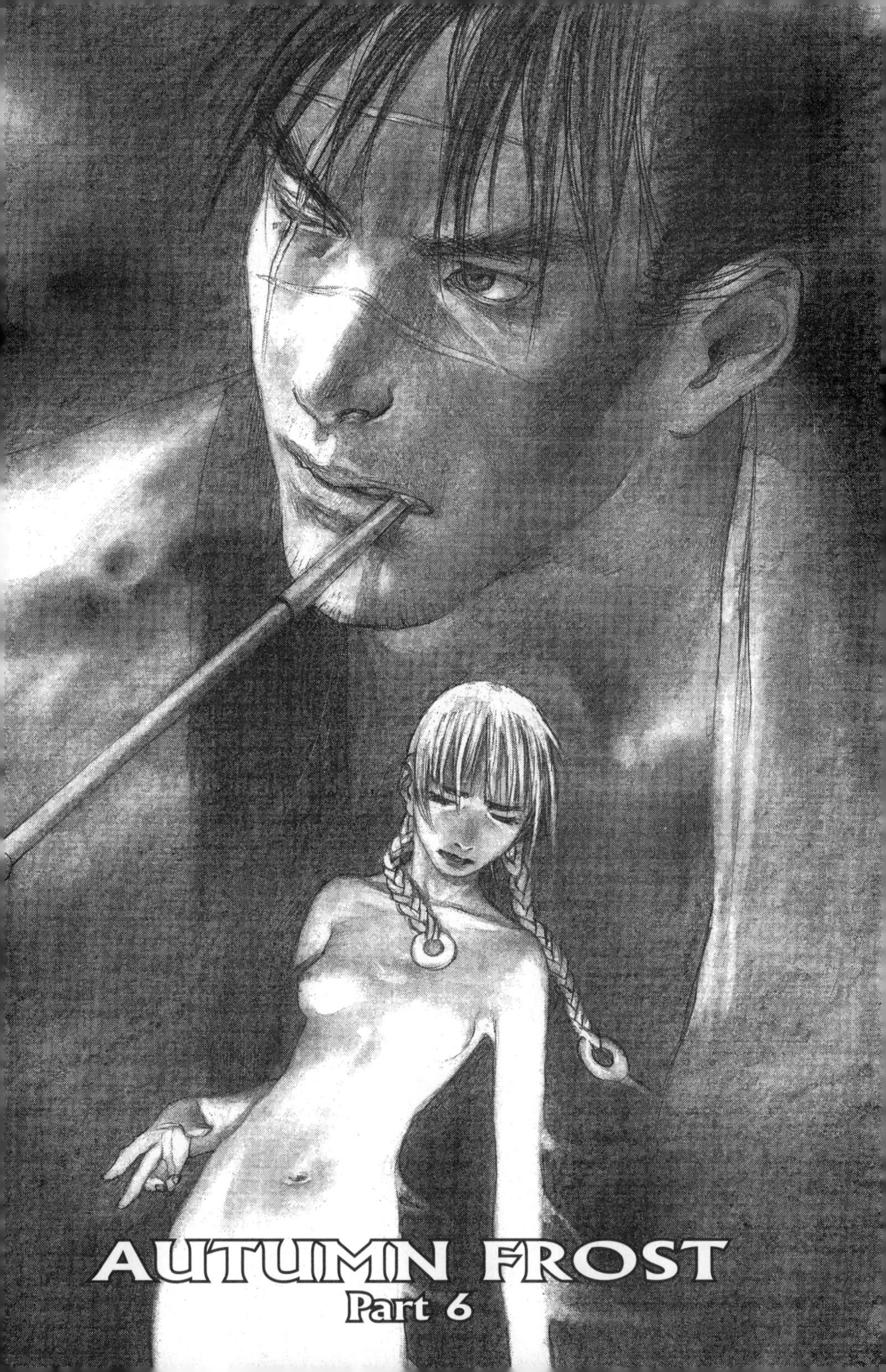
AUTUMN FROST
Part 6

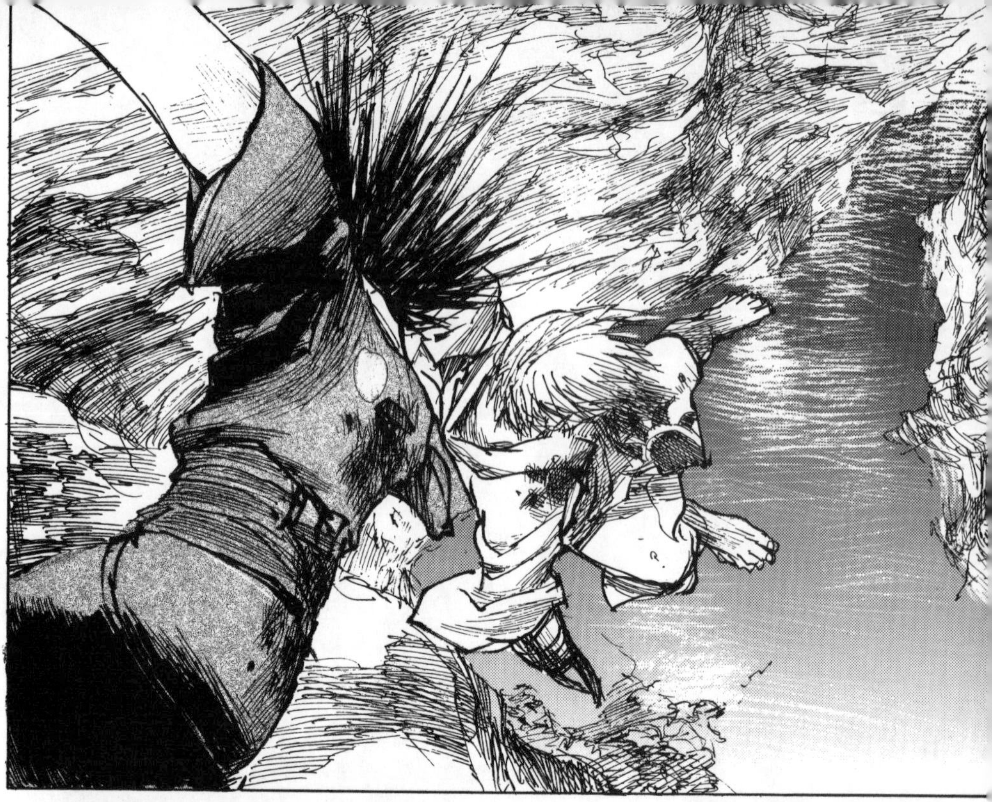

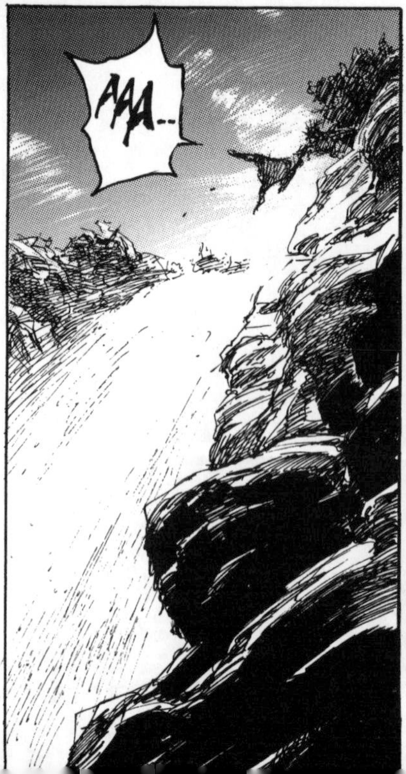
AAA--

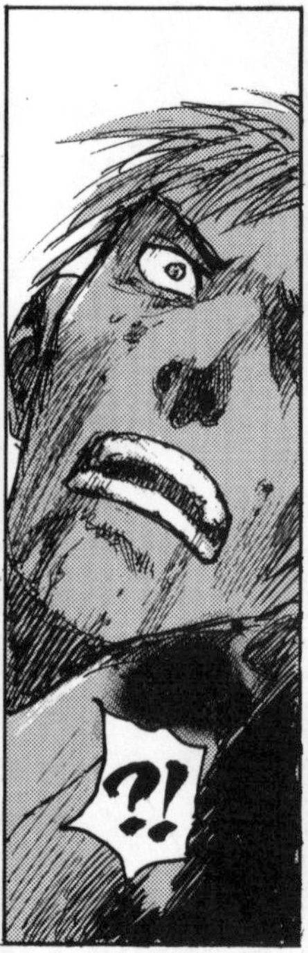
?!

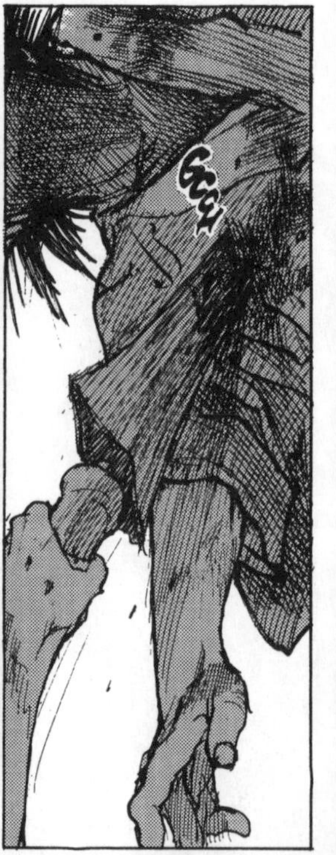

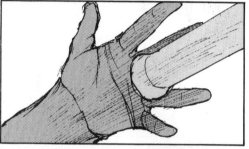

HRGG...
!!

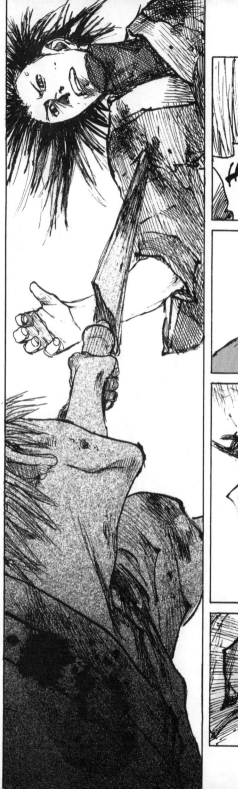

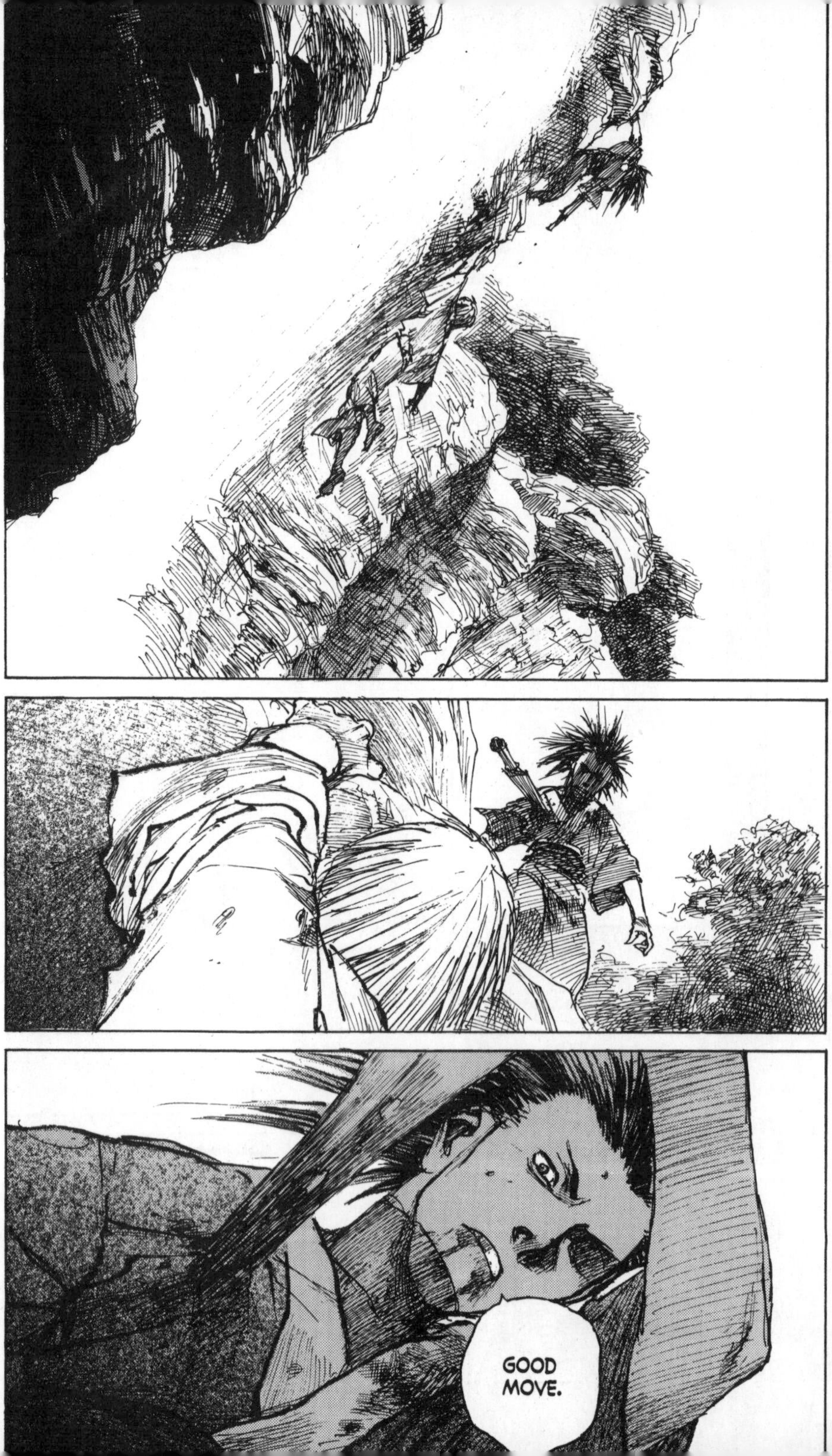
GOOD MOVE.

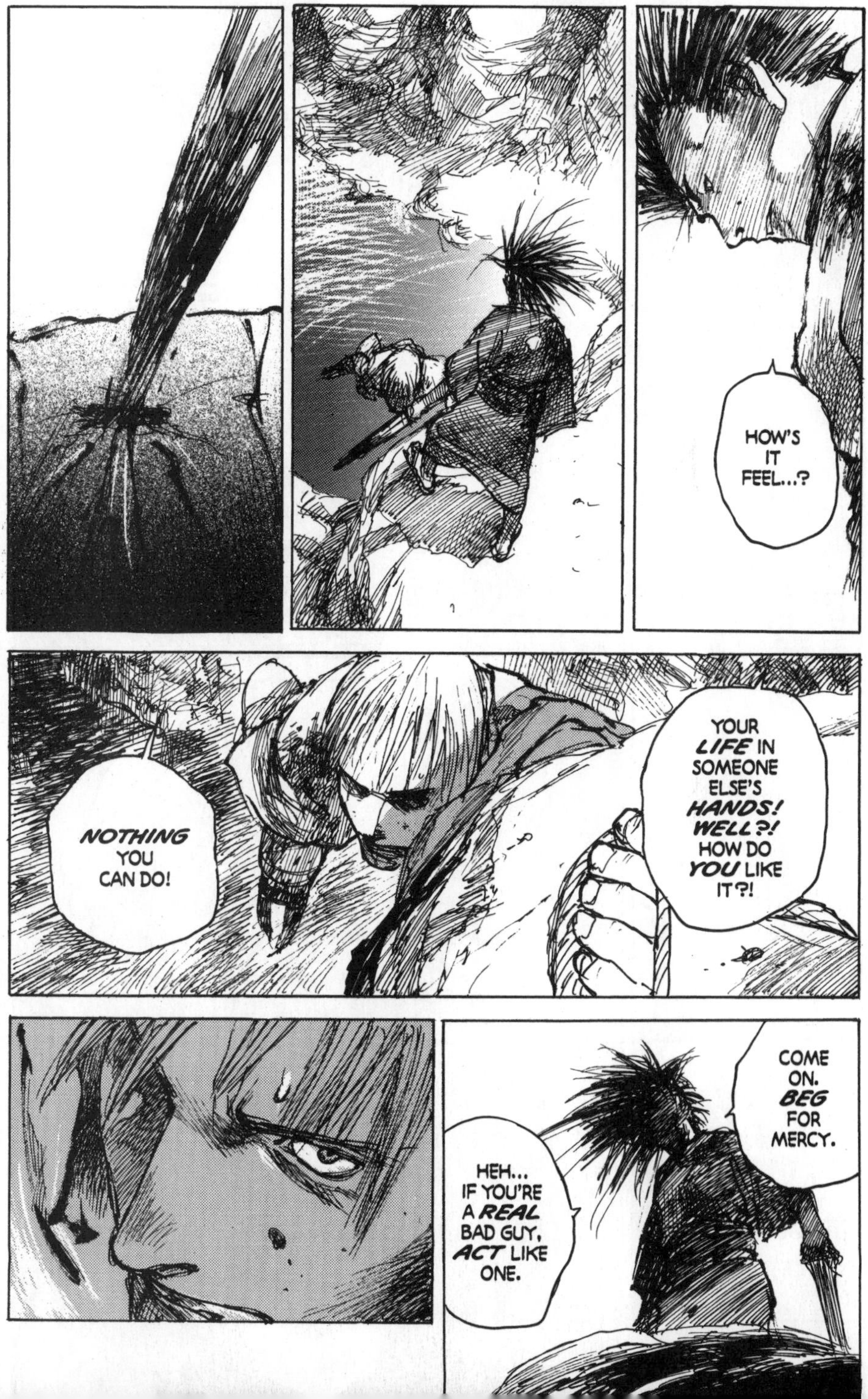
HOW'S IT FEEL...?
NOTHING YOU CAN DO!
YOUR LIFE IN SOMEONE ELSE'S HANDS! WELL?! HOW DO YOU LIKE IT?!
COME ON. BEG FOR MERCY.
HEH... IF YOU'RE A REAL BAD GUY, ACT LIKE ONE.

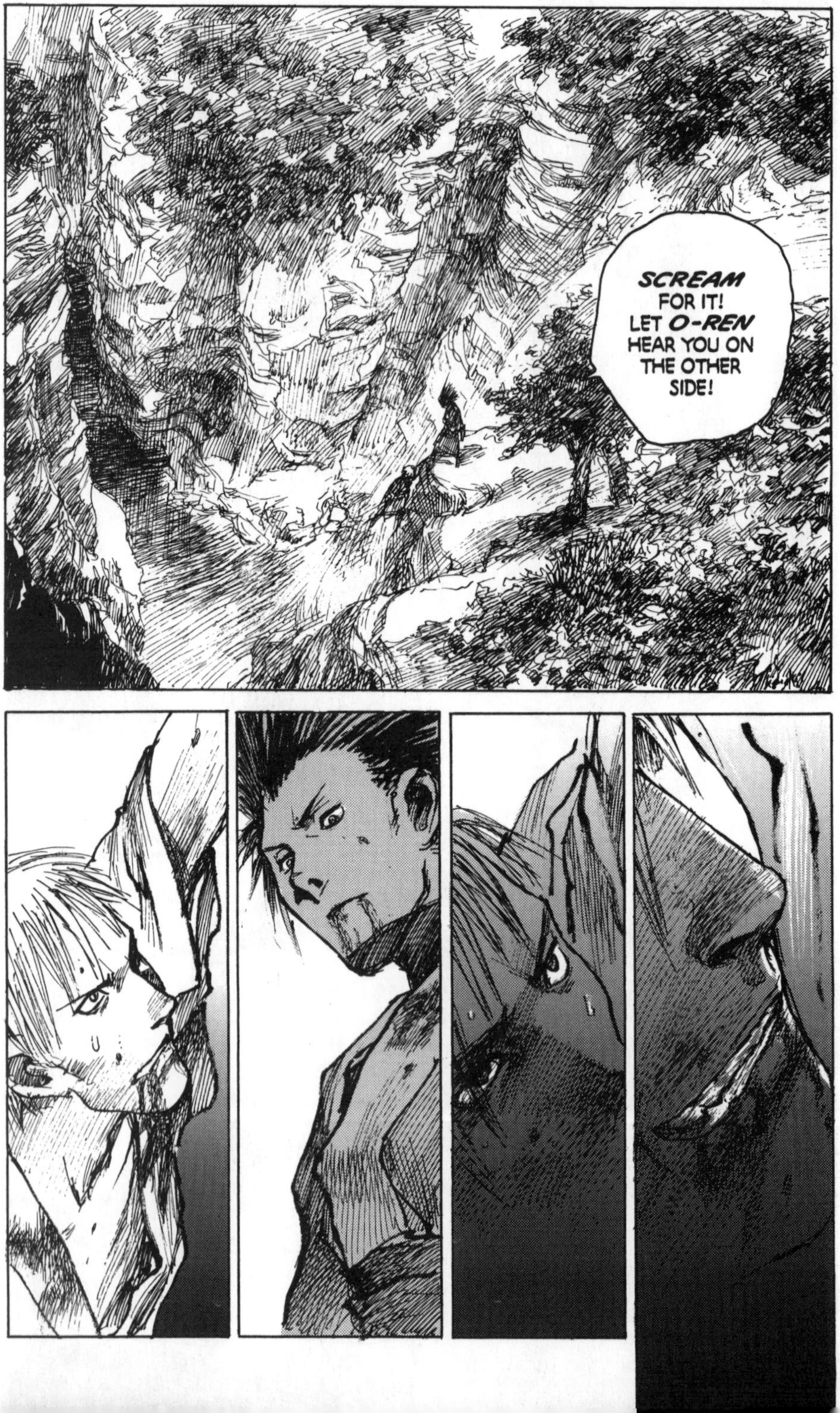
SCREAM FOR IT! LET O-REN HEAR YOU ON THE OTHER SIDE!

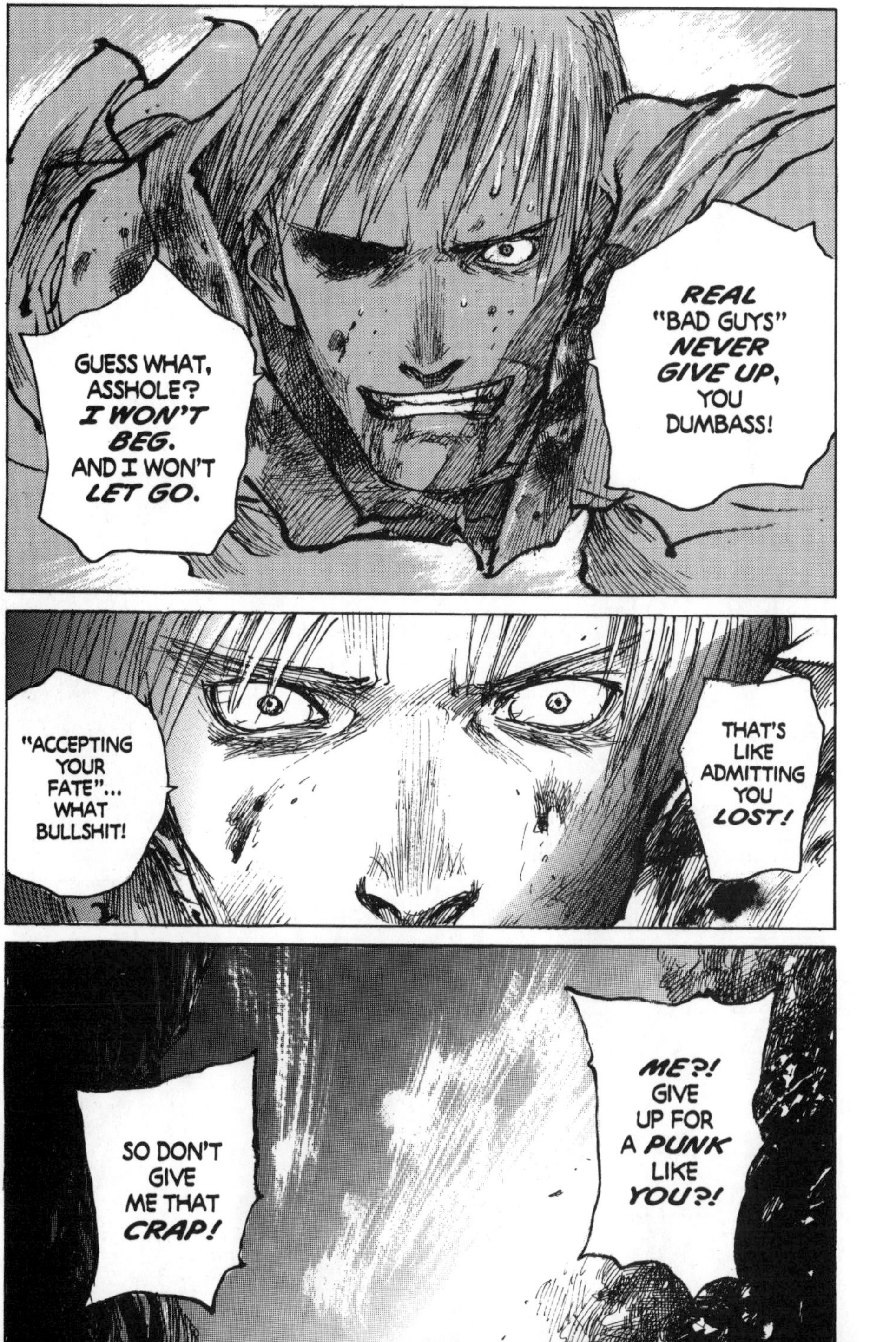
GUESS WHAT, ASSHOLE? I WON'T BEG. AND I WON'T LET GO.
REAL "BAD GUYS" NEVER GIVE UP, YOU DUMBASS!
"ACCEPTING YOUR FATE"... WHAT BULLSHIT!
THAT'S LIKE ADMITTING YOU LOST!
SO DON'T GIVE ME THAT CRAP!
ME?! GIVE UP FOR A PUNK LIKE YOU?!

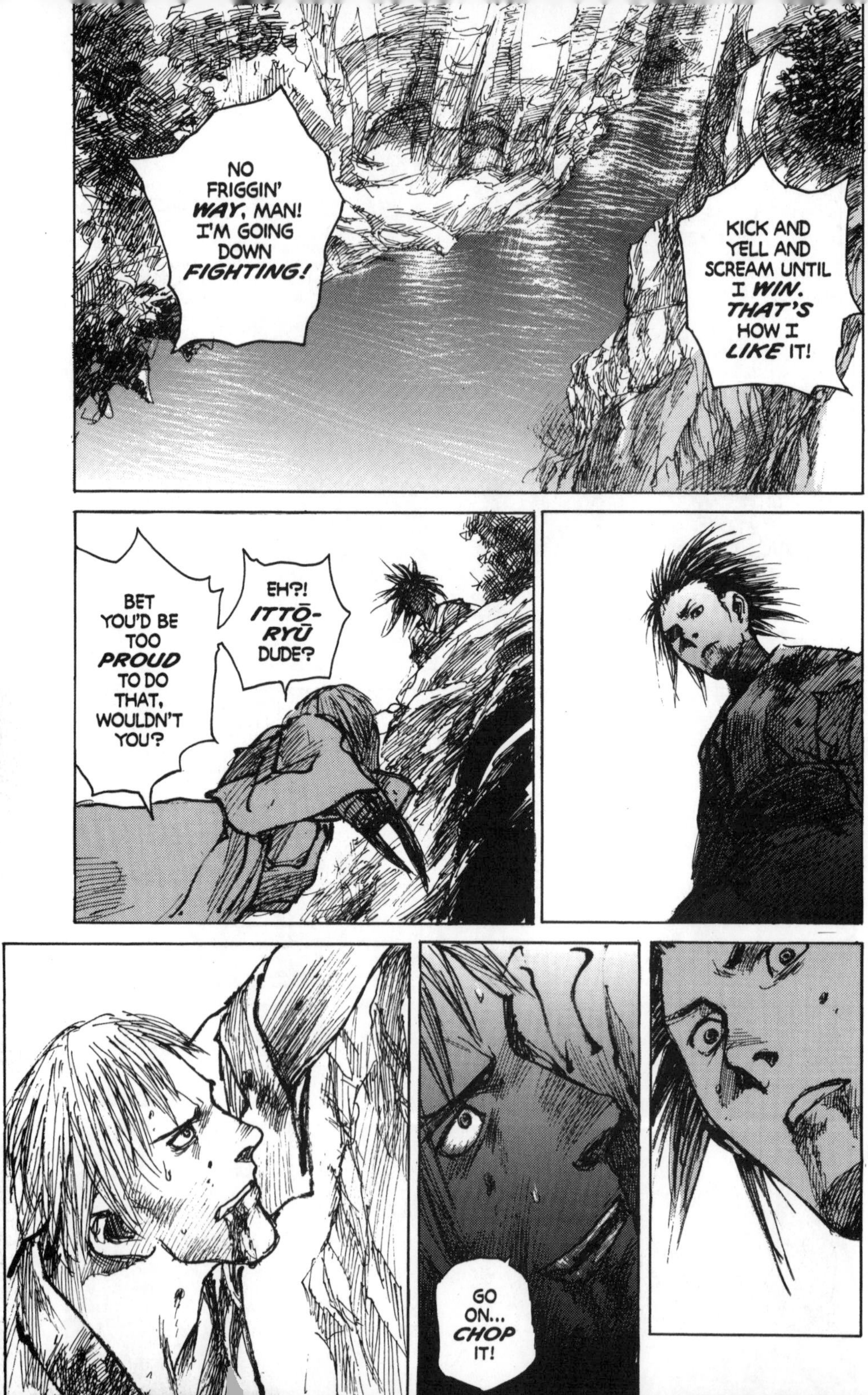
NO FRIGGIN' WAY, MAN! I'M GOING DOWN FIGHTING!
KICK AND YELL AND SCREAM UNTIL I WIN. THAT'S HOW I LIKE IT!
BET YOU'D BE TOO PROUD TO DO THAT, WOULDN'T YOU?
EH?! ITTŌ-RYŪ DUDE?
GO ON... CHOP IT!

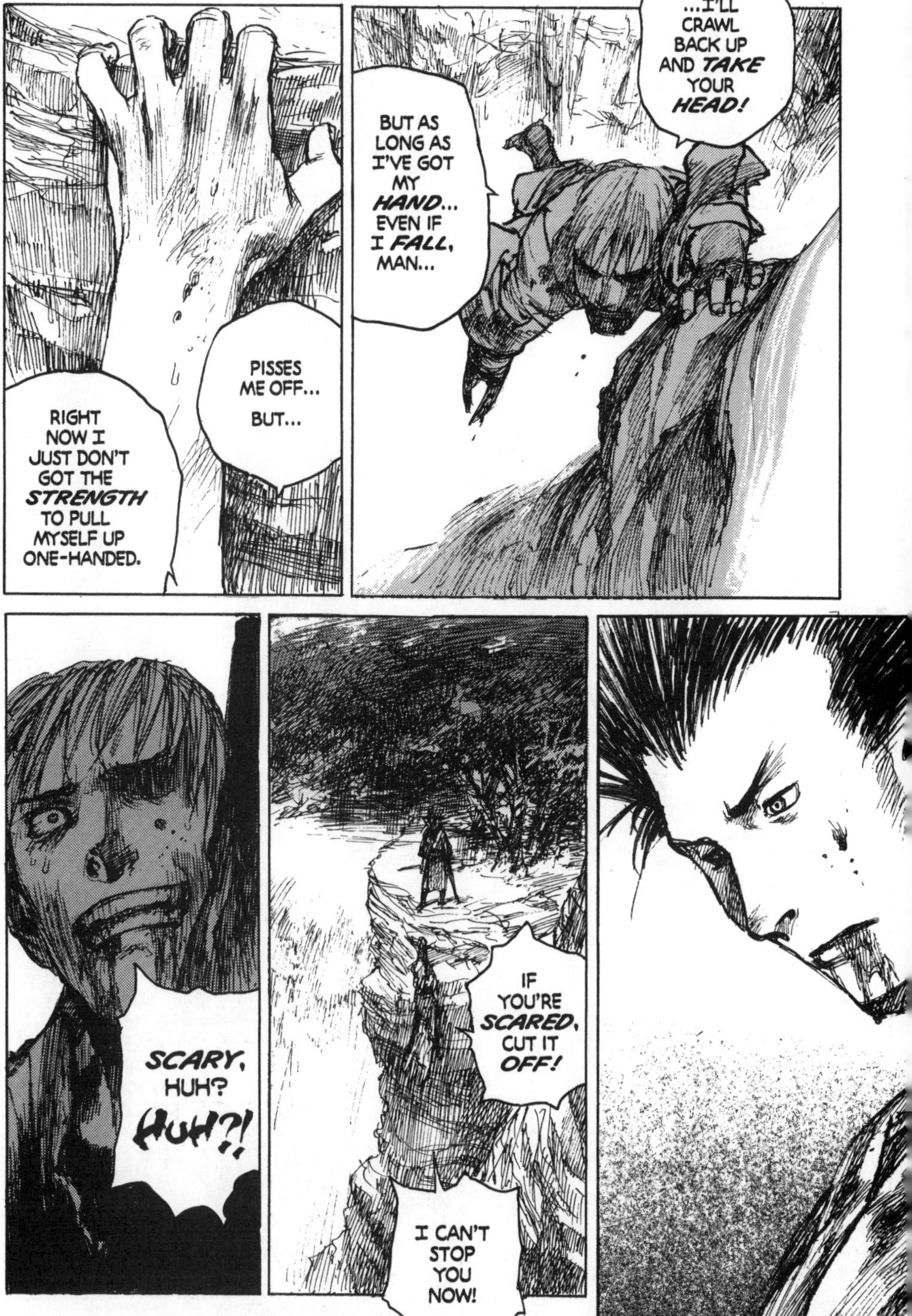
RIGHT NOW I JUST DON'T GOT THE STRENGTH TO PULL MYSELF UP ONE-HANDED.
PISSES ME OFF... BUT...
BUT AS LONG AS I'VE GOT MY HAND... EVEN IF I FALL, MAN...
...I'LL CRAWL BACK UP AND TAKE YOUR HEAD!
SCARY, HUH? HUH?!
IF YOU'RE SCARED, CUT IT OFF!
I CAN'T STOP YOU NOW!

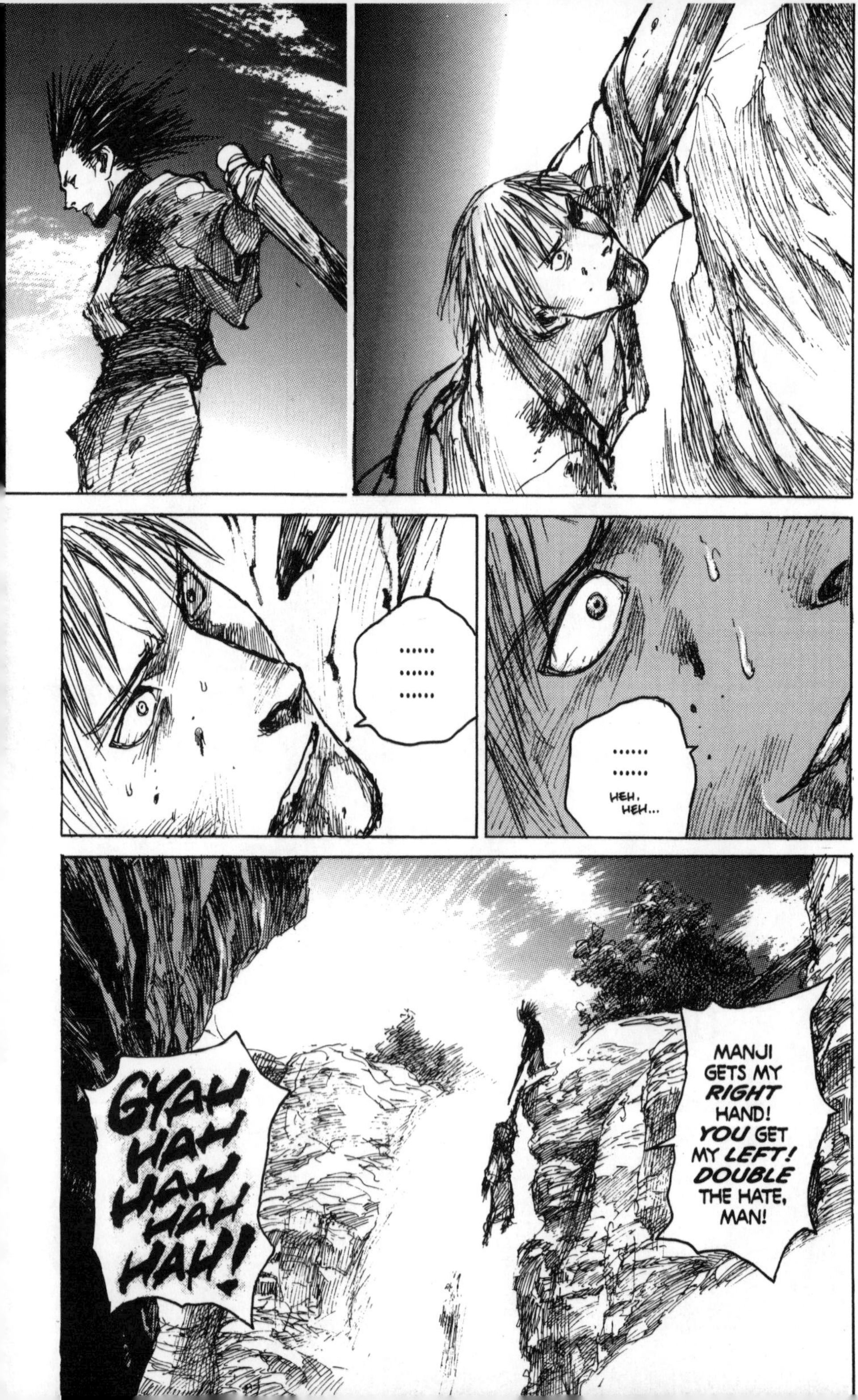
......
......
......
......
......
HEH, HEH...
GYAH HAH HAH HAH HAH!
MANJI GETS MY RIGHT HAND! YOU GET MY LEFT! DOUBLE THE HATE, MAN!

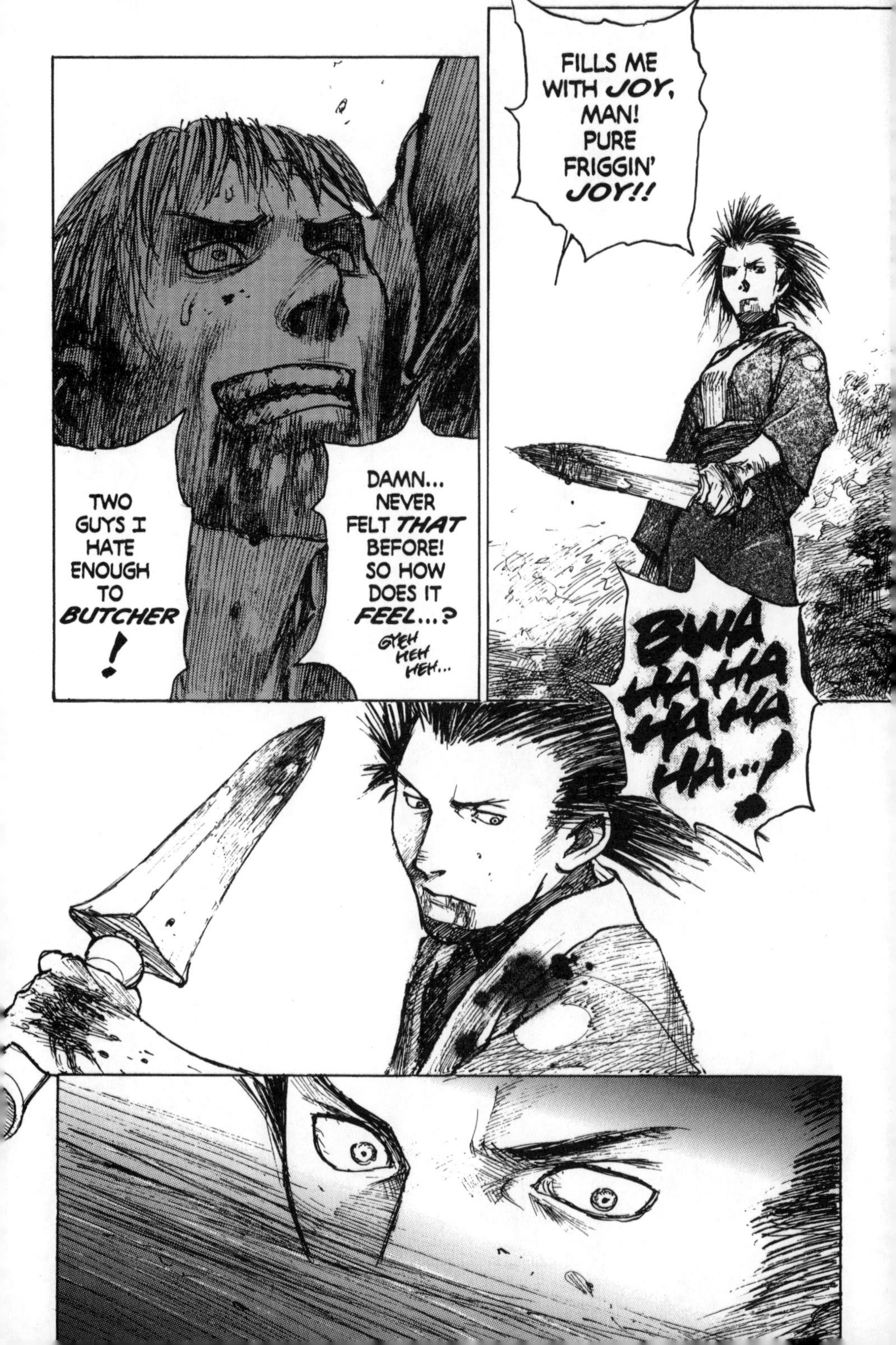
TWO GUYS I HATE ENOUGH TO *BUTCHER*!
DAMN... NEVER FELT *THAT* BEFORE! SO HOW DOES IT *FEEL*...?
GYEH HEH HEH...
FILLS ME WITH *JOY*, MAN! PURE FRIGGIN' *JOY!!*
BWA HA HA HA HA HA...!

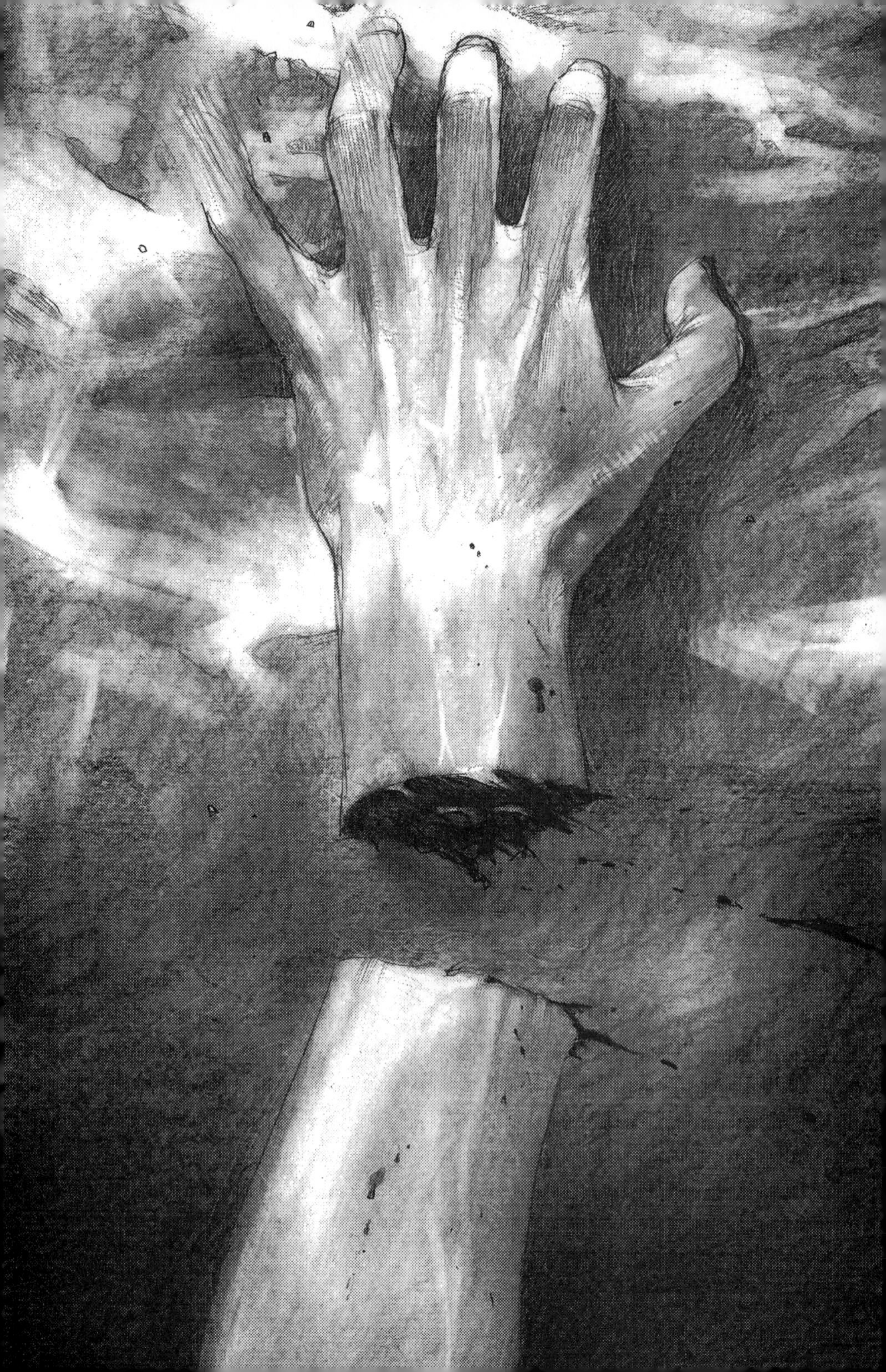

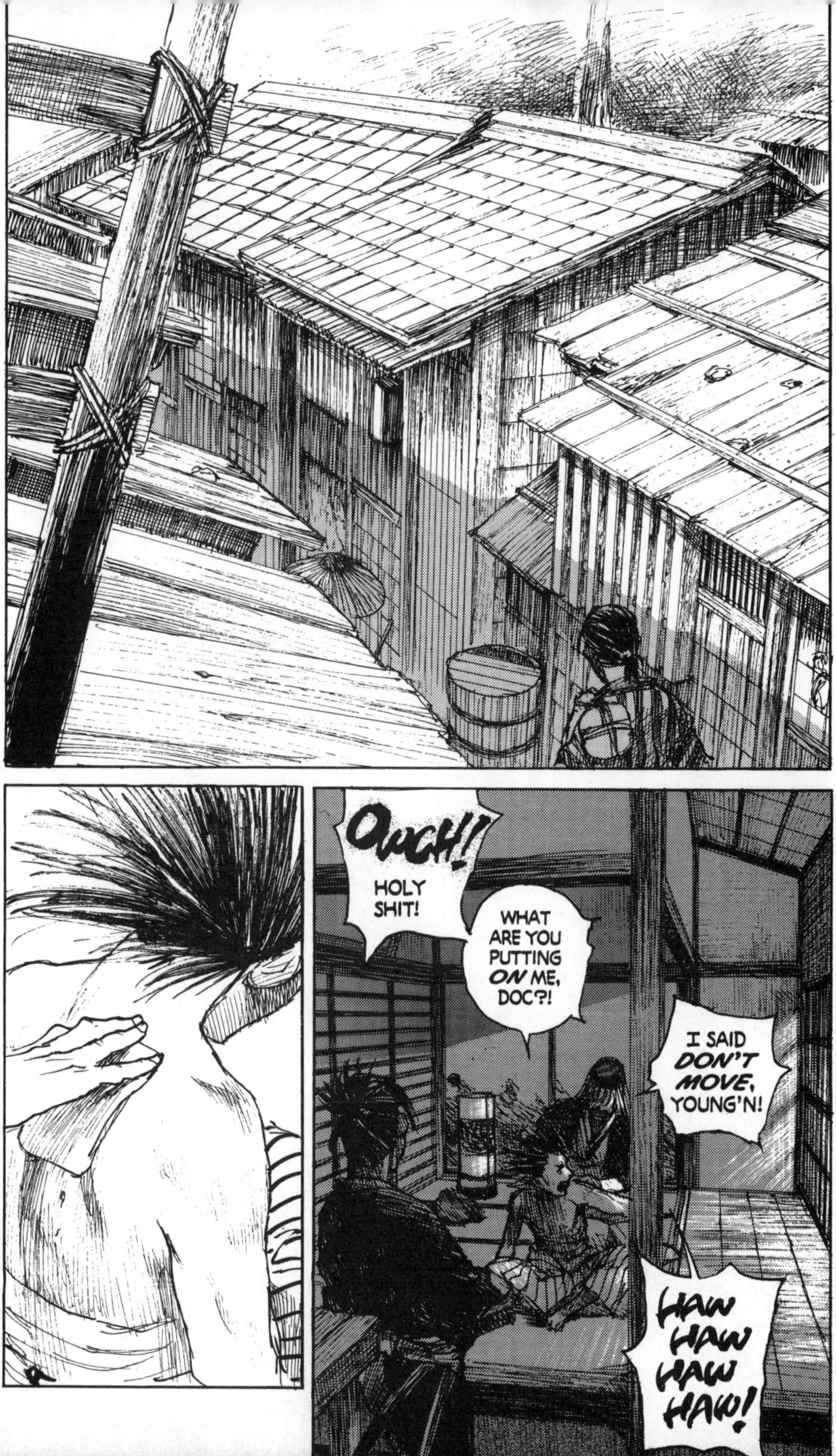
OUCH!
HOLY SHIT!
WHAT ARE YOU PUTTING ON ME, DOC?!
I SAID DON'T MOVE, YOUNG'N!
HAW HAW HAW HAW!

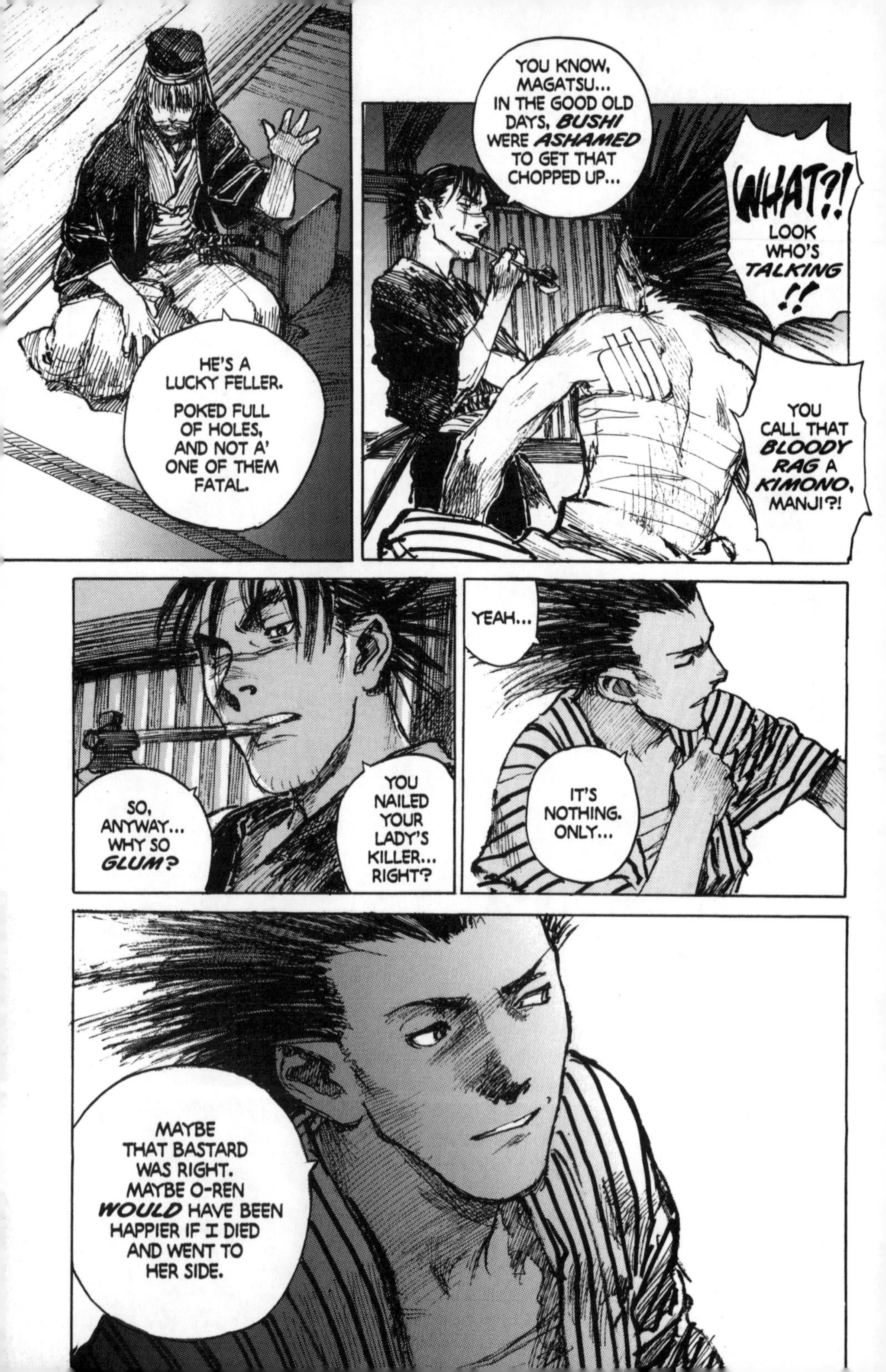
HE'S A LUCKY FELLER.
POKED FULL OF HOLES, AND NOT A' ONE OF THEM FATAL.
YOU KNOW, MAGATSU... IN THE GOOD OLD DAYS, *BUSHI* WERE *ASHAMED* TO GET THAT CHOPPED UP...
WHAT?!
LOOK WHO'S *TALKING* !!
YOU CALL THAT *BLOODY RAG* A *KIMONO*, MANJI?!
SO, ANYWAY... WHY SO *GLUM*?
YOU NAILED YOUR LADY'S KILLER... RIGHT?
YEAH...
IT'S NOTHING. ONLY...
MAYBE THAT BASTARD WAS RIGHT. MAYBE O-REN *WOULD* HAVE BEEN HAPPIER IF I DIED AND WENT TO HER SIDE.

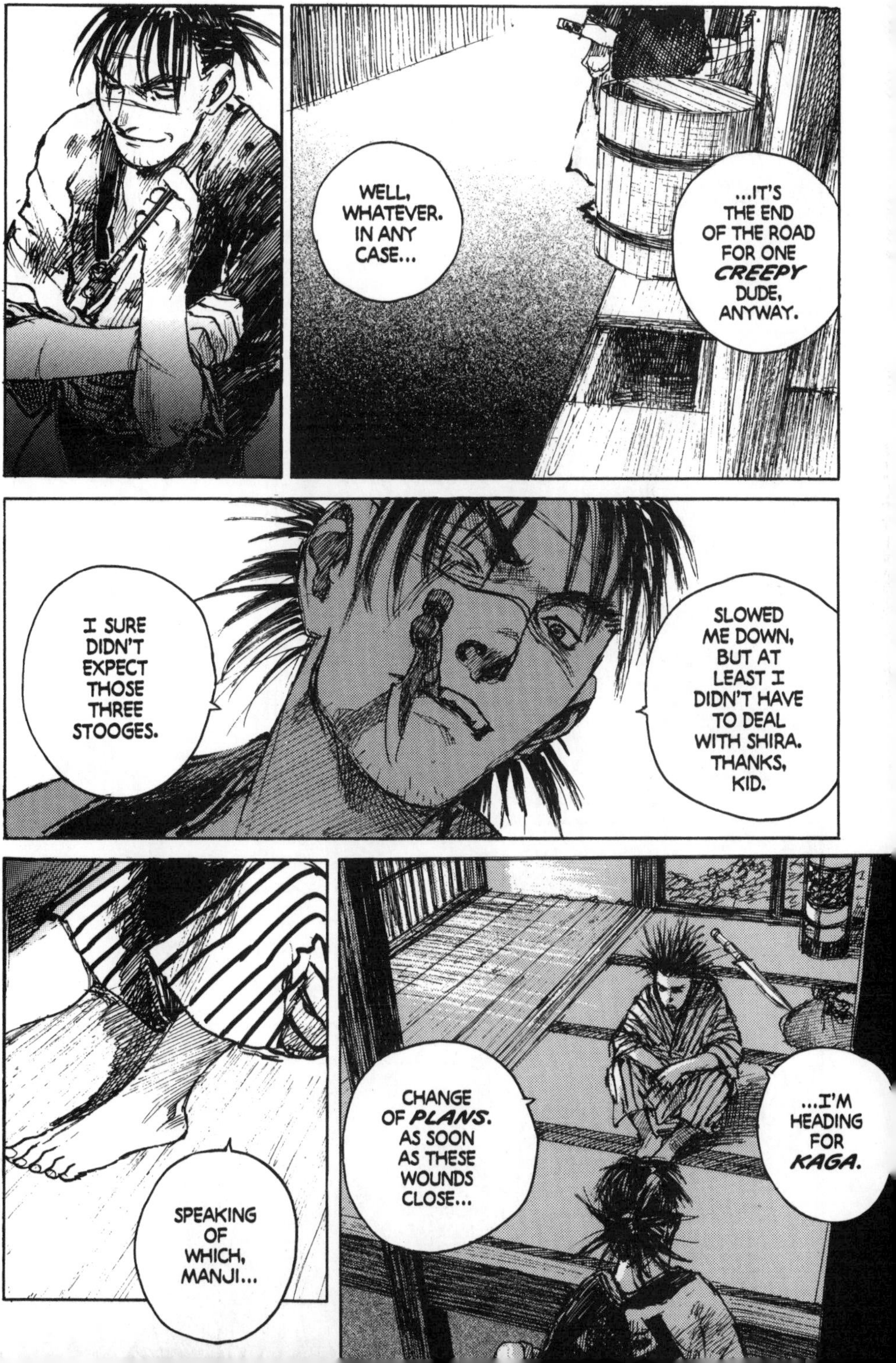
WELL, WHATEVER. IN ANY CASE...
...IT'S THE END OF THE ROAD FOR ONE *CREEPY* DUDE, ANYWAY.
I SURE DIDN'T EXPECT THOSE THREE STOOGES.
SLOWED ME DOWN, BUT AT LEAST I DIDN'T HAVE TO DEAL WITH SHIRA. THANKS, KID.
SPEAKING OF WHICH, MANJI...
CHANGE OF *PLANS*. AS SOON AS THESE WOUNDS CLOSE...
...I'M HEADING FOR *KAGA*.

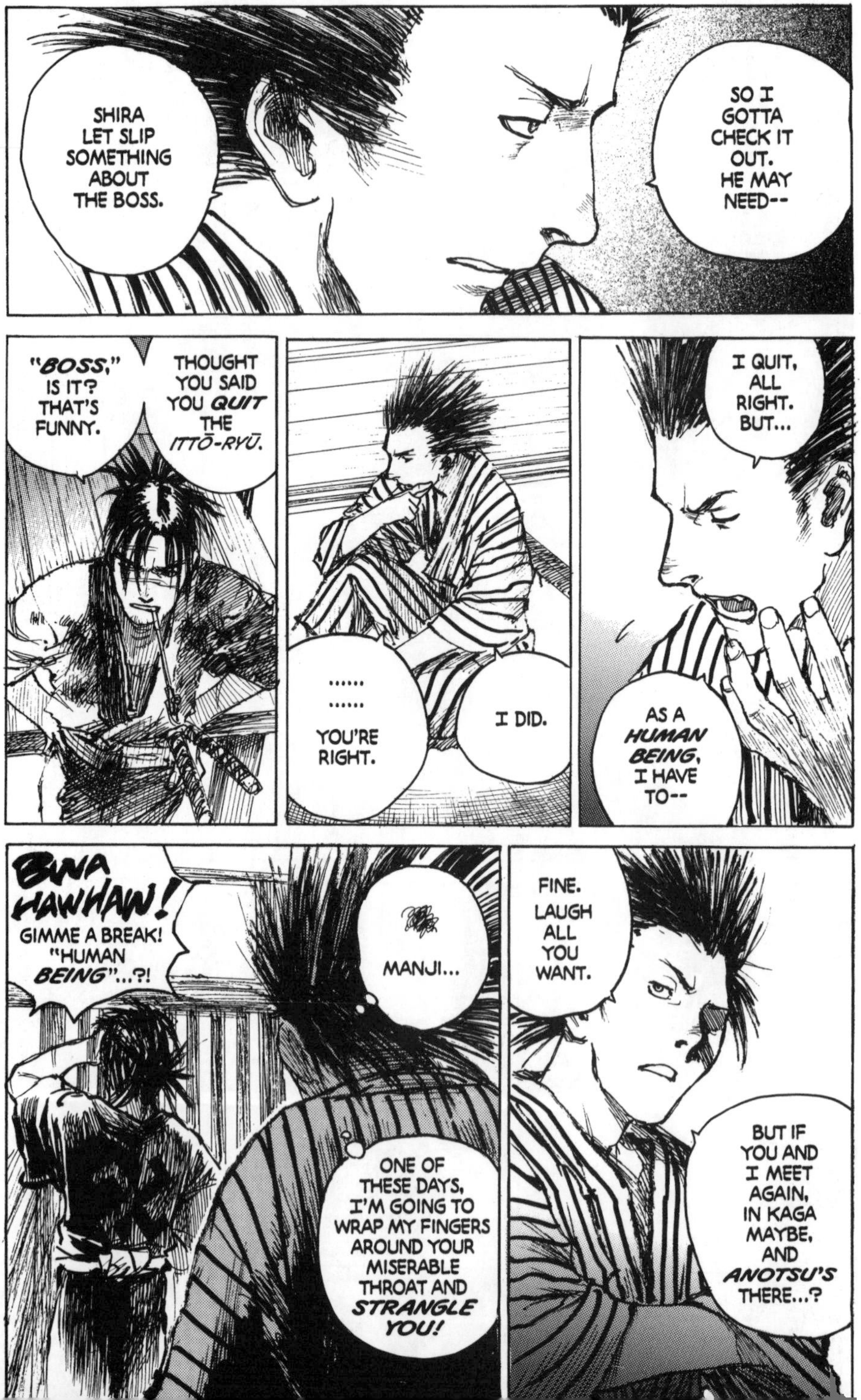
SHIRA LET SLIP SOMETHING ABOUT THE BOSS.
SO I GOTTA CHECK IT OUT. HE MAY NEED--
"BOSS," IS IT? THAT'S FUNNY.
THOUGHT YOU SAID YOU QUIT THE ITTŌ-RYŪ.
.... YOU'RE RIGHT.
I DID.
I QUIT, ALL RIGHT. BUT...
AS A HUMAN BEING, I HAVE TO--
BWA HAWHAW! GIMME A BREAK! "HUMAN BEING"...?!
MANJI...
ONE OF THESE DAYS, I'M GOING TO WRAP MY FINGERS AROUND YOUR MISERABLE THROAT AND STRANGLE YOU!
FINE. LAUGH ALL YOU WANT.
BUT IF YOU AND I MEET AGAIN, IN KAGA MAYBE, AND ANOTSU'S THERE...?

I'LL PROBABLY SIDE WITH HIM.

SO JUST REMEMBER THAT, OKAY?

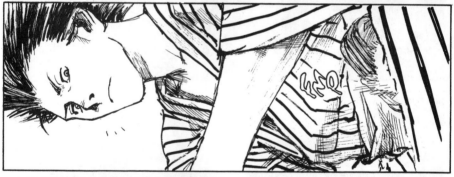

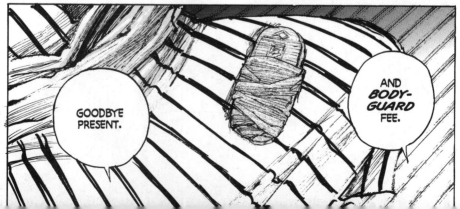

GOODBYE PRESENT.

AND *BODY-GUARD* FEE.

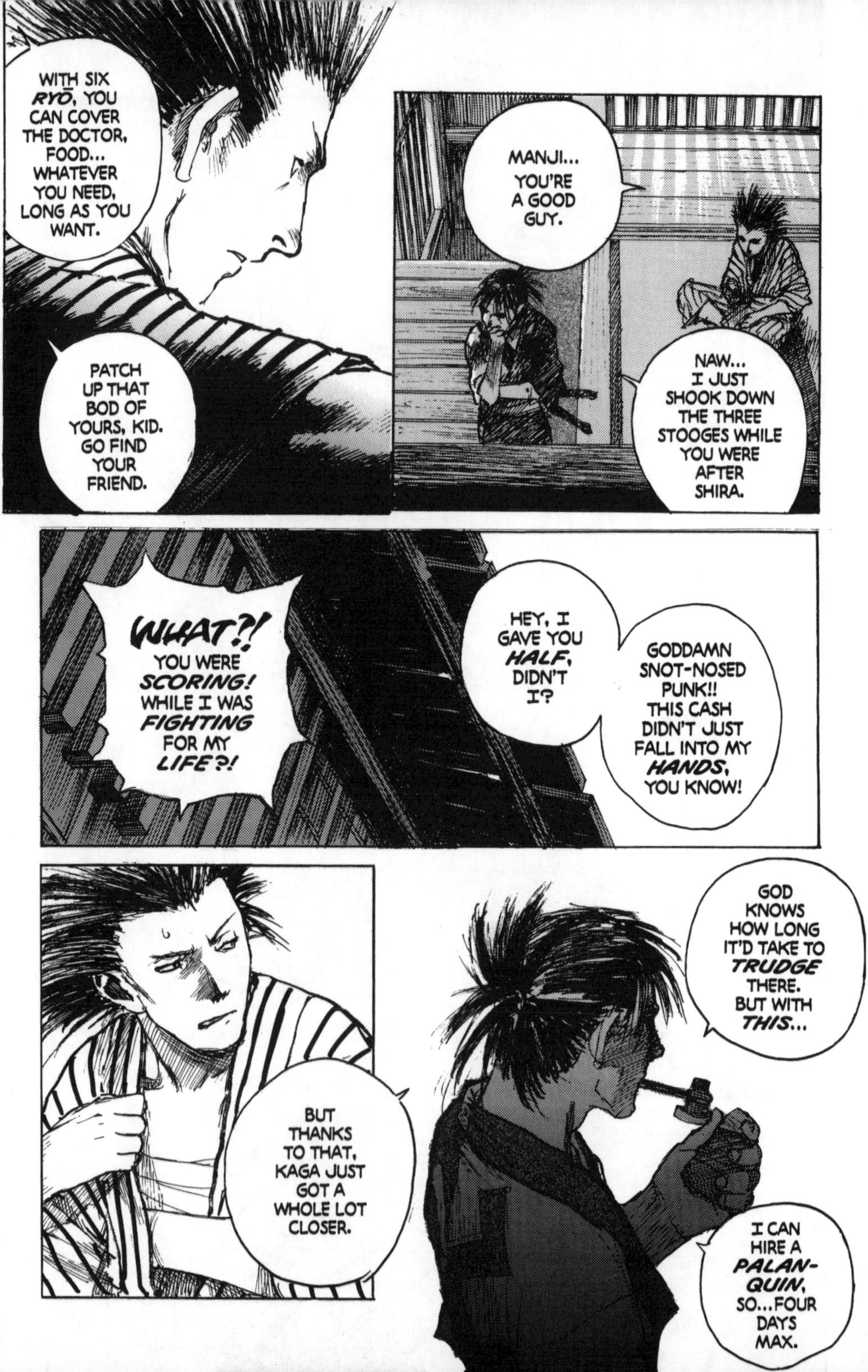
WITH SIX *RYŌ*, YOU CAN COVER THE DOCTOR, FOOD... WHATEVER YOU NEED, LONG AS YOU WANT.
PATCH UP THAT BOD OF YOURS, KID. GO FIND YOUR FRIEND.
MANJI... YOU'RE A GOOD GUY.
NAW... I JUST SHOOK DOWN THE THREE STOOGES WHILE YOU WERE AFTER SHIRA.
WHAT?! YOU WERE *SCORING!* WHILE I WAS *FIGHTING* FOR MY *LIFE?!*
HEY, I GAVE YOU *HALF*, DIDN'T I?
GODDAMN SNOT-NOSED PUNK!! THIS CASH DIDN'T JUST FALL INTO MY *HANDS*, YOU KNOW!
BUT THANKS TO THAT, KAGA JUST GOT A WHOLE LOT CLOSER.
GOD KNOWS HOW LONG IT'D TAKE TO *TRUDGE* THERE. BUT WITH *THIS*...
I CAN HIRE A *PALAN-QUIN*, SO...FOUR DAYS MAX.

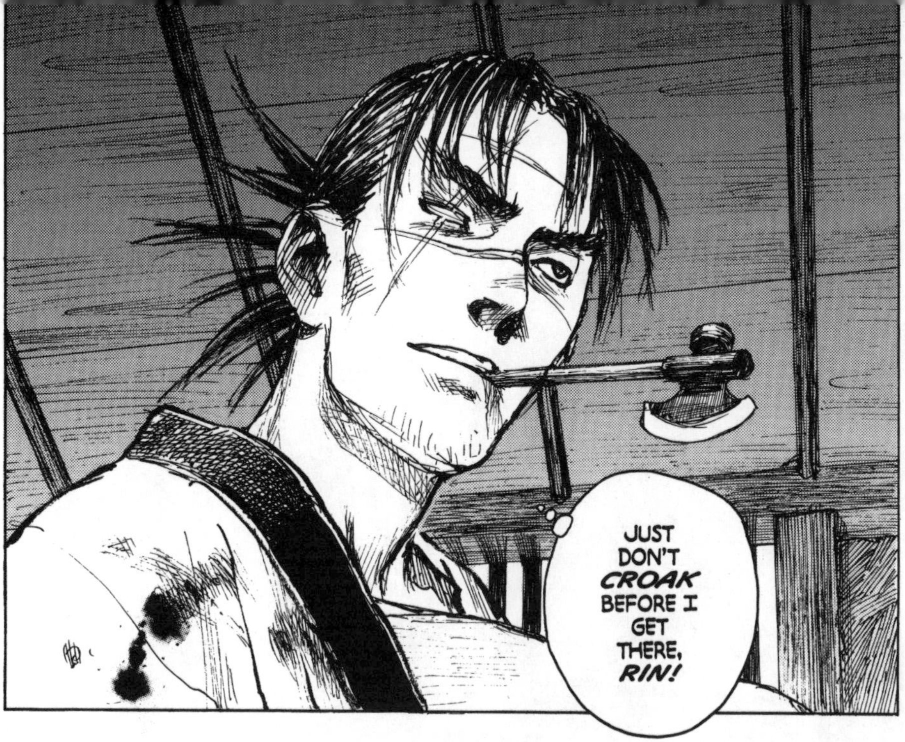
JUST DON'T *CROAK* BEFORE I GET THERE, *RIN!*

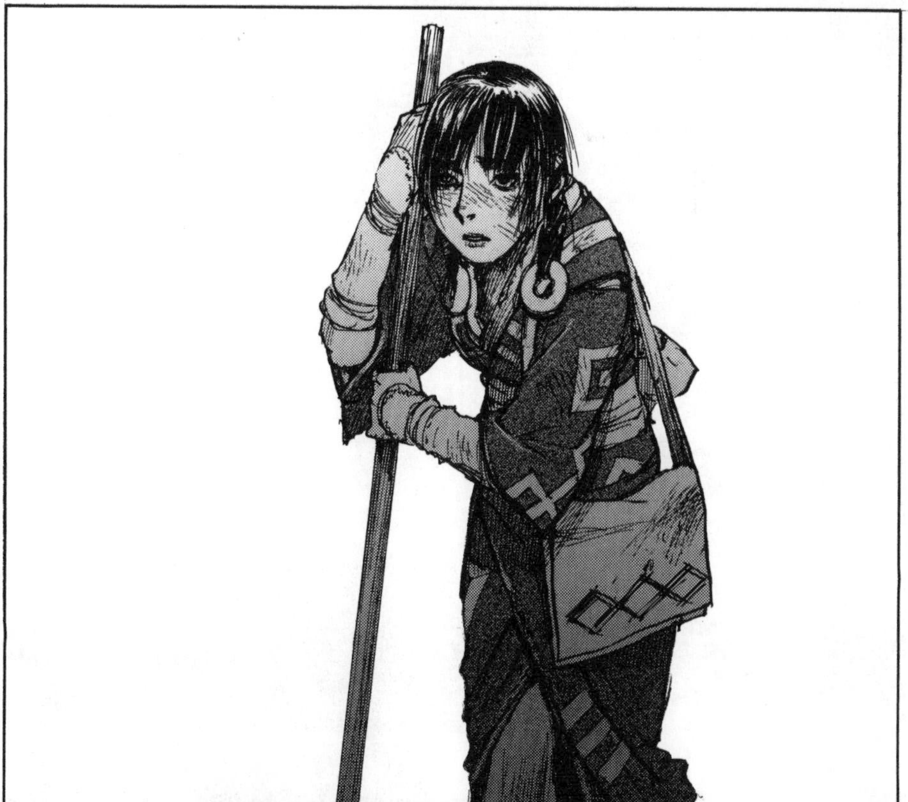

THREE...? FOUR...?

HOW MANY DAYS SINCE I ATE...?

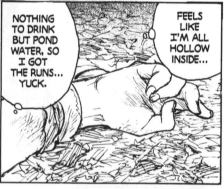

NOTHING TO DRINK BUT POND WATER, SO I GOT THE RUNS... YUCK.

FEELS LIKE I'M ALL HOLLOW INSIDE...

AND WHERE *AM* I? I THINK I'M LOST...

AM I EVEN HEADED TOWARDS KAGA ANY MORE...?

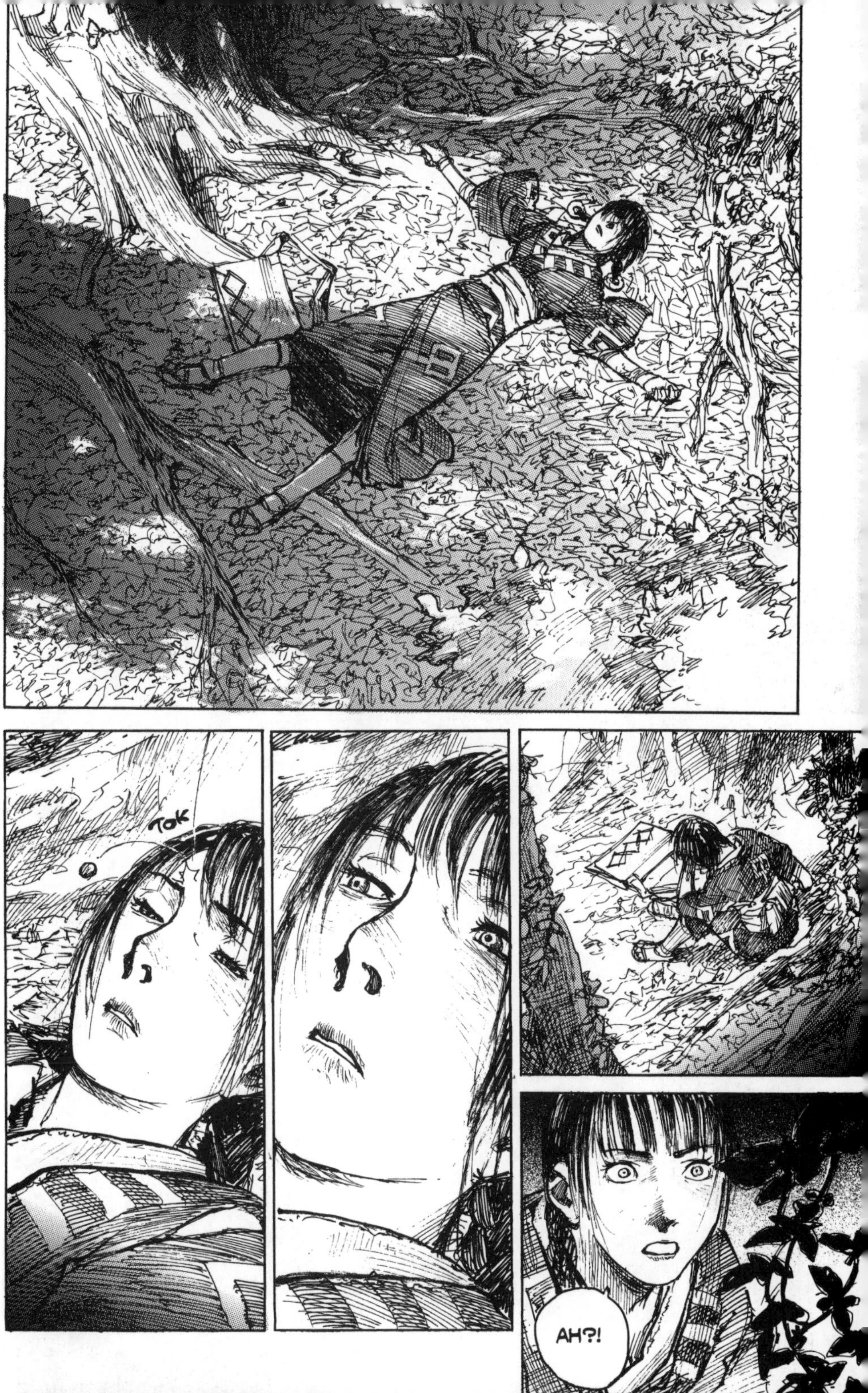
TOK
AH?!

IT'S *MUKAGO*... YOU CAN *EAT* THAT!

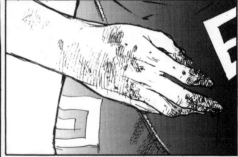

NNGG...
......

......
HHGG!

SHICH

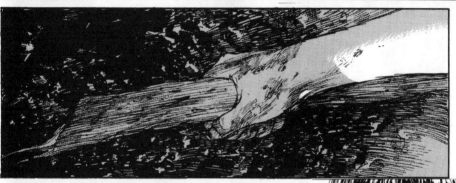

:hahh: :hff:

:hahh:

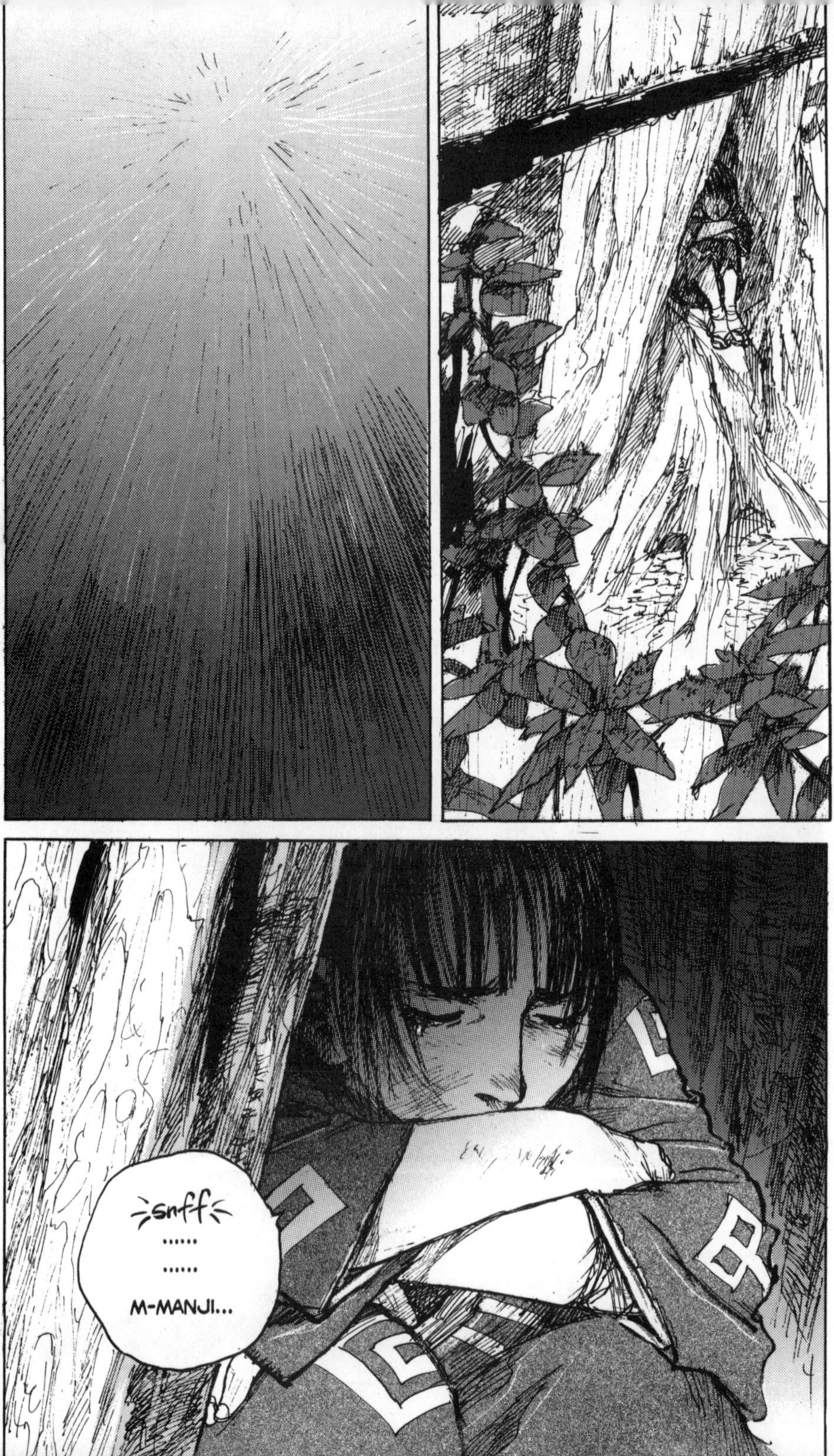
snff
......
......
M-MANJI...

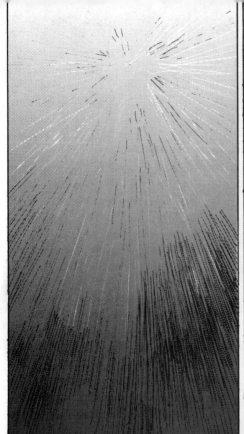

THE WIND AND THE HERON

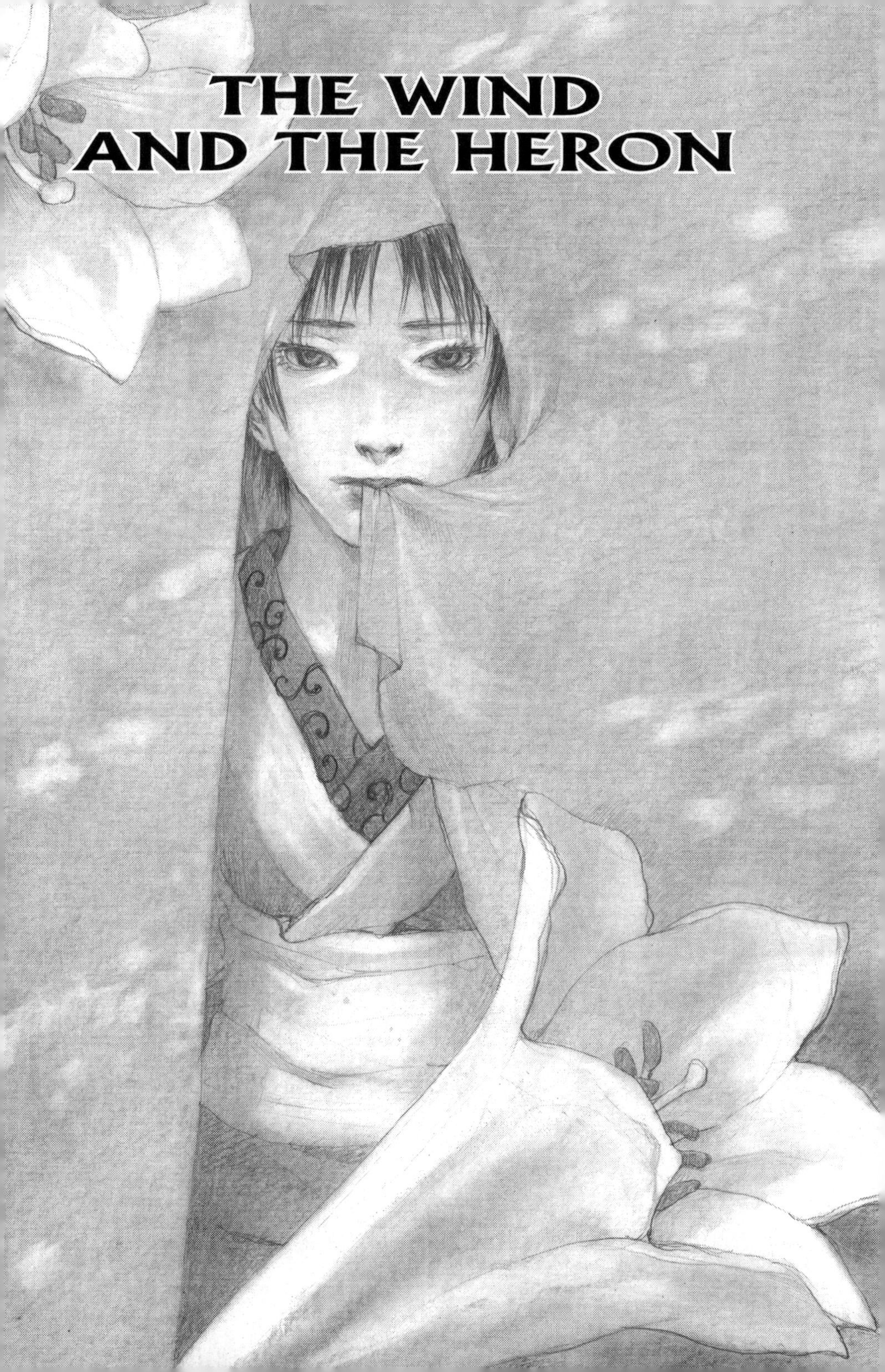

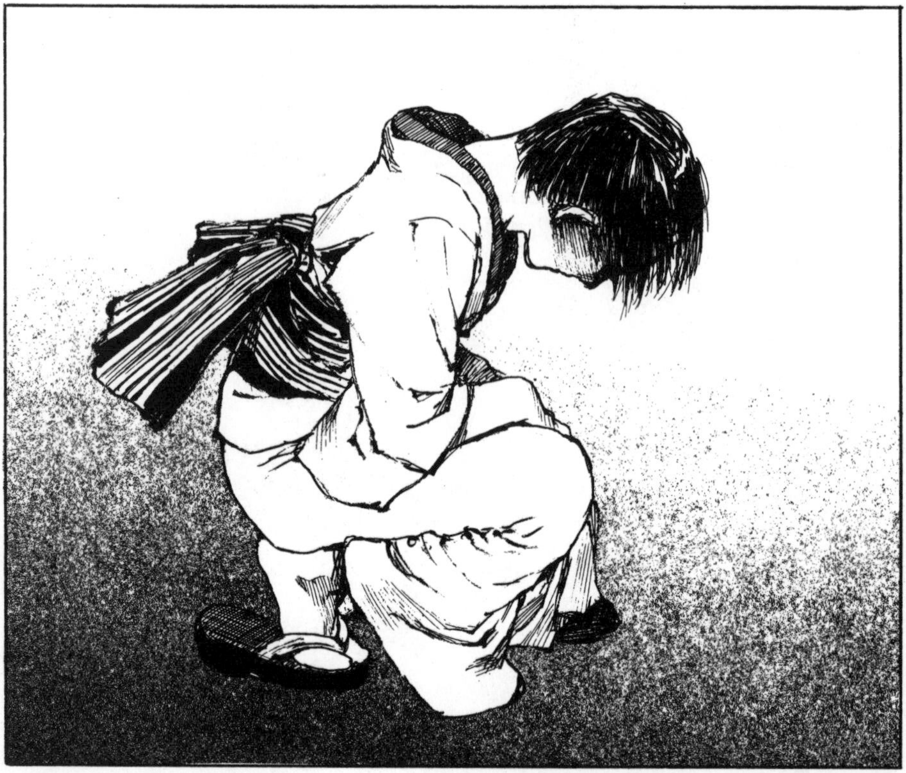

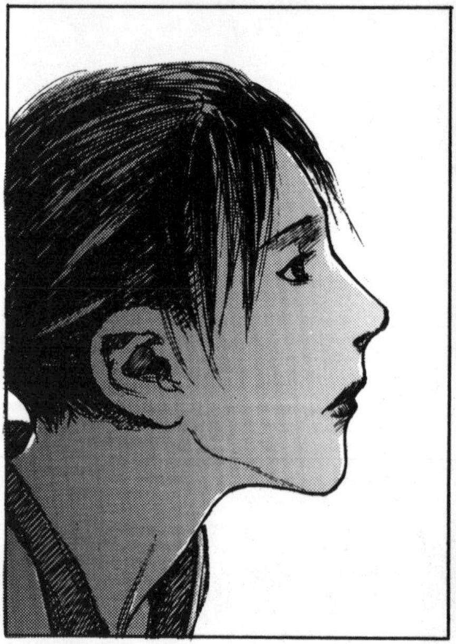

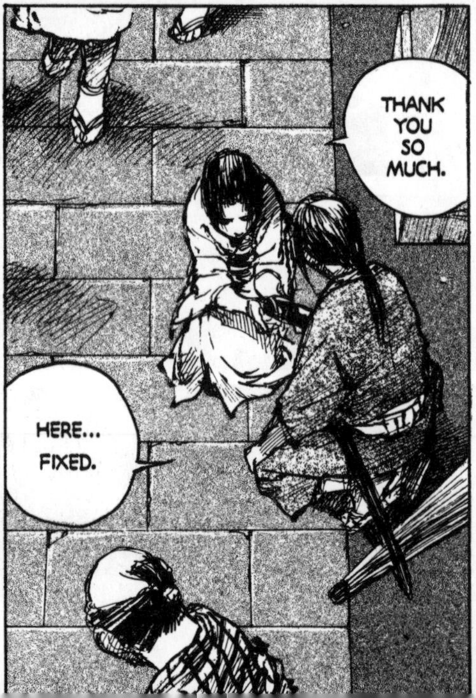
THANK YOU SO MUCH.
HERE... FIXED.

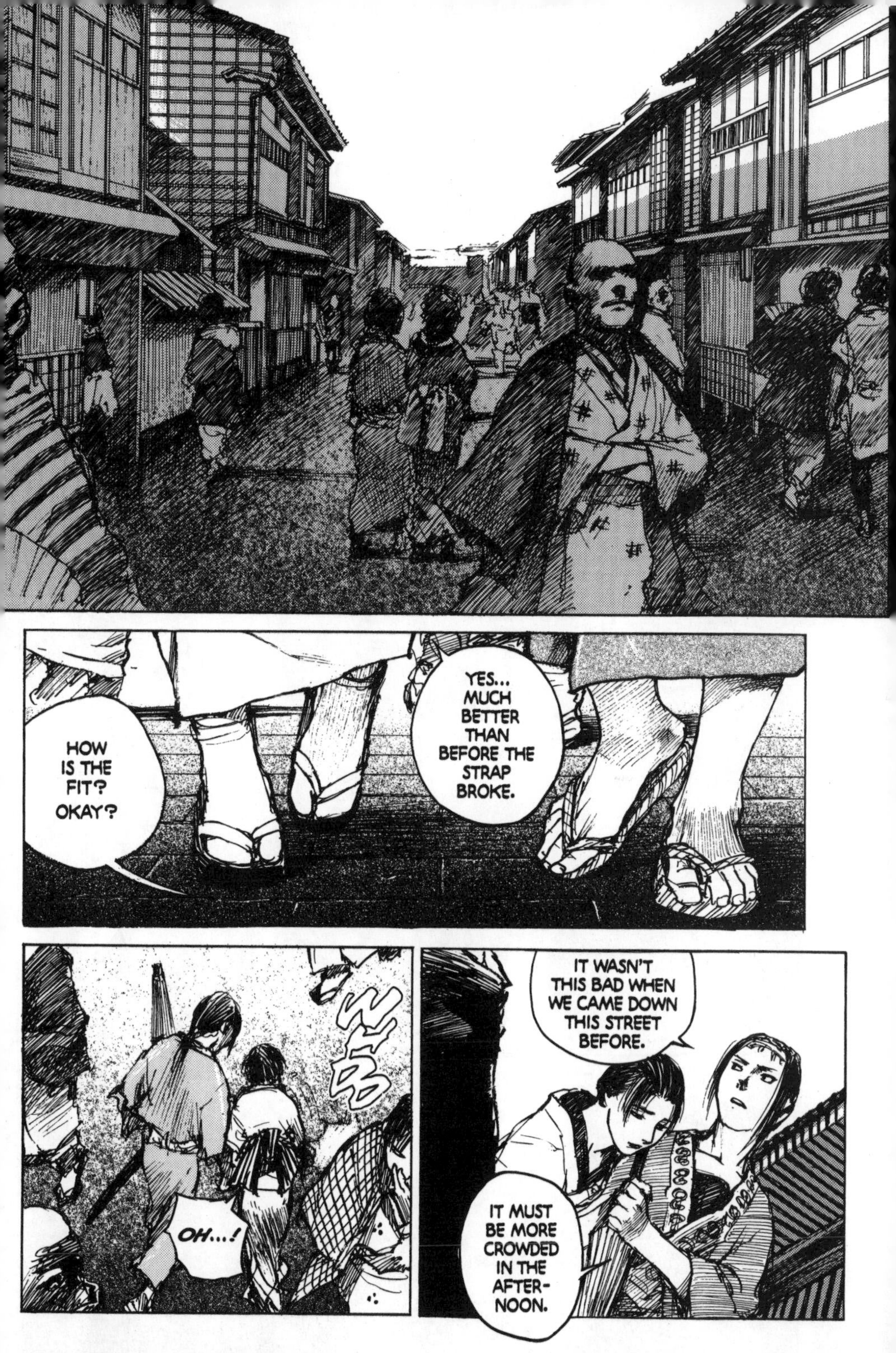
HOW IS THE FIT? OKAY?
YES... MUCH BETTER THAN BEFORE THE STRAP BROKE.
OH...!
IT WASN'T THIS BAD WHEN WE CAME DOWN THIS STREET BEFORE.
IT MUST BE MORE CROWDED IN THE AFTER-NOON.

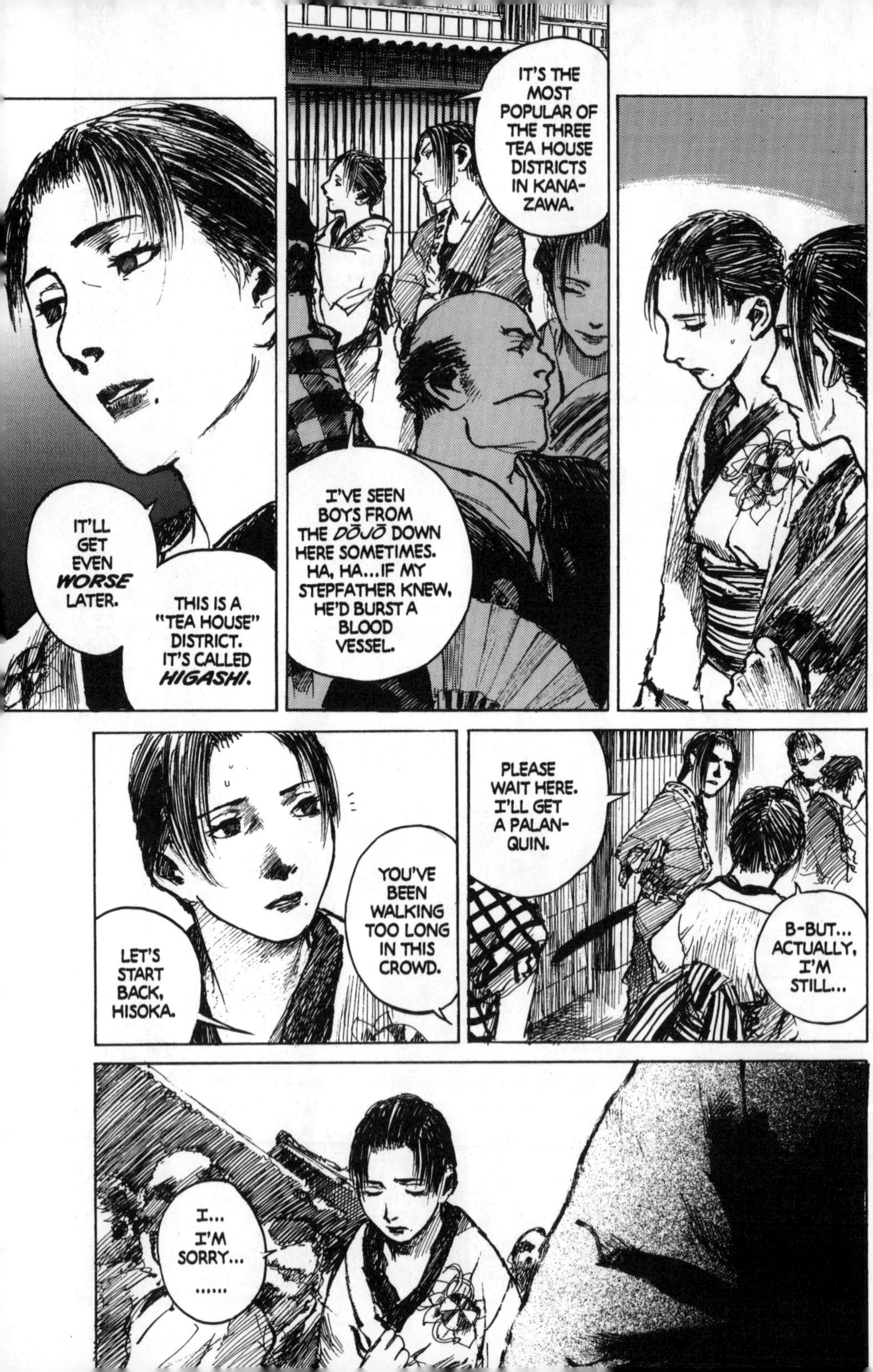

IT'LL GET EVEN *WORSE* LATER.
THIS IS A "TEA HOUSE" DISTRICT. IT'S CALLED *HIGASHI*.
IT'S THE MOST POPULAR OF THE THREE TEA HOUSE DISTRICTS IN KANA-ZAWA.
I'VE SEEN BOYS FROM THE *DŌJŌ* DOWN HERE SOMETIMES. HA, HA...IF MY STEPFATHER KNEW, HE'D BURST A BLOOD VESSEL.
YOU'VE BEEN WALKING TOO LONG IN THIS CROWD.
LET'S START BACK, HISOKA.
PLEASE WAIT HERE. I'LL GET A PALAN-QUIN.
B-BUT... ACTUALLY, I'M STILL...
I... I'M SORRY... ......

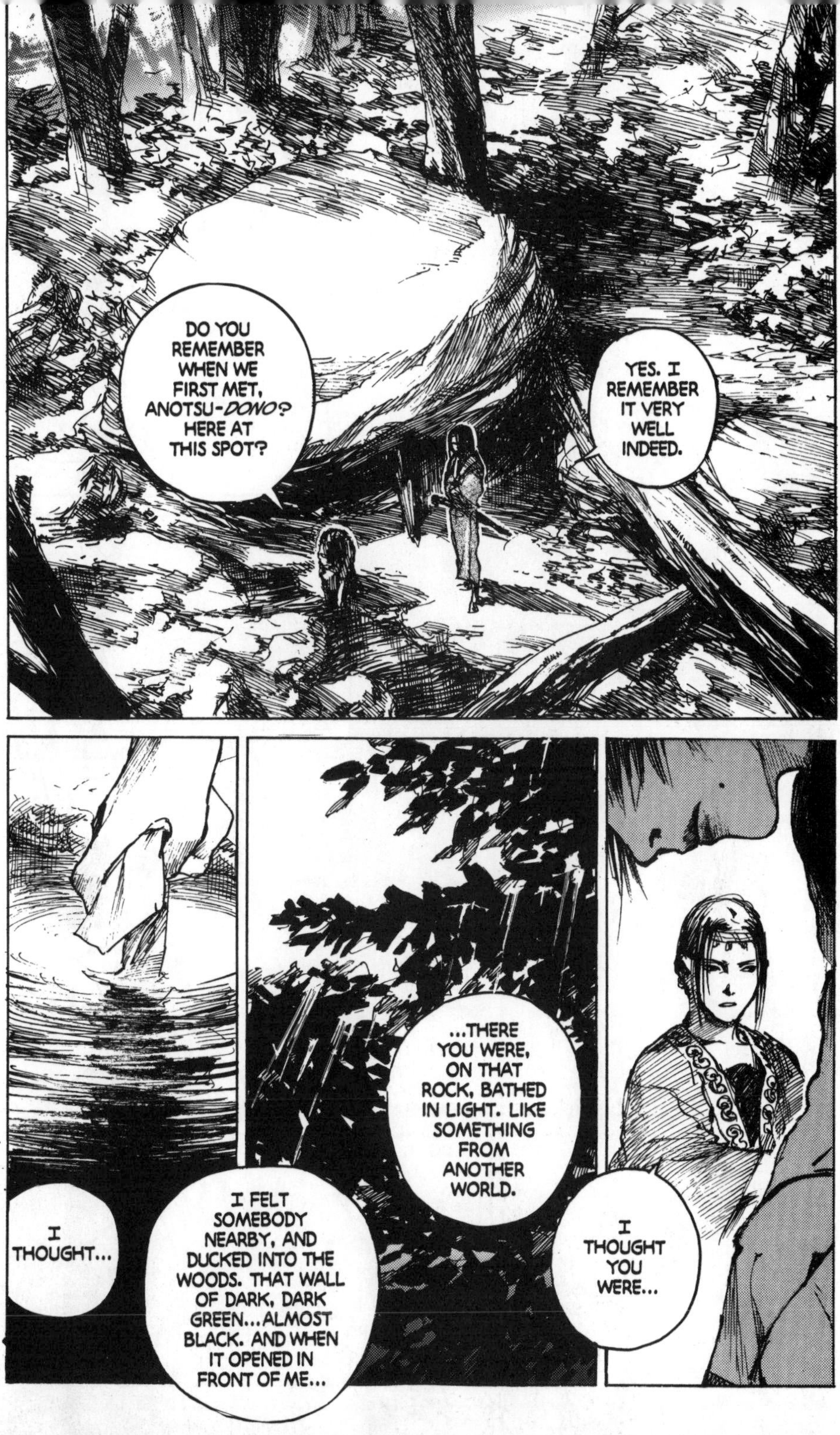
DO YOU REMEMBER WHEN WE FIRST MET, ANOTSU-*DONO*? HERE AT THIS SPOT?
YES. I REMEMBER IT VERY WELL INDEED.
I THOUGHT...
I FELT SOMEBODY NEARBY, AND DUCKED INTO THE WOODS. THAT WALL OF DARK, DARK GREEN...ALMOST BLACK. AND WHEN IT OPENED IN FRONT OF ME...
...THERE YOU WERE, ON THAT ROCK, BATHED IN LIGHT. LIKE SOMETHING FROM ANOTHER WORLD.
I THOUGHT YOU WERE...

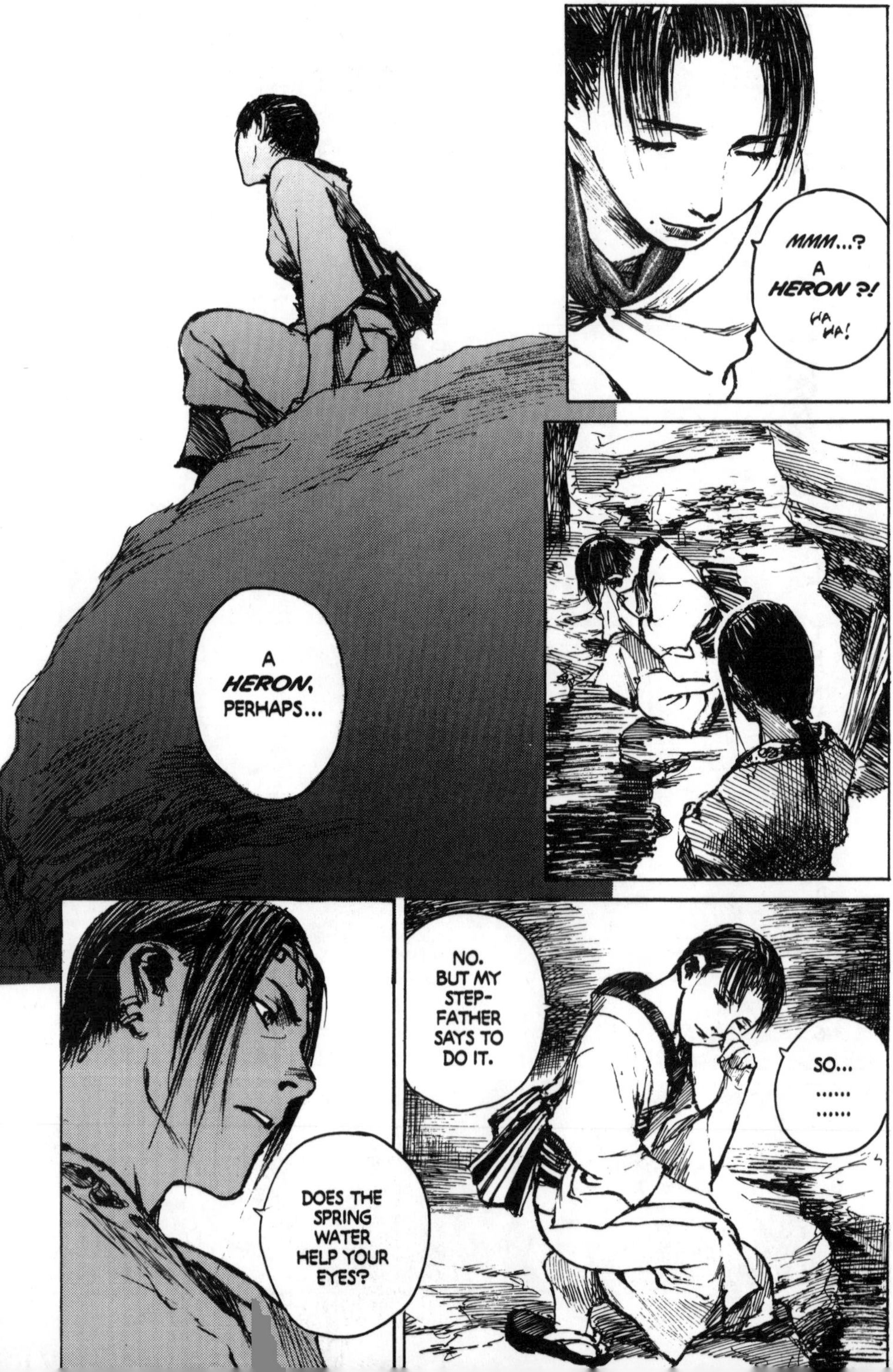
A HERON, PERHAPS...
MMM...? A HERON ?!
HA HA!
DOES THE SPRING WATER HELP YOUR EYES?
NO. BUT MY STEP-FATHER SAYS TO DO IT.
SO... ....

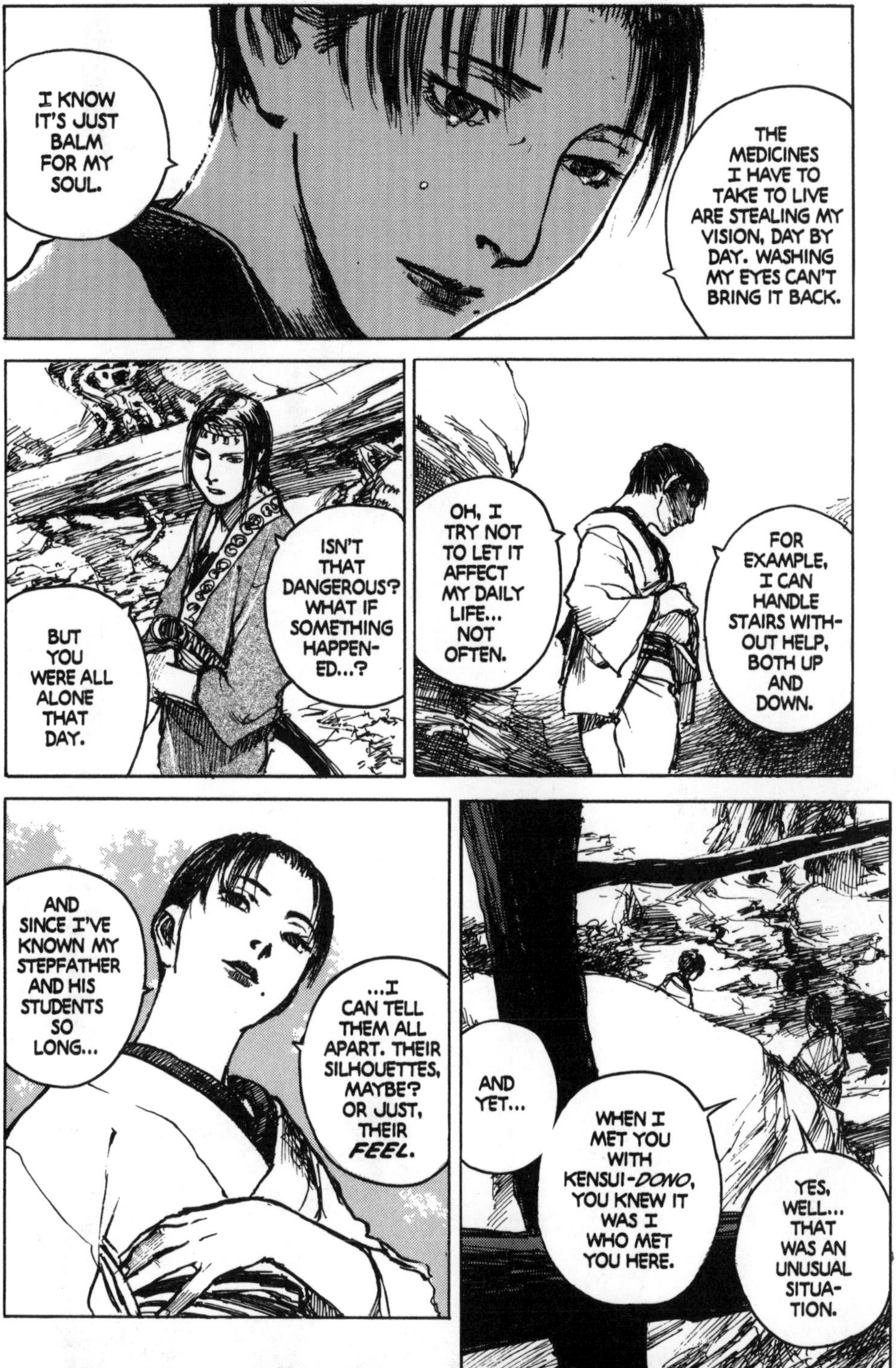
I KNOW IT'S JUST BALM FOR MY SOUL.
THE MEDICINES I HAVE TO TAKE TO LIVE ARE STEALING MY VISION, DAY BY DAY. WASHING MY EYES CAN'T BRING IT BACK.
ISN'T THAT DANGEROUS? WHAT IF SOMETHING HAPPEN-ED...?
BUT YOU WERE ALL ALONE THAT DAY.
OH, I TRY NOT TO LET IT AFFECT MY DAILY LIFE... NOT OFTEN.
FOR EXAMPLE, I CAN HANDLE STAIRS WITH-OUT HELP, BOTH UP AND DOWN.
AND SINCE I'VE KNOWN MY STEPFATHER AND HIS STUDENTS SO LONG...
...I CAN TELL THEM ALL APART. THEIR SILHOUETTES, MAYBE? OR JUST, THEIR *FEEL*.
AND YET...
WHEN I MET YOU WITH KENSUI-*DONO*, YOU KNEW IT WAS I WHO MET YOU HERE.
YES, WELL... THAT WAS AN UNUSUAL SITUA-TION.

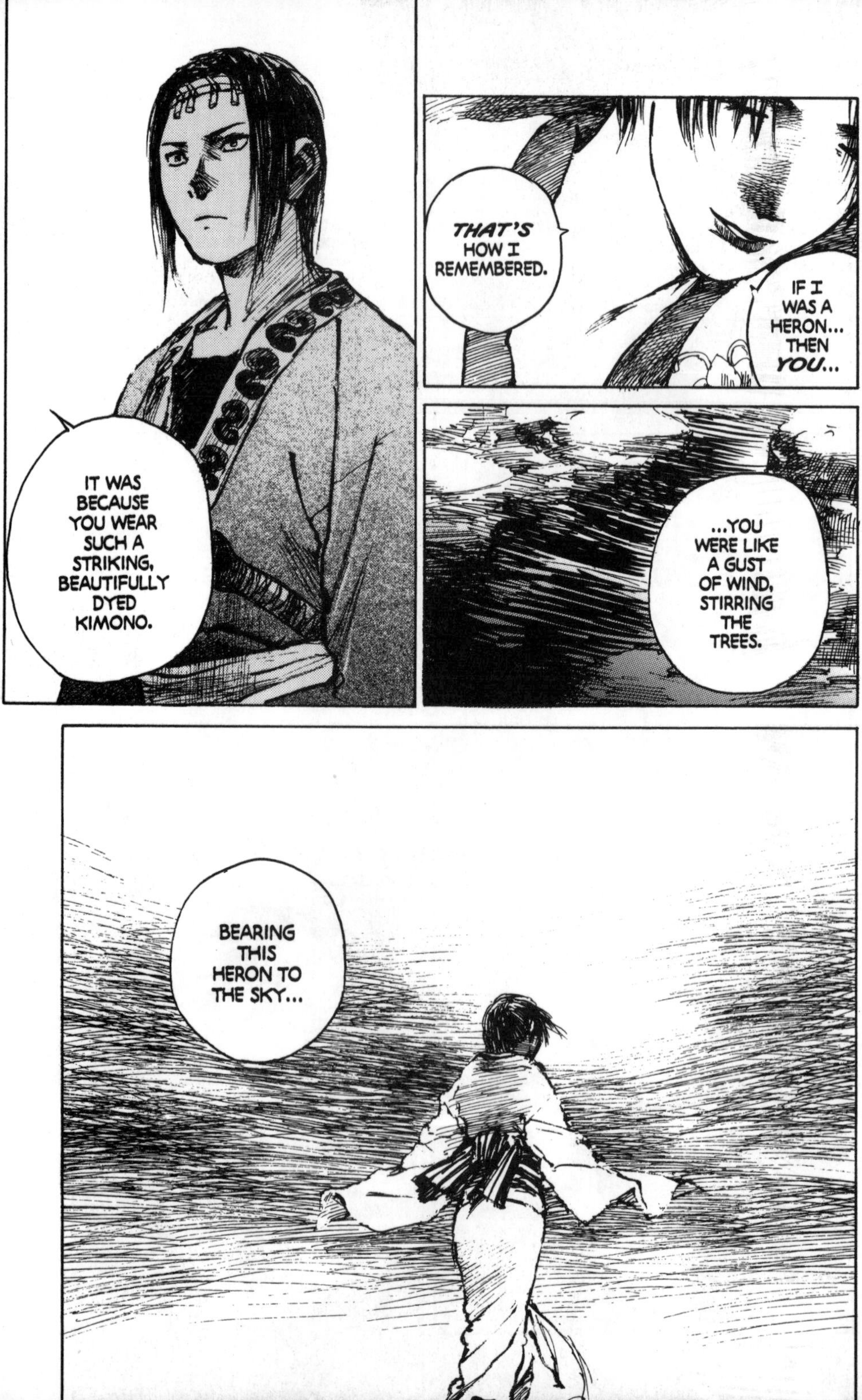
IT WAS BECAUSE YOU WEAR SUCH A STRIKING, BEAUTIFULLY DYED KIMONO.
THAT'S HOW I REMEMBERED.
IF I WAS A HERON... THEN *YOU*...
...YOU WERE LIKE A GUST OF WIND, STIRRING THE TREES.
BEARING THIS HERON TO THE SKY...

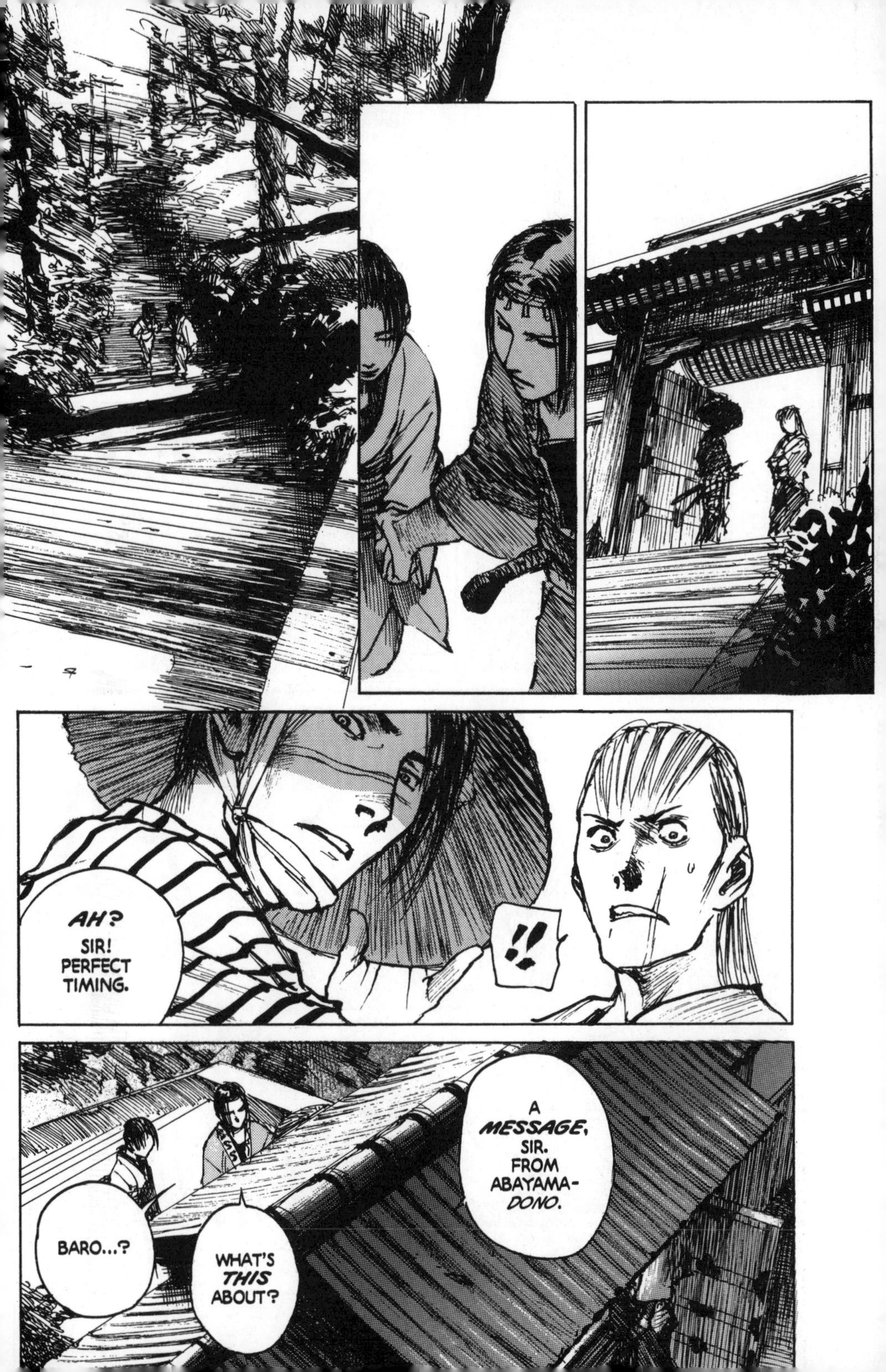
AH? SIR! PERFECT TIMING.
!!
A MESSAGE, SIR. FROM ABAYAMA-DONO.
BARO...?
WHAT'S THIS ABOUT?

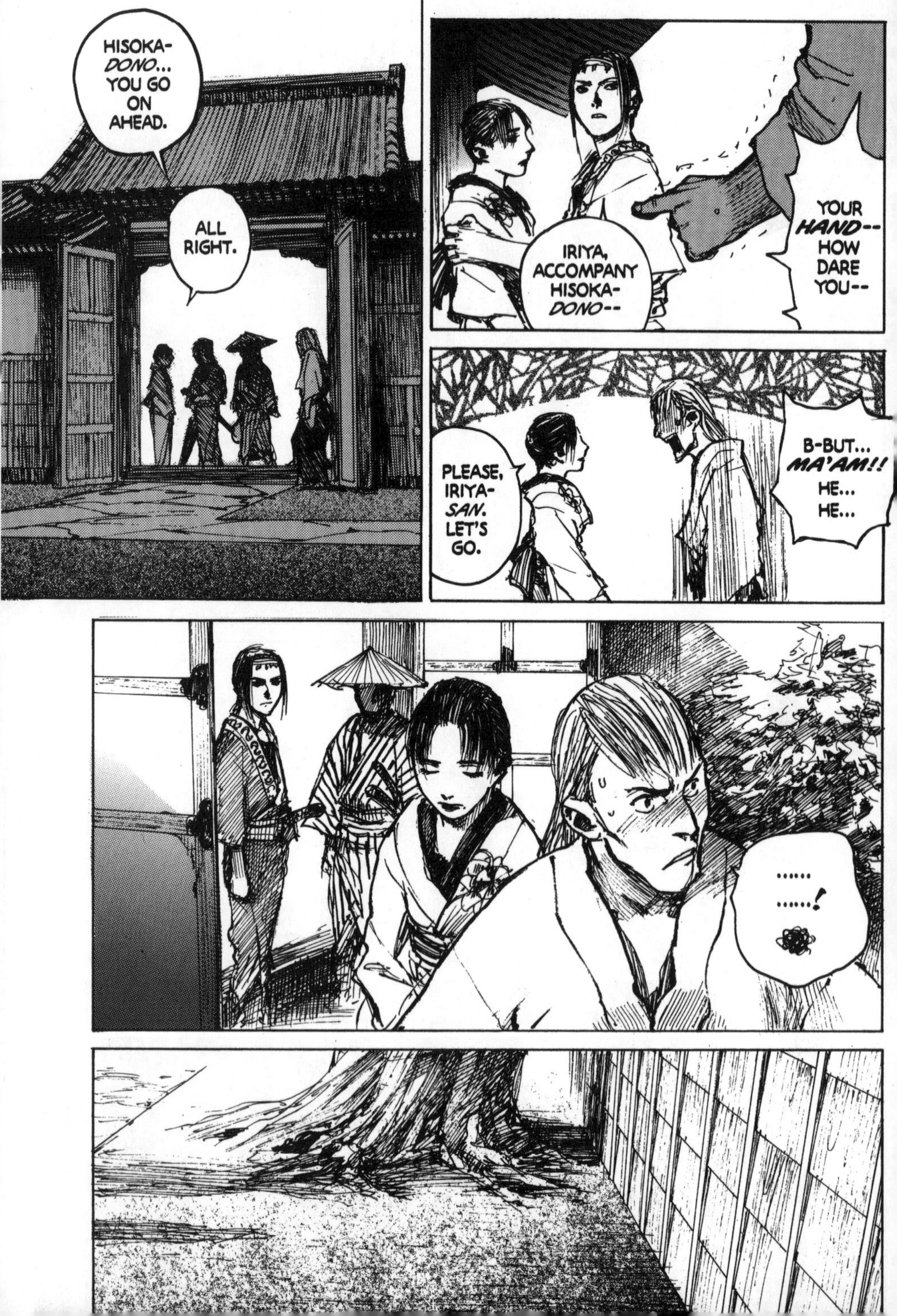
HISOKA-DONO... YOU GO ON AHEAD.
ALL RIGHT.
IRIYA, ACCOMPANY HISOKA-DONO--
YOUR HAND-- HOW DARE YOU--
PLEASE, IRIYA-SAN. LET'S GO.
B-BUT... MA'AM!! HE... HE...
....!

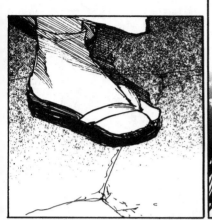

IRIYA...? CAN YOU STOP FOR A MOMENT?

Y-YES, MA'AM!

AH?! M-MA'AM...?

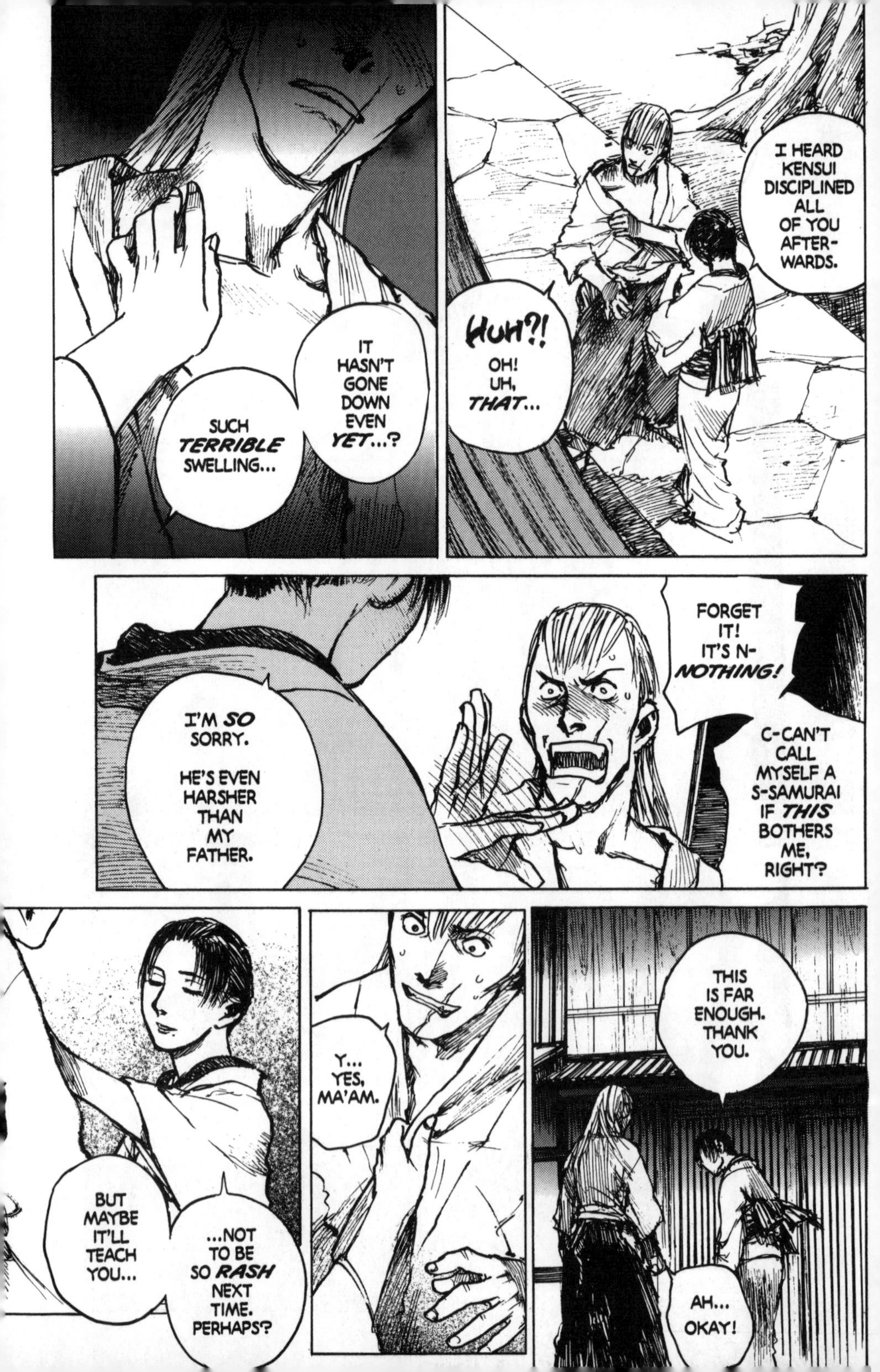
SUCH TERRIBLE SWELLING...
IT HASN'T GONE DOWN EVEN YET...?
I HEARD KENSUI DISCIPLINED ALL OF YOU AFTER-WARDS.
HUH?!
OH! UH, THAT...
I'M SO SORRY.
HE'S EVEN HARSHER THAN MY FATHER.
FORGET IT! IT'S N-NOTHING!
C-CAN'T CALL MYSELF A S-SAMURAI IF THIS BOTHERS ME, RIGHT?
BUT MAYBE IT'LL TEACH YOU...
...NOT TO BE SO RASH NEXT TIME. PERHAPS?
Y... YES, MA'AM.
THIS IS FAR ENOUGH. THANK YOU.
AH... OKAY!

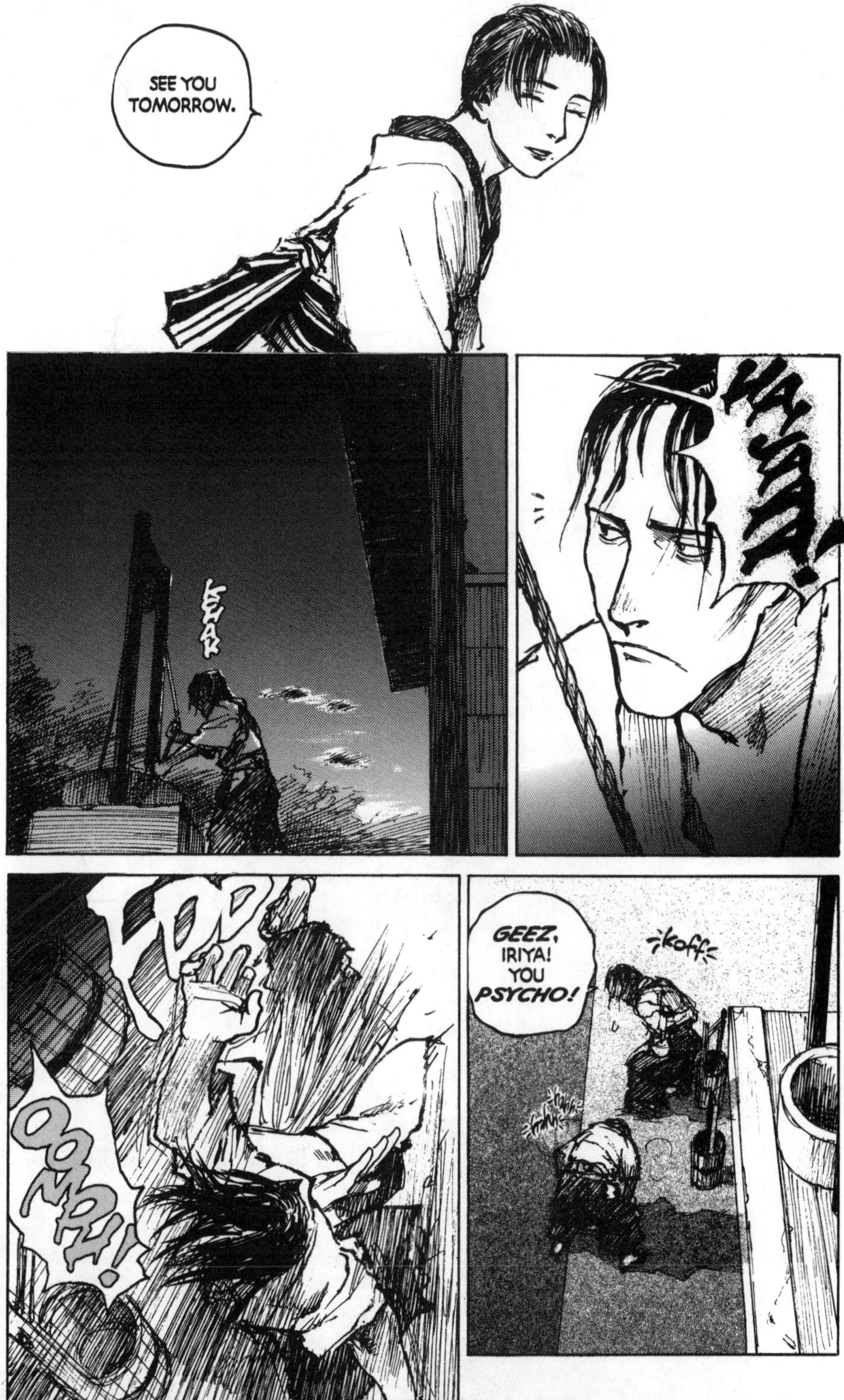
SEE YOU TOMORROW.
KCHAK
OOMPH!
GEEZ, IRIYA! YOU PSYCHO!
koff
hahh hahh

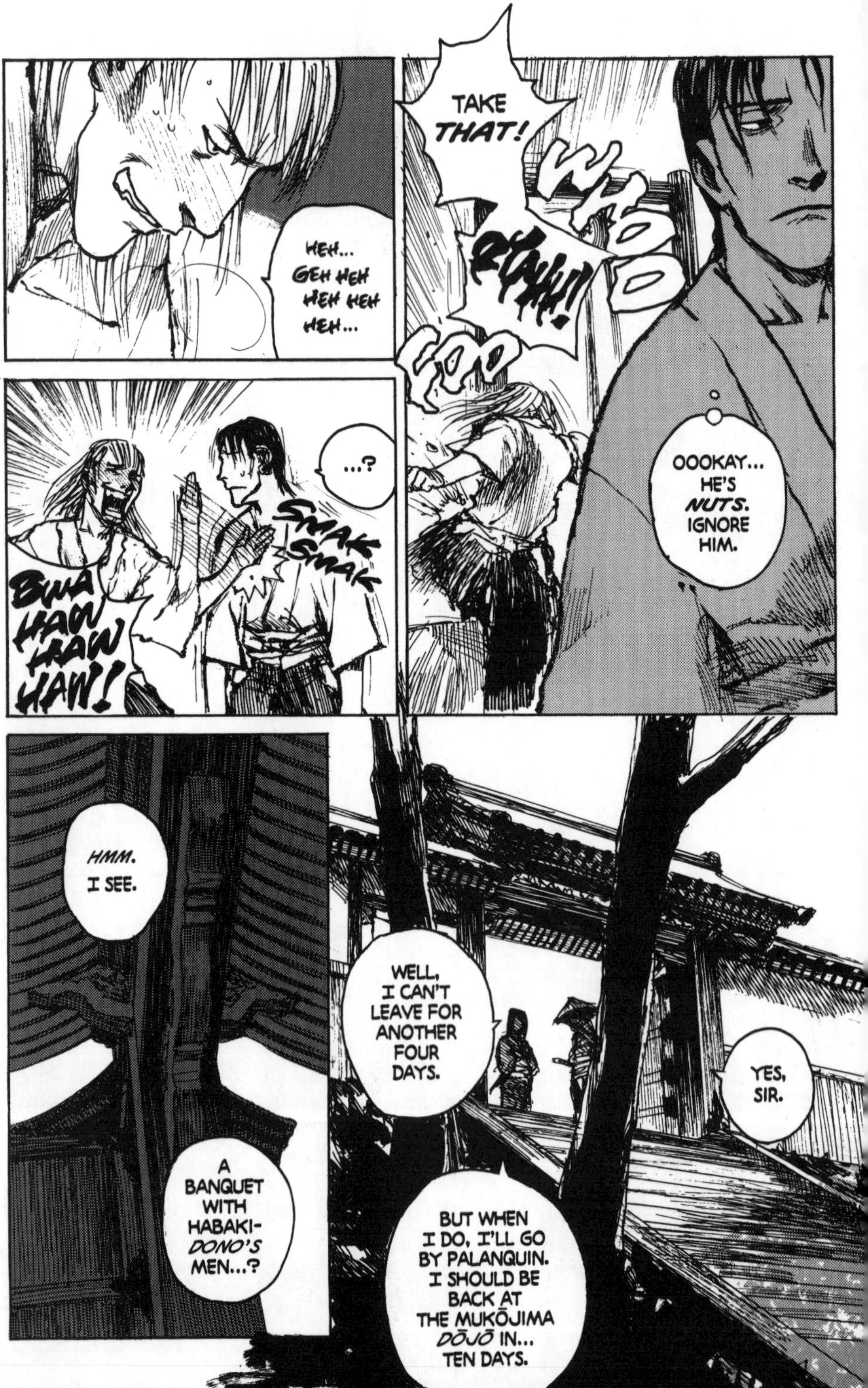
HEH... GEH HEH HEH HEH HEH...
...?
SMAK SMAK
BWA HAW HAW HAW!
TAKE THAT!
OOOKAY... HE'S NUTS. IGNORE HIM.
HMM. I SEE.
A BANQUET WITH HABAKI-DONO'S MEN...?
WELL, I CAN'T LEAVE FOR ANOTHER FOUR DAYS.
YES, SIR.
BUT WHEN I DO, I'LL GO BY PALANQUIN. I SHOULD BE BACK AT THE MUKŌJIMA DŌJŌ IN... TEN DAYS.

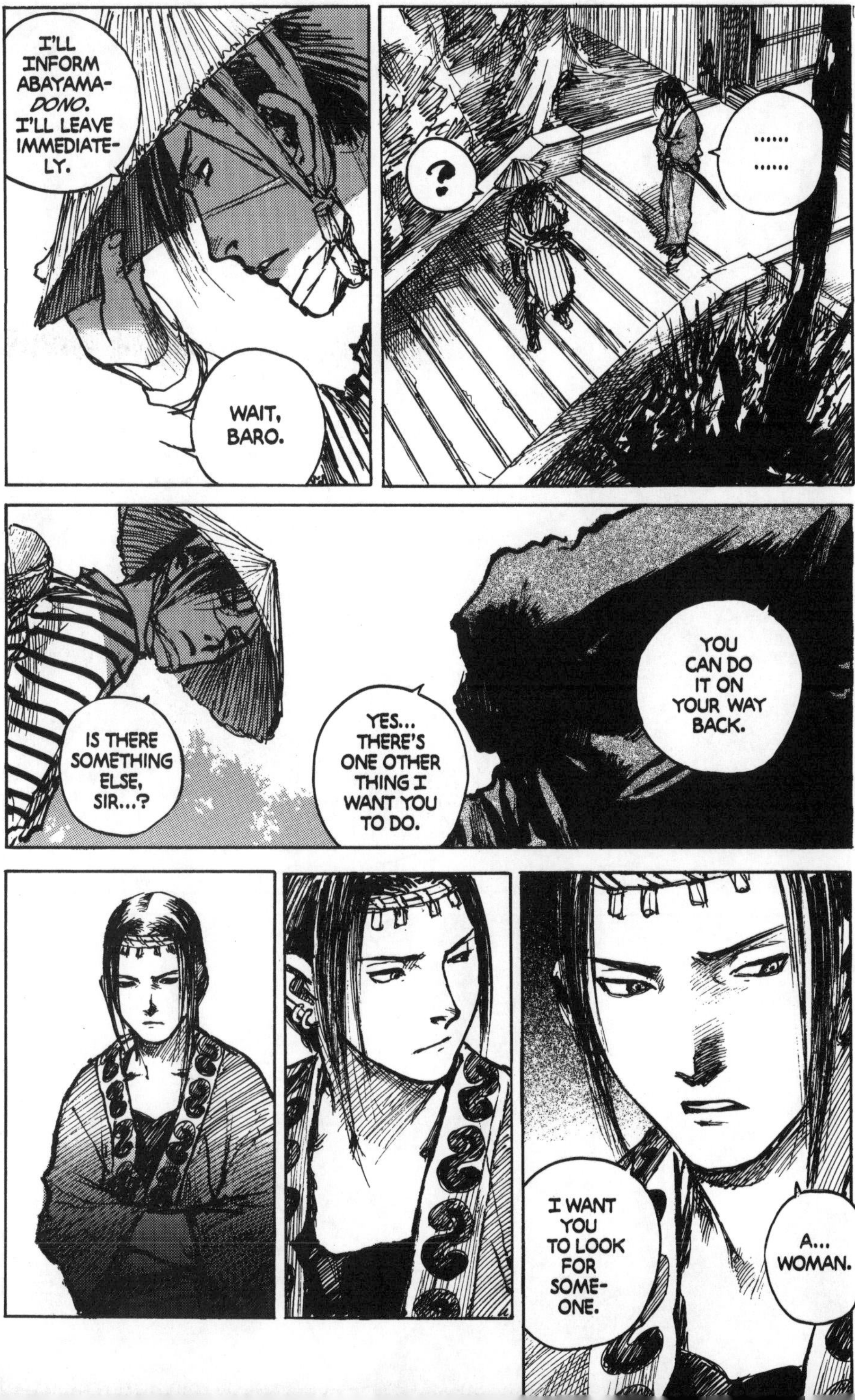
I'LL INFORM ABAYAMA-*DONO*. I'LL LEAVE IMMEDIATE-LY.
WAIT, BARO.
?
......
......
IS THERE SOMETHING ELSE, SIR...?
YES... THERE'S ONE OTHER THING I WANT YOU TO DO.
YOU CAN DO IT ON YOUR WAY BACK.
I WANT YOU TO LOOK FOR SOME-ONE.
A... WOMAN.

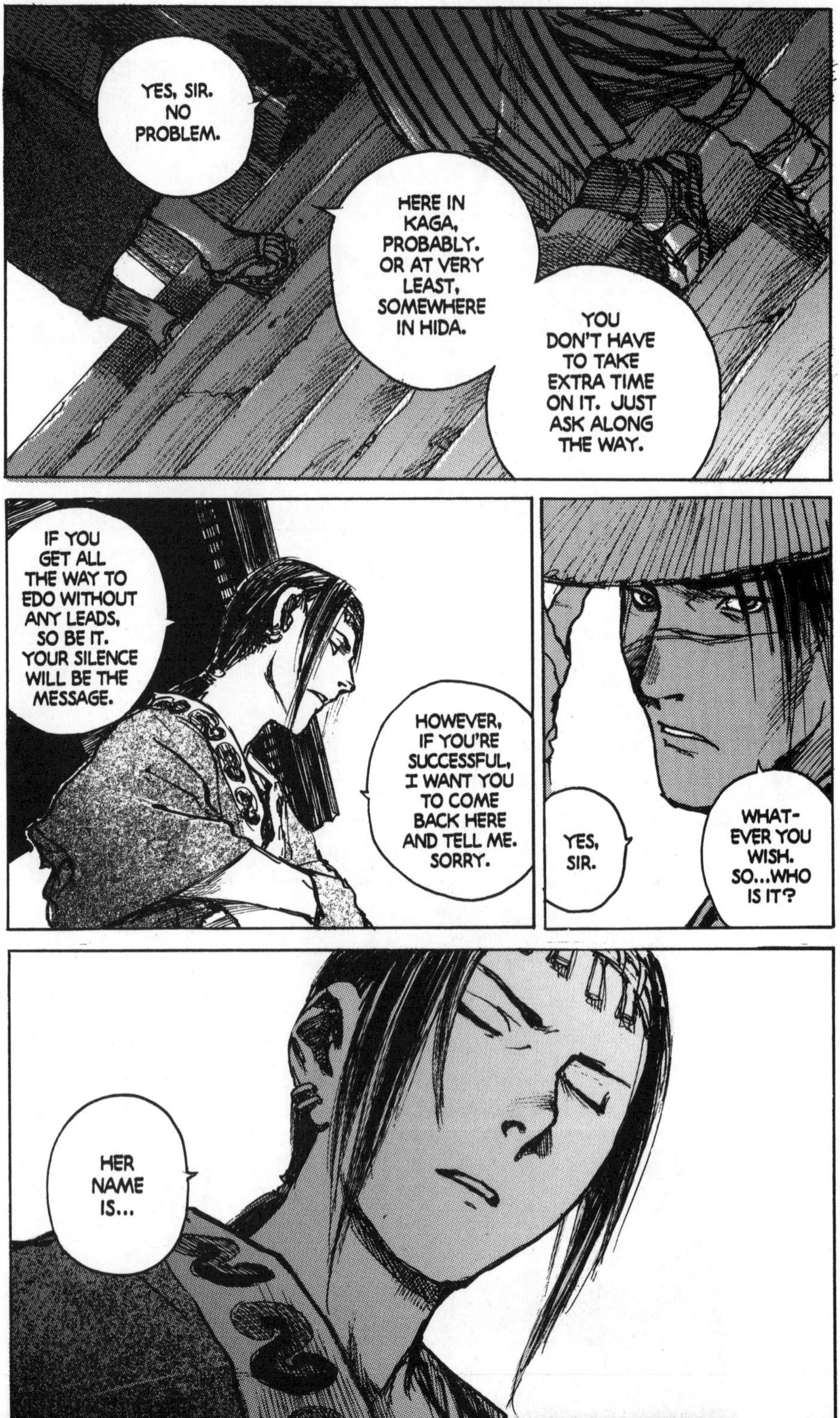
YES, SIR. NO PROBLEM.
HERE IN KAGA, PROBABLY. OR AT VERY LEAST, SOMEWHERE IN HIDA.
YOU DON'T HAVE TO TAKE EXTRA TIME ON IT. JUST ASK ALONG THE WAY.
IF YOU GET ALL THE WAY TO EDO WITHOUT ANY LEADS, SO BE IT. YOUR SILENCE WILL BE THE MESSAGE.
HOWEVER, IF YOU'RE SUCCESSFUL, I WANT YOU TO COME BACK HERE AND TELL ME. SORRY.
YES, SIR.
WHAT-EVER YOU WISH. SO...WHO IS IT?
HER NAME IS...

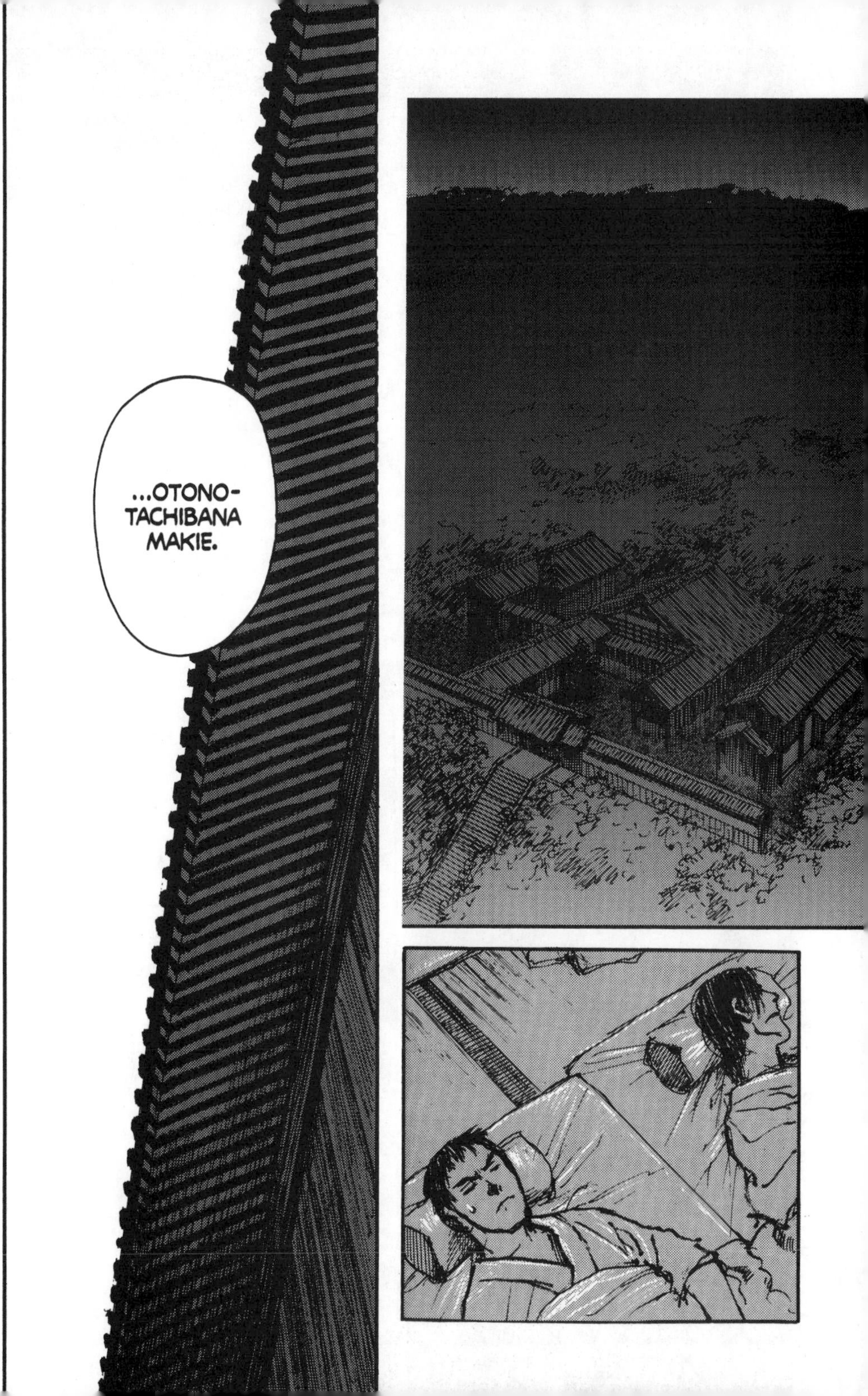
...OTONO-
TACHIBANA
MAKIE.

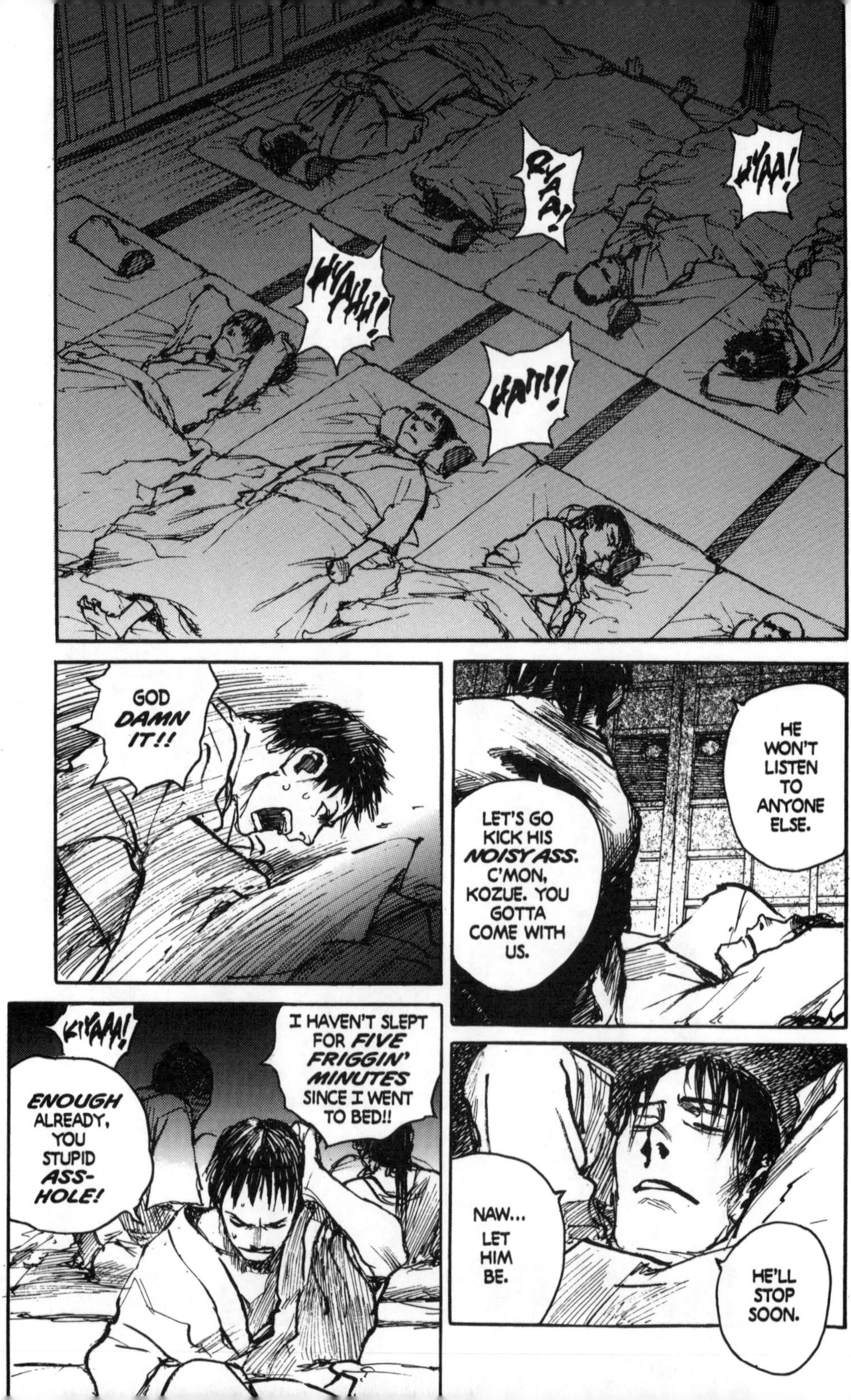

HYAA!
HYAAHH!!
HAII!!
GOD DAMN IT!!
LET'S GO KICK HIS NOISY ASS. C'MON, KOZUE. YOU GOTTA COME WITH US.
HE WON'T LISTEN TO ANYONE ELSE.
KIYAAA!
ENOUGH ALREADY, YOU STUPID ASS-HOLE!
I HAVEN'T SLEPT FOR FIVE FRIGGIN' MINUTES SINCE I WENT TO BED!!
NAW... LET HIM BE.
HE'LL STOP SOON.

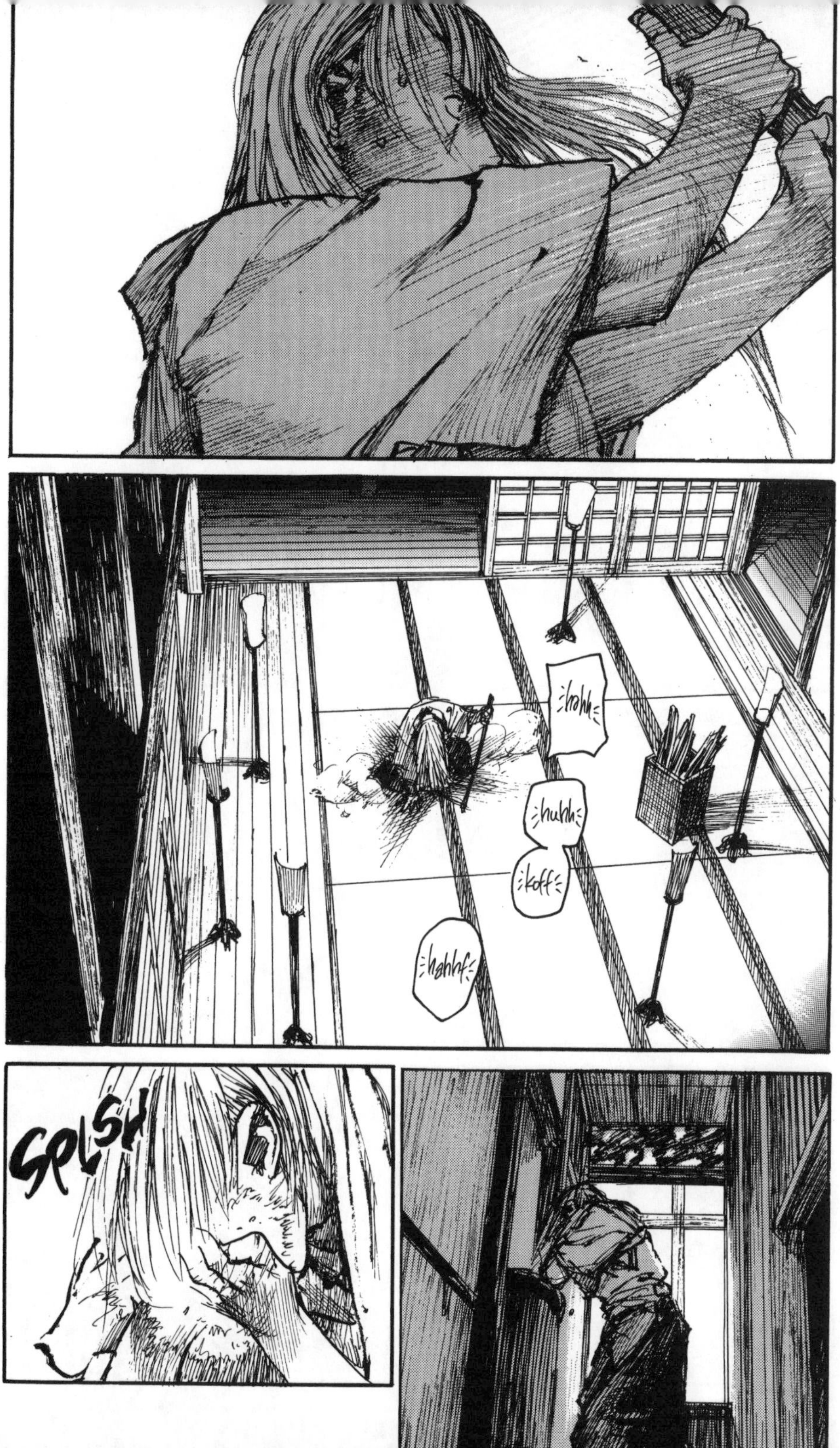
hahh
huhh
koff
hahhf
SPLSH

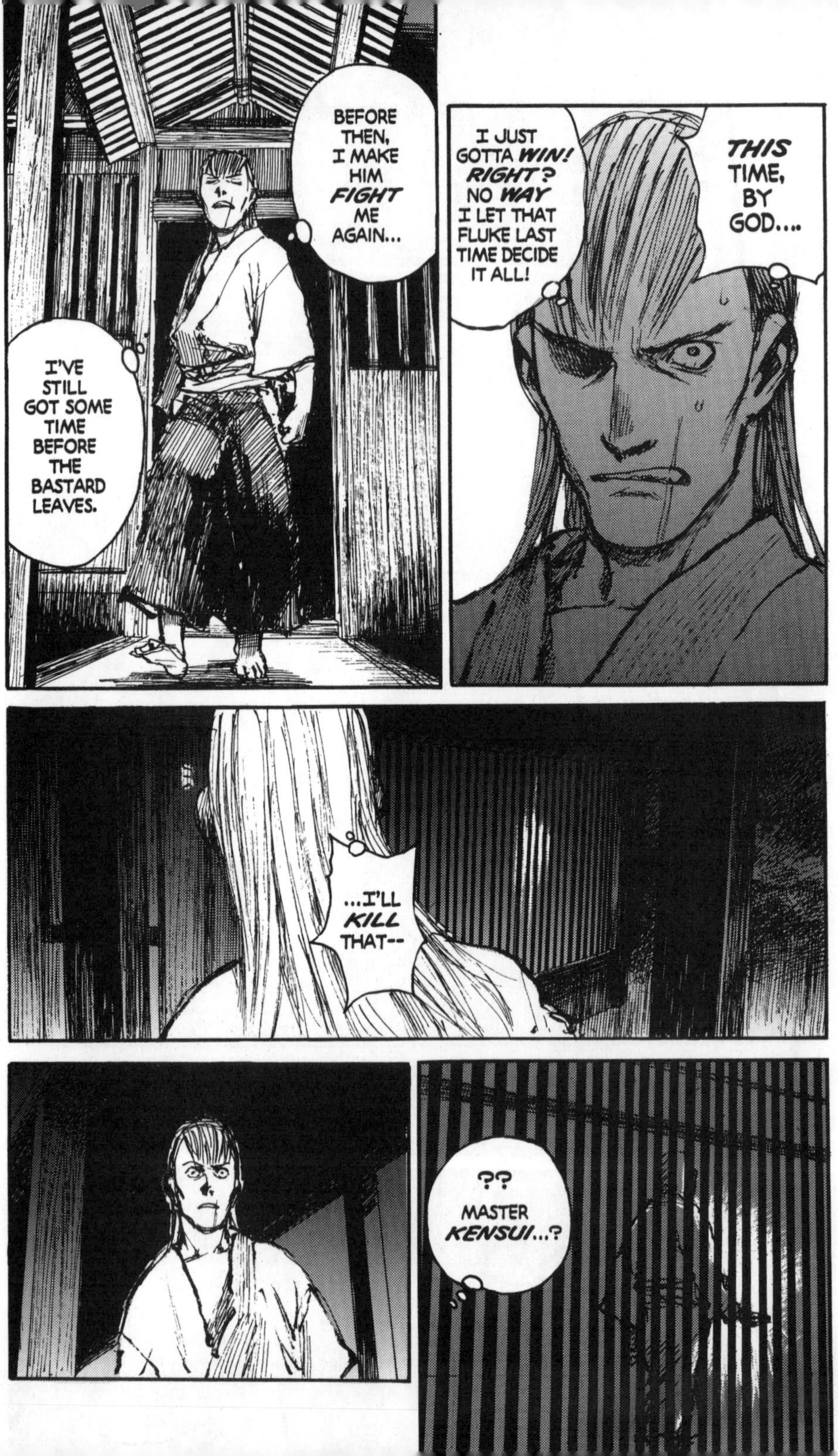
BEFORE THEN, I MAKE HIM FIGHT ME AGAIN...
I'VE STILL GOT SOME TIME BEFORE THE BASTARD LEAVES.
I JUST GOTTA WIN! RIGHT? NO WAY I LET THAT FLUKE LAST TIME DECIDE IT ALL!
THIS TIME, BY GOD....
...I'LL KILL THAT--
?? MASTER KENSUI...?

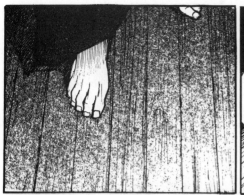

FORGIVE ME FOR ASKING TO SEE YOU SO LATE.

FORGET IT. IT'S *NOTHING.* I DON'T WORK OUT ALL DAY LIKE MY STUDENTS.

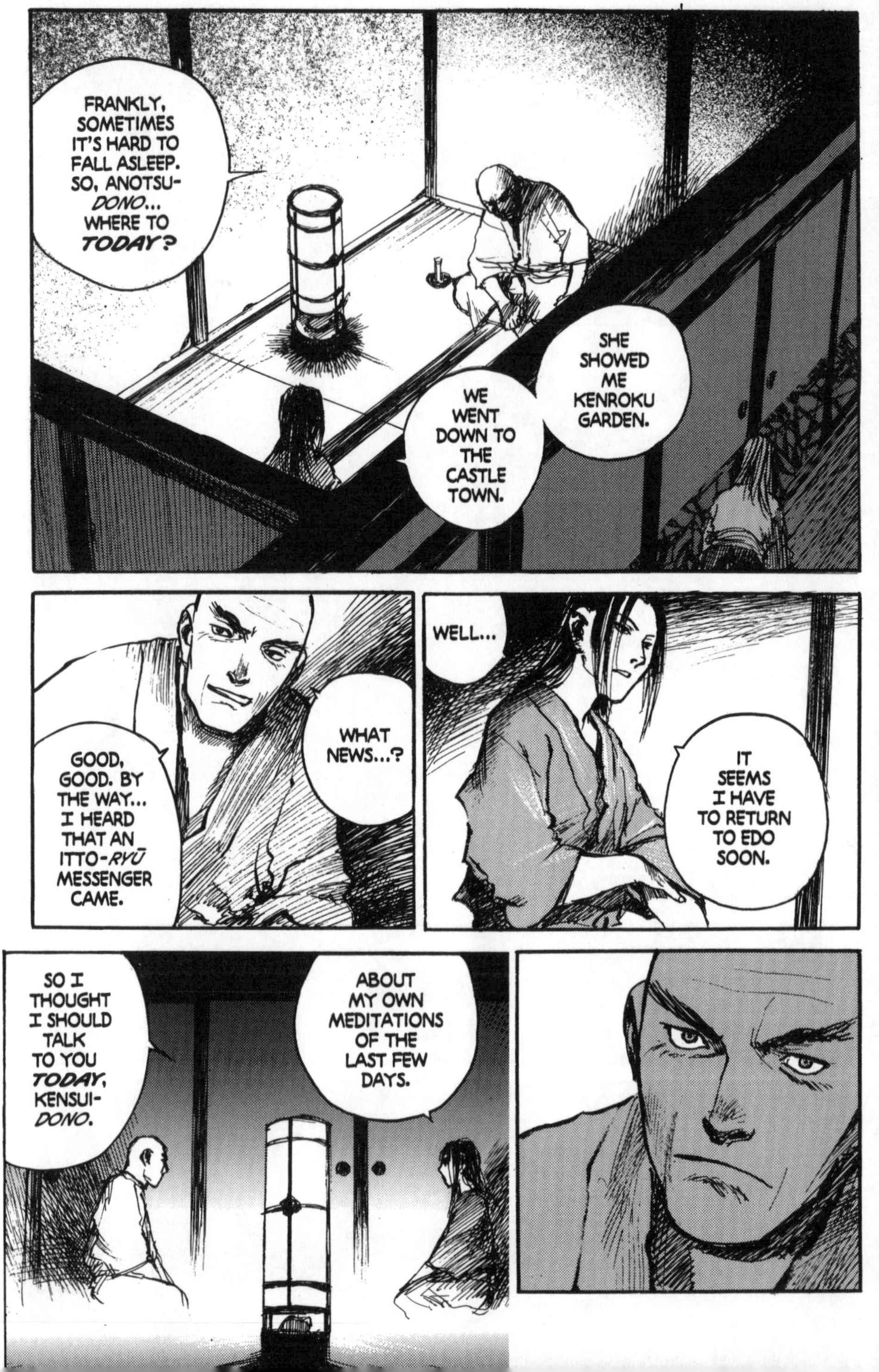
FRANKLY, SOMETIMES IT'S HARD TO FALL ASLEEP. SO, ANOTSU-*DONO*... WHERE TO ***TODAY***?
WE WENT DOWN TO THE CASTLE TOWN.
SHE SHOWED ME KENROKU GARDEN.
GOOD, GOOD. BY THE WAY... I HEARD THAT AN ITTO-*RYŪ* MESSENGER CAME.
WHAT NEWS...?
WELL...
IT SEEMS I HAVE TO RETURN TO EDO SOON.
SO I THOUGHT I SHOULD TALK TO YOU ***TODAY***, KENSUI-*DONO*.
ABOUT MY OWN MEDITATIONS OF THE LAST FEW DAYS.

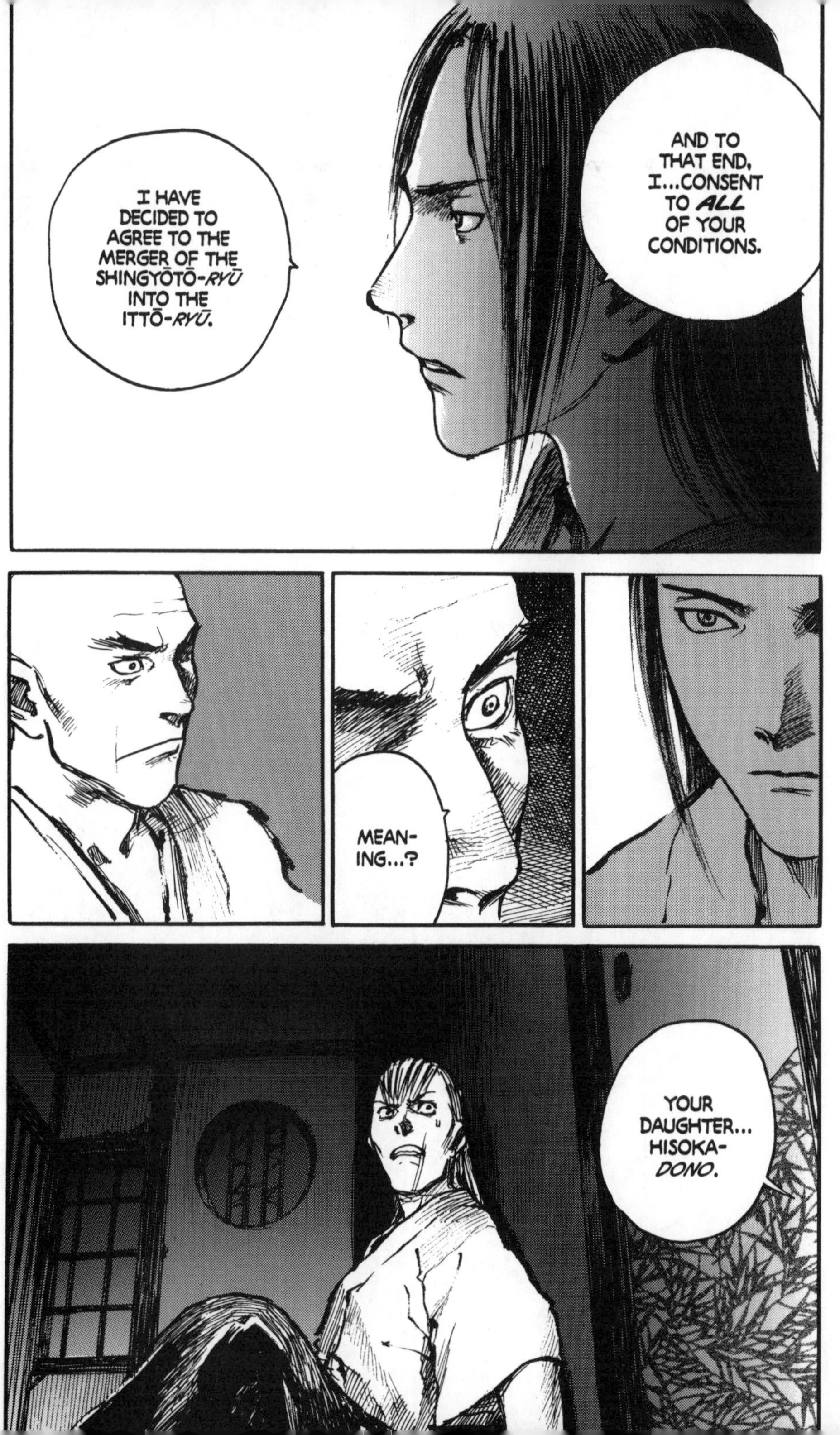
I HAVE DECIDED TO AGREE TO THE MERGER OF THE SHINGYŌTŌ-*RYŪ* INTO THE ITTŌ-*RYŪ*.
AND TO THAT END, I...CONSENT TO *ALL* OF YOUR CONDITIONS.
MEAN-ING...?
YOUR DAUGHTER... HISOKA-*DONO*.

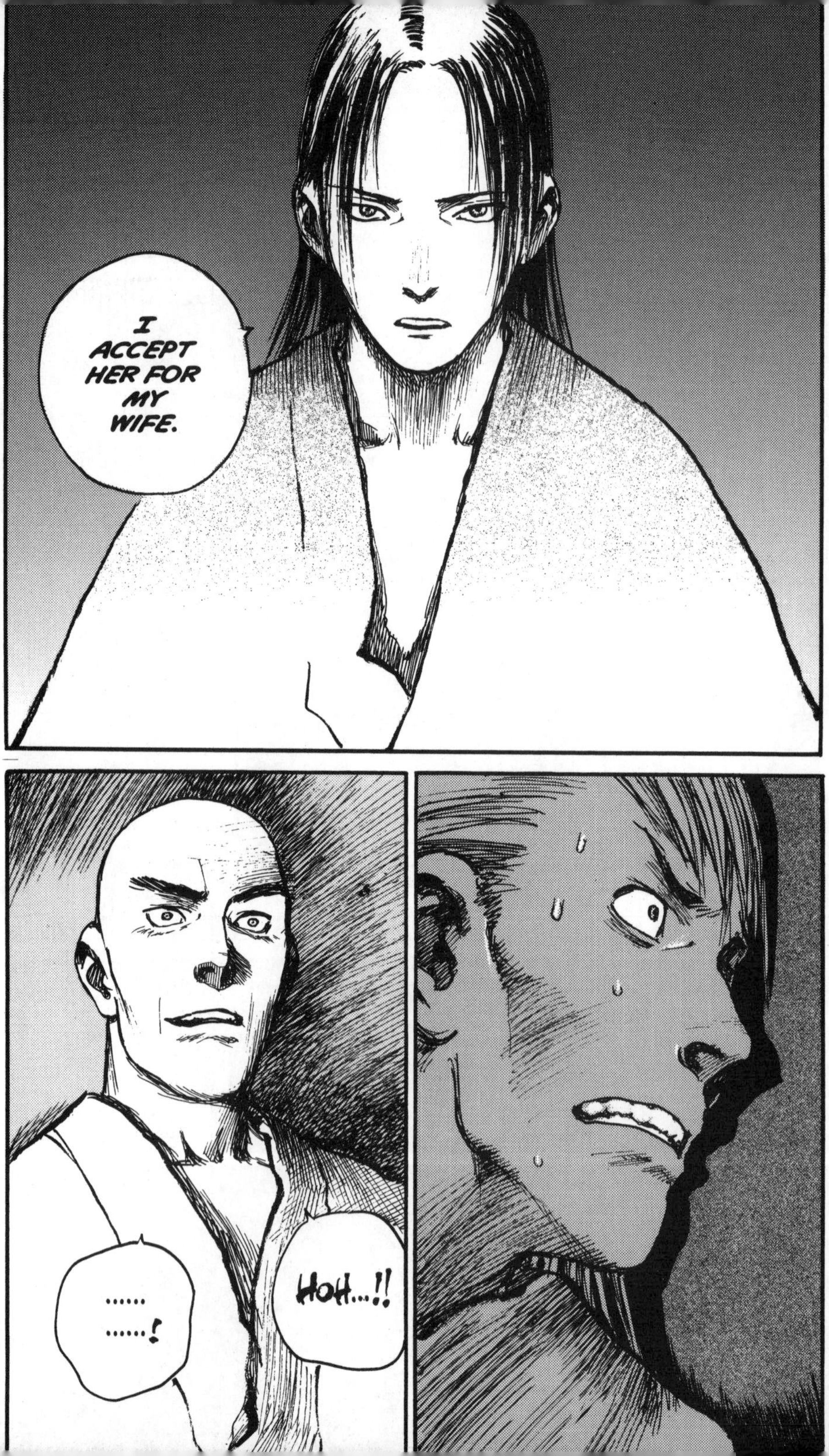
I ACCEPT HER FOR MY WIFE.
....!
HOH...!!

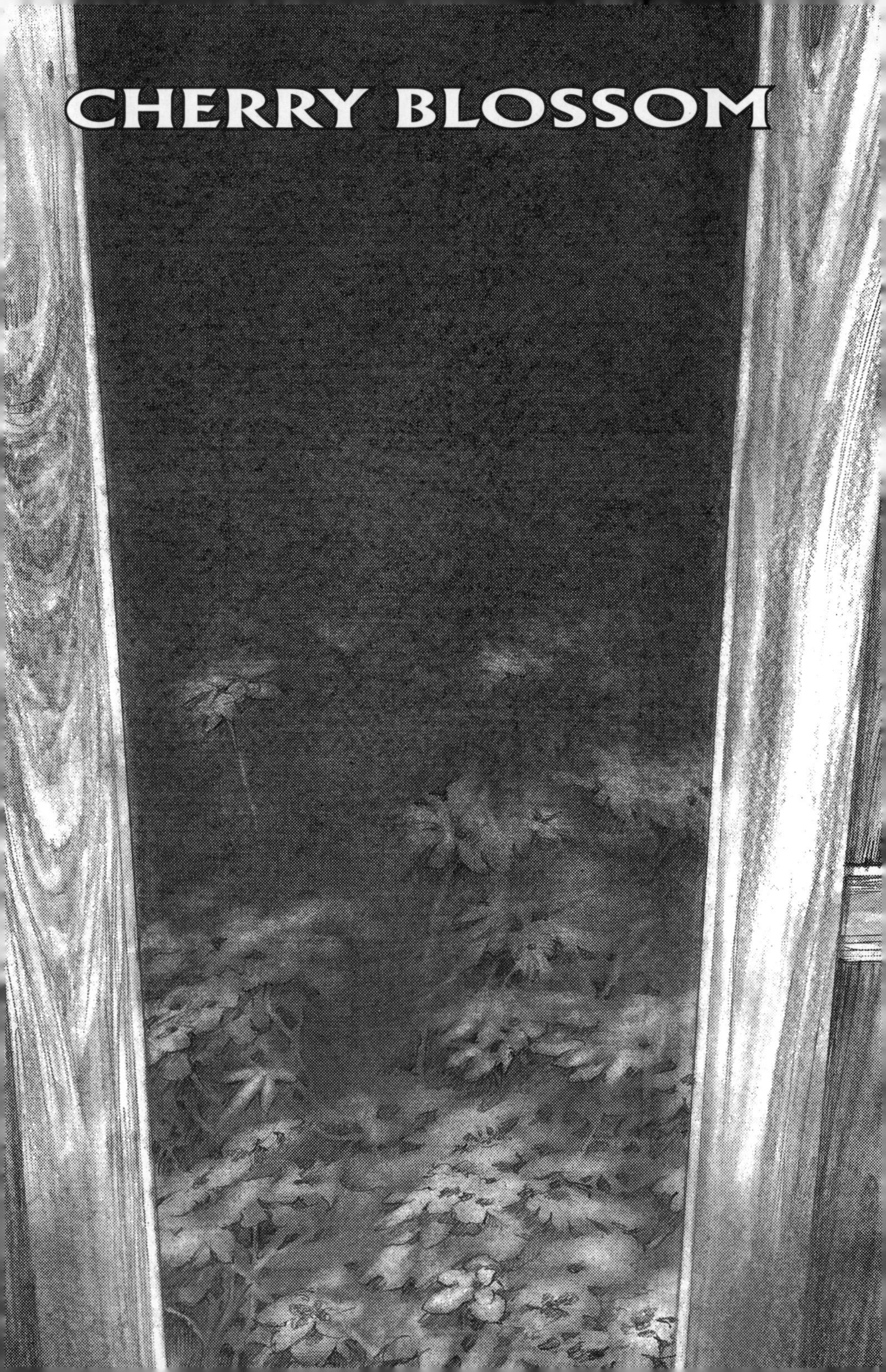
CHERRY BLOSSOM

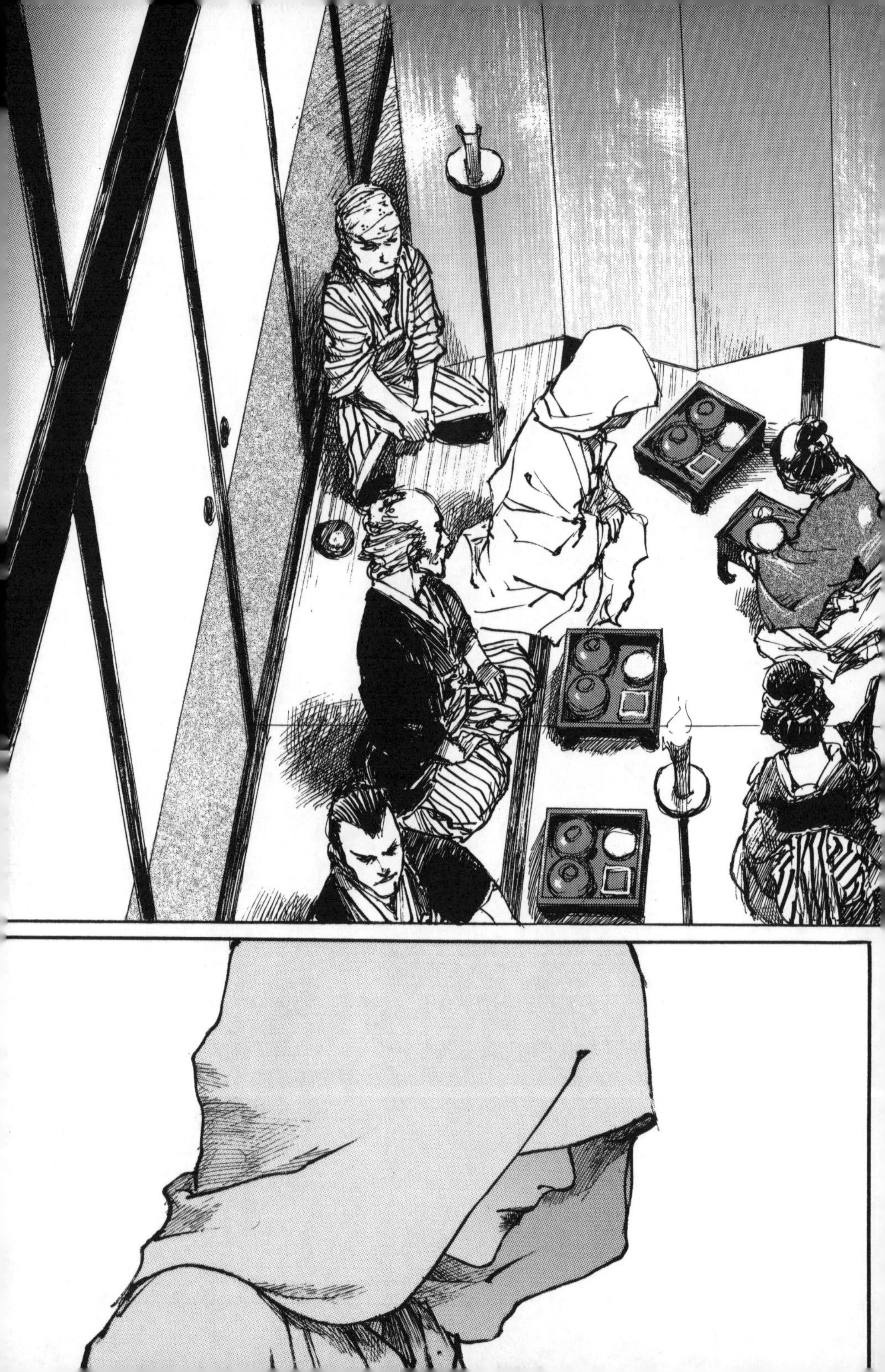

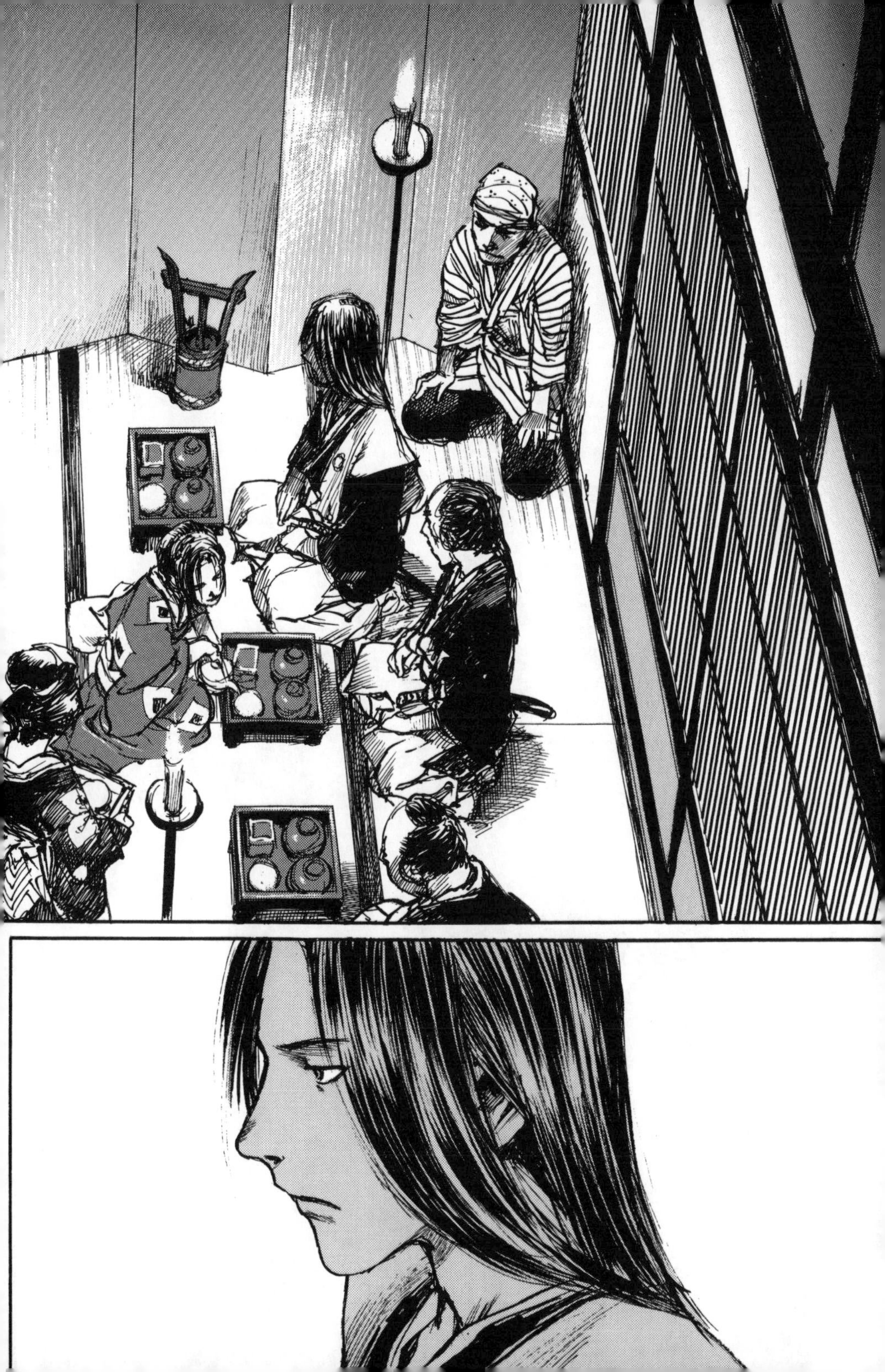

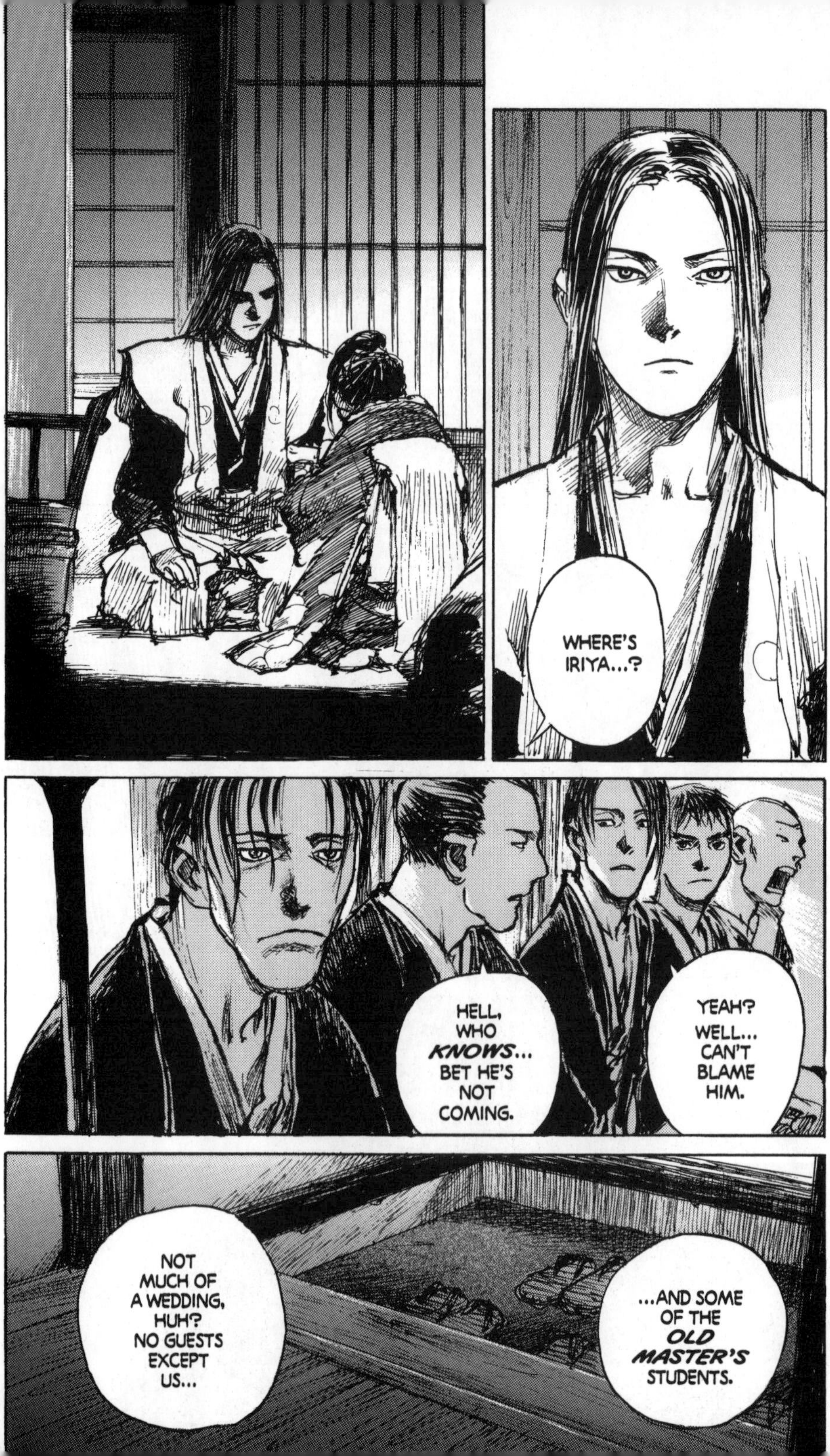
WHERE'S IRIYA...?
HELL, WHO **KNOWS**... BET HE'S NOT COMING.
YEAH? WELL... CAN'T BLAME HIM.
NOT MUCH OF A WEDDING, HUH? NO GUESTS EXCEPT US...
...AND SOME OF THE **OLD MASTER'S** STUDENTS.

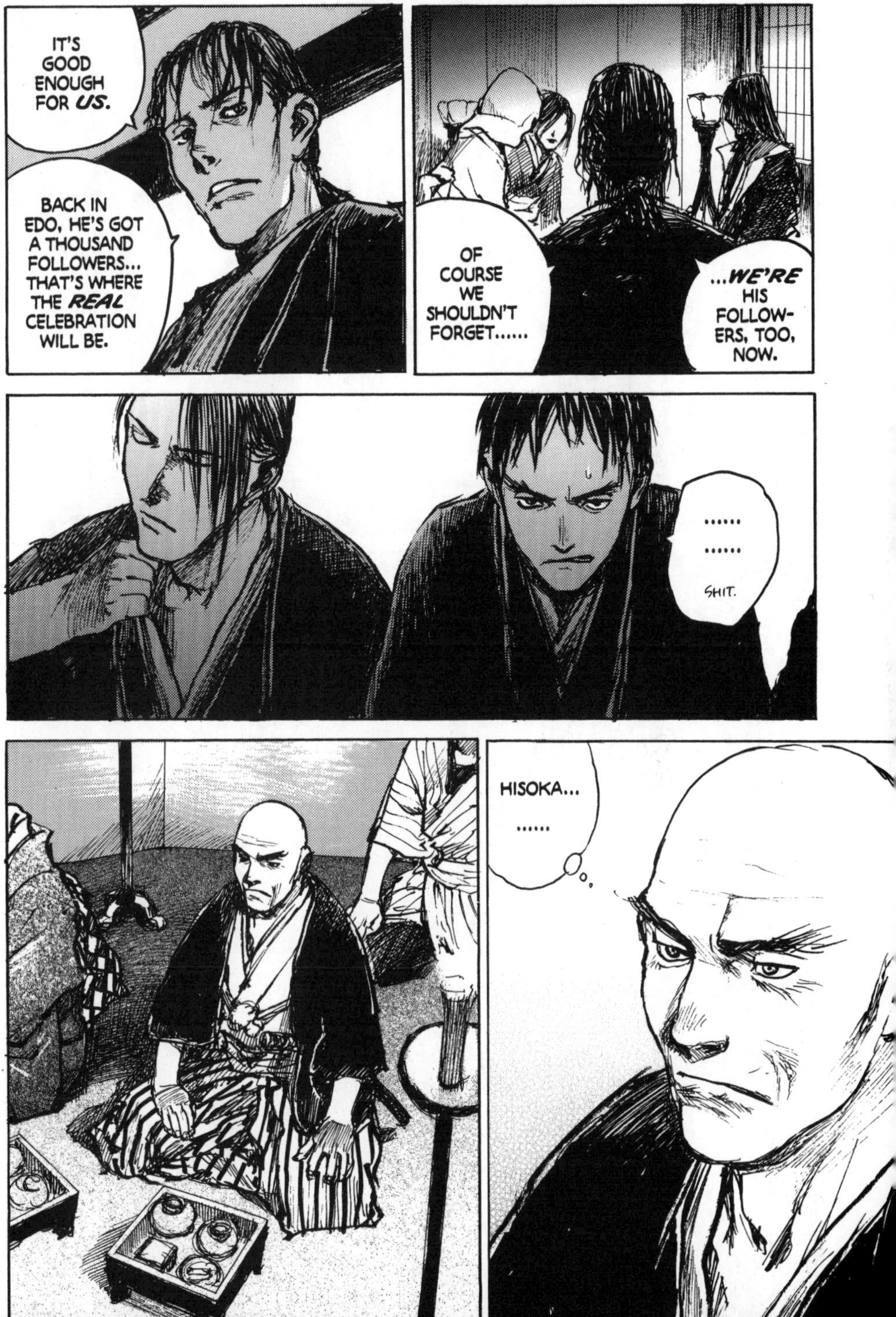
IT'S GOOD ENOUGH FOR *US.*
BACK IN EDO, HE'S GOT A THOUSAND FOLLOWERS... THAT'S WHERE THE *REAL* CELEBRATION WILL BE.
OF COURSE WE SHOULDN'T FORGET......
...*WE'RE* HIS FOLLOW-ERS, TOO, NOW.
......
......
SHIT.
HISOKA...
......

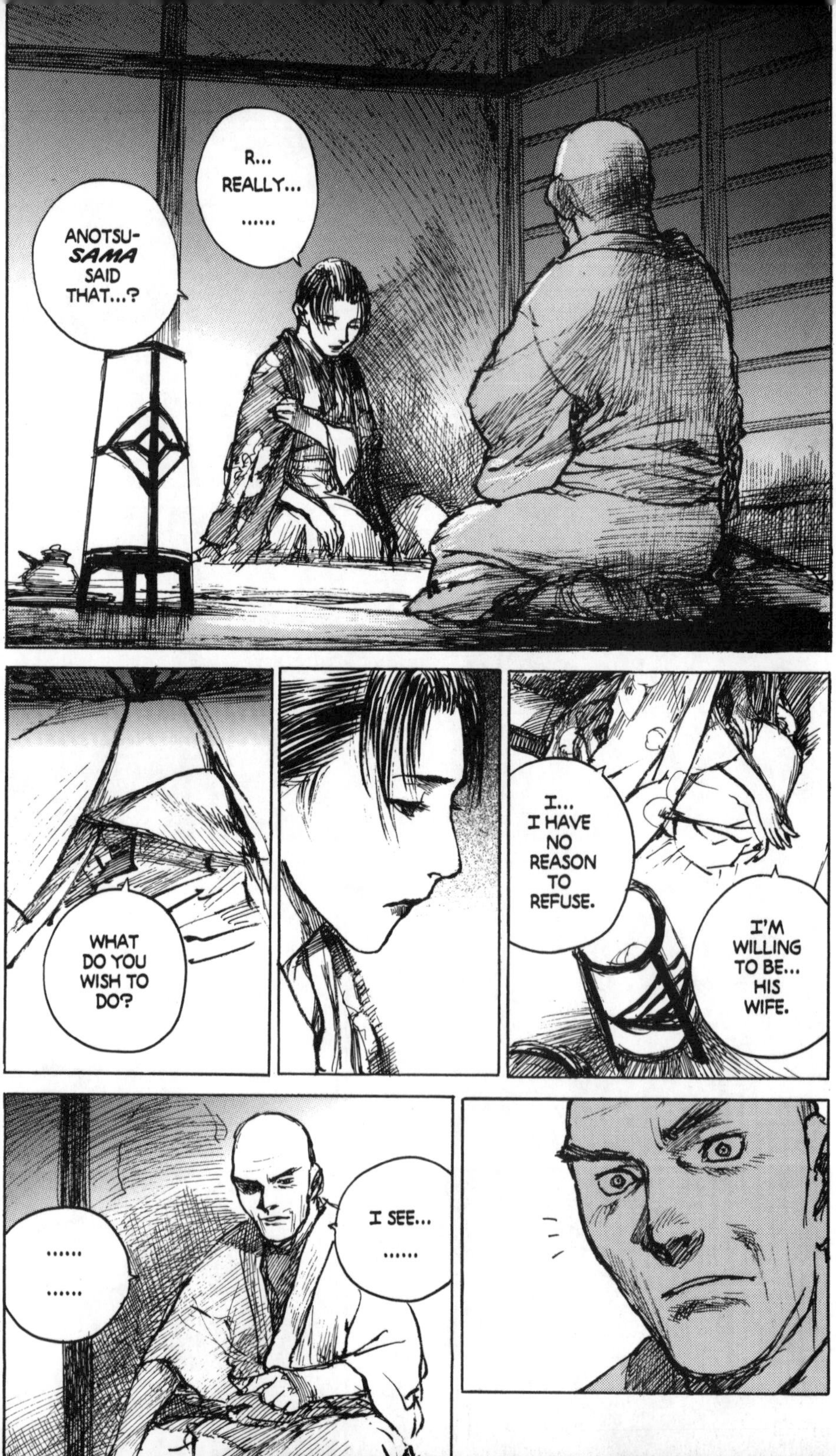
ANOTSU-SAMA SAID THAT...?
R... REALLY... ......
WHAT DO YOU WISH TO DO?
I... I HAVE NO REASON TO REFUSE.
I'M WILLING TO BE... HIS WIFE.
....
I SEE... ......

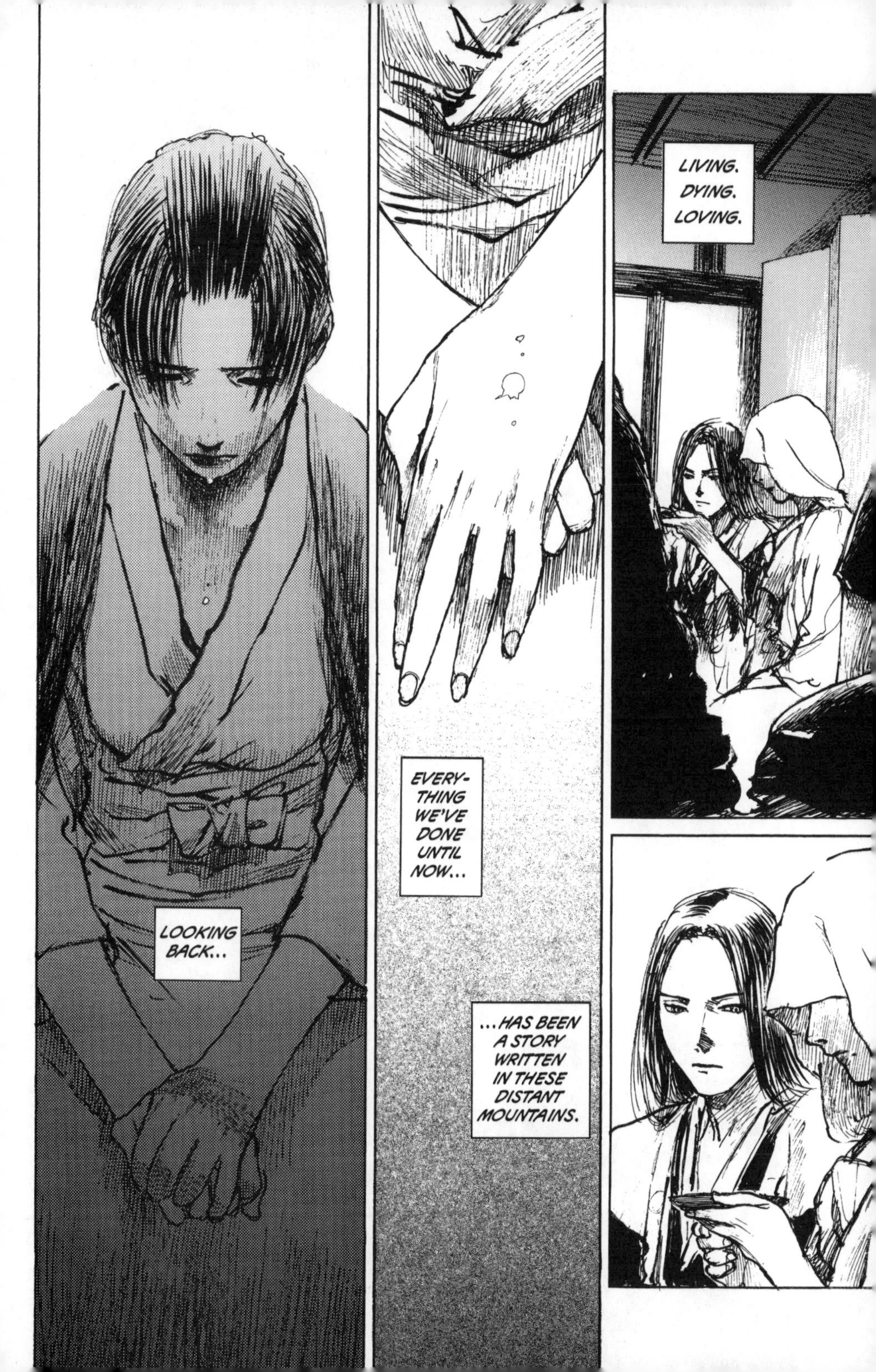
LOOKING BACK...
EVERY-THING WE'VE DONE UNTIL NOW...
...HAS BEEN A STORY WRITTEN IN THESE DISTANT MOUNTAINS.
LIVING. DYING. LOVING.

BUT THAT ERA IS **OVER** NOW.

NO... IT MAY HAVE ENDED LONG, **LONG** AGO.

POWER SHOULD **NOT** BE HIDDEN. IT'S TIME TO LET THESE MEN **LOOSE** ON THE **WORLD**...

...AND PUT OUR SENSEI'S PHILOSOPHY TO THE **TEST!**

MAS-TER...?

A MESSENGER FROM THE **GOVERN-MENT**...?

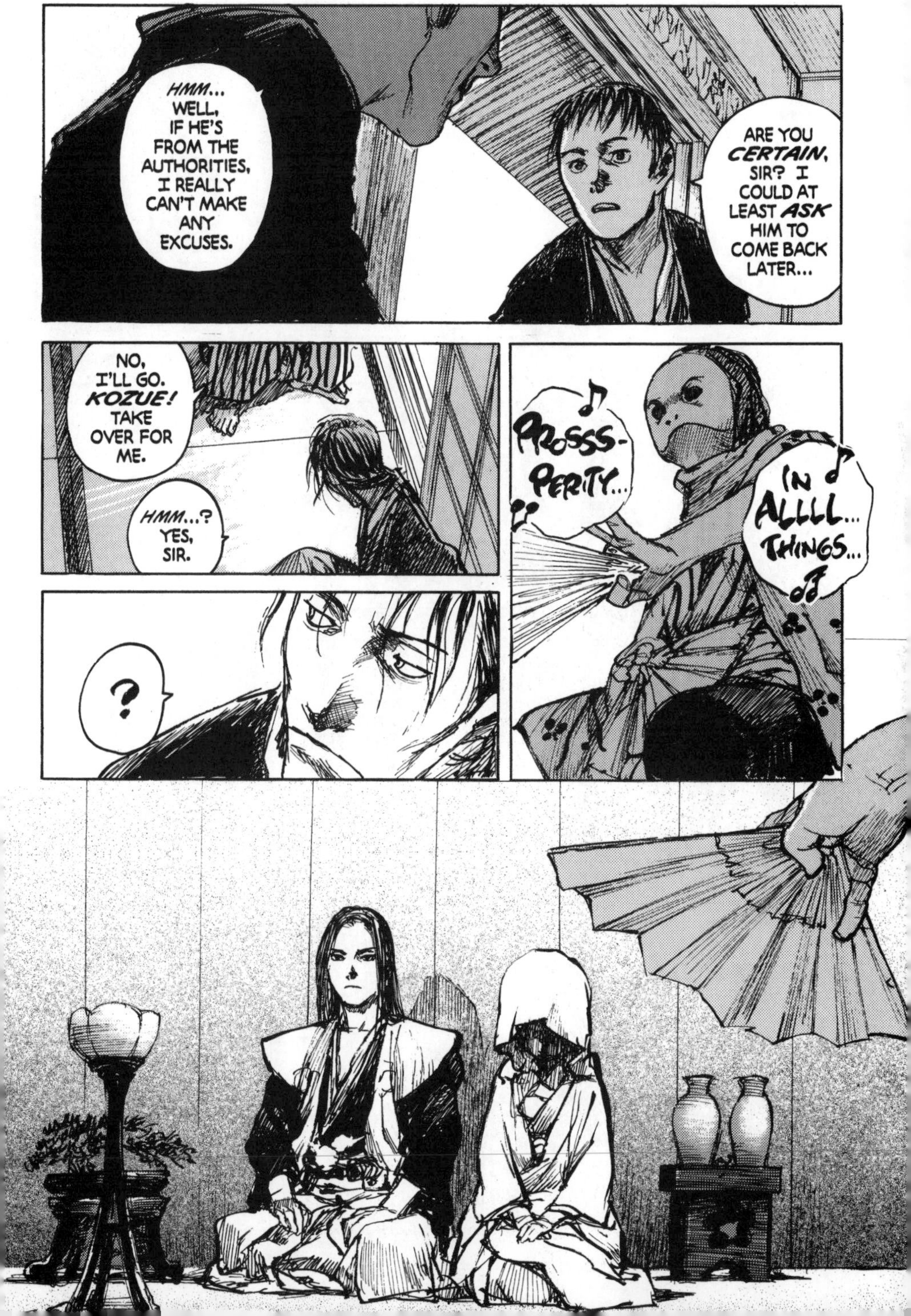
HMM... WELL, IF HE'S FROM THE AUTHORITIES, I REALLY CAN'T MAKE ANY EXCUSES.
ARE YOU CERTAIN, SIR? I COULD AT LEAST ASK HIM TO COME BACK LATER...
NO, I'LL GO. KOZUE! TAKE OVER FOR ME.
HMM...? YES, SIR.
?
PROSSS-PERITY...
IN ALLLL... THINGS...

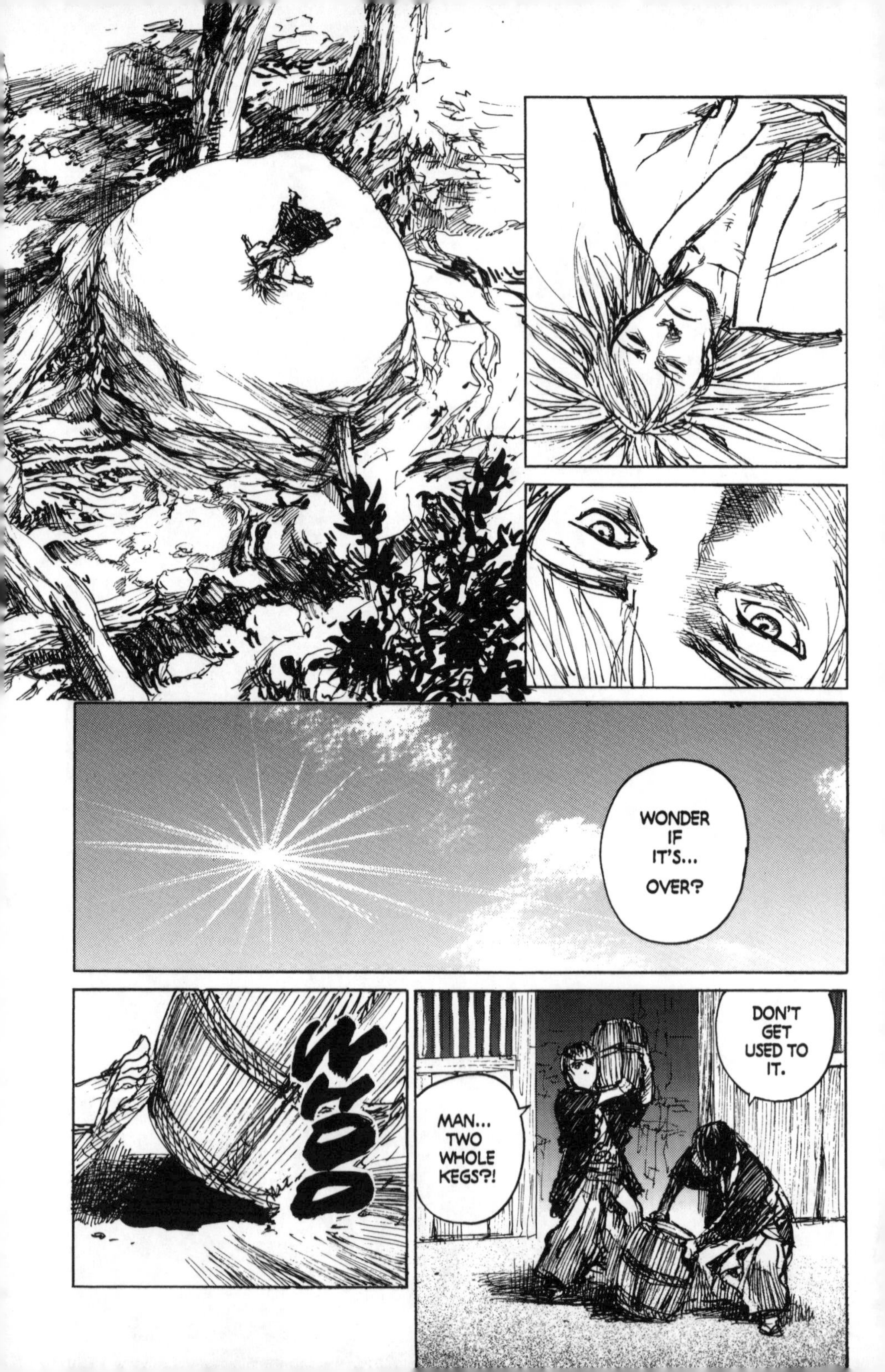
WONDER IF IT'S... OVER?
MAN... TWO WHOLE KEGS?!
DON'T GET USED TO IT.

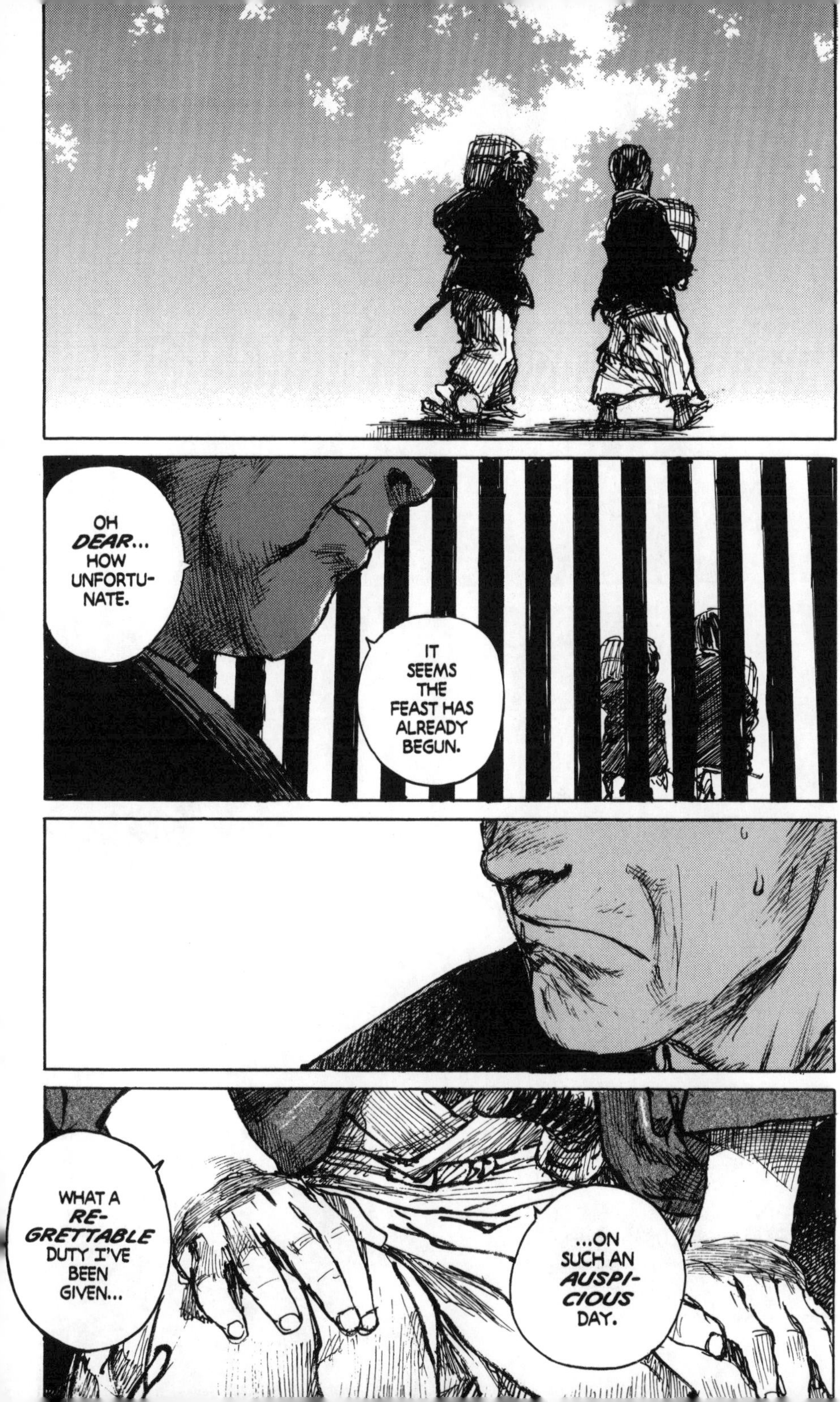
OH DEAR... HOW UNFORTUNATE.
IT SEEMS THE FEAST HAS ALREADY BEGUN.
WHAT A REGRETTABLE DUTY I'VE BEEN GIVEN...
...ON SUCH AN AUSPICIOUS DAY.

SPEAK-
ING
PRIVATE-
LY,
SIR...

...I
CONSIDER
IT
*REPRE-
HENSI-
BLE.*

BUT
THAT'S
NEITHER
HERE NOR
THERE.

THINK
DEEPLY
ABOUT THIS
MATTER,
AND GIVE
ME YOUR
REPLY.

AFTER
ALL, IT'S
FOR THE
*YOUNG
LADY'S*
GOOD,
AS WELL.
NOW, IF YOU'LL
EXCUSE ME...

AH?!

PLEASE
WAIT, SIR!
I'LL GET
A PALAN-
QUIN...

HEAVENS
NO!
DON'T WORRY
ABOUT *THIS*
OLD MAN.
GO! ENJOY
YOUR FEAST!

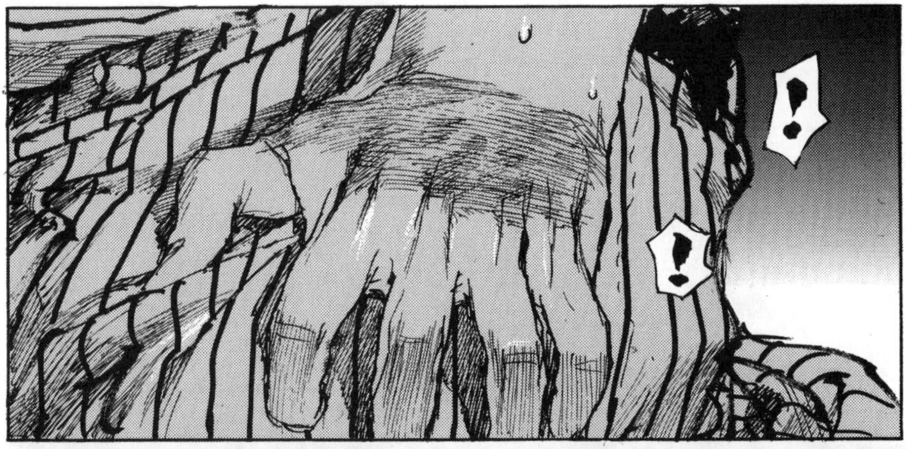
!
!
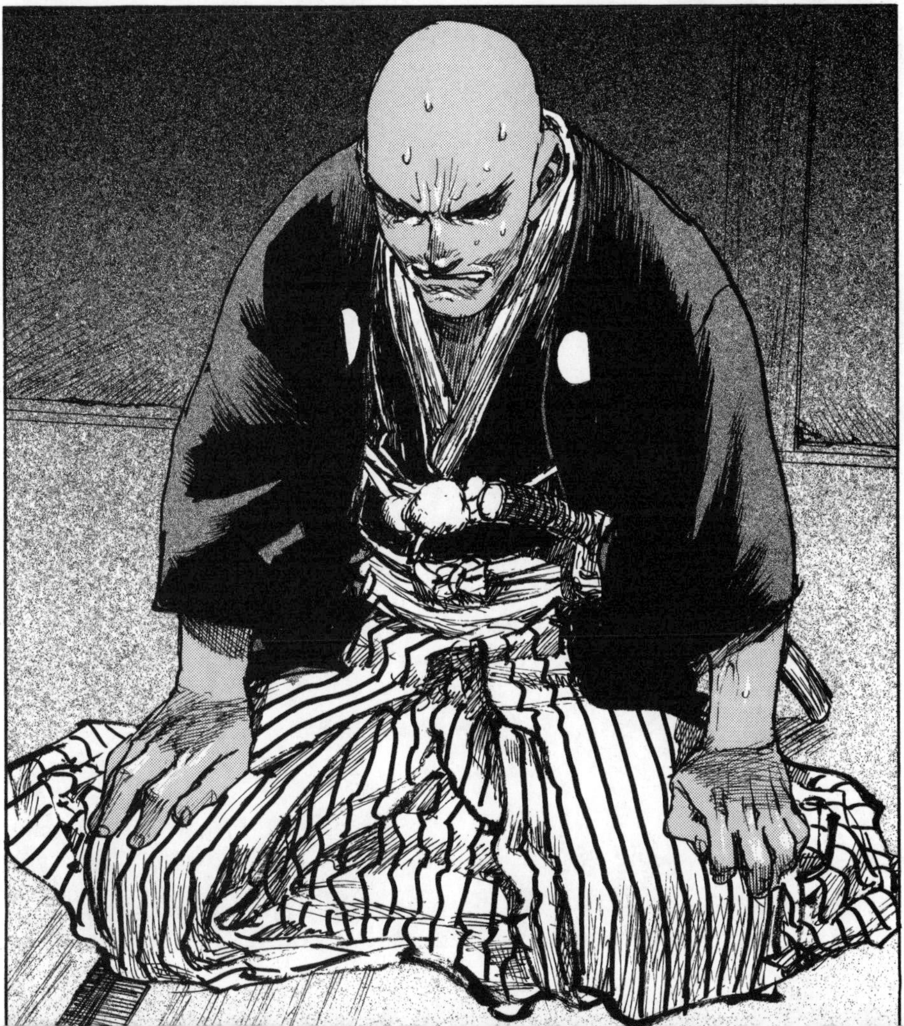

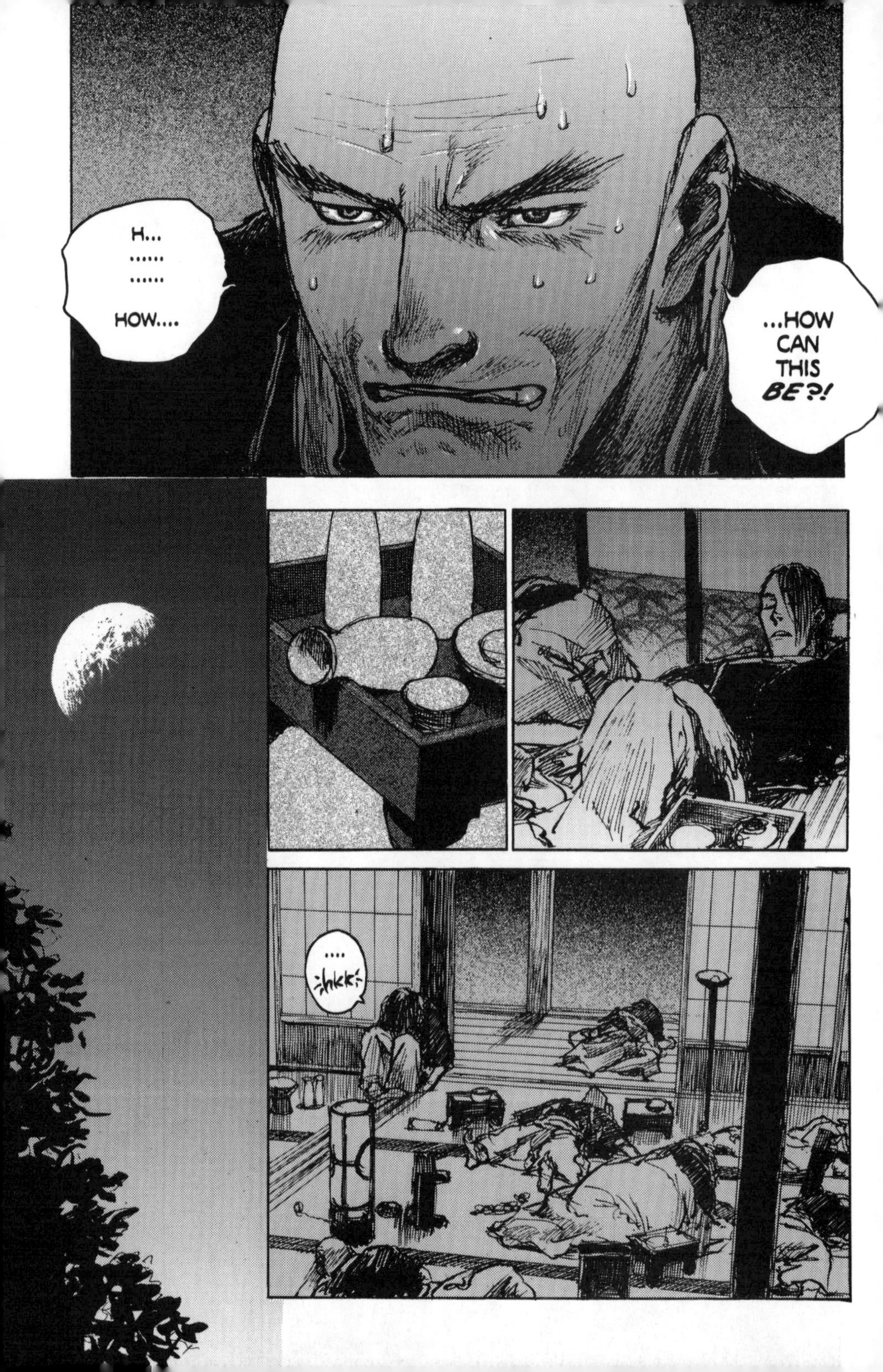
H... .... HOW....
...HOW CAN THIS *BE*?!
.... hkk

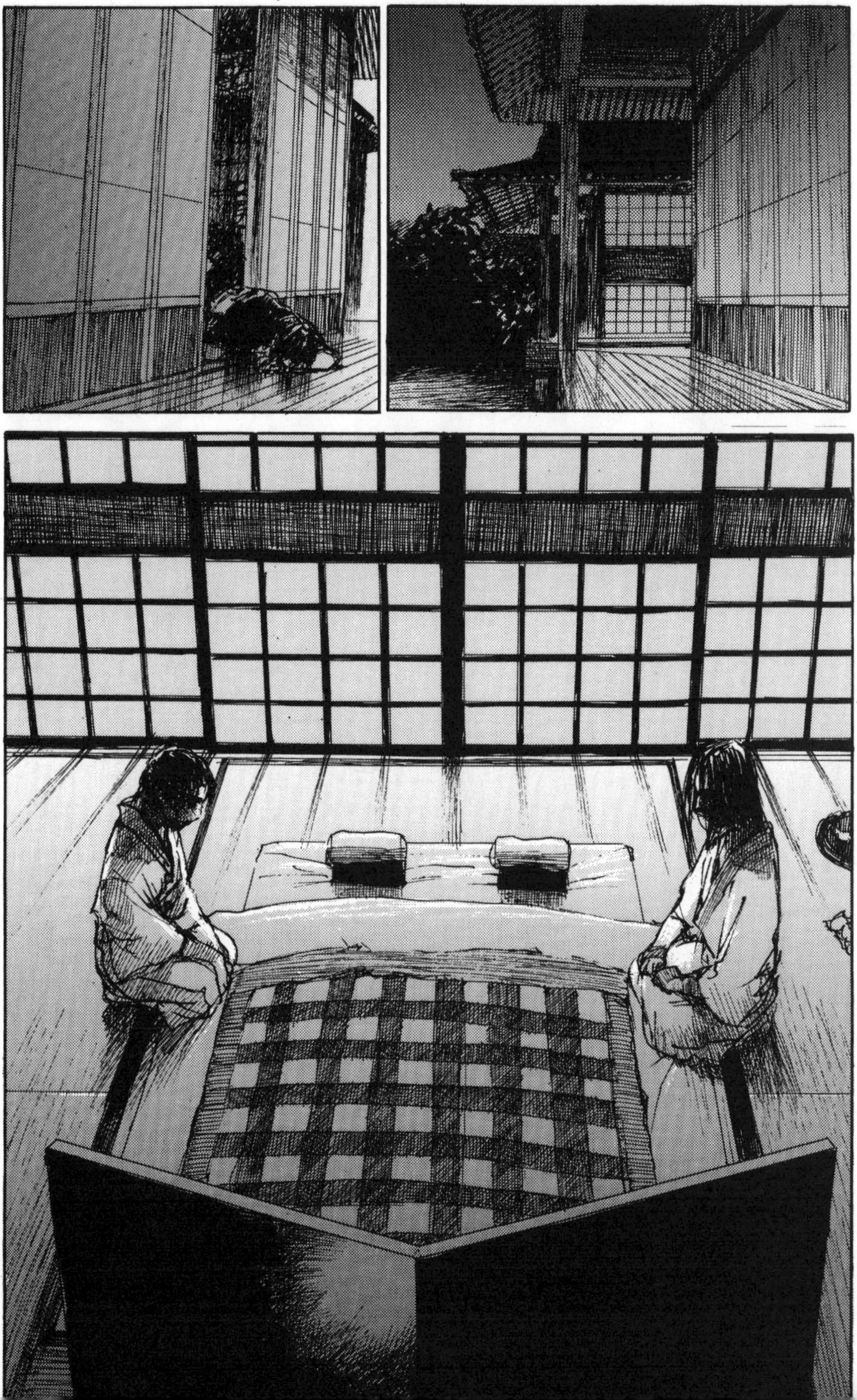

WILL YOU PLEASE PROMISE ME ONE THING...?

...... ANOTSU-*DONO*...?

...WHAT IS IT, HISOKA-*DONO*?

FOR THIS SHORT TIME JUST BEFORE US...

I INTEND TO FORGET ALL TWENTY-FOUR YEARS OF MY LIFE... AND THINK OF NOTHING EXCEPT *YOU*.

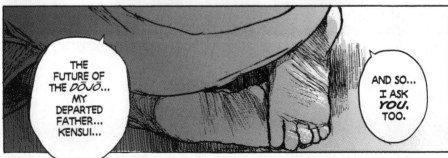

THE FUTURE OF THE *DŌJŌ*... MY DEPARTED FATHER... KENSUI...

AND SO... I ASK *YOU*, TOO.

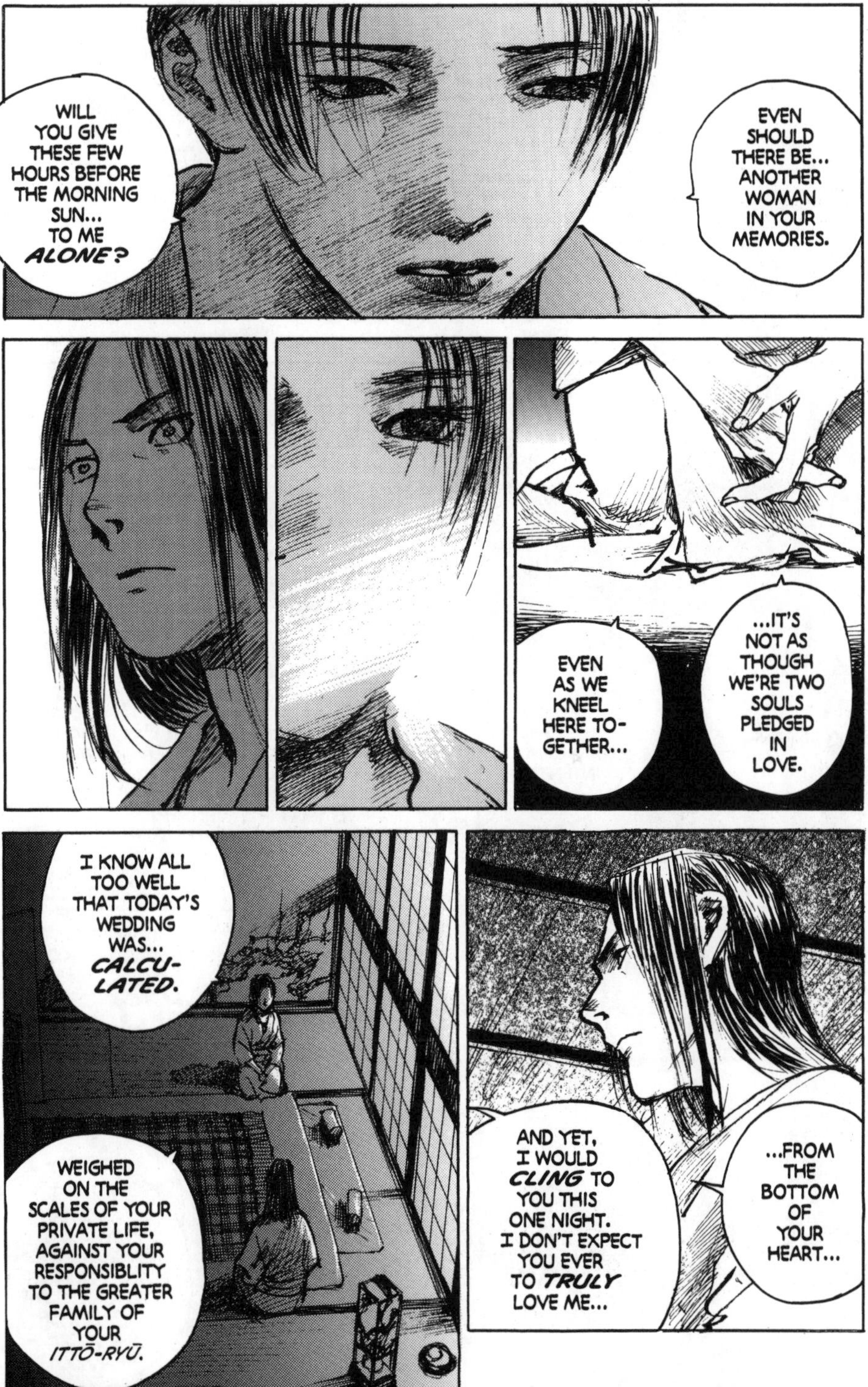
WILL YOU GIVE THESE FEW HOURS BEFORE THE MORNING SUN... TO ME *ALONE?*
EVEN SHOULD THERE BE... ANOTHER WOMAN IN YOUR MEMORIES.
EVEN AS WE KNEEL HERE TO-GETHER...
...IT'S NOT AS THOUGH WE'RE TWO SOULS PLEDGED IN LOVE.
I KNOW ALL TOO WELL THAT TODAY'S WEDDING WAS... *CALCU-LATED.*
WEIGHED ON THE SCALES OF YOUR PRIVATE LIFE, AGAINST YOUR RESPONSIBLITY TO THE GREATER FAMILY OF YOUR *ITTŌ-RYŪ.*
AND YET, I WOULD *CLING* TO YOU THIS ONE NIGHT. I DON'T EXPECT YOU EVER TO *TRULY* LOVE ME...
...FROM THE BOTTOM OF YOUR HEART...

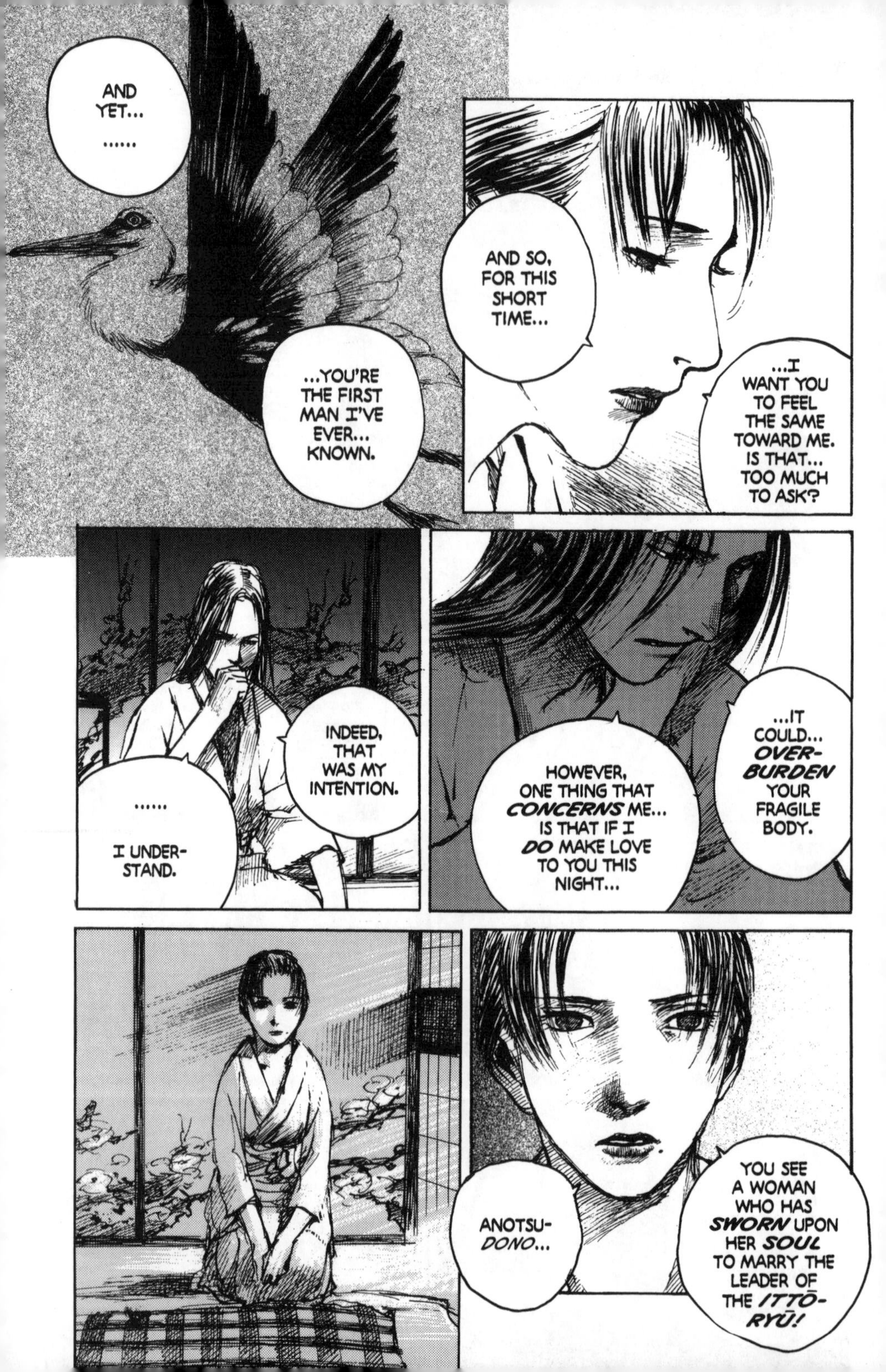
AND YET... ......
...YOU'RE THE FIRST MAN I'VE EVER... KNOWN.
AND SO, FOR THIS SHORT TIME...
...I WANT YOU TO FEEL THE SAME TOWARD ME. IS THAT... TOO MUCH TO ASK?
INDEED, THAT WAS MY INTENTION.
...... I UNDER-STAND.
HOWEVER, ONE THING THAT CONCERNS ME... IS THAT IF I DO MAKE LOVE TO YOU THIS NIGHT...
...IT COULD... OVER-BURDEN YOUR FRAGILE BODY.
ANOTSU-DONO...
YOU SEE A WOMAN WHO HAS SWORN UPON HER SOUL TO MARRY THE LEADER OF THE ITTŌ-RYŪ!

IF I CANNOT EVEN ENDURE LOSING MY *VIRGINITY*...

...HOW CAN I HOPE TO SURVIVE THE *STORMS* THAT WILL SOON ENGULF US?

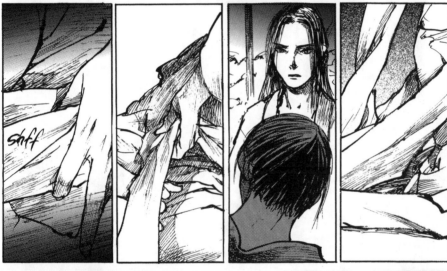

Shrf

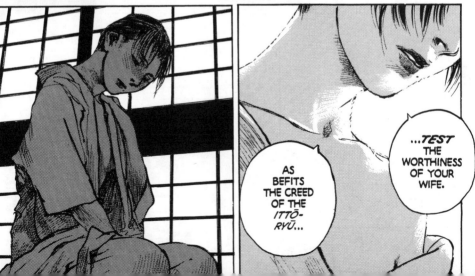

AS BEFITS THE CREED OF THE *ITTŌ-RYŪ*...

...*TEST* THE WORTHINESS OF YOUR WIFE.

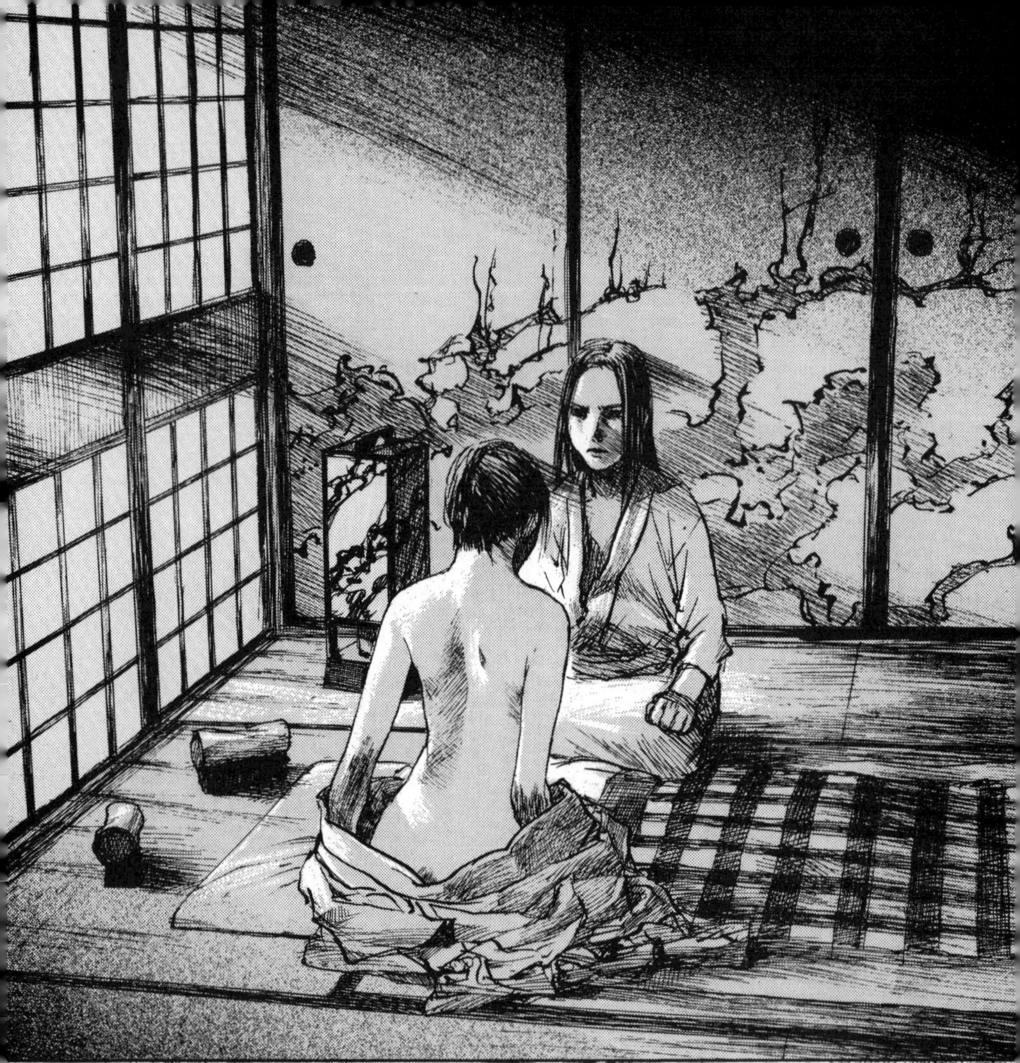

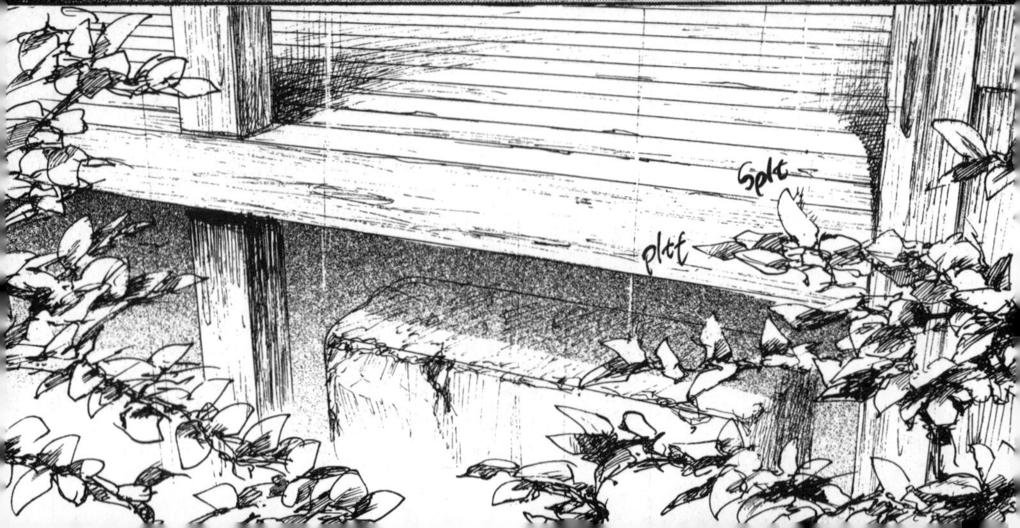
splt
plt

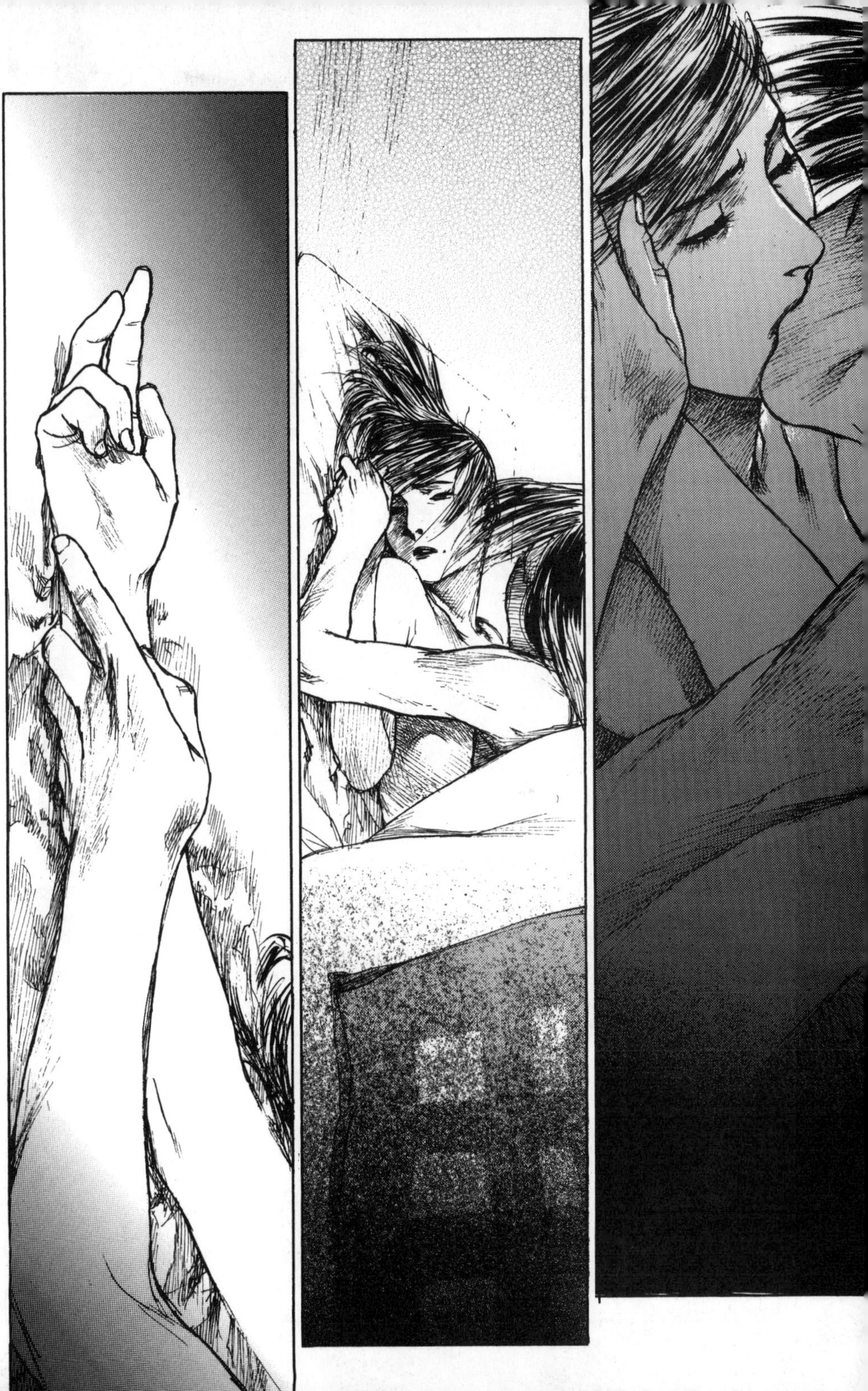

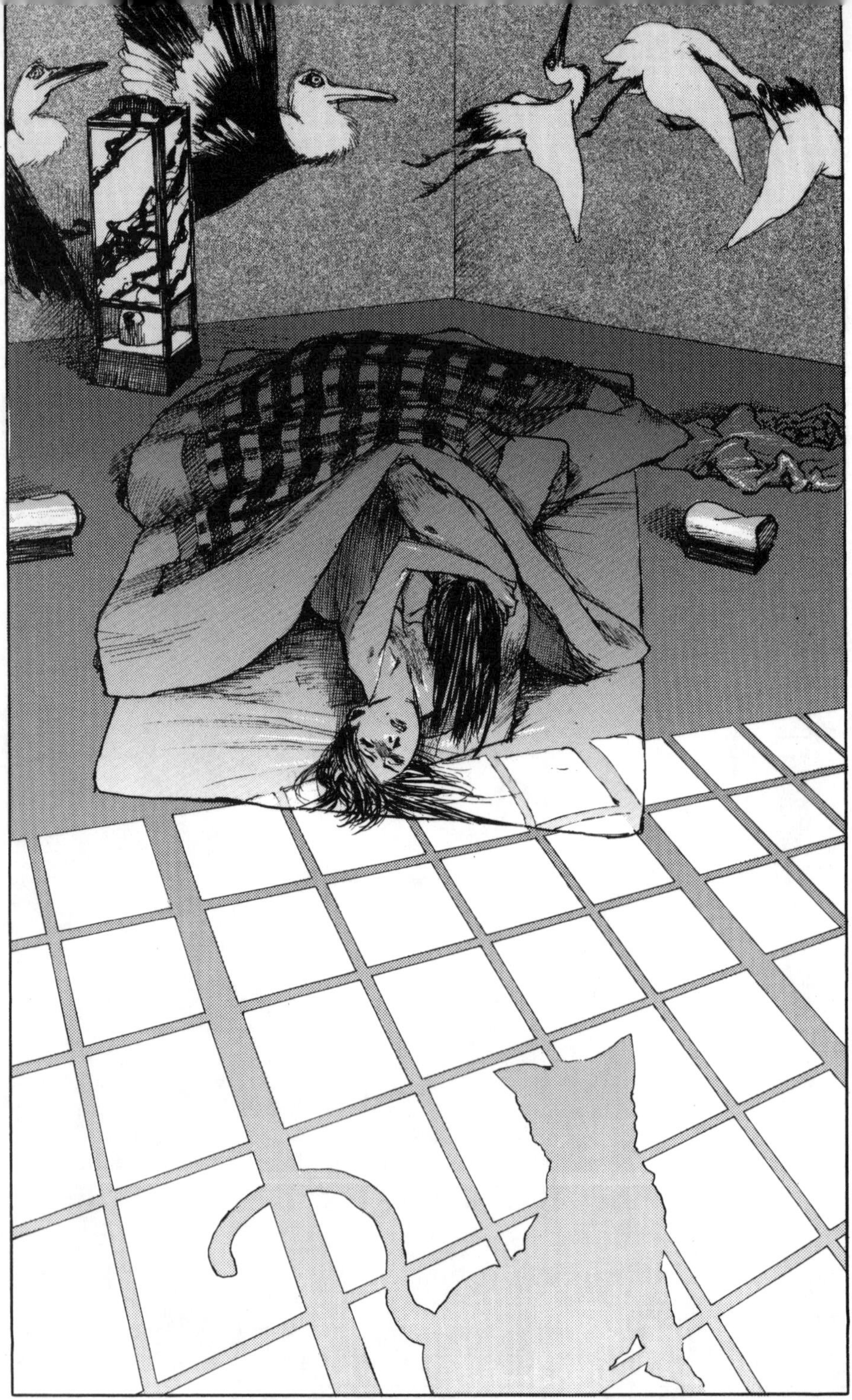

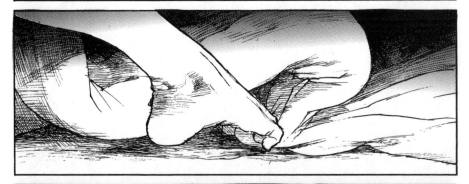

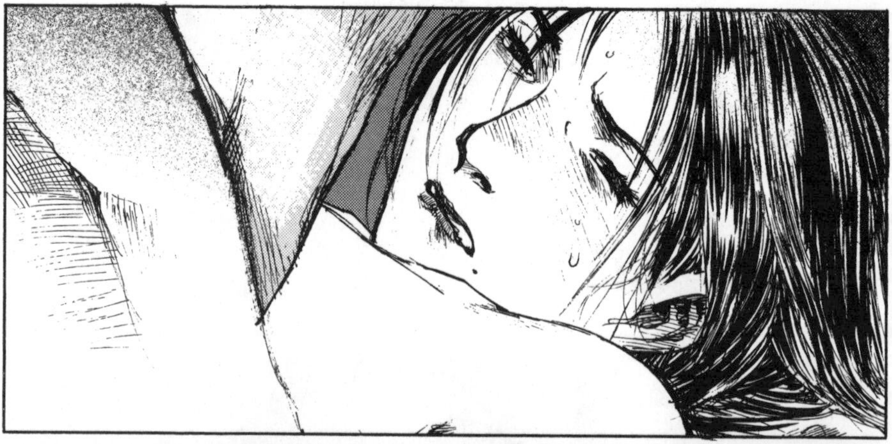

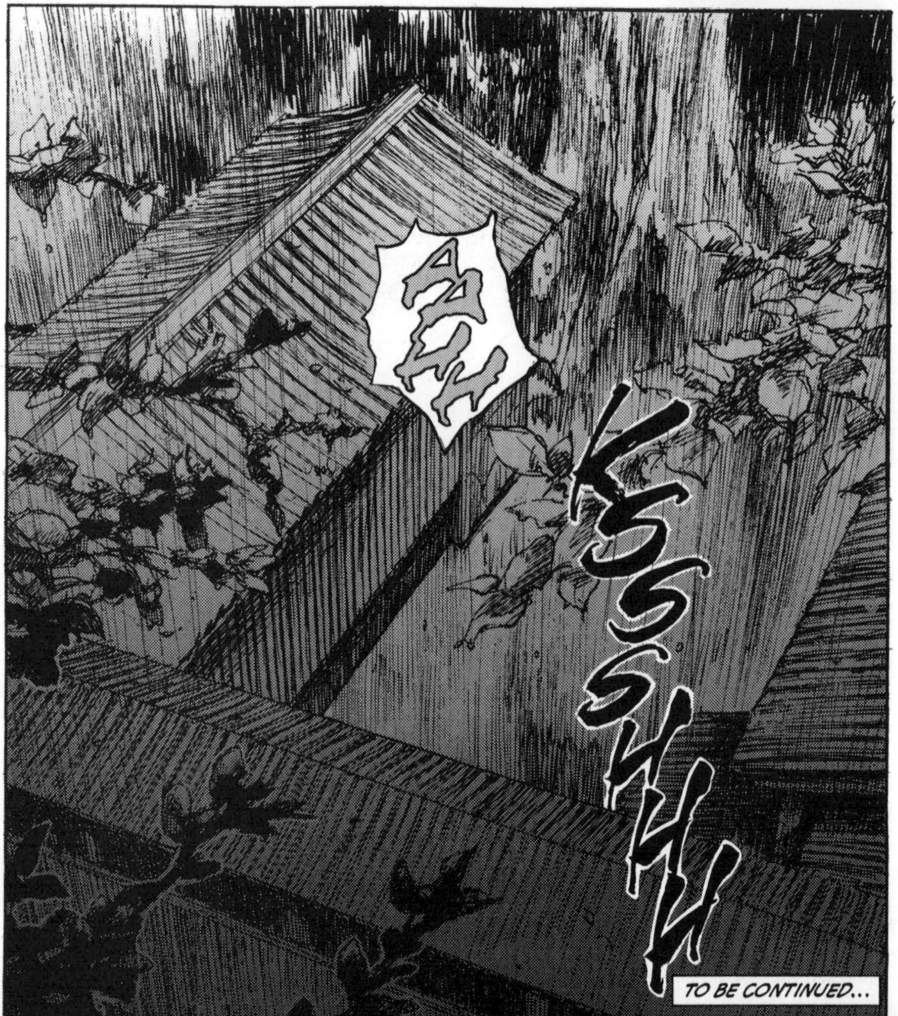
TO BE CONTINUED...

GLOSSARY

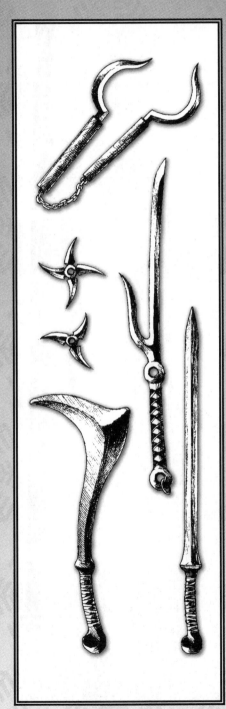

bushi: a samurai; a member of the warrior class

dōjō: a hall for martial arts training; here, centers for swordsmanship

Hakone, Kobotoke: the names of *seki* (checkpoints) along the major byways. Hakone in particular, guarding the mountain approaches to Edo from the south, was one of the most rigorous in feudal Japan.

Ittō-ryū: the radical sword school of Anotsu Kagehisa

Kaga: a remote feudal domain on the Japan Sea coast southwest of Edo

kenkyaku: swordsman; *kenshi*

mukago: a glutinous Japanese yam (*dioscorea japonica*). Edible tubercles (small tubers) grow in the axils of the stem.

rōnin: a masterless samurai

ryō: a gold piece

ryū: a sword school

sekisho: checkpoint regulating travel from Edo to other *han* (feudal domains). All travelers had to submit papers at official checkpoints along the main highways in and out of Edo.

sensei: a teacher, a master

tegata (tsūkō tegata): official travel pass for transiting *sekisho*

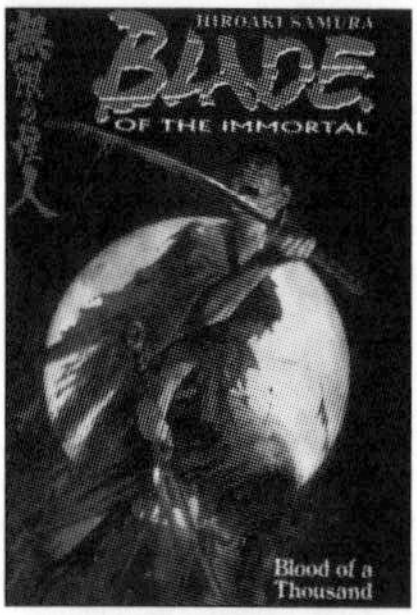
HIROAKI SAMURA
BLADE
OF THE IMMORTAL
Blood of a Thousand

BLOOD OF A THOUSAND
ISBN: 1-56971-239-5 $14.95

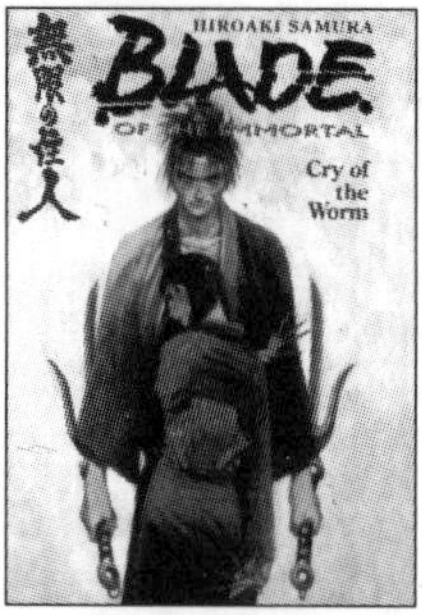
HIROAKI SAMURA
BLADE
Cry of the Worm

CRY OF THE WORM
ISBN: 1-56971-300-6 $14.95

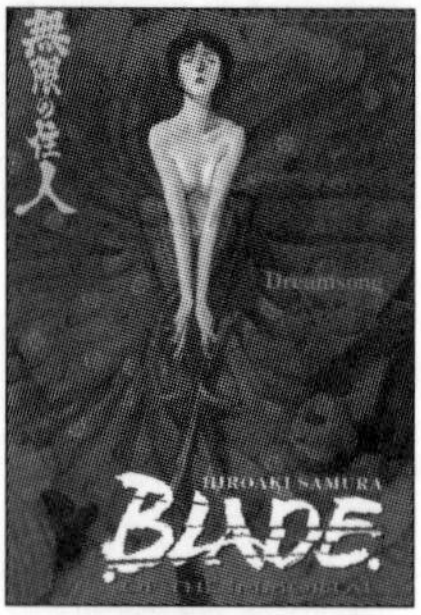
Dreamsong
HIROAKI SAMURA
BLADE

DREAMSONG
ISBN: 1-56971-357-X $14.95

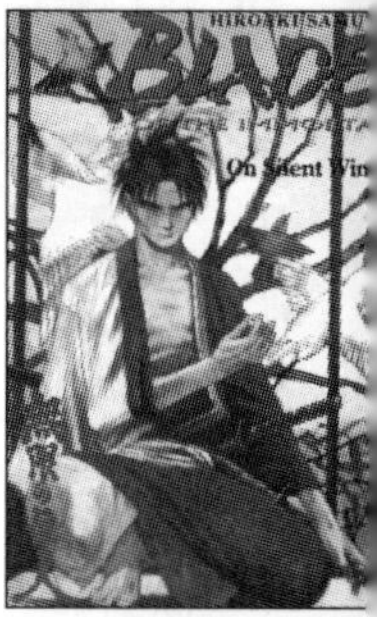

ON SILENT WINGS
ISBN: 1-56971-412-6 $14.9

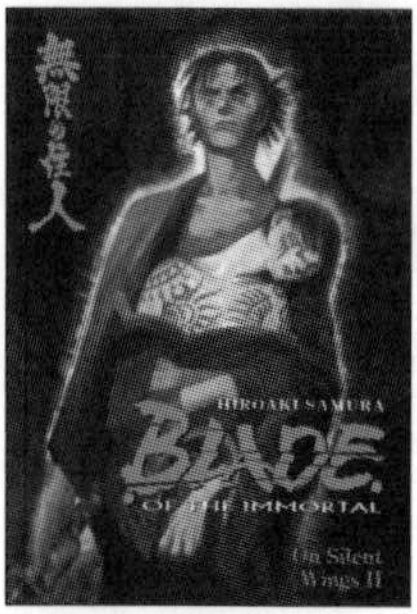
HIROAKI SAMURA
BLADE
OF THE IMMORTAL
On Silent Wings II

ON SILENT WINGS II
ISBN: 1-56971-444-4 $14.95

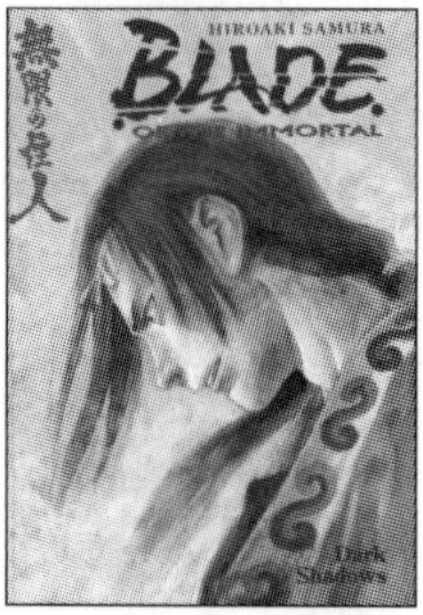
HIROAKI SAMURA
BLADE
Dark Shadows

DARK SHADOWS
ISBN: 1-56971-469-X $14.95

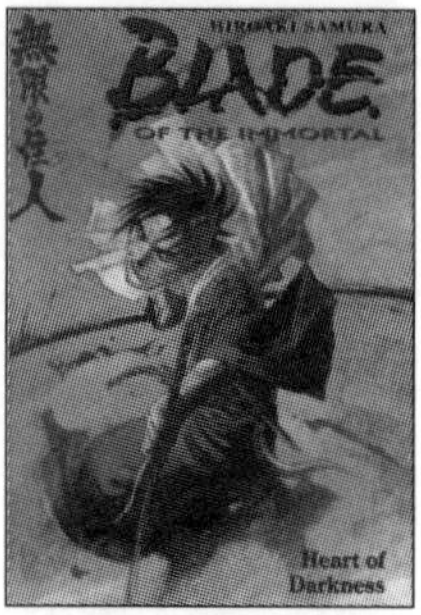
HIROAKI SAMURA
BLADE
OF THE IMMORTAL
Heart of Darkness

HEART OF DARKNESS
ISBN: 1-56971-531-9 $16.95

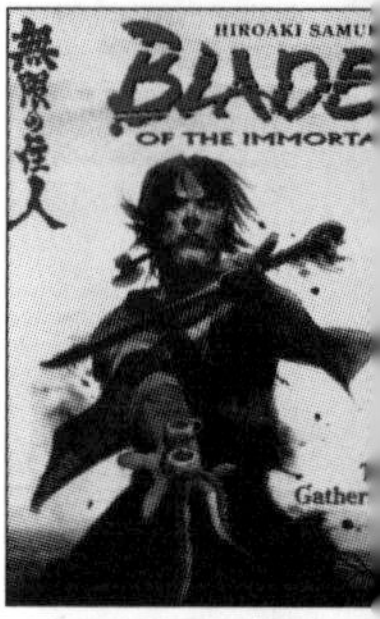

THE GATHERING
ISBN: 1-56971-546-7 $15.9

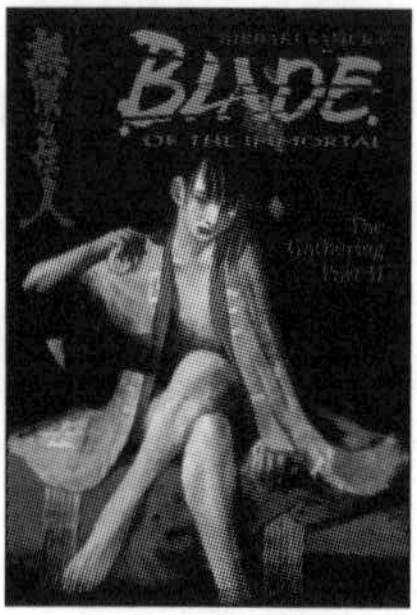
BLADE
OF THE IMMORTAL

THE GATHERING II
ISBN: 1-56971-560-2 $15.95

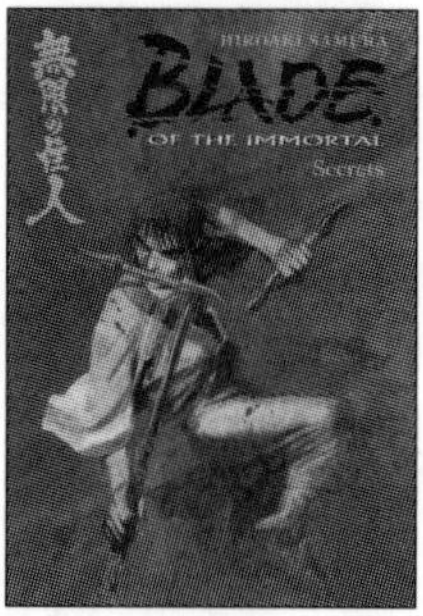
HIROAKI SAMURA
BLADE
OF THE IMMORTAL
Secrets

SECRETS
ISBN: 1-56971-746-X $16.95

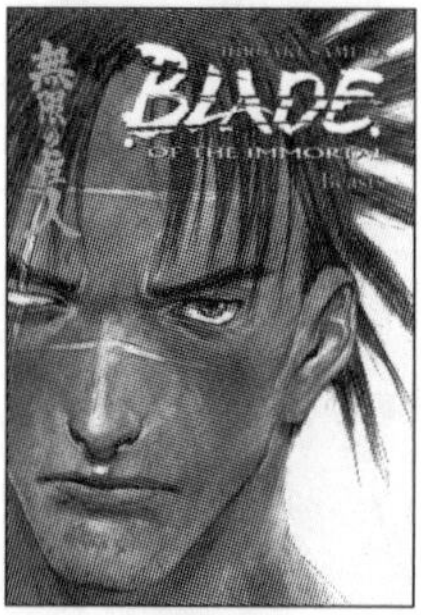
BLADE

BEASTS
ISBN: 1-56971-741-9 $14.95

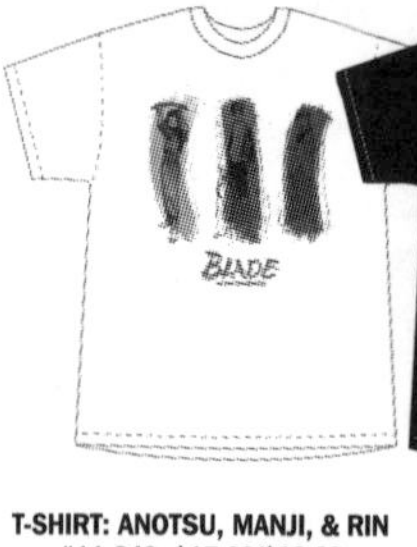
BLADE

T-SHIRT: ANOTSU, MANJI, & RIN
#11-949 $17.99/$19.99

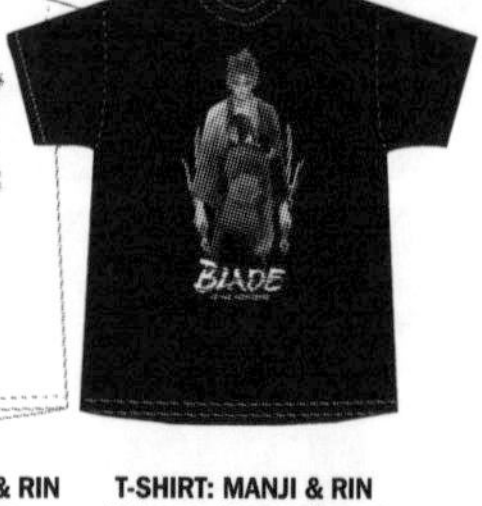
BLADE

T-SHIRT: MANJI & RIN
#11-950 $17.99/$19.99

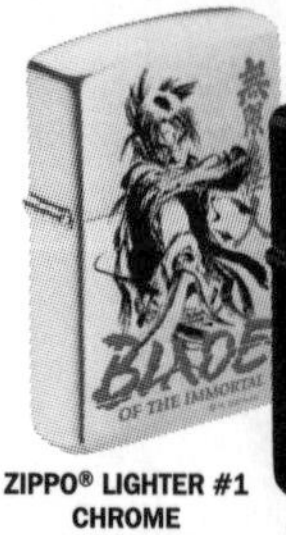
BLADE
OF THE IMMORTAL

ZIPPO® LIGHTER #1
CHROME
#19-063 $29.95

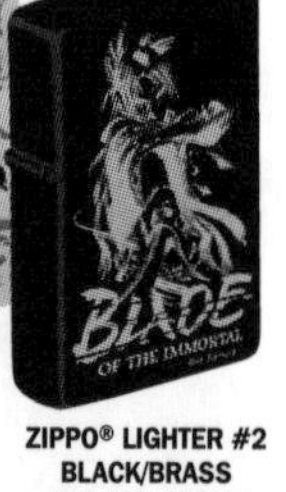
BLADE
OF THE IMMORTAL

ZIPPO® LIGHTER #2
BLACK/BRASS
#19-169 $29.95

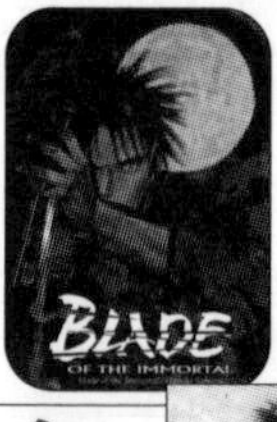
BLADE
OF THE IMMORTAL

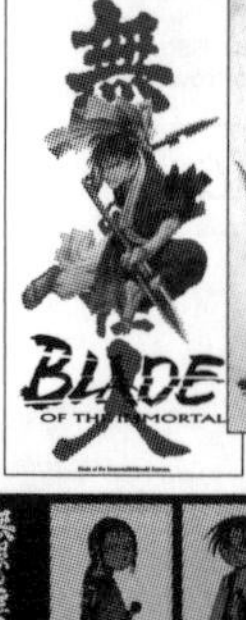
BLADE
OF THE IMMORTAL

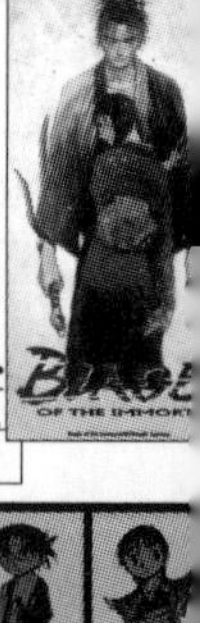

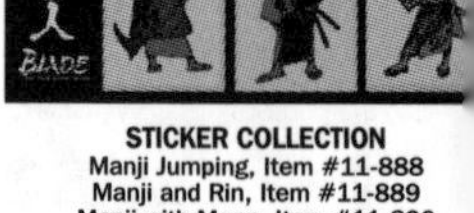
BLADE

STICKER COLLECTION
Manji Jumping, Item #11-888
Manji and Rin, Item #11-889
Manji with Moon, Item #11-890
Superdeformed, Item #11-891
$1.99 each

STUDIO PROTEUS

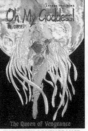